THE RUSSIAN
TWENTIETH CENTURY
SHORT STORY

A CRITICAL COMPANION

Cultural Revolutions: Russia in the Twentieth Century

THE RUSSIAN TWENTIETH-CENTURY SHORT STORY

A CRITICAL COMPANION

EDITED AND WITH AN INTRODUCTION BY
LYUDMILA PARTS

Library of Congress Cataloging-in-Publication Data

The Russian twentieth-century short story : a critical companion / edited and with
an introduction by Lyudmila Parts.
    p. cm. -- (Cultural revolutions: Russia in the twentieth century)
  Includes bibliographical references and index.
  ISBN 978-1-934843-44-4 (hardback : alk. paper) -- ISBN 978-1-934843-69-7
(pbk. : alk. paper) 1. Short stories, Russian--History and criticism. 2. Russian
fiction--20th century--History and criticism. I. Parts, Lyudmila. II.
Title: Russian 20th-century short story.
  PG3097.R88 2010
  891.73'010904--dc22

                                    2009050923

Cover and book design by Adell Medovoy

Published by Academic Studies Press in 2010

28 Montfern Avenue
Brighton, MA 02135, USA
press@academicstudiespress.com
www.academicstudiespress.com

TABLE OF CONTENTS

iv

CONTRIBUTORS

ANDREW BARRATT served as Associate Professor at the Department of Slavonic Languages and Literatures, University of Otago, New Zealand until his retirement. He is the author of *Yurii Olesha's Envy* (1981); *Between Two Worlds: A Critical Introduction to "The Master and Margarita"* (1987); and *The Early Fiction of Maksim Gorky* (1993). He also co-edited and co-translated (with Barry Scherr) *Gorky's Selected Letters* (1997).

FIONA BJÖRLING is Professor of Slavic Languages at the Centre for languages and literature at Lund University, Sweden. Her research areas are Russian literature and Russian cultural history. Her current research on Pasternak is focused on *A Safe Conduct* and concerns Pasternak's aesthetics and his concern with "the language of inspiration." Björling works as well with contemporary Russian cinema, in particular with the films of Andrei Nekrasov and Aleksandr Sokurov. Her most recent article, "Existential Vanishing Points. The Predominance of Visual over Verbal Expression in Sokurov's Films" (in print), is based on her theoretical interest in the specifics of verbal and visual narration.

OLGA BOGDANOVA is Professor at the Department of History of Russian Literature and the Lead Research Fellow at the Institute of Philology at St. Petersburg University. She has published extensively on twentieth-century Russian literature: on Bitov, Venedikt Erofeev, Sorokin, Russian historical fiction and postmodernism. Her most recent monographs include *Историческая проза 1960-90-х годов* (2004); *Постмодернизм в контексте современной руской литературы (60–90-е годы XX века – нач. XXI века)* (2004); and *«Пушкин – наше все...» Литература постмодерна и Пушкин* (2009).

SVETLANA EVDOKIMOVA is Professor of Slavic Languages and Comparative Literature at Brown University. She is the author of *Alexander Pushkin's Historical Imagination* (1999) and of a wide range of articles on nineteenth-century Russian literature (Pushkin, Gogol, Tolstoy, Chekhov). She also published an edited volume, *Alexander Pushkin's Little Tragedies: The Poetics of Brevity* (2003). She is currently working on a monograph about Chekhov and the Russian intelligentsia.

JOHN BURT FOSTER JR. is University Professor in English and Cultural Studies at George Mason University, where he teaches comparative literature, world literature, and literature in translation, with an emphasis on 19th- and 20th-century fiction. He has published widely in these areas, including books on Nietzsche and modernist fiction and on Nabokov's art of memory as it develops during his Russian career and culminates in his autobiography. Other publications on Russian literature include articles on Tolstoy, Dostoevsky, and Bely and a co-edited Forum in the *Slavic and East European Journal* on Slavic identities. He is currently editor of *Recherche Littéraire / Literary Research*, the annual journal of the International Comparative Literature Association.

ERICA GREBER is Professor of Comparative Literature at the University of Erlangen, Germany after eleven years at Munich university and one year at the University of California, Irvine. Habilitation in Slavic Literatures and Comparative Literature, PhD in Russian Literature and Literary Theory, University of Constance. Co-editor of the journal *Poetica*; co-editor of the book series "Münchener Komparatistische Studien". Member of the Munich research group "Anfänge/Beginnings" (2006-2012). Books: *Textile Texte* (On Word Weaving and Combinatorics) (2002); *Manier − Manieren − Manierismen*, ed. with Bettine Menke (2003); *Intermedium Literatur*, ed. with Roger Lüdeke (2004). Special fields of interest: Literary play and experimental literature; self-reflexivity (metafiction, metapoetry, metadrama); intertextuality; minimalism; the sonnet; gender studies; comparative cross-cultural studies, and, of course, cross-media studies (esp. visual poetry).

DIANE IGNASHEV NEMEC is Class of 1941 Professor of Russian and the Liberal Arts at Carleton College, where she teaches Russian language, culture, and cinema and directs Carleton's off-campus studies program in Moscow. She recently completed a translation of Ariadna Efron's memoirs of her mother, poet Marina Tsvetaeva (*No Love without Poetry* (Northwestern University Press, 2009) and currently is researching a study of the film elegies of Aleksandr Sokurov.

MARK LIPOVETSKY is Associate Professor of Russian Studies at the University of Colorado-Boulder. Lipovetsky is the author of six books on Russian literature and culture, which include *Russian Postmodernist*

Fiction: Dialogue with Chaos (1999), *Modern Russian Literature: 1950s-1990s* (co-authored with Naum Leiderman, 2001; second edition in 2003, third edition in 2006), and *Paralogies: Transformation of (Post)modernist Discourse in Russian Culture of the 1920s-2000s* (Moscow: NLO, 2008). He co-edited several volumes including *Dictionary of Literary Biography: Russian Writers Since 1980* (published by Gale Group in 2003), an anthology of Russian and Soviet wondertales, *Politicizing Magic* (Northwestern University Press, 2005), and *Jolly Little Characters: Cult Heroes of the Soviet Childhood* (Moscow: NLO).

ROBERT A. MAGUIRE, the Boris Bakhmeteff Professor Emeritus of Russian and East European Studies had taught at Columbia University until his death in 2005. Maguire's works are classics in the field of Slavic literature. His path-breaking *Red Virgin Soil* (1968) is still the definitive study of Soviet literature in the 1920s, and his *Gogol from the 20th Century* (1974) has introduced generations of Western readers to the Russian scholarly tradition on that author. Maguire's own study of Gogol, *Exploring Gogol* (1994) received the Modern Language Association's Aldo and Jeanne Scaglione Prize for outstanding work in Slavic Languages and Literatures, and his translation (with John Malmstad) of Andrei Bely's *Petersburg* (1978) is widely recognized as the definitive English version of that novel.

ROBIN MILNER-GULLAND learned Russian during National Service in the British Army, subsequently studying at Oxford and Moscow Universities. Since the 1960's he taught in the School of European Studies at the University of Sussex, where after retirement he has been Research Professor in the School of Humanities. His publications include the books *Cultural Atlas of Russia* (1989/98) and *The Russians* (1997/9) and many articles and book-chapters on aspects of Russian literature, art history and general culture, as well as on English Romanesque art. He is a Fellow of the British Academy and of the Society of Antiquaries.

ERIC NAIMAN is Professor at the Department of Slavic Languages and Literatures and Department of Comparative Literature at University of California, Berkeley. His research interests include Early Soviet Culture, Russian Law and Society, Gender Studies, Andrei Platonov, History of Soviet Medicine, and Vladimir Nabokov. He is the author of *Sex in Public:*

The Incarnation of Early Soviet Ideology (Princeton University Press, 1997). Naiman co-edited, with Evgeny Dobrenko, *The Landscape of Stalinism: The Art and Ideology of Soviet Space* (University of Washington Press, 2003) and with Christina Kiaer, *Everyday Life in Revolutionary Russia: Taking the Revolution Inside* (Indiana University Press, 2006).

CATHARINE THEIMER NEPOMNYASHCHY is Ann Whitney Olin Professor of Russian Literature and Culture and Chair of the Slavic Department at Barnard College and Director of the Harriman Institute at Columbia University. She received her Ph.D (1987) and the Russian Institute Certificate (1978) from Columbia University and her M.A. in French literature and B.A. from Brown University (1973). She is co-editor of *Mapping the Feminine: Russian Women and Cultural Difference* (2008), and author of *Abram Tertz and the Poetics of Crime* (1995) and co-translator (with Slava Yastremski) and author of the introduction to *Strolls With Pushkin* (1993). Her most recent books are *Under the Sky of my Africa: Alexander Pushkin and Blackness* (2006) and *Mapping the Feminine: Russian Women and Cultural Difference* (2008). She has authored numerous articles and commentaries on Russian and Soviet literature, culture, intellectual history, and politics.

LYUDMILA PARTS (PhD Columbia, 2002) is Associate Professor at the Department of Russian and Slavic Studies at McGill University, Montreal. Her book *The Chekhovian Intertext: Dialogue with a Classic* (Ohio State UP, 2008) explores the intersection of intertextuality, cultural memory, and cultural myth. Her research and teaching interests include 19th century literature, Chekhov, post-Soviet literature, and the theory of genre. She has published articles on Dostoevsky, Chekhov, Tolstaya, Petrushevskaya, P'etsukh, and Pelevin. Her current research project is on Russian symbolic geography and the provincial topos in contemporary Russian culture.

SVEN SPIEKER is Professor of Russian and Comparative Literature and Affiliate Professor of Art and History of Art and Architecture at the University of California, Santa Barbara. His research interests are Modernism, with an emphasis on the European and American avant-gardes, postwar and contemporary literature and art (especially in Eastern and Central Europe), and media history. He is the editor of *ARTMargins,* an online journal devoted to Central and Eastern European visual culture. His recent book is *The Big Archive. Art From Bureaucracy* (The M.I.T. Press, 2008).

LEONA TOKER is Professor in the English Department of the Hebrew University of Jerusalem. She is the author of *Nabokov: The Mystery of Literary Structures* (1989), *Eloquent Reticence: Withholding Information in Fictional Narrative* (1993), *Return from the Archipelago: Narratives of Gulag Survivors* (2000), *Towards the Ethics of Form in Fiction: Narratives of Cultural Remission* (forthcoming), and articles on English, American, and Russian literature. She is the editor of *Commitment in Reflection: Essays in Literature and Moral Philosophy* (1994) and co-editor of *Rereading Texts / Rethinking Critical Presuppositions: Essays in Honour of H.M. Daleski* (1996). At present she is Editor of *Partial Answers: A Journal of Literature and the History of Ideas*, a semiannual periodical published by the Johns Hopkins University Press.

LEV VYGOTSKY (1896–1934) was a pioneering psychologist and a highly prolific author: his major works span 6 volumes, written over roughly 10 years, from his *Psychology of Art* (1925) to *Thought and Language* [or *Thinking and Speech*] (1934). Vygotsky's interests in the fields of developmental psychology, child development, and education were extremely diverse. His innovative work in psychology includes several key concepts such as psychological tools, mediation, internalization, and the zone of proximal development. His work covered such diverse topics as the origin and the psychology of art, development of higher mental functions, philosophy of science and methodology of psychological research, the relation between learning and human development, concept formation, interrelation between language and thought development, and play as a psychological phenomenon.

ALEKSANDER ZHOLKOVSKY is Professor of Slavic Languages and Literatures and Comparative Literature at the University of Southern California. He graduated from the Moscow Lomonosov University (MGU) in 1959, holds a PhD in African linguistics (Somali) from the Moscow Institute of Oriental Languages (1970) and has published extensively in English and Russian on linguistic theory and Russian literature. He immigrated to the US in 1980. His two major English-language monographs of literary theory and criticism are *Themes and Texts* (Cornell UP, 1984) and *Text counter Text* (Stanford UP, 1994 cloth, 1995 paper). He is also the author of a dozen books of literary scholarship in Russian, of which the latest are: *Selected Essays on Russian Poetry: Invariants, Structures, Strategies, Intertexts* (2005), *Isaak Babel's A Story and a Half: "Guy de Maupassant" and "Answer to Inquiry / First Fee": Structure, Meaning, Background* (2006), and *Mihail Zoshchenko: A Poetics of Mistrust* (2007). In Russia he is also known as a writer of non-fiction: the latest book of his memoiristic vignettes is *Stars and a Bit Nervously* (2008). He lives in Santa Monica, Ca.

ACKNOWLEDGEMENTS

Evdokimova, Svetlana. "'The Darling': Femininity Scorned and Desired." In Robert Louis Jackson, ed. *Reading Chekhov's Text*. © 1993 Northwestern University Press. Reprinted by permission of Northwestern University Press.

Vygotsky, Lev. *The Psychology of Art*. © 1971 The M.I.T. Press. Reprinted by Permission of The M.I.T. Press.

Maguire, Robert. "Ekphrasis in Isaak Babel." In Douglas Greenfield, ed. *Depictions: Slavic Studies in the Narrative and Visual Arts in honor of William E. Harkins*. © 2000 Ardis. Reprinted by permission of The Overlook Press.

Zholkovsky, Aleksander. "Zoshchenko's 'Electrician,' or the Complex Theatrical Mechanism." In *Russian Studies in Literature: a Journal of Translations*. © 1996 M.E. Sharpe. Reprinted by permission of M.E. Sharpe.

Foster, John Burt, Jr. *Nabokov's Art of Memory and European Modernism*. © 1993 Princeton University Press. Reprinted by permission of Princeton University Press.

Bjorling, Fiona. "Child Perspective: Tradition and Experiment. An Analysis of "The Childhood of Luvers" by Boris Pasternak." In Nils Ake Nilsson, ed. *Studies in 20ᵗʰ Century Russian Prose*. © 1982 Almqvist & Wiksell. Reprinted by permission of Almqvist & Wiksell.

Naiman, Eric. "Andrei Platonov and the Inadmissibility of Desire." *Russian Literature*. © 1988 *Russian Literature*. Reprinted by permission of Elsevier.

Milner-Gulland, Robin. "'This Could Have Been Foreseen': Kharms's 'The Old Woman' (*Starukha*) Revisited. A Collective Analysis." *Neo-Formalist Papers. Studies in Slavic Literature in Poetics*. © 1998 Radopi. Reprinted by permission of Radopi.

Toker, Leona "Testimony as Art: Varlam Shalamov's 'Condensed Milk'." In Dominic Rainsford and Tim Woods, eds. *Critical Ethics. Text Theory and*

Introduction:
The Short Story as the Genre of Cultural Transition

LYUDMILA PARTS

During the final decades of the twentieth century short-story criticism went from having to justify its existence as a field of study to being recognized as a prominent area of literary inquiry with its own critical canon. This collection contains some of the most illuminating critical articles treating the short stories that best represent the genre in twentieth-century Russian literature. This introduction focuses on two issues central to the subject at hand: it highlights the main points in short-story criticism and applies them to the Russian short story in particular. However, a definition of the short story is not my aim; rather, I will use others' attempts to define the genre to explore its cultural and sociological function in the Russian context. Is there a specifically Russian short story? And even more to the point, is there something about the twentieth-century cultural and political development that accounts for the short story's prominence in it?

THE SHORT STORY GENRE

A definition of the genre is in order, even if only an elementary one: the short story is a "brief fictional prose narrative" that "usually presents a single significant episode or scene involving a limited number of characters. [...]"[1] Numerous textbooks rely on just that kind of basic formula. Since the short story is very classroom-friendly, a great number of short story collections perform the honorable function of initiating students into the study of literature. These collections open with the building blocks of short-story theory to provide a background for the study of literary texts in general.

A critical inquiry into the short story as a genre takes the basic formula and explicates, develops, or challenges its elements by examining the centrality of brevity, of an episode-focused narrative structure, and of the "limits" upon the number of fictional actors to the definition of this genre.

These are only some of the issues engendering critical debate and enriching our understanding of how a brief narrative attains its power.

Most studies address in some way Edgar Allan Poe's review of Nathaniel Hawthorne's *Twice-Told Tales* (1842), in which Poe advances what has since become a classical definition of the short story. Poe postulates unity of effect as the feature that makes short fiction a unique and superior art form. This "unity of effect or impression" depends on the work's length: if it cannot be "perused in one sitting" (as novels cannot), "it deprives itself [...] of the immense force derivable from *totality*."[2] A successful tale, therefore, is characterized by a clearly-defined movement toward a preestablished effect, with every word or detail contributing to it. Poe positions the tale above the poem and the novel as the only art form capable of sustaining this unity, of controlling "the soul of the reader" in order to produce an effect that is more lasting than that of a brief poem, and less in danger of being counteracted, if not annulled, by the breaks in reading a novel. Poe here mentions the novel only to dismiss it; he positions the tale as equal to the lyric poem as the only other "class of composition [capable of fulfilling] the demands of high genius."[3]

Poe's brief comment prefigures a major trend in short-story criticism: the tendency to discuss the short story in relation and in comparison to other art forms, especially to the novel. The issue in such comparison is invariably whether the difference is one of degree or kind, or, in other words, whether a short story is like a tiny novel, limited in scope and size but not in its relationship to the same material, or whether the short story deals with different material altogether, focuses on subjects that the novel is incapable of addressing, and has a structure that would not work in a novel. Arguing for a difference of degree seems to relegate the short story to the lesser position of a counter genre, merely a step on the writer's path to the "proper" genre of the novel. Mary Louise Pratt examines the link between the novel and the short story in exactly these terms and discusses eight aspects of this unequal relationship. The first four address the incompleteness of the short story in comparison to the novel: 1) the novel tells a life, the short story tells a fragment of a life; 2) the short story deals with a single thing, the novel with many things; 3) the short story is a sample, the novel is "the whole hog"; 4) the novel is a whole text, the short story is not. The other four address thematic and structural features of the short story: 5) its new and often stigmatized subject matter; 6) its inherent orality, that is, its tendency to incorporate oral-colloquial speech forms; 7) its roots in the narrative tradition of folklore and anecdote, whereas the novel originates in history and document; and finally 8) its status as a craft that can be learned and mass-produced.⁴ Pratt's fine analysis, based on the assumption of inequality, identifies those features of the short story that, when taken on their own terms, account for its recognition as a distinct art form.

My preference lies with the critics who undertake the analysis of the short story as an independent genre defined by a set of distinct features – an analysis, in other words, neither anchored in nor impeded by another genre's prestige. These critics see the short story as a genre that precedes the novel in time and essentially differs from it in terms of subject, theme, and structure. The most influential and most anthologized observation on the subject matter unique to the short story is by the writer Frank O'Connor. He comments on the nature of short-story heroes:

> ...the short story has never had a hero. What it has instead is a submerged population group – a bad phrase which I have had to use for want of a better. That submerged population changes its character from writer to writer, from generation to generation. It may be Gogol's officials, Turgenev's serfs, Maupassant's prostitutes, Chekhov's doctors and teachers, Sherwood Anderson's provincials, always dreaming of escape [...]. Always in the short story there is this sense of outlawed figures wandering about the fringes of society, superimposed sometimes on symbolic figures whom they caricature and echo – Christ, Socrates, Moses.⁵

Out of this predisposition toward a special kind of hero comes the worldview embodied by the short story, a worldview that is not exactly hostile to but is somewhat dissociated from the view of society as a civilized community embodied by the novel. As a result, "the short story remains by its nature remote from the community – romantic, individualistic, and intransigent."⁶ Societies interested in their submerged population, communities whose outlook toward themselves sustains a certain degree of reflection and cynicism, produce better short stories.

Charles E. May, the editor of two influential collections of short-story theory, defines the short story by the kind of experience it reflects: "short fiction, by its very length, demands both a subject matter and a set of artistic conventions that derive from and establish the primacy of 'an experience' directly and emotionally created and encountered."⁷ Like O'Connor, May sees a functional link between the subject matter of the short story and the attitude toward everyday reality the short story expresses. The experience reflected in the short story is fragmented, emotional, mythic, and asocial. The kind of knowing embedded in the short story is at odds with a view of reality as well-ordered and secure. It defamiliarizes the everyday and "throws into doubt that our propositional and categorical mode of perceiving can be applied to human beings as well as objects."[8]

Just as the subject matter of the short story is specific to the genre, so are its formal features. The structure of the short story is defined by its brevity: because there are so few details, each one receives additional emphasis. In a short story there can be nothing accidental, nothing that does not contribute to the unity of its effect. This is not to say that the short story must have a neat plot structure that guides the reader through the narration of a single event in the character's life. Most modern short stories abbreviate or distort the traditional plot sequence of exposition, development, culmination, and denouement. This manipulation of the plot in order to foreground the style results in what Susan Ferguson calls elliptical and metaphorical plots. Elliptical plots simply delete some of the expected sequential elements, while metaphorical plots substitute seemingly unrelated events for the ones omitted. The result in both cases is that the reader is invited to infer the missing elements.[9] The most important omission in the modern short story is of the kind of ending that resolves and explains, leaving this task, once again, to the reader. Just like a lyric poem, and much more than a novel, the short story depends for its effect on the ending. Susan Lohafer suggests that the effect of brevity on the short-story reader is to make him or her "the most 'end-conscious' of the readers."[10]

The kind of ending offered by the short story depends more on its subject and theme than on its style: its disenfranchised hero and its limited mode of knowing manifest themselves in the tendency toward endings that refuse to bracket the world with neatly-defined beginnings and ends. Most modern stories are either open-ended or offer an ending that seems unsatisfactory, neither resolving the character's problem nor affirming the reader's sense of logic and order. If the short story describes an experience, *a* moment of truth rather than *the* moment of truth, as Nadine Gordimer puts it, then the ending can only offer a glimpse into an unfolding experience and cannot presume to sum it up. "The short story is a fragmented and restless form," Gordimer continues, "a matter of hit and miss, and it is perhaps for this reason that it suits modern consciousness – which seems best expressed as flashes of fearful insight alternating with near-hypnotic states of indifference."[11]

This point is crucial, in my opinion, to understanding the nature of the modern and postmodern short story: in becoming modern, in shedding the traditional formulaic plot of the fable, the anecdote, and the morality tale, the short story answered the demands of a modern consciousness characterized by a sense of epistemological uncertainty, ambiguity, and fragmentariness. In being "of a moment" the short story is always "of a present moment"; it is a form that responds with immediacy to the sensibilities of its time, to political and ideological climates, and to the way we see the world at large. When our hold on reality is no longer taken for granted, when experience itself becomes fragmented, individualized to the point of dissociation, then the modern short story moves to the foreground of the literary process.

Similar observations are often made by scholars of the American twentieth-century short story; as I intend to show, these apply particularly well to the Russian short story. Richard Kastelanetz defines the American short story from the 1920s to the 1960s by the absence of "the definite moral stance." Even "where one can discern a moral statement in these stories its authority seems pragmatic and tenuous."[12] In this inability to provide a moral message and in the sense of futility of the intellectual quest the short story represents the modern intellectual affliction. As a literary form that takes relatively little time to be written and to be read, the short story functions as a vehicle for a swift inquiry into experience, be it a detached examination or an emotional outburst.

Herein lies a major difference between the short story and the novel: the novel, Frank O'Connor insists, is impossible "without the concept of a normal society."[13] Alberto Moravia makes the distinction between the novel and the short story on the basis that ideology functions as bone structure. The novel possesses this ideological skeleton and the short story does not: "It is the ideology, however imprecise and contradictory it may be, with all the contradictions that are to be found in life itself (the novelist is not a philosopher, but a witness), that begets the things that make a novel a novel."[14] The short story deals not just with events and characters that are unsuitable – insufficient? – for the novel, but also tends to privilege these events and characters precisely because its socio-cultural function differs from that of the novel. The novel enters into a direct relationship with the dominant ideology: it can be supportive of it, hostile to it, or take it for granted; the short story, by contrast, focuses on the individual's moral and emotional experience. The state, society, and ideology enter the short story in the same way good or bad weather, health, or luck do: as external and background factors.

The short story's lack of ideological background accounts for its marginal position in the hierarchy of genres, although there are periods in the development of most national literatures when this very deficiency propels the short story to the foreground of the cultural process. Susan Ferguson traces the rise of the English short story through the literary class system in times of "a certain volatility in the class structure."[15] She concludes that

> the preeminence of the short story as a modernist genre grew out of the modern, highbrow audience's acceptance of fragmentation as an accurate model of the world, with a concomitant focus on 'being' – as in Wolf's 'moments of being' – rather than the 'becoming' that characterizes the plot of the Romantic or the Victorian novel. The brevity that marked 'minor' to earlier generations became a badge of the short story's superior representational capacity. For a brief period, in English literature, at least, the short story became not just a prestige genre but the genre that could be said to represent the essence of the age, as did drama at the end of the sixteenth century.[16]

Ultimately, the short story's rise in prestige, its transformation into a highbrow art form, occurred at a time when modernist artists positioned themselves as the "aristocracy in the arts,"[17] making the modernist short story, with its emphasis on formal and stylistic innovation, an art form for the few.

Before turning to the Russian short story, let me recapitulate several key points. The short story is a distinct genre with its own characteristic subject matter and formal structure. While it shares many of its formal features with other genres, most notably the lyric poem and the novel (all can be relatively brief, have an open ending, and foreground stylistic innovation at the expense of a linear plot), the protagonist of the short story differs from his or her novelistic counterpart, is less a member of society, however defined, than an individuated conscience on a moral and emotional quest. Moreover, the short story (just like the novel) fulfills a socio-cultural function that is unique to its genre; here the differences between the two genres are most clear. The short story rises to prominence during periods of cultural and political transition when literary conventions and ideologies lose some or most of their authority. The Russian twentieth-century short story in particular flourished in a century that saw an abundance of such shifts: cultural, ideological, and political.

THE RUSSIAN SHORT STORY

The history of the Russian short story has yet to be written. Little attempt at a comprehensive analysis of the genre has been made since the groundbreaking work of the Russian Formalists.[18] In "The Literary Fact," Yuri Tynianov provides a useful discussion of the concept of a literary work's size as energy. He proposes that the historical life of genres is characterized by a series of dislocations, that is, changes to what have been considered fundamental signs of a genre. As a result, once-secondary features become responsible for keeping the genre recognizable. The most important of such features is size: "Our expectations of a 'large form' are not the same as of a small form: depending on the size of the construction, each detail, each stylistic device has a different function, a different force, and a different load is laid upon it."[19]

Boris Eikhenbaum's 1925 essay "O. Henry and the Theory of the Short Story" opens by positing an unequivocal division – of kind, not of degree – between the novel and the short story and proceeds to suggest that the short story in general is "a fundamental, elementary (which does not mean primitive) form," and that the nineteenth-century American short story in particular is "built on the principle of structural unity with centralization of basic effect and strong accentuation on finale."[20] In Eikhenbaum's view, this kind of story is not typical for Russian literature. He proposes the sketch or *skaz*-type stories as most characteristic for his native literature.[21]

Formalists considered the novel a composite complex genre that historically developed out of various combinations of short-form narratives. According to Eikhenbaum, the Russian short story appeared at times to merely "create a transition to the novel which it is customary for us to consider the more elevated or the more worthwhile genre." Viktor Shklovsky comments that the modern novel arose out of collections of what he, like Eikhenbaum, calls *novella*s, but takes care to emphasize that there is no "causal relationship" between these genres.[22]

The nature of the novel and of the short story, as well as the very terms applied to these narrative structures, has been changing over the last few centuries. Throughout this time, one can discern a certain kind of interaction – not causal, but one that nevertheless exhibits a definite pattern. The short story accompanies periods of change in literary paradigm when culture develops in new aesthetic, linguistic, and thematic directions. In this way the short story lays the groundwork for the novel, but not by providing shorter pieces to be assembled in a complex plot. Its role is to work out innovative aesthetic and thematic models that the novel can later take into the cultural mainstream.

The end of the eighteenth century was a period when Russian culture needed a new literary structure to enable the reform of literary language and to reflect newly-popular philosophical trends and changes in social life. The second half of the century saw the proliferation of translations and adaptations of foreign adventure and sentimental novels by the likes of Fedor Emin, Nikolai Emin, and Pavel Lvov. Sentimentalism, with its express privileging of the emotional over the social, brought attention to a new kind of hero: an ordinary person from the lower strata of society.[23] With the new protagonist and new literary language came a new genre, the sentimental tale, perfected by Karamzin and popular enough to "decidedly push out the novel."[24] The sentimental tale served as a vehicle for literary language reform as well as a stylistic experiment.[25] This short form was quick to react to socio-cultural changes and was flexible enough to reflect these changes in both subject matter and style.

In the first third of the nineteenth century, the rise of the short-form narrative also accompanied a major shift in the cultural paradigm: from poetry to prose, from élite circles of readers to a massive and dispersed readership, primarily of literary magazines. The word *rasskaz* did not become a widely accepted term for the short story until the second half of the century when it supplanted the eighteenth- and early-nineteenth-century designations such as *istoriia, povest', skazka,* or *anekdot.*[26] Viktor Terras outlines the major types of the short-form prosaic works of the 1820s-50s: the romantic tale, regional and dialect tales, the society tale, and, by the 1840s and 50s, "the story of a superfluous man" and the social tale in the style of the natural school.[27] We of course recognize in this list the familiar concerns of the nineteenth-century Russian novel. Chronologically, the shift toward the novel during the second half of the nineteenth century followed the flourishing of the short form. Yet these tales were not merely a step on the way to the more highly-valued genre of the novel; rather, they were the source of the aesthetic, stylistic, and thematic energy the novel needed to develop over the next thirty years.

In the 1880s, with major novelists either gone or turning, in the case of Tolstoy, to short-form narratives,[28] the short story once again fulfilled its role as the genre of cultural transitions. This time, the shift in literary paradigm – the nascent Symbolist movement with its focus on aesthetic experimentation – was accompanied by a strong sense of political crisis. After the political unrest of the 1870s and subsequent popular disillusionment, writers began to react against the utilitarian critics' demands for social engagement. Moving away from the thematic concerns of the Russian novel also meant turning toward a genre that operates through different thematic and stylistic devices. The Russian Symbolist short story, in a manner akin to its European counterpart, "sought to articulate a more personal perception of human experience and to convey the hidden emanations of [peoples'] psyches."[29] The move from large-scale concepts of nation, history, and social action toward the concepts of individuated conscience, subjectivity, and marginality was at the same time a move from the novel to the short story.

The author who finalized the shift to what we now recognize as the typical concerns of the short story is Anton Chekhov. Just as Pushkin's achievements in prose have been seen to influence the development of the short story throughout the nineteenth century,[30] in the 1880s and 90s Chekhov's stories gave the genre new form, new direction, and new unprecedented prestige. Chekhov's role in the history of the Russian short story and his continuing relevance for short-story writers around the world make it very tempting to suggest that while we cannot define a specifically *Russian* short story, we might consider the twentieth-century short story as such, Russian and otherwise, to be following the paths opened by Chekhov.

The well-documented unease provoked in contemporary critics by Chekhov's poetics is an indication of how drastic this shift seemed at the time. Such was the authority of the novel in Russian literary tradition that Chekhov's stories seemed symptomatic not so much of new directions but of the decline, even destruction, of Russian literature.[31] Most critics found Chekhov's poetics symptomatic of the intelligentsia's social disillusionment and apathy. A 1926 Soviet textbook for adult schools offers a similarly utilitarian explanation by characterizing Chekhov's short stories, and the genre of the short story in general, as exceptionally well-suited to the speed and feel of life in the capitalist epoch: "The age of electricity, express trains, and airplanes created its own literary form."[32]

We can only speculate what new directions the novel might have taken after the modernist / Chekhovian short story had not its development been forcefully redirected. A typical Soviet novel of the 1930s, a thematically and stylistically formulaic text, displays little of the short story's experimentation and freshness of perception precisely because it pushed aside, so to speak, the artistic discoveries of modernism and reached back toward the nineteenth-century Russian novel with its broad social themes and realist poetics.

In Soviet literary criticism, the novel was the preferred genre, with the short story on the defensive. That the "social mandate for a red Leo Tolstoy" (in Mikhail Zoshchenko's phrase) continued to dominate is evinced by Mikhail Sholokhov's famous reprimand to the writers who abandoned the large form during World War II and who, in doing so, lowered their literary standards. Speaking at the Second All-Union Congress of Soviet Writers in 1954, Sholokhov casually equates the length of time devoted to creating a text with its quality.[33] Short stories and poems were the major literary genres of the Second World War, not surprising in wartime conditions when circumstances changed quickly and shortages of time and supplies did not allow for unhurried reflection.[34] Most of the wartime stories did appear in newspapers, and differed only slightly from the journalism of the war effort. Yet a major Soviet writer's call for a return to large-scale works (*krupnye proizvedeniia*) at a forum of great impact (the first major assembly of Soviet writers in the twenty years since the First Congress endorsed socialist realism as the dominant esthetic paradigm) underscores the extent to which the short story was perceived as a suspect genre. When the novel is the officially-sanctioned genre, the short story is forced into the position of lesser and alternative one, and is often perceived as aesthetically and ideologically subversive.

These two features – artistic innovation and ideological unruliness – are most often associated with the short story during the times when cultural and political shifts concur and interrelate. The late 1950s and 60s, with their erratic, short-lived bursts of expansion in the thematic and formal possibilities of works of fiction sanctioned by the literary establishment, provided writers with an opportunity to turn away from the monumental novels of Stalin's time and toward a more nuanced engagement with their experience. Works by young writers and new works by older authors appeared in every popular genre. Poetry enjoyed great popularity. Newly-created literary journals and almanacs served as high-profile venue for the publication of large numbers of short stories and *povesti*.[35] But it was not until perestroika and glasnost', in the 1980s, that critical discourse on the short story showed signs of reevaluating the genre and coming to appreciate its role in times of major cultural and political change.

In 1987, a critic writing in *Novy mir,* a leading magazine of new fiction and a major forum for debates about the state and the future of Russian literature, commented on the short story's socio-cultural function: "The short story strives to indicate new centers of meaning, to capture the nature of interrelated social tendencies. Hence its heightened interest in all kinds of junctions (*styki*): of times, generations, and different layers of society." The short story comes to be seen as a "'demandingly democratic' genre" that helps literature to keep "what architects call the human scale."[36] Another critic sees the "triumph of 'short prose'" in the late 1980s as a deconstruction of the Soviet myth. The short form, in this reading, has undermined the grand metanarratives of Soviet ideology and literature and broken them into basic pieces out of which new myths and new literature (presumably new novels as well) will arise.[37] The focus of most of these discussions remained socio-ideological, but at the time that aspect was inseparable from cultural concerns.

In 2000, *Novy mir* established a literary prize for the best short story named after the short story writer Yuri Kazakov (1927-1982). In 2007, another magazine of new fiction, *Moskva,* dedicated its fiftieth-anniversary issue to the short story, "the capricious genre" that the editors deemed best-suited to represent the history of the magazine and of the last fifty years of the literary process. The novel/short story tension still informs most critical discourse on the genre but with a reversed hierarchy. A critic, commenting on the list of nominees for the 2002 Kazakov prize, dismissed the novel as "a profitable and therefore emasculated genre," and lauded the short story for its "new styles, new kinds of writing, the widening of thematic scope, and syntactic sophistication."[38] While reviewing a collection of short stories about the Chechen war, another critic also denounced the novel but for a different reason: as a genre inappropriate for the unstable and crisis-ridden times.[39] Whether for its artistic sophistication or for its thematic adaptability to periods of crisis, the short story now enjoys the status of a major genre; it is recognized as the source of the artistic energy needed to push the literary process forward.

Multiple anthologies have been published since the beginning of perestroika, most notably of women's prose, and collections of short stories have become increasingly popular. In the Russia of the late 1980s, a number of short story anthologies introduced provincial women writers as a subset of marginalized authors and fictional actors.[40] During this time the short story's subject matter – an individuated and marginalized conscience – was its most distinguishing characteristic. Western feminist and queer scholarship has a rich tradition of considering the short story to be the literary form particularly suited to writing by women and other marginalized groups. The short story as "the outlaw form"[41] or as "the other of fictional prose narrative"[42] undermines a simple linear narrative of culture and challenges the established cultural constructs of norm and identity.

With the proliferation of online journals and libraries, the short story seems to have become a truly democratic genre. Online publishing has practically eliminated the delay between writing a story and delivering it to the reader. It has also done away with discernment, flooding cyberspace with what has already acquired the title of "unprofessional literature."[43] The transition to a new medium has triggered another rise in the popularity of the short story; it has also blurred and reformulated genre distinctions between the short story, diary, blog entry, and works of journalism. The formal signifiers of the short story may change yet again but the genre will remain crucial to the literary process as long as Russian culture sees itself as a culture in transition.

THE PRESENT COLLECTION

The articles in this collection offer analyses of Russian stories that encompass major aesthetic and thematic concerns of the short story genre in the twentieth century. Considering the turbulent historical background, it is remarkable how these authors persisted in preserving the human scale of their texts and in bringing to the fore the "moments of being," the individual search and discovery, often followed by the loss of love, of (meager) personal happiness, and of the means of artistic expression. In choosing these stories I did not look for specific themes, yet it soon became clear that there were recurring motifs that ran through most of them, most notably those of language, childhood, and memory.

The modernist short story's privileging of formal innovation over civic engagement often puts it in explicit conflict with the nineteenth-century realist (and novelistic) tradition. Fiona Bjorling points out how Boris Pasternak's "Childhood of Luvers" diverges form the nineteenth-century "childhood novels" in its composition, its "lack of descriptive exposition, [and] its fragmentary nature." Pasternak chooses a girl for the subject of his "childhood narrative" and foregrounds the physical side of female adolescence. Breaking away from tradition leads the author toward a different type of hero and a taboo subject, and so to the genre best suited for such heroes and subjects: the short story. Svetlana Evdokimova's article on the myth of Echo in Chekhov's "The Darling" – a story built on the complex interplay of desire and scorn for a woman – points out Tolstoy's "misreading" and appropriation of the story at the expense of its textual integrity, a misreading that of course says more about Tolstoy's own moralistic inclinations in his final years than about Chekhov's story. The tension between form and content is the subject of Lev Vygotsky's analysis of Ivan Bunin's "Gentle Breath." This chapter from Vygotsky's influential 1922 study *The Psychology of Art* is a refreshingly lucid approach to the relationship between material and form in literature – an approach that preserves its relevance today. The artistic form – the arrangement of plot elements and the rhythm of poetic language – overcomes the banality of the material, making it "speak the language of gentle breath."

Robert Maguire emphasizes the primacy of language to artistic and personal experience in his analysis of ekphrasis in Isaak Babel's "Pan Apolek." The story is concerned with the transformation of visual into verbal experience. The uneasy relationship between the word and the image parallels the narrator's struggle to both articulate and establish his place in life. The importance and the limits of language in such an attempt are also, as Andrew Barratt shows, a major concern in Yuri Olesha's "Liompa." Mikhail Zoshchenko's "The Electrician," a story set in a theater, in which two media – the verbal and the visual – routinely integrate into a single art form, can also be understood, in Alexander Zholkovsky's reading, as a story of a hierarchical clash: lowly electrician vs. tenor, a short story writer vs. classical novelists, and a satirist vs. ideologically-agreeable realists. In Vasily Shukshin's "Cut Down to Size," the characters' language during their verbal duel reflects their transitional status – the status that marks them as proper short story subjects. Diane Nemec Ignashev points out how language also signals Shukshin's own uneasiness about belonging neither in the village nor in the city. In Viktor Erofeev's "The Parakeet," language is characterized by dissonance and paradox. The seamless conflation of Soviet bureaucratic clichés, "terminology" of torture, and folk poetics, undermines the very concept of a linguistic and social norm, according to Mark Lipovetsky's analysis.

Language as a social and ideological phenomenon is a major theme in

Andrei Platonov's "The River Potudan." The hero's regression into an infantile pre-verbal and pre-sexual state is indicative of Platonov's problematical attitude toward writing and sexuality in the world of utopia. The muteness of the hero, Nikita Firsov, marks his escape from the world and signifies the complete disintegration of language in a utopia. "Utopia," Eric Naiman comments, "connotes a 'withering away' not only of the state and of the phallus but of the tongue and pen as well." Daniil Kharms's experiments with language and subject matter have always been perceived as ideologically charged. Robin Miller-Gulland sums up recent studies of "The Old Woman" and argues that Kharms's testing of the limits of textual cohesion relates to the issue of the status and authority of the writer as much as to the themes of faith, free will, and power. Leona Toker's article on Varlam Shalamov's "Condensed Milk" presents it as a story of limits: of human psyche and of language's ability to convey suffering without trivializing it.

The theme of childhood emerges as related to the problem of language through the frequent association of the child's fresh perception of the world with the artist's perception. The nameless "rubber boy" in "Liompa" stands on the brink of understanding the world just as he is learning to name its parts. In "The Childhood of Luvers" too, the concern with childhood "is not the concern with moral innocence but with perceptive and cognitive innocence." Thus "the comparison between adolescent child and poet lies beneath the surface [...] both are struggling to put words and realties together." Here the theme of poetic expression and just expression come together in the image of "artist as child."

The most persistent theme in twentieth-century Russian literature, I suggest, is the theme of memory: artistic, individual, collective, and cultural. In "Spring in Fialta," Vladimir Nabokov makes use of short fiction's power to contain a glimpse of personal truth. As John Burt Foster demonstrates, such moments of emotional intensity are what Nabokov's protagonist attempts to capture and preserve when he engages memory "as the faculty that preserves the heart's commitments in the wake of immediate emotion." As a result the protagonist achieves an "awareness of an art of memory that would link the heart with the imagination by recollecting sharply focused portions of the past." In Catharine Nepomnyashchy's article on Tertz's "Pkhentz," the alien's memory of his home world constitutes the most important part of his identity. As it fades, so does his very being. Viacheslav Pietsukh sees the historical past as a rough draft for literary texts. As Mark Lipovetsky demonstrates in his analysis of "Central-Ermolaevo War,"

Pietsukh's category of "'national character' [is] a form of ironic compromise with literary tradition, the historical past, and the present," all touched by the absurd and all subject to ironic reevaluation.

Just as the collective memory of a people sorts through past events to privilege those that support the current national identity, cultural memory allots the highest value to texts that confirm and advance this self-image. Pushkin's works, as well as his biography, became a major part of cultural memory and an inexhaustible source of intertextual material for later generations of Russian writers and readers. Andrei Bitov, in "Pushkin's Photograph, 1799-2099," not surprisingly bases his account of a failed attempt to know history actively on the impossibility of knowing the real Pushkin. Sven Spieker describes the cultural quest for Pushkin in terms of a psychotic's inability to accept loss. Tatiana Tolstaya's "The Poet and the Muse" juxtaposes a contemporary poet to the ideal poet, Pushkin, and lays bare the mechanisms by which our cultural myths form our vision of a poet and our own historical, cultural and personal experiences. Erika Greber demonstrates how Tolstaya's carnivalized "critique of socio-cultural stereotypes and norms" results in the blurring of genre boundaries, that is, in carnivalization of the short story genre itself.

Lyudmila Petrushevskaya's story "The Lady with the Dogs," whose first English translation, by Krystyna Anna Steiger, is included in this collection, works with the reader's cultural memory as it both signals an intertextual connection with Chekhov's "The Lady with a Dog" and develops the relationship between Chekhov's story and Tolstoy's *Anna Karenina*. I argue in my article that the result of Petrushevskaya's narrative intrusion into the dialogue between two classics on the nature of love and compassion is a grim pronouncement on the modern world, a requiem for lost or discarded values. Viktor Pelevin's "Nika" also reaches back toward the classics and alludes to both Bunin's "Gentle Breath" and Vygotsky's analysis of the same story. In the process, Olga Bogdanova argues, postmodernist Pelevin "draws a detailed portrait of a contemporary version of the classical hero(es) of Russian literature, modified by time and circumstances, and preserving within itself an inherent dominant idea of a national type."

The protagonists of these stories – children, old people, those who are strangers in their time and place, marginal people with neither full voice nor agency – bring to mind O'Connor's astute observation on the nature of the short story hero. Pelevin's cat protagonist clearly pushes the limits of the short story's unconventional character. The postmodern short story still privileges the marginal subject in a world of (self-imposed) epistemological limits, but its playful self-reflexivity actually reinforces the genre's flexibility and vitality.

The short story has been changing along with other genres; its role and status in various cultures differ, making a trans-historical and trans-cultural perspective on the genre problematic. In a Russian context, the story's relationship to social and literary history brings to light its evolving features as well as its consistent function. On the one hand, the short story flourishes when a shift in cultural paradigm requires new aesthetic means, style and subject matter. On the other, when such cultural shifts are accompanied by socio-political changes the genre's energy puts it at odds with both the aesthetics and the ideologies of the mainstream. In Russian literature (and probably in most literatures in which the novel dominates) the short story serves as a corrective structure; it redirects cultural production toward new developments. Artistically, the short story is often complex, even dense, but thematically it is consistently open-minded: while the novel gives us the world as an object of reflection and possibly understanding, the short story turns our attention back to a moment, an emotion, an experience unmediated, and the human being "as is."

ENDNOTES

[1] Encyclopaedia Britannica, http://www.britannica.com/EBchecked/topic/541698/short-story

[2] Edgar Allan Poe, "Review of *Twice-Told Tales*," in *The New Short Story Theories*, ed. Charles E. May (Athens: Ohio University Press, 1994), 60. Emphasis in the original.

[3] Ibid., 61.

[4] Mary Louise Pratt, "The Short Story: the Long and the Short of It," *Poetics: International Review for the Theory of Literature* 10: 2-3 (1981 June): 175-194. Also in May, *The New Short Story Theories*, 91-113.

[5] Frank O'Connor, "The Lonely Voice," in *Short Story Theories,* ed. Charles E May (Athens: Ohio University Press, 1976), 86-87.

[6] Ibid., 88.

[7] Charles E May, "The Nature of Knowledge in Short Fiction," in May, *The New Short Story Theories,* 133.

[8] Ibid., 137.

[9] Susan Ferguson, "Defining the Short Story. Impressionism and Form," in May, *The New Short Story Theories*, 221.

[10] Susan Lohafer, *Coming to Terms with Short Story* (Baton Rouge: Louisiana State University Press, 1983), 94.

[11] Nadine Gordimer, "The Flash of Fireflies," in May, *The New Short Story Theories*, 265.

[12] Richard Kastelanetz, "Notes on the American Short Story today," In May, *Short Story Theories*, 224.

[13] O'Connor, "The Lonely Voice," 86.

[14] Alberto Moravia, "The Short Story and the Novel," in May, *Short Story Theories*, 149.

[15] Susan Ferguson, "The Rise of the Short Story in the Hierarchy of Genres," in *Short Story. Theory at a Crossroads*, ed. Susan Lohafer and Jo Ellyn Clarey (Baton Rouge/London: Louisiana State University Press, 1989), 180.

[16] Ibid., 191

[17] Ibid.

[18] A number of studies address individual short-story writers' contributions to the genre. There are also numerous surveys of the genre during a particular period. One study, *The Russian Short Story. A Critical History*, ed. Charles A. Moser (Boston: Twayne Publishers, 1986), stands apart as it covers a period of 150 years. It is not a theoretical study but is probably the most comprehensive chronological overview

of the Russian short story to date. The book is a part of the *Twayne's Critical History of the Short Story* series, an accessible introduction to major themes and authors.

[19] Yuri Tynianov, "The Literary Fact," in *Modern Genre Theory*, ed. David Duff (Essex: Longman, 2000), 31-32.

[20] Boris Eikhenbaum, "O. Henry and the Theory of the Short Story," trans. I.R. Titunik, in May, *The New Short Story Theories*, 87.

[21] Usually Eikhenbaum, like most Formalists, differentiates between *novella* and *rasskaz*: the *novella* is an action story with an accentuated ending like the ones he discusses in the O. Henry essay. In this work, however, Eikhenbaum's use of the term *novella* is much more inclusive. He concludes the essay with a reference to the contemporary (in 1925) American *novellas* of Theodore Dreiser, Sherwood Anderson, Waldo Frank, and Ben Hecht, which display "a movement toward the *novella* of manners (*nravoopisatel'naia*) and psychological analysis, in which the material has a more important formal function than the structure."

[22] Viktor Shklovsky, "The Structure of Fiction (*Struktura rasskaza i romana*)," in his *Theory of Prose*, trans. Benjamin Sher (Elmwood Park, IL: Dalkey Archive Press, 1990), 65.

[23] "Ordinary representatives of Russian society – nobility, petty bourgeoisie, merchants, and even peasants – came to replace the heroes of the classical *poema* and tragedy. The peasants soon came to occupy a central place in sentimental literature. P. A. Orlov, *Russkaia sentimental'naia povest'* (Moscow: Izdatel'stvo Moskovskogo universiteta, 1979), 26.

[24] Ibid.

[25] "The appearance of the genre of the sentimental tale was a manifestation of the same basic distinctive feature of the epoch which also figured in the formation of Karamzin's prose: the need for the reform of the literary language. Genre evidences all the distinctive features of an epoch's main impetus." K. Skipina, "On the Sentimental Tale," in Boris Eikhenbaum and Yuri Tynianov, eds., *Russian Prose*, trans. and ed. Ray Parrott (Ann Arbor: Ardis, 1985), 34.

[26] See for instance *Literaturnaia entsiklopedia: Slovar' literaturnykh terminov*, ed. N. Brodksy et al. (Moscow/Leningrad: *Izdalet'stvo L. D. Frenkel'*, 1925).

[27] Viktor Terras, "The Russian Short Story 1830-1850," in *The Russian Short Story. A Critical History*, ed. Charles A. Moser (Boston: Twayne Publishers, 1986), 1-5.

[28] It is remarkable that Tolstoy turned to the short story genre in search of a vehicle for a simple, if not simplistic, moral tale. Tolstoy's later short stories (such as "Master and Man" and "Alyosha the Pot") are an attempt to force the genre into fulfilling a function alien to it: in attempting to embrace a novel-scale philosophical statement they violate the nature of the short story genre.

[29] Julian W. Connolly, "The Russian Short Story 1880-1917," in Moser, *The Russian Short Story*.

[30] Charles A Moser, "Introduction: Pushkin and the Russian Short Story," in Moser, *The Russian Short Story*.

[31] On critical reception of Chekhov's poetics see Lyudmila Parts, *The Chekhovian Intertext: Dialogue with a Classic* (Columbus: The Ohio State University Press, 2008), chapter 3.

[32] Ia. A. Nazarenko. *Istoriia russkoi literatury XIX veka* (Moscow: Gosizdat, 1926), 387.

[33] "It is clear that during the war the majority of the writers could not even imagine creating large works (*krupnye proizvedeniia*) nurtured during hard and lengthy contemplation, written in a well-honed language, and impeccable in style." M. A. Sholokhov, *Sobranie sochinenii v 8-mi tomakh* (Moscow: *Gosudarstvennoe izdatel'stvo khudozhestvennoi literatury,* 1956-1960), vol. 8, 297.

[34] On Soviet war-time story see A. V. Ognev, *Russkii sovetskii rasskaz* (Moscow: *Prosveshchenie,* 1978); E. A. Shubin, *Sovremennyi russkii rasskaz. Voprosy poetiki zhanra* (Leningrad: *Nauka,* 1974).

[35] The twentieth-century *povest'*, a long short story, is usually defined as a genre *between* the novel and the short story. One of the major writers of the period, Yuri Trifonov, worked in the genre of the short story, the novel, and most successfully, the *povest'*. His *povesti* provide an interesting example of the tension between the novelistic impulse to represent on a large scale and the subject's – the private and the quotidian – resistance to the long form. The *povest'*, a long short story, is a compromise of sorts given Trifonov's emphasis on private life.

[36] Vladimir Novikov, "Oshchushchenie zhanra. Rol' rasskaza v razvitii sovremennoi prozy," *Novy mir* 3 (1987): 246.

[37] M. Galina, "Literatura nochnogo zreniia. Malaia proza kak razrushitel' mifologicheskoi sistemy," *Voprosy Literatury* 5 (1997): 4.

[38] Dmitri Bavilsky, "*Znaki prepinaniia #34,*" *Topos* (24/12/02).

[39] "The novel is not the hero of our time. It doesn't belong here for a while." Andrei Rudalev, "Nastoiashchii rasskaz (Aleksandr Karasev, *Chechenskie rasskazy.* Moscow: Literaturnaia Rossiia, 2008)," *Zavtra* 9: 143 (24/09/2008).

[40] See Benjamin M. Sutcliffe, *The Prose of Life. Russian Women Writers from Khrushchev to Putin* (Madison: The University of Wisconsin Press, 2009), chapter 3 and conclusion, ff. 2.

[41] Ellen Burton Harrington, "Scribbling Women and the Outlaw Form of the Short Story," *Scribbling Women and the Short Story Form. Approaches by American and British Women Writers,* ed. Ellen Burton Harrington (New York: Peter Lang, 2008).

[42] Axel Nissen, "The Queer Short Story," in *The Art of Brevity. Excursions in Short Story Fiction Theory and Analysis*, ed. Per Winther, Jacob Lothe, and Hans H. Skei (Columbia: University of South Carolina Press, 2004).

[43] N. A. Konradova, "Neprofessional'noe pisatel'stvo v Internete: o transliatsii 'literaturnosti'," Russian Regional Reading Council http://www.rusreadorg.ru/issues/hl/hl3-09.htm; "O grafomanii v Seti" *Novy mir* 8 (2003): 200-206.

I

"The Darling": *Femininity Scorned and Desired.*

SVETLANA EVDOKIMOVA

"All men are scoundrels, and all women are charming creatures," concluded one of Chekhov's contemporaries after reading "The Darling" (1899). "This is a mockery offensive for a woman," complained another.[1] The way the story was received by Chekhov's contemporaries not only reveals the readers' uncertainty about the role of the woman in society and about the masculine ideal of femininity but also testifies to the inherent ambiguity of the story itself.

When the story first appeared in print, several critics believed that Chekhov's plan was to mock a dependent and unemancipated woman, who had no opinions of her own but was capable only of repeating the words of her husbands, her lover, and even a schoolboy. Critics blamed Olenka for submissiveness. Maxim Gorky supported this negative interpretation: "Like a grey mouse, the Darling anxiously darts about, a sweet, gentle creature who is capable of loving so much and so submissively. One can slap her in her face, and even then she will not dare to let out a moan, the gentle slave."[2] Others, among them Tolstoy, perceived this character as the very embodiment of femininity, as a true ideal of womanhood: "The soul of Darling, with her capacity for devoting herself with her whole being to the one she loves, is not ridiculous but wonderful and holy."[3] Tolstoy not only admired "The Darling," but he proclaimed that, although Chekhov's intent was to curse the heroine, against his will he blessed her.

It is obvious that both Tolstoy and Gorky, to take only two examples, manipulated their interpretations of the text to emphasize one characteristic of the heroine at the expense of others; indeed, they assimilated "The Darling" to their own mythopoetic systems. Thus, when Tolstoy included Chekhov's story in his *Readings for Every Day of the Year* (Krug chteniia), he even went so far as to cut out sentences and passages from Chekhov's text that did not accord with his interpretation.[4] He eliminated Olenka's dreams and all sensual details from Olenka's portrait in order to make his interpretation of the heroine as a "holy soul" more convincing. Gorky, by contrast, was so concerned with the fate of abused and submissive Russian women that he ignored the facts that Olenka is not a victimized wife, that she is not abused, neglected, or misunderstood, that she is financially independent, and that no one in the story ever tries to give her a slap in the face. No matter how interpreters manipulate Chekhov's text, clearly Olenka generates both positive and negative feelings. As Tolstoy himself aptly pointed out about "The Darling," "This is a pearl that similar to litmus paper may produce different effects."[5] Let us analyze the grounds that the text offers for such contradictory interpretations, the sources of the heroine's ambiguity, and the mythopoetic paradigm that lies at the core of Olenka's character and characterization.

"Dushechka," translated traditionally as "The Darling," is a story of a young woman, Olenka (nicknamed *dushechka,* which means "little soul" and is a term of endearment commonly used to address a woman), and of her four loves: two husbands, a lover, and a little schoolboy, Sashenka. The story is constructed as a cyclical, cumulative repetition of the same situation: affiliation and separation. Each time Olenka engages in a relationship, she identifies herself completely with the person she loves, to the extent of assimilating all his thoughts and opinions. Each time she stays alone, she loses all interest in life, all opinions, and she almost ceases to exist.

In his book *The Phoenix and the Spider* Renato Poggioli, inspired by Tolstoy's definition of the heroine as the one who does "what is loftiest, best, and brings man nearest to God – the work of loving," made an attempt to interpret the story as a new version of the myth of Psyche.[6] The very title of the story "Dushechka," a diminutive form of *dusha* (soul, or Psyche), suggests this parallel. In addition, this title brings to mind Bogdanovich's poem *Dushenka,* which is a free version of La Fontaine's *Les amours de Psyche et de Cupidon.* La Fontaine's tale, in turn, goes back to Apuleius's account of the myth of Cupid and Psyche in *Metamorphoses.*

The perception of Olenka as a modern, Russified Psyche, however, is misleading.

The myth of Cupid and Psyche comprises a number of key motifs that are absent in Chekhov's story: Psyche marries outside her community (in folklore variants the girl often marries a monster); she violates the taboo against seeing her husband; she wanders in search of a lost lover, who is Cupid himself; and finally she is happily reunited with him. In Apuleius's version of the myth, Psyche in the end gives birth to a daughter, Pleasure. The heroine of Chekhov's story is the very opposite of Psyche. Olenka marries local residents, violates no taboo, commits no mistake, stays in her own house all the time, and is not happily reunited with her beloved; instead, her last love for a little boy, Sashenka, is full of troubles. Unlike Psyche, Olenka is barren, unable to conceive children with any of her lovers despite her obvious desire to become a mother; while married to her second husband, Pustovalov, Olenka prays to God to give her children.

Whereas the legendary Psyche marries outside her community, that is, into the other world, and then searches for her lost lover, Olenka seeks nothing, never crossing the boundaries of her domestic universe. In this respect she is much closer to Gogol's "old-fashioned landowners" or to the Manilovs in *Dead Souls* (this couple, we may recall, called each other *dushen'ka)* than to the curious and venturous heroine of Apuleius's tale. Like Gogol's old-fashioned landowners, Olenka lives in a secluded world, physically and emotionally limited to her home territory. She seeks her happiness nowhere but in her own house, never leaving the place "where she had lived since childhood, and which was bequeathed to her in the will."[7] Significantly, all Olenka's men come to live in her house: her first husband, Kukin, the veterinarian Smirnin and his son, Sashenka, are all her tenants; Pustovalov, Olenka's second husband, is her neighbor, but he also moves into Olenka's house after their marriage. Olenka has no contacts with the external world, contacts that would take her beyond her familial realm. Father, husbands, a lover, a boy whom she loves as her own son — all of them form one constellation of "relatives." Even Olenka's maiden name is Plemiannikova (from *plemiannik,* "nephew," that is, a person belonging to one *plemia,* "tribe").

The external world beyond her courtyard brings Olenka nothing but troubles. The description of Olenka's marital bliss is immediately followed by the scene in which Olenka receives a telegram informing her of Kukin's death. This news is preceded by "an ominous knock" on her garden gate, that is, by a transgression of the boundary line separating Olenka from the outside world:

> Late on Palm Sunday evening, an ominous knock suddenly was heard at the gate. Someone was banging at the door as though hammering on a barrel: bang! bang! bang! . . . 'Open up, I beg you,' said someone behind the gates in a deep, hollow voice. 'A telegram for you.'

This "ominous knock" brings to mind the man with a little hammer from Chekhov's story "Gooseberries." Chekhov was working on this story at approximately the same time as he was writing "The Darling." In "Gooseberries" Chekhov writes: "Behind the door of every contented, happy man there ought to be someone standing with a little hammer, who would keep reminding him by his knocking that there are unhappy people and that happy as he himself may be, life will sooner or later show him its claws. Disaster will strike – sickness, poverty, losses – and nobody will see him or listen to him, just as now he neither sees nor listens to others."

At the very end of "The Darling," just when Olenka is happy again, she is again reminded of the external world by "a loud knock" on the gate:

> Suddenly a loud knock was heard at the gate. Olenka wakes up and is breathless from fear. Her heart is pounding. Half a minute later, there is another knock.
>
> 'A telegram from Kharkov,' she thinks, beginning to tremble all over. 'Sasha's mother wants him in Kharkov. Oh, goodness me!'

This time the alarm is a false one, but the knock on the gate is a warning. It is obvious that Olenka's last love, too, will abandon her.

The interpretation of the character of the "darling" as Psyche is based on emphasizing only one characteristic of Olenka – her capacity for love – the characteristic that Tolstoy praises so much in his essay. This selfless aspect of Olenka's love makes Tolstoy declare that Chekhov's heroine is an "example of what woman can be in order to be happy herself and to make those happy with whom her fate is united." Tolstoy goes on to develop his thought:

> What would become of the world, what would become of us men if women had not that faculty and did not exercise it? Without women doctors, women telegraphists, women lawyers and scientists and authoresses, *we* might get on, but without mothers, helpers, friends, comforters, who love in man all that is best in him – without such women it would be hard to live in the world.[8]

The ideal of femininity Tolstoy puts forth in his essay is clearly what femininity is for men, or more precisely what it is for Tolstoy; it is defined as "complete devotion to the beloved," literally, "the complete giving up of self to the one you love" *(polnoe otdanie sebia tomu, kogo liubish').*[9] For Tolstoy the ideal of femininity is, in fact, the annihilation of woman's individuality and of her existence as separate from that of man. As opposed to Tolstoy, Chekhov questions this ideal and points to the ultimate danger of Olenka's "complete giving up" to those she loves. The self-abnegating nature of Olenka's love is epitomized in the scene when the "darling" follows the boy down the street to school:

> 'Sashenka, dear,' she calls after him.
>   He looks back, and she stuffs a date or a caramel candy into his palm. When they turn into the street near the grammar school, he feels ashamed that a tall, stout woman is following him, so he turns around and says:
>   'Go home, Aunty. I'll make my own way now.'

Olenka gives Sasha something – a date or a caramel – he does not need. Moreover, the boy wants to "make [his] own way" and perceives Olenka's complete devotion as an assault on his autonomy.

The nature of Olenka's love and character is far more reminiscent of another mythological figure than of Psyche. This is the Greek nymph Echo. In Ovid's account of the myth in his *Metamorphoses,* Juno becomes angry with the nymph Echo for distracting her with chatter, while the rest of the nymphs run off to Jupiter. As punishment, Juno deprives Echo of the ability to initiate discourse, enabling her only to repeat the last syllables of words uttered in her presence. Thus, upon falling in love with Narcissus, she is forced to use his words even for her own declaration of love, as she has no words of her own. When she seeks to embrace Narcissus, he pulls away, saying: "I'll die before I yield to you." She then merely repeats the last part of his sentence: "I yield to you" (*Metamorphoses* 3.391-92). She offers him what he does not need – herself. Her love is rejected, and Echo runs off into the woods and, finally, into rocky caves. In these hollow spaces she withers away with longing for Narcissus, first shrinking to a skeleton and then to only a voice. With no sounds to reverberate, this voice is not heard, and Echo practically ceases to exist; she is reborn, however, each time someone speaks words to echo.

Olenka mirrors the archetypal image of Echo. Like Echo who returns only fragments of speech, Olenka echoes the world around her, but she creates a reduced version of it. People, names, objects, feelings – everything is small and described in diminutive terms: Olenka, Vanichka, Vasichka, Volodichka, Sashenka, little cat (*koshechka*), little window (*okoshko*). Olenka even uses adjectives in diminutive form: *slavnen'kii, khoroshen'kii, umnen'kii, belen'kii*. And of course, Olenka herself is not *dusha* but only *dushechka*. She is not Psyche but only a faint, diminutive echo of Psyche.

Not only does Olenka repeat her men's words, but her very existence is reduced to a form of repetition. Like Echo, she has nothing of her own; she completely lacks any sense of an autonomous self. When she embarks upon a new love, she merges completely with the object of that love. While married to Ivan Kukin, the manager of an open-air theater, she identifies herself as "Vanichka and I" and echoes all his views: "Whatever Kukin said about the theater and the actors she repeated." Exactly the same occurs with Pustovalov, the veterinarian Smirnin, and even the boy Sashenka. Olenka's lack of self is not limited, however, to her lack of opinions. Not only does she not have her own conscious life, but she has no subconscious life of her own either. Even while asleep, she dreams about her husband's business: while married to Pustovalov, the manager of the local lumberyard, she has visions of timber, planks, and boards in her dreams.

Olenka's story, like Echo's, follows a sequence of births and deaths. Olenka is reborn each time she has the opportunity to merge her life with someone else's and to repeat someone else's "word." And Olenka dies an intellectual and spiritual death whenever she is deprived of that opportunity, losing all capacity for judgment and opinion. Like Echo, who shrivels up in the rocky caves after being spurned by Narcissus, Olenka withers away in her empty courtyard when her loves die or leave her:

> Now she really was alone. . . . . She got thinner; she lost her looks. And the passersby in the street would no longer look at her, as they used to before, and would no longer smile at her. . . She would gaze blankly at her empty yard. She would think of nothing. She would want nothing. And afterward, when night came, she would go to bed and would dream of her empty yard. She would eat and drink as if against her will.

By contrast, in those moments when Olenka is full of love, she physically fills out as well: "Looking at her full *[polnye]* rosy cheeks, her soft white neck with a dark mole on it . . . men thought, 'Yes, you'll do!'" After Olenka's marriage to Kukin, her fullness *(polnota)* is stressed again: "He feasted his eyes on that neck and those plump *[polnye]*, healthy shoulders." During this marriage, the narrator notes, "Olenka grew fuller *[polnela]* and beamed with happiness." And when Olenka finds her last love in Sashenka, she is described again as "a tall, stout *[polnaia]* woman."

The opposition full-thin *(polnyi-khudoi)* is further developed in the story into the opposition full-empty *(polnyi-pustoi)*. In "The Darling," emptiness and thinness are observed to accompany the periods of Olenka's spiritual emptiness and solitude:

> When she was with Kukin and Pustovalov, and later with the veterinary surgeon, Olenka could explain everything, and she would give her opinion on any possible subject, but now her mind and her heart were as empty as her yard.

Love for the little boy brings Olenka back to life, once again inspiring her with opinions "after so many years of silence and emptiness *[pustoty]* in her thoughts."

Yet Olenka's fullness turns out to be ambiguous. When Smirnin reappears, bringing his son with him, Olenka's empty courtyard, a metaphor for her soul, is filled with dust:

> On a hot July day, toward the evening, when the town herd
> of cattle was being driven along the street and the whole
> yard was filled [napolnilsia] with dust clouds, someone
> suddenly knocked at the gate.

These dust clouds will inevitably dissipate, though, and the courtyard will become empty again. Likewise Olenka's fullness is always temporary. It is, in fact, itself a cloud of dust. She is doomed to stay forever empty in her empty yard, waiting for someone to come and to give her fullness of being, if only for a brief moment. Such is the fate of the Greek nymph Echo, hiding in hollow caves and waiting for those she can echo in order to become Echo, that is, in order to exist at all.

Given the typological similarity between the Darling and Echo, one can understand why Chekhov's story generated such contradictory responses from its readers. For the myth of Echo itself engendered different and often contradictory interpretations, in part because, in addition to the canonical and better-known tale of Echo and Narcissus discussed above, there exists a distinctly different version of the myth – the tale of Echo and Pan. In this tale, recounted in Longus's *Daphnis and Chloe,* Echo is a wood nymph and an excellent musician. She is a virgin who avoids the company of all males. Pan becomes angry with her because she rejects his advances and because he envies her musical skills. He therefore takes revenge on her by sending shepherds to rip her body apart. The pieces of Echo's body are then flung all across the earth, but they still sing and imitate all sounds as the nymph did before. "Pan himself they imitate too when he plays on the pipe," says Longus in his account of the myth.

Whereas the myth of Echo and Narcissus centers on Echo's reverberative sounds and repetitive language, the fable of Echo and Pan emphasizes the musical and, therefore, creative aspect of Echo. Hence two strands of interpretation – one positive and one negative – derive from the two conceptualizations of this figure. As John Hollander points out in his book *The Figure of Echo,* "in general it is in the milieu of Pan that Echo becomes a credential voice, associated with truth." It is this tradition, then, that led to the adoption of Echo as the symbol of poetry itself. By contrast, the negative readings of Echo arise from Echo's hollowness and repetitiveness, the qualities associated with the other Echo, the spurned lover of Narcissus. Thus Hollander concludes, "Pan's Echo is lyric, Narcissus' is satiric."[10]

The ambiguity of Olenka's character and the differences among its interpreters lie precisely in that Olenka can be seen as both a satiric and a poetic character. The story, indeed, contains both lyrical and satiric overtones. As one Chekhov scholar has noted, at the end of the story the narrator's tone shifts from the satiric to the lyrical, as, for example, in the following passage:

> For this little boy, to whom she was not related in any way,
> for the dimples in his cheeks, for his school cap, she would
> have given her whole life; she would have given it gladly and
> with tears of tenderness. Why? Who can tell why?

Here the narrator's irony gives way to lyrical pathos.[11]

Tolstoy, indeed, perceives Olenka poetically. It is no coincidence that in his defense of the Darling, Tolstoy alluded to "the god of poetry": Chekhov "wanted to ridicule this woman, but the God of poetry took over, and he portrayed her charm and self-sacrifice"; Chekhov, "like Balaam, intended to curse, but the God of poetry forbade him to do so and commanded him to bless." To stress the poetic element of the story, Tolstoy repeatedly refers to Chekhov as a poet. In his afterword to "The Darling" the word *poet* is used five times. In this essay Tolstoy juxtaposes the comic and the poetic in the story. He insists that even though there are many comic elements in "The Darling" and many characters are indeed ridiculous, the heroine herself is not laughable: "Kukin's name is ridiculous, and so even is his illness and the telegram announcing his death. The timber dealer with his sedateness is ridiculous, and the veterinary surgeon and the boy are ridiculous; but the soul of Darling, with her capacity for devoting herself with her whole being to the one she loves, is not ridiculous but wonderful and holy."[12] Thus, the very qualities of Olenka that lend themselves to satire – her dependence, her lack of self – Tolstoy interprets poetically. But while poeticizing the heroine, Tolstoy disrupts Chekhov's text, as Pan did the body of Echo. Fascinated with "The Darling," Tolstoy nevertheless does violence to the text: desiring to possess it, he appropriates "The Darling" and reproduces it in his own *Krug chteniia.* But he eliminates some passages from Chekhov's text; that is to say, he "tears it to pieces." Pan's desire leads to destruction. Incidentally, Tolstoy concludes his afterword to "The Darling" with a story that reveals the connection between desire and destruction: "At the other end of the riding school a lady was learning to ride. I thought of how to avoid incommoding that lady and began looking at her. And looking at her, I began involuntarily to draw nearer and nearer to her, and although she, noticing the danger, hastened to get out of the way, I rode against her and upset her; that is to say, I did exactly the opposite of what I wished to do, simply because I had concentrated my attention upon her." Tolstoy uses this anecdote to illustrate his point that the outcome of Chekhov's story contradicts its intent: "The same thing has happened with Chekhov but in an inverse sense."[13] Best of all, however, this anecdote illustrates Tolstoy's own attitude toward "The Darling": he "concentrated his attention upon her," and as a result he "upset her."

If Tolstoy in his reading of "The Darling" follows the tradition associated with Pan's version of the Echo myth, then satire-oriented readers, such as Gorky, deny the heroine any poetry, scorning her as did Narcissus. They view Olenka as the embodiment of the negative woman-Echo type, emphasizing her vacuity and dependence. I suggest that both types of readings are valid and can be explained by the story's archetypal connections to the same complex myth, that of Echo. In both myths Echo is punished for her creativity either as a storyteller or as a musician, and her autonomy is not tolerated. In both cases Echo's physical being is ultimately destroyed either as a consequence of Narcissus's scorn or as a result of Pan's desire. It is the tale of Echo and Narcissus, however, that most clearly conveys the dynamics between scorn, desire, and destruction associated with the myth of Echo. As Julia Kristeva mentions in her essay on Narcissus, "Narcissus encounters a prefiguration of his doubling in a watery reflection in the person of the nymph Echo."[14] Indeed the figure of Echo in this tale is not limited to the role of a rejected lover and points to the ambiguous nature of Narcissus's attitude toward his own mirror image: Narcissus rejects an acoustic reflection of himself (Echo, or a reflected sound) but falls in love with his visual reflection (reflected light). As the desire for one's reflection leads to destruction, Narcissus's rejection of Echo could be interpreted as an attempt at self-preservation. Hence, we see the inherent tension of Narcissus's love for himself: the reflection of self is both spurned and desired. The way Chekhov portrays the Darling in his story suggests the same tension between desire and scorn of one's own mirror image that is revealed in the myth of Echo. What Tolstoy thought to be a disparity between the outcome of the story and its intent is, in fact, equally present in "The Darling": the author both "blesses" the heroine and "curses" her. He is both attracted to a woman-Echo and scorns her, as he sees the inherent danger of Echo's love and of the love for Echo.

ENDNOTES

[1] A. S. Melkova, "*Tvorcheskaia sud'ba rasskaza 'Dushechka,'*" in *V tvorcheskoi laboratorii Chekhova,* ed., Opulskaia et al. (Moscow: *Nauka*, 1974), 81, 79.

[2] M. Gorky, "A. P. Chekhov," in his *Sobranie sochinenii,* vol. 18 (Moscow, 1963), 14.

[3] See Leo Tolstoy, "An Afterword, by Tolstoy, to Chekhov's Story 'Darling,'" in his *What Is Art? and Essays on Art,* trans., Aylmer Maud (London, 1938), 325.

[4] An analysis of Tolstoy's reproduction of Chekhov's "Darling" in *Krug chteniia* can be found in V. Lakshin, "*Liubimyi rasskaz Tolstogo,*" in his *Tolstoy i Chekhov* (Moscow: *Sovetskii Pisatel'*, 1975), 95-97.

[5] Melkova, "*Tvorcheskaia sud'ba rasskaza 'Dushechka,'*" 78.

[6] Poggioli's interpretation of the "darling" as "one of the Russian equivalents of the Greek Psyche" is elaborated upon by Thomas Winner who points to the "ironic implications of the parallel with the myth; See Renato Poggioli, "Storytelling in a Double Key," in his *The Phoenix: and the Spider* (Cambridge, Mass.: Harvard University Press, 1957), 130; and Thomas Winner, *Chekhov and His Prose* (New York: Holt, Rinehart and Winston, 1966), 215.

[7] All translations of "The Darling" and "Gooseberries" are mine based on A. P. Chekhov, *Polnoe sobranie sochinenii i pisem,* 30 vols (Moscow, 1974-83), *Sochineniia,* vol. 10, pp. 102-13, 55-65.

[8] Tolstoy, "An Afterword, by Tolstoy, to Chekhov's Story 'Darling,'" 326.

[9] Ibid.

[10] J. Hollander, *The Figure of Echo: a Mode of Allusion in Milton and After* (Berkeley: University of California Press, 1984), 11.

[11] See Z. Papernyi, *Zapisnye knizhki Chekhova* (Moscow: *Sovetskii Pisatel'*, 1976)

[12] Tolstoy, "An Afterword, by Tolstoy, to Chekhov's Story 'Darling,'" 324.

[13] Ibid., 327.

[14] J. Kristeva, *Tales of Love* (New York: Columbia University Press, 1987), 103.

II

Bunin's "Gentle Breath"

LEV SEMENOVICH VYGOTSKY

"Anatomy" and "physiology" of the narrative. disposition and composition. characteristics of the material. the functional significance of composition. auxiliary methods. affective contradiction and rejection of the content of form.

In the past decade, the basic elements of the short story have been dealt with in morphological investigations of Western European and Russian poetry and literature. The analysis of any short story deals with two fundamental concepts, which we shall call the *material* and the *form*. We already mentioned that the material is what is readily available to the poet for his story, namely the events and characters of everyday life, or the relationships between human beings – in brief, all that existed prior to the story can exist outside of it or is independent of it. The form of this work of art is the arrangement of this material in accordance with the laws of artistic construction.

We have already established that these terms must not be understood to mean the external, audible or visual, or any other sensorial form accessible to our perception. The form is not a shell which covers the substance. On the contrary, it is an active principle by which the material is processed and, occasionally, overcome in its most involved, but also most elementary, properties. In the short story or novella, form and material are usually taken from certain everyday human relationships. The event, or events, upon which a story is based, comprise the *material* of that story. When we discuss the way this material is arranged and presented to the reader and *how* the event is told, we deal with its *form*. In the existing literature there is no agreement in the matter of terminology. For Shklovsky and Tomashevsky, the plot (*fabula*) is the material of the story, the events from everyday life upon which it is based; the subject (*sujet*), for them, is the formal treatment of the story. Others, such as Petrovsky, use these terms in the opposite sense: the subject is the event that triggers the story, and the plot is the artistic treatment of that event:

> I am inclined to use the term 'subject' (*sujet*) to indicate the material of a work of art. The subject is a system of events, or actions (or else a single event, simple or complex in composition) in a form which is not the result of the artist's individual creative or poetic work. The treated subject, in my opinion, should be called the 'plot' (*fabula*).[1]

However we understand them, it is necessary to distinguish between these two concepts. We shall use the terminology of the formalists, who call the plot, in accordance with literary tradition, the material upon which the work of art is based. The relationship between material and form in the story is, of course, identical to that between the plot and the subject. If we want to know the direction in which the poet's work evolves, we must investigate the techniques he uses: how he treats the material in the course of the story and how he transforms it into the poetic subject. The plot (material) of a story is in the same relationship to the narrative of which it is a part as individual words to a line of verse, the scale to music, colors to painting. The subject (form) is in the same relationship to the narrative as verses to poetry, a melody to music, a picture to the art of painting. In other words, we are dealing with the relationships between individual portions of the material, which means that the subject is in the same relation to the plot in a narrative as the form to its material.

This concept evolved with great difficulty, because the extraordinary rule of art, according to which authors usually treat their material in a fashion concealed from the reader, long misled the theorists when they tried to distinguish between these two aspects of the narrative in order to set up rules for its creation and perception. Writers have long known that the arrangement of the events in a story, the author's method of introducing the reader to the plot, and the composition of the literary work are extremely important tasks in the art of writing. Composition has always been the subject of particular conscious and subconscious care on the part of the poet or novelist. But only in the novella, which evolved from the narrative, did composition achieve its highest development. The novella can be regarded as a pure form of writing, whose main purpose is the formal treatment of a plot and its transformation into a poetic subject. There are a number of sophisticated and complex forms of construction and treatment of the plot. Some writers were quite aware of the role and significance of the techniques they used. The height of this awareness was achieved by Sterne who, as Shklovsky showed, explained the technique of subject composition, and in his *Tristram Shandy* gave five curves for the course of the novel's plot.

> I am now beginning to get fairly into my work; and . . . make no doubt but that I shall be able to go on with my uncle Toby's story and my own in a tolerable straight line.

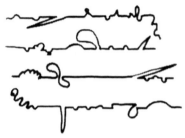

> Now, these were the four lines I moved in through my first, second, third, and fourth volumes. – In the fifth volume I have been very good, – the precise line I have described in it being this:

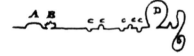

> By which it appears that except at the curve, marked A, where I took a trip to Navarre, – and the indented curve B, which is the short airing when I was there with the Lady Baussiere and her page, – I have not taken the least frisk of a digression, till John de la Casse's devils led me around you see marked D. – for *as c c c c c* they are nothing but parentheses, and the common ins and outs incident to the lives of the greatest ministers of state; and when compared with what men have done, – or with my own transgressions as the letters, *A B D* – they vanish into nothing.[2]

If we take any event of life in a chronological succession, we can represent it as a straight line, where every successive moment replaces the preceding one and is in turn superseded by the next. In exactly the same way we can graphically represent the sequence of sounds in a scale, or the syntactic distribution of words in an average phrase, and so on. In other words, the evolution and development of a material with natural properties can be graphically represented as a straight line. But the artificial (or artistic) distribution of words which determines a verse changes the normal order of their syntactic arrangement. The artificial (or artistic) distribution of sounds which transforms a simple series of sounds into a melody, again changes their order in a scale. The artificial (or artistic) arrangements of events determines an artistic subject and disrupts chronological succession. This artistic distribution, or arrangement, can be graphically represented as a curve traced around a straight line. Thus, we will have curves for verses, melody, or plot. All these curves illustrate the artistic form. The curves which describe the various volumes of Sterne's novel make this point very well.

Before we proceed, we must answer a question that is quite clear when we talk about such well-known artistic forms as melody and verse, but becomes quite intricate when we talk about the narrative. It can be formulated as follows: Why does the artist deviate from the chronological succession of the events in his story, why does he deviate from the rectilinear progression of his story, and prefer to describe a curve rather than move along the shortest distance between two points? Such a preference might easily be taken for a writer's whim, devoid of any rational foresight. If we take the traditional approach to the composition subject, we see that these curves were always wrongly interpreted by the critics. In Russian literature, for instance, the opinion long prevailed that *Eugene Onegin* was an epic poem, adorned with a large number of lyrical deviations. These were regarded as having been separated by the author from the main subject of the story. They were understood to be lyrics or lyrical fragments that had sneaked into the body of the poem without any organic connection to its fabric. These lyrics were believed to have an independent existence and to play the role of an epic interlude, a sort of lyrical entr'acte between the two acts of the story. This view is of course completely wrong. It neglects the purely epic role played by these "digressions." If we take a close look at the economy of the whole story of *Eugene Onegin,* we find that these digressions are a very important technique used by the poet in his development and treatment of the subject. It is just as absurd to consider these devices as digressions as it is to regard as digressions the ups and downs of a melody which, after all, are deviations from the normal course of a scale. Similarly, these so-called digressions in *Eugene Onegin* form the very essence and basic stylistic technique of this work of art. They are the melody of its subject. "One witty painter [Vladimir Miklashevsky]," says Shklovsky, "suggested drawing the main digressions (for instance, as legs); from a compositional viewpoint this would be quite correct."[3] Let us now explain the significance of a subject curve. We know that the dynamic ratio between sounds is the basis of a melody. A verse is not only the sum total of the sounds composing it, but also their dynamic sequence, their specific relationship to one another. Two sounds, or two words, in a specific order, form a definite relation which can be determined by the order of succession of elements. Similarly, two events, or actions, when put together, yield a certain new dynamic relation that is entirely determined by the order and disposition (arrangement) of these events. For instance, the sounds a, b, and c, or the words a, b, and c, or the events a, b, and c, totally change their significance and emotional meaning if we present them in a different order, say, b, c, and a; or b, a, and c; etc. Let us imagine that we are talking about a threat, then about the execution of such a threat, which could be a murder. If we acquaint the reader beforehand with the fact that the protagonist is in danger but keep him in the dark concerning the actual execution of the threat and only after a certain amount of suspense tell him about the killing, we will have achieved one kind of effect. A totally different effect is achieved if we begin our story with the discovery of the corpse, and then, in reverse chronological order tell the reader of the murder and the threat. Disposition and arrangement of events in a story, the combination of phrases and sentences, of concepts, ideas, images and actions is governed by the same rules of artistic association as are the juxtapositions of sounds in a melody, or those of words in a poem.

One last remark on the nature of the method before proceeding with the analysis of the novella: It is useful to distinguish (as many authors do) the static scheme of the construction of a narrative, which we may call its anatomy, from the dynamic scheme, which we may call its physiology. We have already said that every story has a specific structure that differs from the structure of the material upon which it is based. It is also obvious that every poetic technique of treating the material is purposeful; it is introduced with some goal or other, and it governs some specific function of the story. By studying the teleology of the technique (the function of each stylistic element, the purposeful direction, the teleological significance of each component) we shall understand the very essence of the story and witness how a lifeless construction is transformed into a living organism.

We have selected for this purpose Bunin's short story "Gentle Breath." It is convenient for our analysis for many reasons. First, it can be regarded as a typical specimen of the classic as well as modern short story, which clearly reveals the fundamental stylistic elements characteristic of this genre. Artistically, it is most likely one of the best short stories ever written, and by general consensus, it stands as a true model of its genre. Finally, it has not fallen prey to commonplace and vulgar interpretation, the prejudices of which have to be dealt with every time one studies a familiar text, such as Krylov's fables or Shakespeare's tragedies. It is essential to our study to include a work of art that generates an impression which is in no way predetermined by established judgments. We wanted to find a literary stimulant that would be completely fresh and new, unspoiled, not yet reduced to triteness, and therefore unlikely to provoke a preconditioned aesthetic reaction in us.

Now let us take a look at the story:

We begin the analysis by establishing the melodic curve which we find implemented by the words of the text. To this end, it is best to compare the actual events upon which the story is based (events that are certainly possible and probably modeled on real events), which make up its material of the story, with the artistic form into which this material -has been molded. This is a method followed by critics of verse when they try to establish the rules of rhythm that govern certain word arrangements. We shall attempt the same with this story. The material on which it is based is the following: Olia Meshcherskaia, a high-school girl, lives a life which differs in nothing from the usual life of pretty, well-to-do girls living in provincial Russian towns. Then something happens. She has a love affair with Maliutin, a much older landowner and friend of her father's, and then a liaison with a Cossack officer whom she promises to wed. Thus, she "is led astray." The Cossack officer, betrayed yet still in love with Olia, shoots her in a crowded railway station. Olia Meshcherskaia's schoolteacher chooses the deceased as the subject of an almost passionate worship and frequently visits her grave. This is the entire content of the story. Let us now list all the events in the story in the chronological order in which they actually occurred, or might have occurred, in actual life. These events must be divided into two groups, since one is connected with Olia's life and the other with the story of her schoolteacher:

Disposition Scheme	Composition Scheme
I. Olia Meshcherskaia	N. The grave
A. Childhood	A. Childhood
B. Adolescence	B. Adolescence
C. Episode with Shenshin	C. Episode with Shenshin
D. Conversation about gentle breath	H. Last of the winter
E. Arrival of Maliutin	J. Conversation with the principal
F. Liaison with Maliutin	K. Murder
G. Writing in the diary	I. Olia Meshcherskaia
H. Last of the winter	M. Subsequent investigation
I. Episode with the officer	G. Writing in the diary
J. Conversation with the school principal	E. Arrival of Maliutin
K. Murder	F. Liaison with Maliutin
L. Funeral	f. Walks to the cemetery
M. Subsequent investigation	g. At the grave
N. The grave	a. Schoolteaching
II. The Schoolteacher	b. Daydreams about brother
a. Schoolteaching	c. Daydreams about great works
b. Daydreams about brother	e. Daydreams about Olia
c. Daydreams about great works	d. Conversation about gentle breath
d. Conversation about gentle breath	
e. Daydreams about Olia	
f. Walks to the cemetery	
g. At the grave	

This chronological enumeration is known as the *disposition* of the story, i.e., the natural sequence of events, which we may also call the graphic straight line. If we list the order in which the events actually occur in the story *as written,* we have the *composition* rather than the disposition of the material. We notice immediately that the events in the disposition list follow the order of the alphabet, the chronological order, while in the composition list the chronological sequence is completely disrupted. The letters are rearranged in a series without any apparent order. This new series contains all the events we labeled alphabetically. If we denote the progress of the story by two parallel lines, plotting on one of them the individual events, in succession, of Olia's story, and on the other the events in the schoolteacher's story we shall have two straight lines symbolizing the entire disposition of our story.

We will now show what the author has done with this material in order to give it an artistic form. To show this graphically in the composition diagram, we connect the points on these lines in the order in which they occur in the narrative. The bottom curve represents transition to chronologically earlier events (when the author moves backward) and the top curves represent transition to chronologically advanced events (when the author leaps forward). Thus we get two curves. The confused diagram reveals, at first glance, that the events do not evolve in a straight line as would happen in real life, but in leaps and bounds. The story quite unexpectedly drifts from one event to another, connecting the most remote events of the chronologically arranged material. In other words, the curve represents the analysis of the plot and the subject of the story quite faithfully. Referring to the composition diagram, and following the order of succession of the individual elements, we see that our curve, from beginning to end, shows the action of the story as written. This is the "melody." Instead of narrating the content in chronological order, (how Olia Meshcherskaia was a schoolgirl, how she grew up, how she turned into a beautiful woman, how her moral degradation occurred, how her liaison with the officer took place, how she was murdered, how she was buried, and what her grave looked like), the author begins with the description of her grave, switches to her early childhood, suddenly talks about her last winter, describes the conversation she had with her school principal concerning her moral degradation the previous summer. Then he speaks of her death and, at the very end of the story, of an apparently irrelevant episode in her school life which goes back to a more remote past. Our curve reflects this progression or, as some might call it, this deviation from the straight path. The diagrams show what we earlier called the static structure, or "anatomy," of the story. Now we must establish its dynamic composition, or "physiology." We have to find out *why* the author treated the material as he did, for what obscure reason he begins his story at the end, and why he ends it as he does.

In other words, to determine the function of this rearrangement we must find the significance and purpose of the apparently meaningless, confused curve which symbolizes the composition of the story. To do this we must turn from analysis to synthesis to try to gain an understanding of the physiology of the story from its purpose and dynamics.

If we take a look at the content of the story, its material taken per se and the system of events in it, we find that it all comes under the category "troubles of life." There is not a single bright spot in the entire story. There is nothing but the insignificant and rather senseless life of a schoolgirl in a provincial Russian town. It is a life that springs from obviously diseased roots; its outcome is inevitably unhealthy and sterile. Could it be that this troubled life has been idealized, or somewhat adorned, in the story? Could it be that its darker aspects have been made somewhat lighter so that it may appear to be as a "pearl of creation," or could it be that the author represents them in a rosy light? Could it be that the author himself grew up in similar circumstances, and finds a certain charm in these events? Could it be that our evaluation differs from the one given these events by the author?

As we analyze the story, we find that none of these conjectures is justified. Not only does the author not attempt to conceal the gloom of life, he exposes it whenever he can, describes it with graphic precision, lets our sensations and emotions almost touch these events, and, figuratively, allows us to put our hand right into life's festering sores. He underscores the senseless emptiness of this life. This is what he says of the girl:

> . . . her fame at school spread almost imperceptibly, and rumors began to circulate that she was frivolous, that she could not live without admirers, that the schoolboy Shenshin had lost his head over her, that she was also in love with him but was so capricious in her behavior toward him that he attempted suicide. . . .

Bunin uses harsh and brutal terms when he speaks of her liaison with the officer and reveals a truth of life which otherwise might have been somewhat concealed. ". . . Olia had seduced him, had had an affair with him, had promised to become his wife. But on the day of her murder, at the railway station, as she was seeing him off to Novocherkassk, she suddenly announced that she had never loved him, that all the talk about marriage was but a joke. . . . ” Then there is the cruel revelation of the truth as it appears in Olia's diary. Here, she describes her encounter with Maliutin:

> He is fifty-six, but still quite handsome and always well dressed
> – only I didn't like the cape he arrived in – it smells of English
> cologne, and his eyes are quite young and black, and his beard is
> carefully divided into two flowing parts and is entirely silver.

There is nothing in this scene, as recorded in Olia's diary, that makes us feel the existence of any feeling, or somehow brightens the dark and gloomy picture formed in the reader's mind. The word *love* is neither mentioned nor hinted at; one may well think that there is no word more alien to these lines than *love*. Thus, the entire material, all the circumstances of life, all the everyday events, concepts and emotions are described in a subdued tone, without a single bright spot. Thus, as we have stated, the author does not conceal the facts of life but exposes them with a brutality that makes us realize the full impact of the truth upon which his short story is based. We say once again: The essence of the story, viewed from this angle, can be defined as life's troubles, or its turbid waters. Surprisingly, however, the effect of the story, as a whole, is somewhat different.

The story is, after all, called “Gentle Breath.” It produces in us an effect that is almost diametrically opposed to the impression caused by the events themselves. The true theme of this story is the gentle breath, not the muddled life of a provincial schoolgirl. Its fundamental trait is the feeling of liberation, lightness, the crystal transparency of life, none of which can be derived from the literal events. The duality of the story becomes particularly obvious in the part concerning Olia's schoolteacher, which serves as a frame for the entire narrative. This teacher who goes into a stuporlike trance as she beholds Olia's tomb, this teacher who is ready to give half her life if only the funeral wreath would disappear, this teacher who is basically as happy as anyone in love or possessed by a dream, – it is she who suddenly gives a completely different meaning to the story. For a long time she has been living under delusions which she believes to be life. The author is bold enough to name three of them. The first was her brother, a poor, insignificant noncommissioned officer (this is reality) whom she expected to change miraculously her life and fate (this is the delusion). Then, she deluded herself that she was performing some sort of great work, or sacrifice, for an ideal; this served her as a substitute for life for some time. "Olia Meshcherskaia's death provided her with a new dream," says the author, and ranges this third self-deception beside the other two. With this technique, Bunin splits our emotions. He holds up a mirror to the story as he describes the new protagonist and breaks it up into several beams, as with a spectrum. As we read along, we are not only aware, but fully convinced that the story reflects both reality and dreams. From here our mind proceeds easily to the structural analysis mentioned earlier. The straight line is reality as it appears in the story, and the complex structural curve of reality, which we called the composition of the novella, is its light breath. We realize that the events are connected in such a way that they lose their turbidity. They are associated as in a melody, and in their crescendos, diminuendos, and transitions they untie the threads connecting them. They free themselves of the conventional bonds in which they are presented to us in actuality. They divorce themselves from reality, and associate in the same way as words associate and combine into a verse. Now we can formulate our idea and say that the author's reason for tracing such an extremely complex curve is his intent to undo life's turbidity and transform it into a crystal transparency. He did this to make life's events unreal, to transform water into wine, as always happens in any real work of art. The words of a story or verse carry its meaning (the water), whereas the composition creates another meaning for the words, transposes everything onto a completely different level, and transforms the whole into wine. Thus, the banal tale of a frivolous provincial schoolgirl is transformed into the gentle breath of Bunin's short story.

The story itself proves this beyond any doubt. If we take the first step in the composition, we see why the author begins with a description of the grave. We have to simplify matters here and try to reduce complex feelings to elementary emotions. If the story of Olia Meshcherskaia's life were told us in chronological sequence, suspense would be almost intolerable until the moment of her death. The poet would have created that special suspense, the damming up of our interests, which German psychologists like Lipps call a psychological dam, and literary theoreticians call *Spannung,* or suspense. The term means that tension, or suspense, rises exactly at the point where we have encountered the obstacle. The suspense of our interest, which each new episode of the story stresses and directs toward the next solution, would have filled this short story to excess: as stated earlier, the suspense would have been intolerable. The narrative would run somewhat as follows: We would learn how Olia seduced the officer, how she began a liaison with him, how she swore she loved him and talked about marriage, and how she began to make fun of him. We would witness the scene at the railway station, and with almost unbearable suspense would be there watching her for those last moments when the officer, her diary in his hands, steps onto the platform and shoots her. This is the effect this action in the disposition of the story would have on us. It is the culmination, the climax of the narrative around which all the other actions and events gravitate. But at the very beginning the author places us before Olia's grave and we learn about her life after she is dead. We learn first that she was killed and only later how it happened; we realize that the composition already gives the solution of the tension inherent in the events, if we take them per se. We read of the killing and the writing in the diary with completely different feelings than if the events had been developed rectilinearly, in chronological sequence. Thus, step by step, from episode to episode, from one phrase to another, we can show that the events were selected and connected in such a way that through the suspense they caused, all the dark, confused feelings are released to produce an effect completely different from the one we would have felt if the action had been narrated in its natural sequence. Following the structural diagram of the narrative, we can show that all the artificial leaps of the story have but one purpose, the neutralization of the first impression provoked by an event and its transformation into another, in contrast to the first.

This destruction of content by form can be illustrated with individual scenes and episodes from the narrative. For example, we learn of Olia's tragic death in a very peculiar fashion. The author has already brought us to her grave, we have learned of her depravation from the talk with the school principal, Maliutin was named for the first time.

> A month after this conversation took place, a Cossack officer, ugly and coarse in appearance and having nothing in common with the class of people to which Olia Meshcherskaia belonged, shot her on the platform of the railway station, in the midst of a large crowd which had just arrived on a train.

The structure of this sentence reveals the teleology of the author's style. Notice how the main word is lost in the agglomeration of descriptions which apparently have nothing to do with the narrative. The word "shot" is completely lost; and yet, it is the most terrible, sinister word not only of this sentence, but of the entire story. It is lost in the middle of the long, calm, placid description of the Cossack officer and the railway platform, and the large crowd just arrived on a train. We can say that the structure of this sentence damps the sound of this terrible shot to near imperceptibility, deprives it of its impact, and transforms it into an imitative sign or symbol. The emotional stress of this event is released, pushed aside, and destroyed. Note how we learn for the first time of Olia's moral depravation: in the cozy office of the school principal, filled with fresh lilies of the valley, amidst talk of expensive slippers and hairdos. And the terrible, or, as the author says, "the incredible confession which stunned the school principal" is described thus:

> At this point Olia, without losing her calm and simplicity, suddenly but politely interrupted her: 'Excuse me, Madame, but you're making a mistake. I am a woman. And do you know who is to blame? A friend and neighbor of Papa's, your brother Aleksei Mikhailovich Maliutin. It happened last summer, in the country...

The shot is described as a minor detail in the scene of the arrival of the train. The shocking confession is placed as an insignificant detail in a conversation about slippers and hairdos. The purpose of the meticulous detail, "a friend and neighbor of Papa's, your brother Aleksei Mikhailovich Maliutin," is to eradicate the impact caused by the confession. But the author does not fail to emphasize the realistic aspects of both the shot and the confession. In the cemetery scene Bunin describes in plain words the true significance of the events. He tells us of the state of mind of Olia's teacher, who cannot associate with this pure, innocent look all the horror now connected with Olia Meshcherskaia's name. Yet this horror, undiminished, follows us throughout the narrative. The story, however, does not strike us as a horror story; the horror is transposed to another level where we experience it differently. For some reason, this narrative of a dreadful event has the strange title "Gentle Breath," and for some reason the entire story is permeated with the breath of a cold, clear spring.

Let us look at the title. A title is given a story for the purpose of disclosing its most important theme, the dominant which in turn determines the structure of the narrative. This concept, which Christiansen introduced into aesthetics, is an extremely useful one, without which no serious analysis is possible. A work of art – a narrative, painting, or poem – is a complex whole which consists of heterogeneous elements organized in different ways and according to different hierarchies. In such a whole there exists always some dominating element which determines the structure of the entire story, as well as the significance of each of its parts. The dominant of our narrative is, of course, the *gentle breath*. It appears at the very end, the schoolteacher's reminiscence of a conversation she once overheard, between Olia Meshcherskaia and her girlfriend. It is a conversation about feminine beauty, and it proceeds in a semicomical style with reference to funny antique books. It happens to be the *pointe* of the story, the catastrophe which reveals its true significance. The "funny antique book" places the greatest emphasis on "gentle breath": "A gentle breath! I have it, don't I? Listen, how I sigh. It's there, isn't it?" It is as if we heard the sigh. . . . And in this trivial description, we suddenly discover its other significance, as we read the concluding words of the author: "And now this gentle breath is again dissipated in the world, in this cloud-covered sky, in this cold-spring wind..." These words complete the circle and bring the end back to the beginning. Frequently, one small word in an artist's hands can have great significance and tremendous impact. Such a word in this context is "this." It carries the outcome of the story, *this* gentle breath. We are talking about the sigh, we are talking about the gentle breath that Olia Meshcherskaia asked her girl friend to listen to. Further on we again meet significant words: ". . . in this cloud-covered sky, in this cold spring wind." The very last three words establish the whole idea of the narrative, which begins with a description of a cloudy sky and cold spring wind. Bunin uses the same mood in the beginning and end of his narrative, thus summarizing all that has happened, all that amounted to the life, love, and death of Olia Meshcherskaia (all this, in essence, is but one single event). And now *this* gentle breath has again dissipated in the world, in *this* cloud-covered sky, in *this* cold spring wind. All the earlier descriptions of the grave, the April weather, the gray days, the cold wind, all this is suddenly compressed at one point and introduced into the narrative. The story acquires a new significance, a new meaning. This is no longer a Russian provincial landscape, this is no longer a Russian provincial cemetery, this is no longer the sound of the wind in the porcelain wreath. No, it is the gentle breath, all the gentle breaths dissipated in the everyday world of the shot, Maliutin, and the horror associated with the name of Olia Meshcherskaia. Literary theoreticians characterize the *pointe* as the finale of a story at an unsettled point, or the finale in music ending with a dominant chord. At the very end of the narrative, when we know everything, when the story of the life and death of Olia Meshcherskaia has passed before our eyes, when we know all that could possibly interest us about the schoolteacher — at this point an unusually bright new light is cast upon the entire story. The transition from the tomb to the gentle breath is decisive for the composition of the narrative, inasmuch as it suddenly shows us the whole story in a completely different light.

The concluding sentence, which we called catastrophic, resolves this unsteady finale with a tonic chord. This unexpected and rather flighty confession of the light breath brings together the two levels of the narrative. Bunin does not conceal reality here, nor does he confuse it with invention. What Olia tells her friend is funny in the precise sense of the word. When she quotes from the book, "... black eyes, of course, gleaming like boiling pitch, that's the way it was written: gleaming like boiling pitch! Eyelashes as black as night . . ." and so on. It is amusing, it is simple, and it is true. And the real sigh ("listen, how I sigh"), so long as it is a part of reality, is but a small detail of this strange conversation. Taken in another context, however, it makes it possible for the author to bring together the scattered parts of his story, so that in its catastrophic concluding lines we see with unusual conciseness the whole story once again, from *this* gentle sigh to *this* cold spring wind on the tomb. And we are satisfied that the story is about gentle breath.

The author has used quite a number of auxiliary devices and techniques in this narrative. We have mentioned only one, that of the artistic treatment, or subject composition. It appears to be the most obvious and clear-cut of all the techniques used by Bunin. But there are of course many others, such as the manner in which the author narrates the events, the language he uses, the tone, the mood, his choice of words, his construction of sentences, whether he describes scenes or gives only a brief summary, whether he transcribes the dialogues of his characters or just tells us what they have said, and so forth. All of this is quite important and has a great bearing on the artistic treatment of the subject. Of similarly great importance is the choice of facts. For the sake of our argument we proceeded from a comparison between disposition and composition, assuming that disposition is the natural element and composition the artificial, or art one. We did not mention, however, that disposition in itself, that is, the choice of the facts to be treated, is already a creative act. In Olia Meshcherskaia's life there were thousands of events, thousands of dialogues. Her liaison with the officer included dozens of quarrels. Among her school loves, Shenshin was not alone. She mentioned Maliutin more than once to the principal. But for some reason, the author chose precisely some of these facts and episodes, and rejected thousands of others. This selection and screening, is, of course, a creative act. A painter portraying a tree cannot paint its every leaf, but gives a general impression by means of spots of color and draws a few leaves here and there. In the same fashion, the writer selects only those events that characterize best and most convincingly the real life material with which he is dealing. Strictly speaking, we already step outside the limits set by this selection when we begin to apply our own viewpoints about life to this material.

Blok has quite successfully described this rule in a poem:

> Life has no end and no beginning.
> Chance waits for us at every step. . . .

On the other hand Blok says:

> Erase sometimes the chance —
> And thou shalt see:
> The world is beautiful.

Particular attention must be paid to the organization of the writer's language, rhythm, and melody. In the calm, flowing, almost classic phrasing used by Bunin in his short story we find all the elements of power, strength, and eloquence necessary for an artistic treatment of the subject. To determine the importance of the effect produced on our breathing by the language used by the writer, we have made experimental recordings of our breathing while reading excerpts of prose and poetry with different rhythms, in particular while reading Bunin's story. Blonsky claims that we feel the way we breathe, and he is right. We can determine the emotional effect of a work of literature from the breathing that corresponds to it. When the author makes us breathe in short intervals, he creates a general emotional atmosphere corresponding to a sad and somewhat withdrawn mood. When he makes us exhale all the air we have in our lungs and then take another deep breath to refill them, he creates a completely different emotional mood for our aesthetic reaction.

At some later stage we shall discuss the meaning of these recordings of our breathing. It is significant, however, that the pneumographic recording made during the reading of the story under discussion shows a *gentle* breathing, which means that we read about the murder, the death, the troubles, and the horrors associated with Olia Meshcherskaia's name and breathe as if every new sentence brought us release from these horrors. Instead of painful tension and suspense, we experience an almost pathological lightness. This illustrates the affective contradiction, the collision between two contrasting emotions which apparently makes up the astonishing psychological rules of the aesthetics of the story. Astonishing, because traditional aesthetics prepared us for a diametrically opposite understanding of art. For centuries, scholars of aesthetics have told us of the harmony of form and content. They have told us that the form illustrates, completes, or accompanies, the content. And now we suddenly discover that this was an error, that the form may be in conflict with the content, struggle with it, overcome it. We discover in this dialectic contradiction between content and form the true psychological meaning of our own aesthetic reaction. It would seem that to represent gentle breath Bunin should have chosen a lyrical, calm, peaceful, and un-troublesome event in life. Why did he not tell us about some transparent, airy, and lofty first love, pure and untouched? Why did he choose terrifying, vulgar, turbid, and troublesome events to develop his theme of gentle breath?

We seem now to have reached the point where we can say that a work of art always contains a certain amount of contradiction, a certain inner incongruity between the material and the form. We can say that the author intentionally chooses a difficult, brittle material which will resist his efforts to say what he wants to say. The more brittle and hostile the material, the more suitable will it be for the author. The form given by the author to this material is not intended to reveal the feelings hidden in the material itself. It is not intended to expose the life of a Russian schoolgirl in a provincial town in all its depth. On the contrary, its purpose is to overcome these properties, to compel the horror to speak the language of gentle breath, and to induce the trouble, the pain, and turbidity of life to breathe and move like the cold spring wind.

ENDNOTES

[1] M. Petrovsky, "Morphology of Pushkin's 'The Shot,'" in *Problemy poetiki (Problems in Poetics)*, ed. V. I. Briusov (Moscow-Leningrad: *Zemlia i fabrika*, 1925), 197.

[2] V. Shklovsky, Tristram Shendi *Sterna i teoriia romana (Sterne's , Tristram Shandy' and the Theory of the Novel)* (Petrograd: *Opoyaz*, 1921), 38-39.

[3] *Ibid.*, p. 39.

III

Ekphrasis in Isaak Babel

ROBERT A. MAGUIRE

Toward the beginning of Babel's "Pan Apolek," one of the longest and most complex stories in *Red Cavalry*, the narrator, Liutov, pauses to describe a painting he sees hanging on the wall of a fugitive priest's house in Novograd-Volynsk:

> I remember: the spiderweb stillness of a summer morning hung between the straight and bright walls. A straight shaft of light had been placed at the bottom of the picture by the sun. In it swarmed sparkling dust. The long figure of John [the Baptist] was descending straight down upon me out of the dark-blue depths of the niche. A black cloak hung in triumph from that implacable, repulsively thin body. Drops of blood glittered in the round clasps of the cloak. John's head had been cut off at an angle from the flayed neck. It lay upon an earthenware dish that was held tightly by the large yellow fingers of a warrior. The dead man's face looked familiar to me. I felt a touch of mystery in the offing. On the earthenware dish lay a head that had been copied from that of Pan Romuald, the fugitive priest's assistant. From between the bared teeth of the mouth hung the tiny body of a snake, its scales glittering colorfully. Its small head, delicately pink, full of animation, powerfully set off the deep background of the cloak.[1]

This is an instance of the device known in Greek (and usually in English) as *ekphrasis*, in Latin as *descriptio*. Ernst Robert Curtius has defined it succinctly as "the elaborate 'delineation,'" verbally, of "people, places, buildings, works of art."[2] It takes its origin in the Greek and Roman classics. We all remember famous instances like Achilles's shield in Book 18 of the *Iliad*, or the murals depicting the fall of Troy in the temple of Venus in Book 1 of the *Aeneid*. So graphic are these instances that they can be readily translated into paintings and drawings.[3] And they serve more specifically literary purposes too: varying the narrative pace, furthering the characterization of the heroes involved, invoking a larger world that lies outside the text.

Over the centuries, writers have borrowed lavishly from Homer and Virgil, replicating or varying the famous scenes, and taking for granted that readers would remember the originals. No such assumption is possible today, of course. Yet the classics live silently on in literature, and ekphrasis is as vigorous as ever. We are often surprised at the lengths to which writers of the late twentieth century will go to give it prominence. In ancient times, ekphrasis could serve as a visual record of things otherwise unrecordable and therefore unpreservable. Obviously that is no longer the case; yet writers apparently still feel the need to create verbal equivalents of that which can be registered on film, canvas, or computer disk, and made available, through inexpensive reproductions and the internet, to millions of people throughout the world. We must also wonder why ekphrasis, as both a literary and rhetorical device, has recently engendered an enormous resurgence of interest – along with the related topic of *ut pictura poesis* – among critics and theorists. During the 1990s alone, many books and articles have been devoted to explorations of a device whose very name, a generation ago, would have been unfamiliar to most scholars who were not professional classicists.[4]

Broad questions of this kind can best be addressed through specifics, like the passage I have just quoted from "Pan Apolek." It not only draws on some of the traditional uses of classical ekphrasis, but gives them a modern spin. One of these uses is to amplify the personage most closely associated with the object being described. In the *Iliad*, for example, the new shield marks the true coming-of-age of Achilles. In the *Aeneid*, the murals reassure Aeneas that he is on friendly territory, and also embed some of the paradoxes and ironies that will complicate his physical and psychological journey to Italy. The Liutov who contemplates the painting of John seems more self-aware than his classical predecessors – at least, more neurotically self-preoccupied – but he is not very perceptive about ways of dealing with the chaotic world of war he encounters in *Red Cavalry*. The fact that it is he who describes the painting, and not an anonymous narrator, as in Homer and Virgil, subjects what he sees to his own limitations. Perhaps, then, he is not much "fuller" a character at this point than Achilles or Aeneas toward the beginning of their stories. Yet precisely because his perspective is narrow, and because any specimen of ekphrasis tends to take on a life independent of its observer, the "real" author, Babel, can enter silently into the narrative and show us sides of Liutov that would otherwise remain dim, if not invisible. In the process, Liutov does become fuller, and we readers gain in our understanding of certain issues that inform the book as a whole.

Liutov tells us that the "dead man's face looked familiar." Presently he connects it with Pan Romuald. But the word "mystery" suggests a more important connection, which he does not see but may intuit. As every reader of the Bible knows, John the Baptist was the last of the prophets of Israel, a transitional figure between an old way of life and a new one, often called the Kingdom, where there would be no differences between Jew and Gentile. Specifically, his role was to prepare the way of the Lord, by preaching repentance and administering baptism. Some parallels with Liutov immediately suggest themselves. He too is a Jew, and in his role as a Bolshevik political officer he preaches repentance, as it were, of the old ways of life as a prerequisite to entering a new order, where all distinctions of class, social standing, ethnic origin, and religion will disappear. The first story, "Crossing the Zbruch" (*Perekhod cherez Zbruch*) has already evoked mythologies of initiation and baptism, in its emphasis on the water-crossing and the entrance into a new realm (Poland) that is very different from the ones in which the Cossacks, not to speak of Liutov himself, have passed their lives. And the immersion in the river contains one specifically Christian reference, albeit blasphemous, which points ahead to the subject of the "icon" just a few pages later: "Someone was drowning, and loudly defaming the Mother of God" (23). We remember that Mary is told by the Angel Gabriel not only that she will bear a son, but that her cousin, Elizabeth, "has conceived a son in her old age" (Luke 1:36-63). That son is John, and the most important baptism he performs is that of Jesus himself (Matthew 3:13-17). But ironies abound. John the Baptist never doubted for a moment what his mission was, succeeded in accomplishing it brilliantly, and was fully prepared to die for it. Liutov quickly discovers that the Cossacks are singularly unreceptive to his message, and he progressively loses confidence in the validity of his mission. Finally, if anyone is a candidate for baptism in this book, it is Liutov himself, as the "old" identities he brings to the land across the river – Jew, Russian, Bolshevik, urbanite, intellectual – are challenged and found wanting; yet every step he takes toward a "new" life is marked by a hesitation and fear that make regeneration impossible. Whether he sees either the parallels or the ironies is unclear. But we readers do, and we understand that the painting of John the Baptist stands in mute reproach to a vocation imperfectly conceived and incompetently pursued, and as a challenge to rethink and remake it in creative and productive ways.

The problem of Liutov's vocation is preponderantly a problem of language. Let us recall how the first story begins: "The Sixth Divcom reported that Novograd-Volynsk was taken today at dawn." This has all the gray impersonality of any military dispatch. In its colorless certitude, the language conveys the kind of impersonal, abstract actuality that can account for all situations, because it ignores the messiness of actual experience. It is a language that generals and commissars understand well. But the rest of the story deconstructs this statement, as Liutov (who as yet has no name) comes to understand that it is inadequate to the many ways in which a town's capture can be described. He tells the same story over and over again in a variety of styles and from different points of view, without arriving at any definitive version. Struggling with the soul of the ideologue is the soul of the poet, which understands that reality is composed of particulars, each of which has a name that the poet feels bound to find, record, and communicate. This struggle creates the main dynamic of the book. But it is a dynamic that inspires profound disquiet in Liutov; for as an ideologue, he has been trained, to reapply the apt words of E.H. Gombrich, to cultivate "the art of imposing a pattern on reality, and to impose it so successfully that the victim can no longer conceive it in different terms."[5] One reason he is drawn to visual artifacts, like the painting of John, is that they do not move, and are thus more susceptible to receiving prefabricated patterns than is the welter of experience which imposes itself on him in baffling, often dangerous ways.

"My First Goose" (*Moi pervyi gus'*) deals with this struggle in an especially rich and nuanced way. Liutov's task is to bring the word of Bolshevism to the Cossack division commanded by Savitskii. But he is frustrated from the outset as Savitskii and other soldiers make it brutally clear that he is out of place. Assailed by "an unparalleled feeling of loneliness," he then "lay down on the ground to read in *Pravda* Lenin's speech at the Second Congress of the Comintern." That is to say, he resorts to the soothingly familiar rhetoric of ideology. But to no avail: "the beloved lines came toward me along a thorny path and could not reach me" (50-51), because they do not account for the situation with which he must deal in this particular Cossack camp at this particular time. The seemingly helpful quartermaster proposes what amounts to an initiation (already hinted at by the word "first" in the title): "Just go and mess up a lady, a real pure lady, and the boys will treat you good." Liutov does no more than kill a goose, but that apparently suffices. The Cossacks now listen to him read the speech and even comment on it: "Truth tickles everyone's nostrils." What really matters to Liutov, however, is the pleasure he derives from "spying out exultingly the secret curve of Lenin's straight line," a pleasure he cares nothing about communicating to his audience, as he himself suggests when he tells us that he declaimed the speech "loudly, like a triumphant deaf man," a man, that is, who remains "deaf" and presumably blind as well (his eyes being fixed on the "secret curve" of the speech) to the still elusive realities of this particular slice of Cossack life, and who has therefore not found a language that can convey them.

As an ideologue, Liutov has learned a language which purports to explain everything about the world. As a highly sensitive observer, he understands that this is not the case, that other languages must be sought and found, but that none of them suffices. Whether the fault lies in the way he perceives the world or in the linguistic resources at his command is never offered as an alternative in these stories. In his famous essay on the Laokoon group (1776), Lessing had argued that literature and the visual arts reflected different modes of perceiving the world, the one sequential, the other spatial, and therefore required different means of expression. The distinction has not prevented writers from attempting to employ the perceptions and techniques of the visual arts as one way of coping with the problems posed by the slippery, elusive ways of language. Babel is one such writer. Many of the stories in *Red Cavalry*, like "Crossing the Zbruch," rely heavily on the kind of spatial juxtapositions we associate with painting.[6] The use of ekphrasis, as in the painting of John, is technically less sophisticated, but psychologically more gratifying to Liutov. It represents a verbal imitation of a solid object, which, as an "icon," has the additional advantage of incorporating the eternal and unchanging truths of religion. Babel may not have been thinking of Gogol; but the parallel is intriguing, for painting, in particular religious painting, attracted Gogol as a wish-fulfilling alternative to the verbal medium he found increasingly unsuited to the kind of iconic art he wished to create. It functions as a wish-fulfillment for Liutov too, a vivid and colorful affirmation of the Tightness of the mind-set of the ideologue.

But why does Liutov call it an "icon?" This term has long been reserved to designate a particular kind of Eastern Orthodox religious art, and is not now properly used of Western art at all, regardless of subject-matter. Liutov's misuse of the term hints at a failure to understand not only what icons are all about, but what this particular painting could reveal to him if he had the eyes to see. Least of all is an icon intended to serve as a mirror of an individual's psyche. Rather, in Egon Sandler's words, it "introduces another dimension to the image, transcendence, and thus projects itself beyond the forms of our world, making God's world present.... The icon points to a dimension which goes beyond the natural; it pushes out toward the ineffable. This ascension toward the Beyond is a communion with eternity."[7] Babel's non-Jewish Russian readers are presumably more competent than Liutov. They also know that even though the painting in question is Roman Catholic in origin, the decollation of John the Baptist is a frequent subject of Orthodox icons too. But Babel may be inviting us to "read" this painting as we would an icon, appealing to what any Orthodox Russian reader would know: that, as Leonid Ouspensky puts it, the Church "attributes to the icon the same dogmatic, liturgie and educational significance as it does to the Holy Scriptures. As the word of the Holy Scriptures is an image, so the image is also a word."[8] The equation extends to the creative act too, as suggested by the verb *pisat'*, which means both "paint" and "write." In these ways we are instructed that whatever the "icon" of John "means," that meaning informs Liutov's acts of verbal creation as well.

Presently the title character, Pan Apolek, appears. The name is charmingly odd. "Pan" is of course the normal Polish word for "mister." "Apolek" is an affectionate diminutive of the name of Apollo, who is associated with the arts and with the sun, among other things, and who therefore epitomizes two of this wandering painter's main qualities. Once the mythological subtext has been brought into play, however, "Pan" becomes more than just an honorific, and summons up yet another ancient Greek figure. Half-man and half-goat, Pan is a pastoral god who is famously lustful, a quality that in his Polish namesake has been sublimated into a joyous celebration of the sensualities of nature and ordinary human life. "Pan" is supposedly derived from a word designating "feeding" or "nourishing," but readers ignorant of the niceties of classical philology will almost certainly associate it with the word for "all," as did the Greeks themselves. "Allness" hints at Apolek's ability to meld, through his art, puzzlingly different realms of being, particularly the spiritual and the fleshly, into an integral and apparently authentic whole.

But there are troubling things about his names. We soon learn that he was baptized "Apollinarius." This is a peculiar name for a Christian, since it is most notably borne by the exponent of the first great Christological heresy (fourth century). Apollinarius taught that "in man there coexist body, soul, and spirit. In Christ, however, were to be found the human body and soul, but no human spirit, the spirit being replaced by the Divine Logos." What this means is that "while He possessed perfect Godhood, He lacked complete manhood." This is inimical to Roman Catholic teaching because "if there is no complete manhood in Christ, He is not a perfect example for us, nor did He redeem the whole of human nature but only its spiritual elements." In what sense might Apolek/Apollinarius be a "heretic" in this story? Presumably we are being invited to seek a parallel in the painter's life and work that would show him to be favoring the spiritual over the fleshly, or the saintly over the merely human. Yet his religious pictures appear to combine all those qualities successfully, most of all in the "icon" of John the Baptist, which we soon learn is a product of his brush. A hint may lurk in the Vicar's objection to Apolek's making "saints" of the townsfolk "in their lifetime." Our first impulse is to dismiss him as narrow-minded and formalistic. After all, Roman Catholic artists have for centuries been using live models for works commissioned by the highest ecclesiastical authorities, without much fuss about their manners or morals. What he specifies as the sins that disqualify those who have sat for Apolek – "disobedience, secret distillers, pitiless moneylenders, makers of false weights, and sellers of the innocence of your own daughters" – are mere rhetorical tinsel, the stuff of bad Sunday sermons: we are offered no evidence that these people are any worse than human beings generally (39). Even so, the Vicar may have a point. His outrage suggests that he is not concerned with these paintings as much as with the danger that at a stroke of the brush, anyone can be turned into a saint, human qualities aside. Catholics know that only the Church can make saints, and only posthumously. Quite apart from questions of sin, true personhood is regarded as a process which ends only with death. A human being who is incomplete in the eyes of the Church would be passed off as complete, and in that sense, would represent a counterpart of the operation performed upon Christ by the fourth-century Apollinarius. To a man like Liutov, who is uncomfortable with the ambiguities of raw experience and yearns for quick solutions, Apolek's way is tempting. But we see that it is dangerous because it brings spiritual death, as Faust, among the many literary prototypes of Liutov, discovered. Can it be mere coincidence that Apolek/Apollinarius is also phonically suggestive of Apollyon or Abbadon, "the angel in charge of the abyss" in Revelation 9:11?[9]

Troubling too is the way in which Apolek tells the Jesus/Deborah story. Of course he wants to shock Robatskii, the beadle, and he succeeds; but it does not take a very sensitive ear to detect a smacking of the lips, and to wonder whether Apolek is not just an esthetic lecher, who ogles life as material for his paintings, paintings which, furthermore, are rendered according to formulas, and thus are mere cartoons, not even imitations of life. The fakery is hard to see because it is so engagingly brought off – who can fail to like Apolek? – and it represents still another temptation to Liutov because it is the way of the ideologue too. Yet Liutov is constantly forced to experience more authentic versions of sensuality, because they are more immediate, and often life-threatening.

Once again, the first story poses the problem in a dramatic way. The pregnant Jewess removes a blanket from what the narrator thinks is her sleeping father, and reveals "a dead old man," whose "throat had been ripped out, and his face cleft in two, and dark blue blood lay in his beard like a piece of lead." She then tells the narrator that it was the Poles who had cut his throat, while he begged them to kill him "in the back yard so that my daughter won't see me die." The old man is anxious that his daughter *not* see what is being done to him. But she does see, and in seeing, achieves the kind of wisdom expressed in her final cry: "where on all the earth will you find another father like my father?" (24) In effect she seems to be saying that it is only as a result of violent death that the otherwise insignificant, anonymous old Jew becomes special, a "father," someone whose memory will be perpetuated in and through the child that is yet to be born. This particular episode does not seem to touch Liutov personally; he remains an onlooker, as nameless at this point as the daughter and the father. In the three stories that follow – "The Church at Novograd" (*Kostel v Novograde*), "A Letter" (*Pis'mo*), and "The Remount Officer" (*Nachal'nik konzapasa*) – he comments, muses, reports, but feels at best an intruder into an alien world. The fourth story, however, is "Pan Apolek," and the icon of John, with which it opens, poses the problem of sensuality and violence in a way that begins to touch him more deeply and directly.

The beheading of John, and the events that led up to it, are related in Matthew (14:1-12), Mark (6:14-29), and Luke (9:7-9), and are commemorated by the Church on August 29. For all its brevity, it is one of the most fruitful stories of the New Testament, as countless paintings, novels and operas attest. The Gospel tells us only that Herodias's marriage to Herod is illegal, since he is her brother-in-law, and (in Mark) that her daughter, Salome, performs a dance, which "delighted" her stepfather, and for which she is rewarded by being given John's head on a platter. What most readers remember, however – Babel surely among them – are the later, secular versions, where Herodias takes a carnal interest in John (as in Flaubert's story), or where Salome is depicted as a Lolita type (as in the Oscar Wilde play and the Richard Strauss opera based on it). For all but the most literal-minded readers of the Bible, a sexual element is subtextually present in the painting that Liutov contemplates. We will remember that in the first story, "Crossing the Zbruch," violence is also directed at the head and inflicted with a blade, and that the result is the ennoblement of the victim, and a flash of wisdom in the daughter, who is also the "victim" of the thrusting, sword-like act of sex that produces a new life. Where is the "wisdom" of the event portrayed in the painting? Perhaps it is suggested in the detail of the snake that hangs from the mouth of the decapitated head. Of course, we associate the snake with temptation and evil, which certainly figure in the death of John. But the snake is also a traditional emblem of wisdom and healing. The fact that the snake is leaving the head, however, suggests that wisdom and healing do not depend on cerebral activity, as an ideologue like Liutov might wish them to, but are bound up with sensuality, especially in the form of sex and violence.

It is not until "My First Goose," however, that Liutov is compelled by circumstances to act upon these dimly intuited verities. As the story opens, he stands in the presence of Savitskii, the commander of the Sixth Division, and "marveled at the beauty of his giant's body. He rose, and with the purple of his riding-breeches, with the little crimson cap that had been knocked to one side, with the decorations hammered into his chest, he clove the hut in two, as a standard cleaves the sky. From him wafted the smell of perfume and the cloying coolness of soap. His long legs were like girls who had been sheathed up to the shoulders in gleaming jack-boots" (49). The sexuality is blatant and violent ("knocked," "hammered," "clove," "sheathed"); but because it is also predominantly homoerotic – we might easily encounter it in a specimen of gay sado-masochistic fiction – it cannot be biologically productive. As such, it is admirably expressive of the voyeuristic proclivities of Liutov. His glasses keep him safely distanced from Savitskii, the object of his fantasy; yet they instantly mark him as an ogler, and open him to discovery and danger. "People get their throats cut for wearing glasses," Savitskii observes contemptuously, the implication being that not only is Liutov an outsider of an especially undesirable kind – Jew, intellectual, and propagandist – and as such is incapable of taking the kinds of action incumbent on a real soldier in this war, but that he cannot even properly see – in the sense of observing and understanding – how things really are, or, in the homoerotic context of the opening paragraph, possess what Savitskii represents: manliness, strength, beauty, and membership in a vital collective.

Possession is also denied a few paragraphs later when Liutov encounters "a young lad with long flaxen hair and a beautiful Riazan' face," who "turned his rear end toward me and with special skill began emitting shameful sounds" from it, which an onlooking Cossack laughingly compares to the firing of a cannon (50). It is as if Liutov's homoerotic contemplation of Savitskii is being mocked by the lad, who announces in effect that this particular rear end is unavailable for any purpose other than that for which it was originally designed. The lad's actions also reinforce the solution that the quartermaster has just proposed to enable Liutov to win acceptance by the Cossacks. "Just go and mess up a lady, a real pure lady, and the boys will treat you good." Liutov is hereby put on notice that the male bonding of the Cossacks, which he yearns to share, is not an expression of homoeroticism, but requires an assertion of maleness in the most obvious way. His response is curious, because it does not literally fulfill the requirements of the statement. The only female present is the old Polish landlady, who, being almost blind too, is another version of Liutov himself and therefore cannot be directly assaulted. Instead he picks a goose, whose whiteness endows it with symbolic purity, crushes its head beneath his boot, impales it on "someone else's sword" ("*chuzhuiu sabliu*"), and orders the landlady to cook it for him. The Cossacks watch this series of ritual displacements "like pagan priests" ("*kak zhretsy*"), and appear to extend acceptance, as they invite him to share their meal, and then listen to him read aloud from Lenin's speech.

In the final scene, the Cossacks allow him to sleep with them, legs intertwined. As he sleeps he dreams that he "saw women, and only my heart, blood-stained with murder, squeaked and flowed over" (51). "Murder" (*ubiistvo*) is of course too strong a word for the killing of a goose. But it is no more of a mismatch than Liutov's response to the quartermaster's challenge. We are prompted to ask: what *is* being "murdered," if not the goose? The fact that the Cossack "priests" "did not look at the goose" suggests that their "acceptance" of Liutov is provisional at best, condescending at worst. This is a truth he sees in the discomfiting dream, and it tells him that his debut as a man of action is bogus, that the goose-killing is perverse sexuality, with its hints at fetishism and cannibalism, and that the intertwined legs represent not bonding, but the temporary gratification of an adolescent fantasy of belonging. Ironically, Liutov has declined to violate his self in the alter-ego of the landlady, only to violate, or "murder" it far more fundamentally in the substitution he chooses.

Yet Liutov does act, however absurdly. That is why his experience is more authentic than Apolek's, and why it brings him closer to the figure of John in the icon than to the painter who created him. He is beginning to see that spirituality grows out of the lives of ordinary people, especially those who are violated in one way or another, and that he must accept his own ordinariness – as Jew, Russian, and soldier – if he is to achieve integration into the human community as represented, with all its imperfections, in these stories. Spirituality cannot be imposed by formula, whether iconographic or verbal. As one who imposes, Apolek is a heretic, as his baptismal name suggests, and so is Liutov whenever his psychological need for certainty draws him to ideological solutions. From this point on, he displays a greater willingness to engage himself, though never fully, and with frequent and disastrous setbacks, as in "The Death of Dolgushov" (*Smert' Dolgushova*). Never does he attain the level of fearless commitment exemplified by John, which depends on an order of spiritual maturity he never even approaches. Nor does he ever understand that a true sense of mission inescapably involves knowing what that mission is *not*. John certainly does, as a particularly vivid account in the Fourth Gospel attests. His initial responses to the question "Who are you?" are framed as denials: "I am not the Christ . . . I am not [Elijah] ... No, [not the Prophet]." This opens the way for a clear statement of who he is and what he does: "I baptize with water," in preparation for the one "who comes after me, the thong of whose sandal I am not worthy to untie" (John 1:19-27, Revised Standard Version). Liutov knows that he is not a Cossack, of course, but it is the Cossacks themselves who provide constant reminders of that, while he wishes with all his heart that he were one of them. What makes his emotional and moral flaccidity even more striking, and rather funny too, is his name. It is obviously one of those revolutionary pseudonyms that were in vogue among the early Bolsheviks. Being derived from *liutyi*, "fierce" – a word often used of predatory animals – it attributes to its bearer qualities which in this case he certainly does not possess, but would like to. What he admires about Savitskii and the Cossacks is their *liutost'* (although he does not call it that), their capacity for direct, purposeful, and, if need be, "fierce" action. He has to learn, again and again, that such qualities, in this story and throughout the cycle, spring from an honest understanding of one's purpose in life and a willingness to see it through, with no concern for unpleasant consequences.

He must also learn to endure the knowledge that this self is actually two. One is the self which believes in, yearns for, and strives toward essences. The other is the self which is obsessed with observing the existential world and trying to render it as precisely as possible. The two selves have opposite aims, and are inevitably in conflict. Liutov is tormented by the anxiety that the world before his eyes may disappear into a rhetorical sea of ideological dicta and military dispatches, two of the prime genres of essentialism. (It is useful to remember that Babel was a contemporary of the Acmeist poets, who were intent on celebrating the thinginess of the world.) Conversely, he often seems overwhelmed by the plethora of particulars, and fearful that nothing can knit them together. This conflict takes many forms, among them his increasingly troubled questioning of his Jewish identity: Judaism is not only a religion of rules and practices, and thus a rival to the new religion of Bolshevism, but is also a religion of the book, that is, of the word.

In any event, Liutov begins to find a voice in the process of creating these stories. Babel's brilliant touch is to make him a reluctant creator, who is thrown into situations for which his gift seems utterly inadequate, yet for which it could not be better suited. Quite against Liutov's will, words become the vehicles of flux and process; they cannot create an iconic reality. Probably no Russian writer since Gogol has had a keener sense of the flaws of the verbal medium in which he is condemned to work. For Gogol, however, the icon was perfect and exemplary, and because he could not translate its lessons into the terms of his own art, he ended by abandoning his writing and dying shortly thereafter. By contrast, Liutov discerns the limitations of the visual media – whether the "icon" in "Pan Apolek" or the stagecraft in "Italian Sunshine" (*Solntse Italii*) – yet reaches a solution, one that is not satisfying to most readers, who tend to perceive it as a cop out. In "Argamak," a story added to the 1931 edition of *Red Cavalry*, he finally learns to ride like a Cossack, whereupon "[my] dream came true. The Cossacks stopped following me and my horse with their eyes" (152). The writer disappears into his material, and the stories must come to an end.

Isaak Babel was not the only Russian writer of the 1920s to explore the tensions between word and image. We could profitably look at Evgenii Zamiatin's *We* (*My*, 1920) or Iury Olesha's *Envy* (*Zavist'*, 1927), among many interesting instances. Nor was this a uniquely Russian preoccupation. It had surfaced internationally around the turn of the century, and was engaging the talents of some first-class writers. Virginia Woolf's *To the Lighthouse*, for example, appeared in 1927, one year after the first publication in book form of *Red Cavalry*. It bears many similarities, albeit coincidental, to Babel's story-cycle: the prominence of mythic motifs, including water-crossings; the crucial importance of "moments" – scenes in Woolf, whole stories in Babel – in which private sensibilities and disparate images of the outside world meld to create an integral, albeit fleeting vision. Other similarities can be detected in the ways Woolf uses her characters to represent different ways of perceiving reality. For Mrs. Ramsay, words serve to register the ebb and flow of the minutiae, mental and physical, that comprise the world yet are "ephemeral as a rainbow." Her husband, Mr. Ramsay, is a professional philosopher of great repute, obsessed with creating a grand scheme of thought as represented by the twenty-six letters of the alphabet, and bitterly frustrated that in his intellectual quest he may possibly move beyond "Q" to reach "R," but never the "Z" of full understanding, let alone the sudden "flash" which "lump[s] all the letters together" (part 1, section 6). In short, he is an essentialist, who, like Liutov, is aware not only of the limitations of his mind, but also of his inability to deal with the necessary bustle of life he affects to despise yet desperately craves. It is he who most resists undertaking the "expedition" to the Lighthouse, "distant and austere," which the children and Mrs. Ramsay constantly urge, in their deeply rooted sense that such an undertaking confirms one's commitment to life as a journey in all its puzzling variety, and its inevitable finiteness.

The third major character, whom we might conveniently if inaccurately call the "heroine," is the painter Lily Briscoe. She is shown throughout the novel attempting to paint a picture of Mrs. Ramsay and her young son James. It is not to be representational but abstract; and the purple triangle that represents a first effort is promising. But she cannot make it come right. The reason is that she is unable, until nearly the end of the novel, to understand that art is not a question of personal feelings and emotions, but of insight born of detachment, distance, and impersonality. (Coleridge's famous distinction, in *Biographia Litteraria*, between "fancy" and "imagination" works very well here.) As that begins to happen, the particulars of her vision arrange themselves in shapes and lines that move as if by an inner rhythm and strike the eye as "greens and blues," "brown running nervous lines," "a red, a grey." The result, she hopes, comprises something "[b]eautiful and bright ... on the surface, feathery and evanescent, one color melting into another like the colors on a butterfly's wing" (part 3, section 5). Painting does seem to be privileged; but it is meant to stand for all art, regardless of medium. Woolf uses a painter to make her point perhaps because a painting, especially if abstract, more readily stands apart from the creator and the viewer, who are otherwise tempted to "read" art in terms of personal needs, aspirations, and urgings. But the same should be true of a work of verbal art, as the method Woolf employs in *To the Lighthouse* is meant to demonstrate. No doubt that is why we do not really know what Lily's painting looks like: there is no ekphrasis where we expect it. The denial of visual specificity further makes the point that painting should convey none of the sense of permanence that a describable artifact would, for each work of art is unique and unrepeatable, being the product of a specific time and place. Lily's slow arrival at that truth is the mark of her achievement. Her picture "would be hung up in the attics, [Lily] thought; it would be destroyed." But she knows that this does not matter: "It [the painting] was done; it was finished ... I have had my vision," (part 3, section 13).

Undoubtedly Woolf s novel is more "modernist" than Babel's story-cycle in its calm acknowledgment of ambiguity and impermanence, in its strong but unspoken conviction that there is a "language" common to both graphic and verbal discourse, but reducible to neither, and in its cultivation of distance and impersonality as the only way the artist – represented in Woolf by an anonymous third-person narrator with no describable personality – can achieve the right kind of vision. Detachment and impersonality may often be desiderata for Liutov, but in his passionate, agonized attempts to make sense of life and his place in it, he can never rise above his insatiable involvement with the immediacies of situations and people, as the very fact of his being his own narrator emphasizes. Still, his yearning for mutually exclusive alternatives strikes us as modern, if not modernist. Perhaps "Argamak," written when Stalinism was already ascendant, can be read as a prophecy of things to come: not only does the wielder of words disappear into the mute mass of the Cossacks, but their "eyes" cease to register his existence, as his do theirs. With the imposition, a mere three years later, of socialist realism as the official and therefore exclusive guide to artistic creation, word was made iconic, and privileged over image, which became merely illustrative of truths that supposedly could find full expression verbally. (In an even grimmer irony, Babel began complaining about his inability to write fiction, and put his talent to the service of a visual art, in the form of film scenarios.) Not surprisingly, ekphrasis virtually disappeared. The only striking instances in all of Stalinist literature that I can recall are associated with "negative," that is, anti-Soviet characters and situations, precisely because the kind of graphic detail essential to ekphrasis was deemed alien to the esthetics of socialist realism.[10]

With the passing of socialist realism, the graphic arts are reappearing in Russia with a vigor that they have not displayed since the 1920s. It remains to be seen whether the complex relationship between word and image, which Babel so brilliantly explored more than seventy-five years ago, will also revive, and whether ekphrasis will again take an honored place in the arsenal of literary devices.

ENDNOTES

[1] In I. Babel, *Konarmiia. Odesskie rasskazy. P'esy* (Letchworth (Hertfordshire): Bradda Books, 1965), 35-36. (Reprinted from *Izbrannoe*. Moscow, 1957.) Hereafter, page references will be given in the text.

[2] Ernst Robert Curtius, *European Literature and the Latin Middle Ages*, trans. Willard R.Trask (London: Routledge and Kegan Paul, 1979), 69.

[3] See, e.g., the drawing of Achilles's shield in Malcolm W.Willcock, *A Companion to the Iliad* (Chicago and London:The University of Chicago Press, 1976), 210.

[4] On ekphrasis, three books have recently appeared from the University of Chicago Press alone: James A.W. Heffernan, *Museum of Words.The Poetics of Ekphrasis from Homer to Ashbery* (1993); John Hollander, *The Gazer's Spirit. Poems Speaking to Silent Works of Art* (1995); W.J.T. Mitchell, *Picture Theory. Essays on Verbal and Visual Representation* (1994). On ut pictura poesis, see Wesley Trimpi, "Horace's 'Ut pictura poesis:' The Argument for Stylistic Decorum." *Traditio* 34 (1978): 29-73. For Russian literature, see Amy Mandelker, *Framing Anna Karenina.Tolstoi, the Woman Question, and the Victorian Novel* (Columbus: The Ohio State University Press, 1993), esp. Ch. 5. Of the many books on rhetoric that have appeared in the last fifteen years or so, one of the best is Brian Vickers, *In Defence of Rhetoric* (Oxford: Clarendon Press, 1988).

[5] E.H. Gombrich, "Renaissance and Golden Age," in *Studies in the Art of the Renaissance.Vol. I* (Chicago: University of Chicago Press, 1985), 31.

[6] Cf., e.g., Joseph Frank, "Spatial Form in Modern Literature," in *The Widening Gyre* (New Brunswick, NJ: Rutgers University Press, 1963), 3-62.

[7] Egon Sandler, *The Icon. Image of the Invisible*, trans. Steven Bingham (Redondo Beach, CA: Oakwood Publications, 1988), 1-2.

[8] Leonid Ouspensky and Vladimir Lossky, "The Meaning of Icons," in *The Meaning of Icons*, trans. G.E.H. Palmer and E. Kadloubovsky (Crestwood, NY: St. Vladimir's Seminary Press, 1983), 30.

[9] For the characterization of Apollinarius, see *The Oxford Dictionary of the Christian Church*, ed. F.L. Cross (London: Oxford University Press, 1958), 70.The quotation from Revelation comes from *The New American Bible*, which defines the Hebrew "Abaddon" as "destruction or ruin," and the Greek Apollyon as "destroyer."

[10] See Robert A. Maguire, "Literary Conflicts in the 1920's," *Survey* 18.3 (1972): 98-127.

IV

Zoshchenko's "Electrician," or the Complex Theatrical Mechanism.[1]

ALEXANDER ZHOLKOVSKY

In memory of Iu. V. Tomashevsky

Somehow we got to talking about... the concept of Jungian archetypes... [according to which] all people have an archaic... psychic layer dating from the Paleolithic era, which once gave birth to myths and now gives birth to works of art... Zoshchenko felt that the writer should portray in man not only the personal but also the "generic," what history had deposited in his psyche. Writers in pursuit of fashion did not satisfy him because they ignored the generic and historical for the sake of the temporary and individual. (G. Gor, "*Na kanale Griboedova*")[2]

[A] very powerful pre-Revolutionary picture. It captures very accurately the moments of that era... It is instructive to see this picture in all historical periods. (M. Zoshchenko, "I Won't Allow It" (*Ne pushchu*))[3]

Once we put on a play... from the old life... In it,... a merchant is robbed right in public... I play... the merchant. I shout...: "Help..., citizens, they're robbing me blind"... I see my shouts won't help. Because no matter what I shout, everything falls right in with the play. (M. Zoshchenko, "The Actor" (Akter))

The Serapions had a refrain that went...: "Zoshchenko took offense"... Yes,... he would have grounds to be offended by us, because we knew his work better than anyone and had no right to interpret it so superficially. (K. Fedin)

Who the hell cares whether the Art History Institute praises or damns me? Do you really think I don't know what my things are worth? (M. Zoshchenko)[4]

PART ONE

"The Electrician" (*Monter*) is one of Zoshchenko's fifteen or so "theatrical" stories, which typically ignore, purposely distort, and significantly refract what is happening on stage.[5] The plot of the story, which runs for all of a page and a half, consists of the following. When

> "the whole theater... was having its picture taken, the electrician... was crammed in somewhere on the side, as if to say, technical staff. And in the middle... they put the tenor. The electrician... didn't say a word to this loutishness, but in his soul he harbored a certain rudeness... And then this started happening... Two young ladies he knew walked up to this electrician... and basically they asked to be seated with everyone in the hall," but the administrator refused, because "each chair has been accounted for." Then the electrician refused to "play": he "turned off the lights to the entire theater and it served them right, the bastards... and he sat there flirting with his young ladies.

A "total impediment" arises:

> The tenor... goes right to the management and says in his tenor voice: "I refuse to sing tenor in the dark... Let that son-of-a-bitch electrician sing." The electrician says, "Since he's... photographed in the middle, let him sing with one hand and switch the light on with the other... Nowadays there are no more tenors!"

The administrator relents and seats "the young women in prominent positions." Since the electrician's claims have been satisfied ("Only the ruin is not through them, the ruin is through me...I have nothing in principle against using the energy"), he gives them light, and the show begins all right.[6]

Interpreting the story in a cultural-sociological key takes one only so far.[7] Naturally, we have Zoshchenko's characteristic variations on contemporary themes:

- equality: "No more tenors" (*Tenorov nynche netu*);[8]

- the latest technology, especially electrification and its costs: "I have nothing in principle against using the energy" (compare "Telephone" (*Telefon*), "Dictaphone" (*Diktofon*), "Scientific Phenomenon" (*Nauchnoe iavlenie*), "Electrification" (*Elektrifikatsiia*), "Poverty" (*Bednost'*), and especially "Summer Break" (*Letniaia peredyshka*), where we find this passage: "We would economize like rascals, but the others have nothing against using the juice, so we won't either"[9];

- embezzlement: "The cashier screams, afraid they'll filch his money in the darkness" (compare the classic "Theft" (*Krazha*), or "An Interesting Theft in the Cooperative" (*Interesnaia krazha v cooperative*) in *The Sky-Blue Book*);

- squabbles: "At this, of course, the electrician lashed out at the tenor" (and many similar such passages).

From this thematic cluster, the story's main "cultural" conflict is formed by centering on the issue of "equality/leveling," which provides the narrative's frame: the story begins with the words: "Who is more important in the theater, the actor, the director, or perhaps the stage carpenter? The facts will tell," and ends with essentially the same question: "Now figure out for yourselves who is more important in this complicated theatrical mechanism." The facts seemingly demonstrate that the electrician is just as important as the tenor, that it is not a good idea to scorn the virtue of the "little man," and that in general it is time to put an end to mutual boorishness:

> The tenor... says: "Let that son-of-a-bitch electrician sing." The electrician says: "Spit right in his kisser. If he's going to be such a pig and stand in the middle of the picture... What a jackass you've got there!"... The manager says: "Where the devil are those two broads...They could use a swift kick in the pants!"

Nonetheless, this somehow doesn't amount to a full-blown moral for the story.

On the formal level, Zoshchenko's filigree work with verbal and thematic motifs is remarkable as always. The indecision over "who is more important... the actor, or the director, or maybe the stage carpenter," is picked up by the rhythmically similar vagueness, or rather "alternativeness," of the place of action: "This affair occurred in either Saratov or Simbirsk, in short, somewhere not far from Turkestan."[10] The word "outstanding" from the second paragraph ("Besides the *outstanding* acting by the artists, this theater had... an electrician") returns to its mirror image in the penultimate ("They then seat his young ladies in *outstanding* places"). The motif and root *igr-* (from *igrat'*, "to play, to act") carries through the main episodes, effectively standing out thanks to the awkward combinations that arise:

> They *acted* an opera in this municipal theater; Besides the outstanding *acting* by the artists, this theater had... an electrician; Today, for example, they are *acting Ruslan and Liudmila;* Well, in that case, I refuse to *act.* I refuse, in short, to illuminate your production. *Act* it without me.

The seating leitmotif, which carries the theme of human dignity, is less conspicuous but even more consistent:

> But in the center, on the chair with a back, they *sat* the tenor; the young ladies... asked to be *seated* with everyone in the hall; I'll whip up a pair of tickets for you right now. *Sit* down here, by the booth; Then we'll see... who to photograph on the side and who to *seat* in the middle; He's locked the booth with all the keys and is *sitting* − flirting desperately; I'll *seat* them somewhere right away; Then they *seat* his young ladies in outstanding places and begin the performance.

Ironically, as the electrician sits in his booth flirting he assumes the privileged position of an aristocratic theatergoer who has a reserved box for receiving his guests, ladies etc.

Attesting to the consummate stylistic and compositional structuring of the text as they do, these effects, however, do not give us the key to interpreting its content.

PART TWO

Following up on the hypothesis about the importance for Zoshchenko of existential as well as socio-cultural and stylistic problems (see note 7), let us take a closer look at the plot of "The Electrician" in this context. The main conflict arises if not "through" the young ladies, then in any case in connection with them. The electrician's ego, already injured when he was marginalized in the photograph, is further insulted by the manager's refusal to find a place for his lady-guests. The hero is publicly humiliated along the most banal but also most offensive – "amorous" – lines and responds with the no less public preference he shows for flirting with the ladies over his job obligations.

The public aspect of humiliation is a frequent theme in Zoshchenko's stories (see "The Aristocratic Lady" (*Aristokratka*), for one). Here it is graphically presented in the beginning of the story, thanks to the collective nature of the event as well as to its "artistic registration" in the photograph ("In the *entire group,* when the *whole theater...* was *photographed...*"). In the main story, the public element is taken to an extreme when the scandal plays out with the participation of the "extraneous" young ladies, the behind-the-scenes stage personnel (the electrician, the cashier, the manager, the administration), and finally the entire theater hall ("The audience is shouting").[11] What happens on stage is not irrelevant either – despite its almost total inconspicuousness.

Zoshchenko often resorted to the traditional "mousetrap" motif of play-within-a-play, having the "real" events echo the theatrical performance (see the quotation from "The Actor" in the epigraph). In "The Electrician," the content of the opera, mentioned only briefly and comically ("Today, for example, they are playing *Ruslan and Liudmila*. Music by Glinka. Directed by Maestro Katsman"),[12] is not at all irrelevant to the squabbling between the protagonists.

On the most general level, both plots feature a conflict over women: in the story, around the two young ladies; in the opera, around Liudmila. In the story, the conflict pits the electrician against the manager, then the tenor, and then again the manager, the last time coming to a satisfactory resolution. In the opera, Ruslan has to deal successively with Golova, Chernomor, and Farlaf, and constantly with Svetozar, who in the beginning and the end gives him Liudmila, but through all the peripeties promises her to any successful rescuer. With respect to the evil wizard Chernomor as well as the Grand Prince Svetozar, Ruslan is, if not a "little man," then in any case a personage of lesser rank, and his victory proves possible only thanks to the help of a more powerful ally – the good magician Finn. Corresponding to this in the story is the intervention of the manager, who in this way combines the features of Svetozar and Finn.

The relevance of these rather trivial similarities is reinforced by one more specific resonance. The turning off of the light, naturalized by the electrician's job, creates an unexpected parallel to the episode at the end of the opera's first act, where the wedding feast is interrupted by thunder, "the stage is in absolute darkness, all the characters are stunned, rooted to the spot," and it is discovered that Liudmila has been abducted.[13] At the same time, the electrician, plunging the theater in darkness switches, so to speak, from the role of Ruslan to that of Chernomor, rendering the mythological connotations of his action more salient.

The light/dark opposition is at the center of Glinka's opera (even the name of the grand prince is noteworthy, Svetozar (*svet* meaning "light"), contrasting with Chernomor (*chern* meaning "black"); in the corresponding Pushkin narrative poem (where the contrast is between Vladimir-the-Sun and Chernomor) the opposition involves also the motif of "invisibility" granted by the magic cap that conceals first Liudmila, then Chernomor. In the Zoshchenko story, darkness is caused by the electrician and is played up in several ways: "in the dark" money can be stolen from the cashier; the tenor balks at "singing in tenor in the dark"; the title character himself, having turned off the "light all over the goddamn theater," attempts, like Chernomor, to reap the amorous fruits of his black magic by "sitting – and flirting desperately." The "diabolical" motif returns later in the remarks of both the manager and the electrician about the "damn (*chertovy*, lit. "devil's) young ladies." Finally, the "supernatural" power over light is underscored one more time in denouement, this time in a positive, "divine" key – by an almost Biblical phrasing: "'Right away,' he says, 'I'll give you light'... And he gave them light that very minute. 'You can start,' he says." Cf: "In the beginning... God said: let there be light. And there was light" (Gen. 1:1-3).[14]

Even the inimitably Zoshchenkovian phrase, "Let him sing with one hand and switch on the light with the other," seems to have a highly poetic source. In Pushkin's *Ruslan and Liudmila*, the same syntactic construction is used at the high point of the combat between Ruslan and Chernomor (Canto Five):

Then Ruslan with one hand
Took the sword of the vanquished Head
And, seizing the beard with the other,
Severed it, like a tuft of grass.[15]

Zoshchenko's referencing not only Glinka but also Pushkin seems natural, as does his special interest in the theme of "hand," especially a punishing one.[16]

The ambiguity of the electrician's intertextual projections — on both Ruslan and Chernomor — is aggravated by yet another discrepancy. The narrative presents the tenor as the principal, virtually the sole, performer in the opera. But *Ruslan and Liudmila* hardly warrants such casting. The opera's title male protagonist, Ruslan, is a baritone; his magician antagonist Chernomor is an extra without a singing part; Ruslan's rival Farlaf, is a bass; the ambivalent father figure Svetozar is a bass too; and Ruslan's ally Ratmir is a contralto. Only more or less episodic characters are indeed tenors: the singer Baian, who appears only in the first act; the helper-magician Finn, who appears mostly in the second and only briefly in the fifth; there is also the hostile donor of the sword Head (*Golova*), performed by a chorus of tenors (in the second act). In this way one more intentionally implausible element is introduced in the plot, one to be noticed and appreciated by connoisseurs only. Indeed, Zoshchenko was a man of refined cultural tastes, a friend of Dmitry Shostakovich; he frequented concerts and theaters, often in the company of the women he courted.[17]

The blurring of the correspondences between the story and the opera does not seem to undermine the interplay itself, especially given the general "alternativeness" and "approximateness" of the Zoshchenko narrative. The word "tenor" may not so much designate here an operatic singer with a specific voice range as refer — in a vague and ignorant way — to the traditional star of the show, the *jeune-premier*, and thus to Ruslan, after all. Similarly, appearing in the story as a modest "electrician" is a theater worker whose job is officially described as *zaveduiushchii osvetitel'noi chast'iu*, "chief of the lighting department." The emblematic opposition of the story's two central figures gains also from sound orchestration: the words *monter* ("electrician") and *tenor* ("tenor") repeatedly collide in the text, producing a paronomastic effect, especially striking when *tenor* occurs in the Instrumental case: *Tut, konechno, monter skhlestnulsia s tenorom* ("Then, of course, the electrician barreled into the tenor").

On the whole, the intertwining of the conflict over a woman and the abduction of light creates an impressive overlap of the two plots, one unfolding conspicuously in the wings, the other implicit in the meager references to what is happening on stage.

PART THREE

From the intertextual links that reinforce the love-and-prestige theme of "The Electrician" let us proceed to the next step in our search for the story's existential meaning. Correlation of Zoshchenko's comic stories with his autopsychoanalytical memoir *Before Sunrise* suggests the possibility of identifying Zoshchenko's heroes with the author himself, who endowed them with his own passions and traumas – but, as Gogol famously put it, "demoted from generals to enlisted men."[18]

It stands to reason that we should look for the author in the story's title protagonist. The electrician's interest in the young ladies, his thin skin, and his peripheral position in the theater give certain grounds for this. As is well known, Zoshchenko had the reputation of a ladies' man, he took offense easily (among the Serapions, his thin skin became proverbial[19]), and he was deliberately practicing a "disreputable" literary genre. To this could be added his fixation on the motifs of "hand," "thunder," and "light/darkness," as painstakingly analyzed in *Before Sunrise*.

The light/dark opposition is implicit even in the title of his autobiographical novella, and he persistently plays with the "light of reason" metaphor:

> What could have illuminated these scenes [of infancy]? Fear perhaps?.. Now these stories are cast in an entirely *different* light. Now *you can see* almost everything in them... The light of logic expels or excludes these [basest of] forces...
>
> Disaster, it seemed, was unavoidable... But I managed to cross the threshold of that world. *The* light of my reason lit up the horrible slums where the fears were lurking... But the battle was uneven. I had already suffered defeat in the darkness... But now, as the sun lit up the dwelling place, I spied my enemy's pathetic and barbaric mug...
>
> The old fears said farewell to my person... only because the light of my reason illuminated the illogic of their

existence... I have already recounted my dream of how water once filled my room... Even in this clumsy dream I had to *see* the infant's fear.[20]

In a more ambiguous vein the same "enlightenment" motifs[21] are played out in Zoshchenko's 1924 story "Electrification" (also reprinted under the title "Poverty" (*Bednost'*) and included in altered form in the "Amazing Events" (*Udivitel'nye sobytiia*) section of *The Sky-Blue Book* under the title "The Last Story" (*Poslednii rasskaz*):

This business... to *illuminate* Soviet Russia *with light*...

And they started *bringing in light* here... [T]he little landlady... suggested they *illuminate* the apartment... They did, and goodness gracious *[batiushki svety,* lit. "fathers-lights"], *the lights did illuminate* it! Mold and filth all around us... *You couldn't see* any of it with kerosene... *A nauseating* spectacle...

I *lit* the electricity... Well, well!... "It's *disgusting* to *look* at it all." And all this was *filled with bright light,* and everything *leapt into the eye...* I started coming home bored. I arrived, *didn't light the light,* and burrowed into my cot...

[T]he landlady cut the line... "It hurts," she said. "It all looks so poor *in that light.* Why *illuminate* that kind of poverty with *light* for the bedbugs' amusement..? I don't want to *live with light,*" she said.

Hey, lads, *light's fine but lighting it up is bad!...* Everything that's *good in the dark is bad in the light.*[22]

A variation on the theme of "anti-enlightenment" can also be seen in the preventive unscrewing (and eventual crushing) of a light-bulb by the protagonist of "Guests" (*Gosti*).[23]

Enough has been written about the "hand" and "thunderclap" motifs in *Before Sunrise,* but a few words may be in order regarding their behind-the-scenes role in "The Electrician." In Glinka's opera, the scene of thunder, gloom, general freeze, the abduction of the bride (right before the consummation of the marriage) is followed by the words of the chorus: "What happened? The wrath of Perun?" and those of Ruslan (supported by other characters):

"What a wondrous moment! What does this marvelous dream mean? This freezing of emotions! And the mysterious gloom all around? Where is Liudmila?" (Chorus: "Where is our princess?") "She was speaking to me here with quiet tenderness."[24]

This famous scene (involving also the chorus' address to Lel' the arbiter of love, jealousy and death) bears an almost uncanny resemblance to a recurrent cluster of motifs in *Before Sunrise*:

I recalled a dream of long ago.,. An enormous arm stretches toward me out of a dark wall... I cry out. I wake up in terror... Evidently, during the day a hand... had taken something away from the infant. But what... ? The mother's breast?.. Perhaps the father's hand, which was once placed on the mother's breast... scared the child...

Lightning struck in the yard of our *dacha*... Terrible thunder shook our whole *dacha*. This coincided with the moment when my mother began breast feeding me. The clap of thunder was so powerful and unexpected that my mother lost consciousness for a minute and dropped me. I fell on the bed... I hurt my arm...

The hand can come... take, carry away, punish... And suddenly the hellish clap of thunder, the falling, my mother's senseless body...

Later the mother's breast came to embody woman, love, and sexuality... There is no doubt about it – I was avoiding women... and at the same time yearning for them... in order to run away, frightened by the expected retribution... Won't it be followed on its heels... by a clap of thunder...?[25]

Here we have the dream, the clap of thunder-cum-lightning (= the wrath of Perun), the frozen senselessness, and the loss of the woman. It would be only natural to assume that Glinka's opera was a favorite of the author of *Before Sunrise*.

As for the "arm/hand" motif in "The Electrician," it is threaded through the text rather subtly. The original turning on of the light by the electrician is not mentioned at all. In the episode of the defiant extinguishing of the light and shutting up of the booth, the hand is implied but not named. The same is true of the final giving of light. But the mocking retort about the suggested turning on of the light by the tenor is features the close-ups first of one, "singing" hand and then of the other, "lighting" one.[26]

Comparing these situations with the traumas analyzed in *Before Sunrise,* one is struck by the power that the electrician, standing in for author's ego, wields over his formidable antagonist. The control over light, darkness, and women is shown to be "in the hands" of the hero, and all the antagonist gets is his absurdly hypothetical lighting of the light. In other words, the "hand/ arm trauma" is presented here as successfully overcome by the "patient."[27] This may help interpreting the electrician's Ruslan into Chernomor metamorphosis.

In *Before Sunrise,* Zoshchenko focuses on the moral dilemma that arises as a result of his successful vanquishing of, but by the same token unique identification with, the baser forces of his psyche:

> I got up from my bed no longer the man I had been. Unusually healthy and strong… I rose from my bed… I was just about to start rushing about, not knowing what to do with my barbaric strength… Like a tank, I advanced across the fields of my life, easily overcoming all obstacles… I seemed to have started to bring people more grief than before, when I was… weak.[28]

Zoshchenko finds the solution to this Nietzschean problem of amorality – he had been infatuated with Nietzsche's teachings in his youth, and his constant striving for a healthy, barbaric, "anticultural" simplicity is permeated with latent Nietzscheanism – in channeling his newly found strength into the handling of his art:

> Now, however, my reason was liberated. I was free to do with it what I liked. Once again I took what I held in my own hands – art. Only now I did not take it with trembling hands or with despair in my heart.[29]

In this passage, there is a sense of creative omnipotence akin to the divine giving of light at the close of "The Electrician," a parallel whose meaning will soon become clear.

PART FOUR

To resume the discussion of Zoshchenko's "thin-skinnedness," in *Before Sunrise*, there is a string of episodes from the author-narrator's (henceforth — MZ) childhood that illustrate his aggressive-defensive reaction to humiliation by authority figures, in particular, those connected with the hero's "cultural" activities:

- After his father's death, the young MZ accompanies his mother to see the arrogant artist (P. P. Chistiakov), on whom the amount of the pension depends. All his life MZ would remember the humiliation they suffered.[30]

- MZ attempts to poison himself over a flunking grade in Russian composition and the instructor's commentt: "Drivel." "True, it was a composition on a Turgenev theme, 'Liza Kalitina.' What did that have to do with me?.. But this was unbearable."[31]

- The editor-in-chief [according to Zoshchenko, Mikhail Kuzmin, which seems historically implausible – A. Zh.] rejects "the five best little stories" as unsuitable for his journal. "I left the editorial offices. I no longer had the same feelings I once did in gymnasium. Not even irritation. 'God be with him,' I thought. 'I'll get along without these journals... They want it to be "classical" . . .' 'I'm not bitter. I know I'm right.'"[32]

- Insulted by the mocking tone of the schoolteacher, MZ chases him in the hallway: "If you taunt me like that one more time, I'm... I'm... I'm going to spit on you." The teacher was about to take MZ to the principal's office but let him go and from the next time on changed his tone to one of respect. He mistakenly assumed that the main source of MZ's reaction was the prospect of a low grade.[33]

In one of these episodes, MZ so to speak "suppresses his rudeness"; in others, he vented it desperately and was even ready, like the electrician, "to spit in the face" of his mighty antagonist. Reminiscent of "The Electrician" are also the themes of the boss's false interpretation of the offense (it wasn't a matter of a low grade in history – or of the "damned ladies" – but of the protagonist's hero's self-respect) and of the specialist's hyper-sensitive reaction to disrespect of his professional dignity (as his contribution is deemed "drivel").

The latter theme was close to the writer's heart. In his introduction to a collection of essays about him, which was first given as a paper at the Art History Institute in February 1927, that is, soon after "The Electrician" was written, Zoshchenko said:

Critics don't know actually where to anchor me – in high
literature or in petty literature, unworthy, perhaps, of criticism's
enlightened attention... But since most of my things are written
in a disreputable form – of the magazine feuilleton and the very
short story – my fate is usually predetermined... There is an
opinion that what is required now is a red Lev Tolstoy...

[But] all our life... and all the surroundings the writer lives
in do not of course "place an order for" a red Lev Tolstoy...
What is ordered is a piece in that disreputable minor form
with which... worst literary traditions have been connected.

I contracted to meet this order. I don't think I was
wrong.[34]

In light of this, the conflict between the electrician and the tenor acquires unexpected significance. The importance of peripheral "technical
staff' turns out to be similar to the relevance of the "disreputable, minor
form" of Zoshchenko's "very short story," and out from behind the figure
of that "tramp, the opera's principal tenor, who is used to being always
photographed in the center,"[35] emerges that of a representative of "high
literature" – Lev Tolstoy, or rather, the highly placed customer for a "red Lev
Tolstoy," a "thick-journal" editor like Kuzmin or Voronskii.[36] By facing down
his omnipotent antagonists (the tenor, the manager, the administration)
right in front of the public, the electrician fulfills Zoshchenko's authorial
dream of recognition validating his creative agenda.[37]

The figure of the stage electrician-lighting man suits this role both
because of its obvious marginality as well as its resemblance to the real
person in charge of a theatrical performance, the director, who, after
all, does not appear on the stage. Remarkably, Glinka's Chernomor is
characterized by similar features; he is a character without a singing part
but responsible for the powerful stage effects: thunder, darkness etc. (in
the first act) and the "staging" of the three oriental dances that are supposed
to bring about Liudmila's seduction (in the fourth).[38] The plausibility
of Zoshchenko's symbolic self-identification with the electrician is also
buttressed by the following passage from one of the concluding chapters
of *The Sky-Blue Book,* saturated with enlightening, inflammatory, and
"marginal" motifs:

In his day, the French writer Voltaire with his laughter extinguished the bonfires that burned people up. But we, with our weak and insignificant powers, take on a much more modest task. We hope with our laughter to light at least a small splinter-candle, by the light of which some people might notice what is good for them, what is bad, and what is in between.

If this happened, then in the overall spectacle of life we would consider fulfilled our modest role of a laboratory assistant and lighter of the performance. [39]

Incidentally, the modesty of this lighting role is, of course, deliberately exaggerated here in a pride aping humility move. Zoshchenko's narrator picks up here on a motif mentioned half a hundred pages earlier, in the introduction to the "Amazing Events" section, where he discusses with a "bourgeois philosopher" the meaning of life's spectacle, striking a note similar to the "The Electrician":

"Yes," said the philosopher. "In essence, life is unreal... So let the people have fun, enjoy operettas, all those kings, and soldiers, and merchants..."

And we say to him...:

"Here's what, sir. Even if your amusing definition of life as operetta stands... Still... you are in favor of an operetta in which one actor sings and the rest raise the curtain for him. Whereas we..."

"Whereas you," he breaks in, "are in favor of an operetta in which all the actors are extras... and want to be tenors."

"By no means. We are in favor of a spectacle in which the roles are all correctly distributed among the actors – according to their talents."[40]

Developing the idea of the electrician as the embodiment of the author's "creative ego,"[41] one can say that his "refusal to act" not only echoes the numerous childish "refusals" and "departures" of MZ the first-person protagonist hero of *Before Sunrise*, but also anticipates the famous rebuff given by Zoshchenko himself to his official persecutors in June 1954. Speaking at a meeting in the House of Leningrad Writers, the disgraced author defiantly insisted on his refusal (in a recent conversation with visiting

British students) to recognize the correctness of Zhdanov's reviling. As Daniil Granin recalled,

> It suddenly turned out that Zoshchenko was not defending himself, was not asking for leniency; he was on the offensive. One man against the entire organization with its powerful secretaries, departments, editors-in-chief... He had been invited to the podium in order to bow his head in public and repent...
>
> "I can say that, given this situation, my literary life and fate are over... A satirist must be a morally pure man, and I have been humiliated like the worst son of a bitch... I have no intention of asking for anything. I don't need your leniency" – he looked at the presidium – "or your Druzin, or your abuse and shouts... I will accept any fate other than the one I have..."
>
> Not cowed, he said what he wanted to say... he defended his honor. For the first time, someone had dared to speak out against one of the Loyal Disciples [i.e., Zhdanov] of the Follower [i.e., Stalin, Lenin's heir]. The Twentieth Congress [of the Communist Party] hadn't happened yet. And the words of either were not subject to doubt.
>
> This was a victory. It was clear that it would cost him dearly. But the price did not concern him. There was nothing stopping him anymore.[42]

PART FIVE

But let us return to the 1920s. An episode preserved by memoirists resonates tellingly with "The Electrician" and the entire *topos* outlined above. Recalling the times of the Serapion Brothers, Valentin Kaverin wrote:

> There were no "crummy guests", and I especially liked those kinds of gatherings – I was a proponent of our "order" being closed... my imagination glimpsed something knightly, requiring rituals and "initiations"...
>
> Then Zoshchenko came, dressed up like a dandy. His first book had just come out, *The Stories of Sinebriukhov*. It was very good that Zoshchenko had come, but unfortunately he had invited three actresses from some theater touring in Petrograd...

as well, and this, from my point of view, was bad. The girls were quite pretty, actually, especially one... who apparently liked my gloomy, furrowed face because, while her girlfriends were reciting poetry, she was making goo-goo eyes to me...

Did I think that the unceremonious invasion of the pretty actresses, whom Zoshchenko should not have invited, was an insult to our "order"? I don't know. But I listened with revulsion to our guests' trite poems, and when the reading was over, I attacked them scornfully and sharply... Without waiting for the other readings, the girls took offense and left. Zoshchenko saw them home.

The Serapions chewed me out unanimously, and I defended myself... when he returned. Everyone fell silent... [No one] had ever seen him like that before. His swarthy face was white, his handsome dark eyes slightly squinted. He was enraged. Without raising his voice, he said that I had behaved like a sanctimonious hypocrite... and he demanded that my comrades condemn my behavior.[43]

Later Kaverin challenged Zoshchenko to a duel, studied the dueling code, and prepared for death, but at the next meeting of the "order" they were reconciled. Moreover, Zoshchenko reported that he too had been "expecting seconds."

The parallels to "The Electrician" are obvious:

- the ladies, who also came illegitimately (compare in the story: "But at a quarter to eight two young ladies the electrician knew turned up. Either he had invited them before, or else they had barged in – no one knew");
- the "theatrical" element: the actresses;
- a rival insisting on a prescribed artistic exclusiveness (although not his own, but rather of the entire "order");
- the furious offense driving the conflict to an extreme: a duel (compare Ruslan's "knightly" combats); and
- the appeal to a higher authority: the fellow Serapions (compare the manager, the administration, and the public in "The Electrician").[44]

The incident with Kaverin occurred in January 1922, soon after the publication of *The Stories of Sinebriukhov* (December 1921). The events described in "The Electrician" refer to roughly the same period: "when the entire theater was photographed *in 1923.*" "The Electrician" was written in 1926 and appeared in the journal *Behemoth* (*Begemot*) (no. 43) as "A Complicated Mechanism" (*Slozhnyi mekhanizm*). It was also published as "A Theatrical Mechanism" "*Teatral'nyi mekhanizm.*"[45] As we can see, the "minor" anecdote does indeed conceal quite a complicated mechanism – theatrical, psychobiographical and metaliterary.

ENDNOTES

[1] Russian text © by the author. *'Monter' Zoshchenko, ili slozhnyi teatral'nyi mekhanizm,"* in *Tynianovskii sbornik* 10, ed. E. A. Toddes (Moscow, 1998): 335-56; authorized English translation by Marian Schwartz. Revised Russian version in A. Zholkovsky, *Mikhail Zoshchenko: poetika nedoveriia* (Moscow, 2007 [1999]), 132-44, 330-35.

English translation of "Monter" by Sidney Monas is in Mikhail Zoshchenko, *'Scenes From the Bathhouse' and Other Stories from Communist Russia* (Ann Arbor: The University of Michigan Press, 1961), 47-48.

[2] In Iu. V. Tomashevsky, ed. *Vspominaia Mikhaila Zoshchenko* (Leningrad: Khudozhestvennaia literatura, 1990), 211-12.

[3] Ibid., 105-6.

[4] Ibid., 97.

[5] On this group of stories, see A. Zholkovsky, *Bluzhdaiushchie sny i drugie raboty* (Moscow: Nauka/Vostochnaia literatura, 1994), 124-27; Cathy Popkin, *The Pragmatics of Insignificance: Chekhov, Zoshchenko, Gogol* (Stanford: Stanford University Press, 1993), 76-79.

[6] M. Zoshchenko, *Sobranie sochinenii v trekh tomakh,* ed. Iu. V. Tomashevsky (Leningrad: *Khudozhestvennaia literatura,* 1987), vol. 1, 355-56. Further cited as Zoshchenko 1987.

[7] As exemplars of the "cultural-sociological" approach to Zoshchenko, one could cite the following: Ts. Vol'pe, *Iskusstvo nepokhozhesti* (Moscow: *Sovetsky pisatel'*, 1991 [1940]); M. O. Chudakova, *Poetika Mikhaila Zoshchenko* (Moscow: *Nauka,* 1979); Iu. K. Shcheglov, *"Entsiklopediia nekul'turnosti. Zoshchenko: rasskazy dvadtsatykh godov i* Golubaia kniga,"in A. K., Zholkovsky and Iu. K. Shcheglov, *Mir avtora i struktura teksta. Stat'i o russkoi literature* (Tenafly, N.J.: Hermitage, 1986), 53- 84; A. K. Zholkovsky, *Bluzhdaiushchie sny,* 35-39, 122-38; Popkin, *The Pragmatics of Insignificance,* 52-124. For a revision of such a treatment of Zoshchenko (i. e., as a critical realist, portrayer of the "new philistines" and their lowbrow discourse) with a view to a more "existential" interpretation of Zoshchenko's oeuvre, see A. K. Zholkovsky, "Aristokratka," in *Litso i maska Mikhaila Zoshchenko,* ed. Iu. V.Tomashevsky (Moscow: Olimp-PPP, 1994), 331-39; his *"Ruka blizhnego i ee mesto v poetike Zoshchenko," Novoe literaturnoe obozrenie* 15 (1995): 262-86; and his "What Is the Author Trying to Say with His Artistic Work? Rereading Zoshchenko's Oeuvre," *Slavic and East European Journal* 40: 3 (1996): 458-74.

[8] Compare: "'I am no gentleman. All gentlemen are in Paris!' Sharikov howled" (Mikhail Bulgakov, *Heart of a Dog (Sobach'e serdtse)*, chap. 8).

[9] Zoshchenko 1987, vol. 1, 432.

[10] On the "alternativeness" of the Zoshchenko narration, see Shcheglov, "*Entsiklopediia nekul'turnosti,*" 73-74.

[11] On the "public" dimension of what happens in Zoshchenko's stories, see Shcheglov "*Entsiklopediia nekul'turnosti,*" 67, and Popkin, *The Pragmatics of Insignificance*, 118.

[12] There is a similar quasi-antisemitic" wisecrack in Zoshchenko's sentimental story "Apollo and Tamara" (1923), in a reference to the male protagonist's fortunate rival as music performer: *"Maestro Solomon Belen'kii has now pursued his occupation on every evening with two first violinists, a contrabass, and a cello... Maestro Solomon Belen'kii and the disappearance of the velvet jacket made Apollo Perepenchuk a spineless observer"* (Zoshchenko 1987, vol. 2, 38, 41).

[13] M. I. Glinka, *Ruslan i Liudmila. Volshebnaia opera v 5 deistviiakh,* in his *Polnoe sobranie sochinenii,* vol. 15, ed. G. V. Kirkor (Moscow: Muzyka, 1967), 80.

[14] Compare the conceit likening of the theater, director, prompters etc. to the creation of the world in Boris Pasternak's poem "To the Meyerholds" (*Meierkhordam*) (1928). Broader mythological parallels could be drawn between the "abduction of light" by the electrician/Chernomor and such mythological figures as Lucifer and Prometheus.

[15] A. S. Pushkin, "*Ruslan i Liudmila. Poema,*" in his *Polnoe sobranie sochinenii v 10 tomakh,* 4th ed., vol. 4: *Poemy. Skazki* (Leningrad: Nauka, 1977), 58.

[16] On the "arm/hand" motif in Zoshchenko, see A. K. Zholkovsky, "*Eccola! (K donzhuanskoi teme u Zoshchenko),*" in his *Inventsii* (Moscow: Gendal'f, 1995), 57-71; and Zholkovsky, "What Is the Author Trying to Say." Zoshchenko's references to Pushkin are a promising topic; in the context that concerns us here, note the allusion to the *Stone Guest (Kamennyi gost')* in Zoshchenko's story "Private Life" (*Lichnaia zhizn'*) (included in *The Sky-Blue Book's* "Love" section as "A Trivial Event from [my] Private Life" (*Melkii sluchai iz lichnoi zhizni*)): the protagonist's amorous designs on a woman's love are crushed — right in front of the statue of Pushkin! — as she identifies his fancy overcoat as stolen from her husband (see Zholkovsky, *Bluzhdaiushchie sny,* 229-30). As for the poetic formula "with one hand — with the other hand," parodied by Zoshchenko, it can be traced from Pushkin all the way back to Ovid's classical line about the Scythians who were forced to be always prepared for enemy attack: *Hac arat infelix, hac tenet arma manu,* "unhappy, plows with one hand and holds a weapon with the other" (*Tristia,* V, 10.24).

[17] See, for example, Tomashevsky, 307, 314, 329, 340; Zoshchenko was also a circus fan (ibid., 167-68). Later, he also wrote for the stage and gave readings of his stories in opera halls (ibid., 192 – 93).

[18] For the argument in favor of seeing Zoshchenko himself in his comic characters, see Zholkovsky "Aristokratka," "Ruka blizhnego," "What Is the Author Trying to Say." A similar point was earlier made by Valentin Kaverin: "[Zoshchenko] saw the similarity to Gogol's moral tragedy very early on. Their shared characteristics consisted in… their tormented focus on themselves and their effort to reduce the distance between themselves and the 'little man.' Both scrutinized the character the way they did themselves" (V. A. Kaverin, *Epilog: Memuary* (Moscow: *Moskovskii rabochii*, 1989), 62.) In his note "On the Novel" (*O romane*) (1955), Kaverin uses almost the same words regarding the blows dealt by Knut Hamsun and then James Joyce to the conventions of the novel: "Interest arose in the author as an individual and his biography, at the price of reducing the distance between the author and the hero" (Kaverin, 173). This is fully applicable to *Before Sunrise*. Moreover, one can assume that Kaverin's insistence on "reducing the distance" can be traced back to Tynianov's 1924 essay, "Staff Reduction" (*Sokrashchenie shtatov*), in which he mentions Zoshchenko (Iu. Tynianov, *Poetika. Istoriia literatury. Kino,* eds. E. A. Toddes, A. P. Chudakov, M. Chudakova (Moscow: Nauka. 1977), 145-46). Among the 1930s critics, it was Tsezar' Vol'pe who came closest to a serious – rather than not disparaging – realization of the closeness between the "Zoshchenko types" and their creator (Vol'pe, 220-21, 209, 228-29, 235, 252, 273-74).

[19] See the epigraph to this essay as well as Tomashevsky, 76, 80, 85-86, 103-5, 110, 129.

[20] Zoshchenko 1987, vol. 3, 558, 619, 622, 625-28. Note a favorite little word of Zoshchenko's, "ruin" [*gibel'*] which pops up several times in connection with the childish fears of the MZ protagonist of *Before Sunrise* and resonates with that "ruin" on the brink of which the electrician places the entire performance.

[21] On Zoshchenko's "enlightenment" (as opposed to "dialectical," whether Hegelian or Marxist) approach to history in *The Sky-Blue Book,* see Vol'pe, 278-85. According to memoirists, one of Zoshchenko's favorite writers was Voltaire (see Tomashevsky, 372).

[22] M. Zoshchenko, *Uvazhaemye grazhdane* (Moscow: Zemlia i fabrika 1927), 150-51.

[23] Zholkovsky, "*Ruka blizhnego.*"

[24] Glinka, 81-85.

[25] Zoshchenko 1987, vol. 3, 607-15.

[26] Compare the subtle use of the arm/hand motif in the "El'vira" chapter of *Before Sunrise,* involving a subtextual reference to Mozart's *Don Giovanni,* which in its turn features numerous arms/hands. See Zholkovsky, "*Eccola*." In Glinka's opera, the arm/hand motif sometimes comes to the fore, especially in the second act, as Ruslan gets the magic sword from the Head [Golova]: "I shall crush all before me, if only the sword suits my hand... Oh, the long-desired sword! In my palm I sense your full worth" (Glinka, 181,184).

[27] On other instances of such overcoming, see Zholkovsky, "*Eccola*."

[28] Zoshchenko 1987, vol. 3, 607-15.

[29] Ibid., 627.

[30] Ibid., 590-91.

[31] Ibid., 467.

[32] Ibid., 506; compare the last quote in my epigraph – *A. Zh.*

[33] Ibid., pp. 549-50.

[34] Ibid., M. Zoshchenko, "*O sebe, o kritikakh i o svoei rabote,*" in his *Uvazhaemye grazhdane,* ed. M. Z. Dolinsky (Moscow: *Knizhnaia palata,* 1991), 585.

[35] Ibid., Zoshchenko again used the entire cluster of "artistic photographing," "challenging authority," "center/margins opposition," and "struggle for women's attention" in his comedy *Respected Comrade (Uvazhaemyi tovarishch)* (1930); its negative protagonist, Barbarisov, is a to-be- purged party bureaucrat who is also a household tyrant and a womanizer:

> *Rastopyrkin:* The tenants are simply burning to be photographed together. With you, surrounded, so to speak... And we'll hang the group in the front room... Especially in such an ominous... hour, getting photographed is instructive... Anyway, your pretty face... wouldn't have such a bold expression if this happened after the purge...
>
> *(Rastopyrkin moves the chair closer to the camera.)*
>
> *Barbarisov.* So why a chair for me in the center? What about the others? This means the others are going to be standing?.. No, then let everyone be sitting... Equality is more important to me. Lately I have taken a great interest in equality... [NEP man Patrikeev too] can be photographed. Maybe not all the way to the center, but he can be seated to the side of me. The vermin wants to have a little breather, too...
>
> *Rastopyrkin:* Petr Ivanovich, the tenants are exceedingly weary from their poses...You... are being practically torn apart by the ladies.

Barbarisov: Yes!.. Everyone loves and adores me, but the ladies – that is something special.

Rastopyrkin: Please, here, take this nice chair... Is that a good seat for you, Petr Ivanovich? Or perhaps you will tell the tenants to hold the chair by the legs?.. And so you're not bored being photographed, that nice teacher, Madam Ershova, by way of her civic duty, can perform something divine for us on the piano, some unimaginable Chopin waltz...

Rastopyrkin (laughing): Petr Ivanovich... We forgot to photograph Madam Barbarisikha...

Barbarisov (waving his hand): Oh, who cares, honest to God..

[Zoshchenko 1987, vol. 3, 211-19]

Zoshchenko also elaborates on the "photography" motif in connection with the existential problem of self-image in "The Photograph" (*Fotokartochka*) (1945), see Zholkovsky, *Bluzhdaiushchie sny*, pp. 230-31. And there is the portrayal of a photo retoucher as a kind of artist ambiguously akin to the author in the "sentimental" *povest'* "Lilac in Bloom" (*Siren' tsvetet*); see also Vol'pe, 209.

[36] A typologically likely prototype of the "tenor" character is Aleksandr Blok, who (albeit only in hindsight, after Zoshchenko's death), was dubbed, by Anna Akhmatova, "the tragic tenor of the epoch" (see her *Three Poems* (*Tri stikhotvoreniia*), 2 ["And in black memory, after groping about, you will find..."] (1960); A. Akhmatova *Sochineniia*, vol. 1, 1967; vol. 2, 1968, eds. G. P. Struve and B. A. Filippov (*Mezhdunarodnoe literaturnoe sodruzhestvo*, 1967-68), vol. 1, 316. The moniker goes back to the hasty exchange between the two poets that took place in the wings before a performance at an evening concert held at the Bestuzhev courses (1913), as recalled in her *Reminiscences of Al. Blok* (*Vospominaniia ob A. Bloke*) (1965):

A young student walked up with her list and said that my turn was after Blok's. I implored him: "Aleksandr Aleksandrovich, I cannot read after you." He reproached me in reply: "Anna Andreevna, we are not tenors." At that time he was already Russia's most famous poet. For the past two years I had recited my poetry quite frequently at the Poets' Studio... and at Viacheslav Ivanov's Tower, but here everything was completely different. It is very difficult to hold a hall – Zoshchenko was a genius at that... No one knew me, and when I walked onto the stage a voice rang out: "Who is this?" (Akhmatova, vol. 2, 191-92).

Let us point out the "famous/unknown" opposition emphasized by Akhmatova, as well as the unexpected mention of Zoshchenko. The appearance of Zoshchenko's name in the context of Blok is all the more intriguing as for Zoshchenko, Blok, with his decadent grandeur, decline and fall, had always been an fascinating but also problematic figure; see his early essay "The Demise of the Knight of the Sorrowful Countenance" (*Konets rytsaria Pechal'nogo Obraza*) (1919), his *Mishel' Siniagin* and *Before Sunrise*. The image of Blok as a "tenor" may have entered the cultural vocabulary of the era; also, Zoshchenko could have heard about Blok-the-tenor from Akhmatova.

[37] Cathy Popkin draws a similar parallel between Zoshchenko and his characters who tend to violate the accepted order, which is often represented by the strictly codified theatrical decorum; in particular, she notes the affinity between the author and the title character of "The Electrician" in terms of her concept of Zoshchenko's "poetics of the insignificant" (Popkin, 76-79). On the relationship between Zoshchenko and Tolstoy, see Zholkovsky, *Bluzhdaiushchie sny*, 122-38.

[38] The "authorial-directorial" behavior that propels the action is a characteristic function of negative and ambivalent characters: the evil magicians, villains, provocateurs, and clowns, such as Mephistopheles, Khlestakov, Petr Verkhovensky, Ostap Bender, and many others.

[39] "Afterword to the Whole Book" (*Posleslovie vsei knige*), (Zoshchenko 1987, vol. 3, 441-42). In Zoshchenko's poetic world, the spiritual-intellectual status of electricians is quite high. Compare the following dialogue in one of the stories in *The Sky-Blue Book*." 'But perhaps he is not an intellectual... maybe he's a street scavenger?'... 'Why a street scavenger? He's quite an intellectual. He's an electrician'" (Zoshchenko 1987, vol. 3, 207). The electrician's refusal to "light your production" can be construed in an Aesopian vein, as a disinclination to participate in the glorification, mandatory for Soviet writers, of the vaunted triumphs of socialist production (on Zoshchenko's strategy for evading themes foisted on him by official ideology, see Popkin, 106-9). Incidentally, the lexical substitution of "illumination, lighting" [*osveshchenie*] for "enlightenment" [*posveshchenie*] can also be found in Zoshchenko's early texts, e. g. in the speech of Nazar Il'ich Sinebriukhov: "I'm an unilluminated man"; "I don't know, I'm not illuminated, I say," "I, although a man not illuminated... but I know culture" ("A Fashionable Story" (*Velikosvetskaia istoriia*), Zoshchenko 1987, vol. 1, 310-32).

[40] Zoshchenko 1987, vol. 3, 396.

[41] The combination in the electrician of the "little man" and the "artist" can be traced typologically to Gogol's "The Overcoat" (*Shinel'*): Akakii Akakievich is also a kind of "master" (of writing/copying) who gives a surreal "rebuff to the bosses." The ironic mixture of the "artist" and "artisan" was a favorite device of

Zoshchenko's; compare above on the retoucher and also in *Mishel' Siniagin*, the line about "some unusual acts… of a brilliant artist, pianist, or tuner" (Zoshchenko 1987, vol. 2, p. 176).

With respect to the intertextual links between "The Electrician" and Glinka's *Ruslan and Liudmila,* note the foregrounding in the opera (as distinct from the Pushkin poem) on the meta-artistic theme: not only does it feature a special singer character Baian, but he also foretells (as a tenor!) the appearance many centuries later of his double, the author of *Ruslan and Liudmila,* i. e. Pushkin: "There is a desert land, a cheerless shore, there in faraway midnight realms. The summer sun there glances on the valleys through a fog without rays. But ages will pass, and on this poor land a miraculous lot will descend. There a young singer on golden strings will sing glory of the homeland, and will preserve Liudmila for us and her knight from oblivion. But a singer's time on earth is brief; all immortals are in heaven" [Glinka, 28-31]. In terms of the "light/darkness" opposition, the young singer contrasted to the sunless northern land clearly belongs in the zone of "light." The opposition itself is, of course, among the staples of Pushkin's poetry (see "The Bacchic Song" *Vakkhicheskaia pesn'*)). The anachronistic connection between Baian and Push-kin is also Pushkin-like; see the "legend" about Ovid supposedly preserved in the collective memory of 19th-century nomads and recounted to Aleko by the Elder in "The Gypsies" (*Tsygany*).

[42] Tomashevsky, 425-26.

[43] Ibid., 118-23.

[44] G. Munblit recalls how Zoshchenko "decisively and angrily" rebuked him for a mocking review he wrote: "This is the first thing by a young woman writer! And you have insulted her. Publicly insulted her!" (Tomashevsky, 238). Here is one more case of Zoshchenko defending a woman and a modest artistic output, complete with the motifs of insult, publicness, and defiant reaction.

[45] See the commentary in Zoshchenko 1987, vol. 1, 548.

V

Yury Olesha's Three Ages of Man: a Close Reading of "Liompa."

ANDREW BARRATT

In Yury Olesha's small corpus of literary works "Liompa" occupies a special place. Not only was it the first of the writer's mature stories to see publication, but it has also been acknowledged, by Western critics at least, as one of his finest achievements in the genre.[1] Existing studies of "Liompa" have tended to concentrate almost exclusively on thematic elements, indicating in particular the central importance to Olesha's overall worldview of the problem of perception as articulated in the story.[2] My purpose in this article is to attempt a more detailed and comprehensive reading of "Liompa." By examining the formal and stylistic elements of what is possibly Olesha's most complex and elusive story I hope to throw some light on certain residual problems of interpretation.

"Liompa" is a story which yields its meaning only after considerable effort on the part of the reader. This point should be emphasized, as it is this very difficulty of comprehension that constitutes the first, and most lasting, impression upon the reader, and hence forms a vital element in the story's meaning.[3] The prime importance of such an initial response to the text is stressed by L. M. O'Toole, who puts the case for attempting to state the theme of a story on the basis of a first reading:

> There seems to be value in attempting to state the theme first,
> before analyzing the structure, partly because one's first reactions
> have a special validity in any art, and partly because one thereby
> gains a point of reference for the analysis which follows.[4]

This argument is developed, in a different context, by Roger Fowler who insists on the importance of recent attempts by certain structuralist critics to reinstate the concept of the reader as a crucial element in the process of literary signification.[5] Fowler himself begins a detailed and impressive analysis of a Shakespearian sonnet by recording his first impressions. By passing from the surface to the deeper structures of the text in this way the critic is able to establish a firm point of departure for the subsequent discussion.

What exactly does the reader gain from a first reading of "Liompa"? The broad outlines of the story are clear enough. The juxtaposition of three views of the world (represented by the dying Ponomaryov, the young boy Aleksandr, and the unnamed "rubber" boy) is foregrounded quite sharply, as is the story's central event – the crisis that afflicts Ponomaryov and the truth which is revealed to him on his deathbed. Yet, if this much is evident, there is a great deal more that is far from obvious, disturbingly puzzling even. What is the connection between Ponomaryov's crisis and the behavior of the two young boys ? What is the significance of the lengthy description of the kitchen? How are we to account for the Isaac Newton passage which intrudes upon the narrative seemingly without motivation? And, perhaps most important of all, what are we to make of the highly dramatic moment when the old man utters the name "Liompa"? These general difficulties are compounded by numerous details at the level of the sentence, the clause, or even the phrase, which contribute further to the reader's sense of bewilderment at the seeming incoherence of Olesha's narrative. The magnitude of the problem is such that there would probably be few readers able, on the basis of a first reading, to formulate the story's theme in terms other than a résumé of Ponomaryov's last thoughts.

On the surface level "Liompa" seems puzzling to the extent that one suspects deliberate perversity on the part of the author. Indeed, there are certain signs that Olesha does set out to thwart our conventional notions of fictional coherence and unity. Perhaps the most obvious of these is the very title of the story. The function of titles in literary texts is a subject which has as yet attracted little, if any, systematic critical attention. The structural importance of the title is, of course, self-evident. As the first element in the text it is, inevitably, the first factor also in determining the nature of the reader's response to the narrative proper which is to follow. The title "Liompa" is an example of what might conveniently be termed an enigmatic title; that is, a title whose meaning, without further contextual clues, is at first uncertain. Commonly, the enigmatic title is a proper name, such as Gorky's "Chelkash." Even to the native Russian reader this title poses a puzzle: is Chelkash the name of a person, or of a place, or is it perhaps not a proper noun at all, but simply a foreign word of unknown meaning?[6]

The title "Liompa," initially at least, functions in precisely the same way.[7] Just like the title of the Gorky story, Olesha's too is, to the Russian ear, an alien word whose semantic connotations are immediately unclear. Yet the very use of such a title leads to certain predictable expectations. By marking the title in this way the author draws attention to its importance, and we tacitly assume that the story itself will render the title and its thematic significance fully intelligible. Gorky satisfies our curiosity; in his story we learn quite quickly that Chelkash is a person, although the aura of mystery surrounding his personality continues to exercise the reader's imagination. Olesha, on the other hand, reneges on this implicit contract. Our expectation that the significance of the title will be revealed in the course of reading the story is undermined. Having aroused interest in the exotic word "liompa," Olesha builds up suspense by carefully avoiding any clue to its meaning until very late in his story, where its appearance is quite unexpected. The very unexpectedness of the context in which the word appears creates an oddly contradictory effect. On the one hand our curiosity is satisfied; we do at least understand how the story came to receive its unusual title. Yet this satisfaction is somehow deficient, as the meaning of the utterance and its context has still to be penetrated.

Olesha challenges our conventional expectations in other ways too. The choice of the springtime setting for a story about death offends against one of the most pervasive literary traditions. And the entire text, with its disjointed syntax and radical disruptions of "flow" – the constant shifts of viewpoint, the intrusion of seemingly irrelevant details – contributes to a sense of dislocation, confronting the reader with fresh and unexpected difficulties in almost every paragraph, and frustrating his initial attempts to discover any obvious pattern of coherence.

If I have taken what might seem excessive pains to emphasize the difficulties facing the reader of "Liompa," it has been in order to indicate that these problems of intelligibility contribute not only to the story's aesthetic impact, but also to its central theme. By refusing to give his story an immediately apparent communicative focus, Olesha provides a surplus of potential meaning which forces the reader to examine the very process by which he assigns meaning to literary texts. That this bears directly upon the story's central theme, the problem of how man assigns meaning to the phenomena of the physical world, is a point which hardly needs to be labored.

The cause of much of the difficulty in reading "Liompa" is that Olesha, like many other modernist writers, has created a text in which the story element itself is not the primary source of coherence. Although the account of Ponomaryov's crisis is clearly central to the meaning of "Liompa," this story alone cannot account for the presence of a large amount of material that is extraneous to it. We must look elsewhere, therefore, for the key to textual organization. On this subject the work of Lotman seems to be of help:

> The ordered quality of any text can be realized along two lines. In linguistic terms it can be characterized as ordering in terms of *paradigmatics* and *syntagmatics,* in mathematical terms – of equivalency and order. The character and function of these two types of ordering are different. If in narrative genre the second type predominates, then texts with a strongly expressed modeling function (and it is precisely here that poetry, especially lyric poetry, belongs) are constructed with marked predominance of the first.[8]

The same basically valid distinction is made by Barthes, whose views are neatly summarized by O'Toole

> Within a literary text, Barthes claims, we may distinguish two types of function: (a) those properly labeled 'function', which relate units in sequence through the narrative (i.e. syntagmatically) and (b) those which he labels 'indices' which relate a given unit to the more general, abstract purposes of the story (i.e. paradigmatically).[9]

The crucial notion in paradigmatic ordering, as Lotman explains, is that of binary opposition, by means of which patterns of parallel and contrast are established at all levels of the text. In the remainder of this essay I will attempt to demonstrate that "Liompa" is organized according to this principle, and displays a discernible tripartite structure. In the opening section (paragraphs 1 to 10) Olesha develops a series of polar oppositions which constitute the thematic "core" of the text, a fundamental revelation about the nature of human existence, the full implications of which are subsequently revealed to the reader in the second and third parts (paragraphs 11 to 17, and 18 to 30, respectively).

In the first ten paragraphs of "Liompa," Olesha establishes a pattern of polar opposition which is realized at many levels of the text. Perhaps most immediately striking is the contrast of setting, between the kitchen and the bedroom. The details, although not fully explicit, make it evident enough that the characters inhabit a communal dwelling of the type that was only too common in the urban centers of Russia in the early years of Soviet rule. What is striking, however, is that Olesha transforms the mundane, even squalid conditions of the kitchen into a positive hymn to life.

The kitchen is the realm of bustling communal activity: the young Aleksandr works on his model plane, other occupants of the house prepare food, eat sunflower seeds, and sing songs. Even the rat in the rubbish bin seems somehow to participate in the joyous celebration of the beautiful spring evening. The season is itself symbolic; spring is the time of rebirth, and the details of the description convey a vitality that is almost physically tangible. The predominance of food (potatoes, eggs, crayfish, sunflower seeds) emphasizes the physiological process of human life, as do the references to sun and water, the life-giving elements. These are present not only in the natural world, but also in the man-made environment. Water, in particular, features prominently here, gurgling in the pipes, escaping from the taps, and boiling on the primus to cook the crayfish. Colors too are the colors of life: gold, yellow, and green. The one exception is the color of the primus flame. Here, significantly, the color blue is explicitly linked with the notion of death: "It died as a meek blue flame" (191). The choice of vocabulary, with a strong emphasis on verbs of action, and the cluster "life, lodger, live crayfish" *(zhizn', zhilets, zhivogo raka)* also contributes strongly to the air of joyous vitality which pervades the kitchen scene.

Ponomaryov's bedroom, by contrast, is introduced at once as the scene of lonely death; food is replaced by medicine, the bright yellow light by a flickering candle, the movement and vigor by the motionless figure of the room's solitary occupant:

> In the room next the kitchen lay Ponomaryov, critically ill. He lay in his room alone. There was a candle burning; a medicine bottle with a prescription attached to it stood on the table at his head. (141)

Here not only the vocabulary but even the intonation conveys a feeling of inertia. The phrases of the second sentence conform to a rhythmic pattern of masculine endings, the tendency towards regularity culminating in the perfectly regular anapestic meter of "*ot flakona tyanulsya retsept.*"

The kitchen is part of the wider universe; its doors stand symbolically open. Olesha's description leads us beyond the confines of the building into the yard; we are offered glimpses of the pavement and of the food store opposite. The bedroom, on the other hand, is remote from the world outside and represents the totality of Ponomaryov's drastically restricted and impoverished universe.

The juxtaposition of kitchen and bedroom is further emphasized by a radical shift in point of view, which brings into focus other important aspects of the polar opposition between the two symbolic realms. Although the entire narrative is conveyed in the third-person, omniscient mode, Olesha alternates, within this framework, between the poles of objectivity and subjectivity. These two terms are much abused: the precise sense in which they are intended here will become apparent in the course of the following discussion.

I will begin with the description of the kitchen and its occupants, and a statement by Alain Robbe-Grillet which seems apposite to our present concern. Writing on the role of description in the New Novel, Robbe-Grillet comments:

> Many specialists still deprecate them; they find them pointless
> and chaotic. Pointless, because they have no real relation to the
> action, and chaotic, because they don't fulfill what is thought
> to be their fundamental purpose: to make the reader see.[10]

These remarks (like so many in the French writer's theoretical articles) seem especially relevant to Olesha's work. The description of the kitchen in "Liompa" is precisely such a "pointless and chaotic" passage, and these features contribute in no small way to the story's difficulty.

Description in the pre-modernist novel and short story normally serves two basic functions. The first is to provide a readily recognizable picture of reality ('to make the reader see', as Robbe-Grillet puts it). The second is to endow this fictional world with order and perspective, hence permitting the reader to discern the relevance of what is being described. To illustrate the point I cite the following passage from Chapter

11 of Turgenev's *Fathers and Sons,* in which the interior of Kukshina's house is described. Arkady and Bazarov are led into the drawing-room by Sitnikov:

> The young people went in. The room in which they found themselves looked more like a study than a sitting-room. Papers, letters, thick issues of Russian magazines, mostly uncut, were spread about the dusty tables; scattered cigarette butts were everywhere to be seen.[11]

Turgenev's description, like Olesha's, relies on impressionistic details rather than an exhaustive catalogue of furnishings. Yet it has none of the "pointlessness" or "chaos" of the Olesha passage. The details recorded are not random; they display a readily discernible "logic." The general impression of the room, introduced in the second sentence, is supported and amplified by the specific details presented in the third. There is obvious purpose here too; objects are described not for their own sake, as the backcloth for the action, but rather as factors indicating the essential characteristics of the room's occupant. The dusty tables, the scattered cigarette-ends, and the untidy heap of journals reveal Kukshina's slovenly nature. The fact that she smokes cigarettes at all is a sign of her ostentatious "emancipation," whilst the uncut journals invite a certain skepticism about her pretensions to culture. Turgenev's description, then, is unashamedly anthropocentric: the physical environment is of importance only inasmuch as it reflects the character or mood of the human protagonists.

Before returning to the Olesha passage, I wish to mention one further aspect of description which is well illustrated by the famous passage from the beginning of Lermontov's "Bela":

> This valley is a wonderful place! Inaccessible mountains on all sides, reddish cliffs covered in green ivy and crowned with clumps of plane-trees, yellow precipices, furrowed with gullies, and high, high up there the golden fringe of snow, while below, the Aragva, embracing another nameless river, which bursts loudly from a dark ravine full of mist, stretches like a silver thread and sparkles, like the scales of a snake.[12]

Both the tone and the focus of this description are quite different, the effusive, poetic expression of this piece contrasting strikingly with the neutral, prosaic manner of the Turgenev passage. So infectious is the narrator's enthusiasm for the awesome beauty of the Caucasian scenery that the entire piece is dominated by his personality. Yet the description is not anthropocentric in quite the same way as the Turgenev passage. Despite the bold anthropomorphism of the metaphor 'embracing', which is reinforced by the humanizing metaphor 'crowned', the impressive contours of the Koyshaur valley are primarily of importance in their own right. Of particular interest to our present discussion, however, is the prominence in Lermontov's description of spatial perspective, which allows the reader both to identify, and to identify with, a human point of view which is both emotional and physical.

When viewed against this background the unconventionality of Olesha's kitchen description is readily apparent. The Olesha extract is neither anthropocentric in the manner of the Turgenev passage, nor "humanist" in the manner of the Lermontov.[13] The details of the kitchen tell us nothing of those who use it, except that they eat. Similarly, the neutrality of the third-person narrative makes it impossible to draw any conclusion as to the personality of the narrator. What is more, there is very little in the passage to "help the reader to see." The details we have are too fragmentary, and too unspecific, to create a precise visual impression of the setting.

The passage, then, seems deprived of any evident "logic": it serves neither to characterize the actors, nor to establish a dramatized narrative consciousness, nor even to create that vivid visual impression of reality so important to narrative fiction. Equally, there is no obvious attempt to exploit the description for the purpose of social criticism; on the contrary, the squalid conditions of the communal kitchen combine to form a positive celebration of life. Yet this very absence of "logic," although at first perplexing, is the key to the rationale of the passage. By depriving the description of any sign of ordered perception, Olesha rids it of a recognizably human viewpoint, intellectual, emotional, or physical. Both the nature of the items recorded and the order of their presentation create the impression of total randomness. Details are highly concrete,[14] being composed almost entirely of visual and audible sense impressions, with a strong emphasis on the former. Together with the highly disjointed syntax,[15] this has the impact almost of mechanical perception: it is as if a camera had been placed in the kitchen, its position and the focus of its zoom lens continually changed, and its shutter released at random intervals, whilst, independently, a tape-recorder had been switched on at various moments to capture sounds. In this way the description achieves a unique kind of objectivity, which seemingly excludes the mediating influence of the human mind, to present a more "pure" perception of the phenomenal world.

Given the general simplicity and concreteness of the extract, the cluster of anthropomorphic metaphors at the end of the second paragraph invites special comment: "The tap was discreetly *blowing its nose* quietly. Then, upstairs somewhere, pipes *began talking* in a variety of voices. [...] The taps *chattered*" (141). The notion of animation is also present in the sentence: "Two or three drops of their own accord *(sami po sebe)* shot out of the tap" (141). The kitchen thereby emerges as a universe in which inanimate objects live their own lives, independent of man. The active role of human beings is correspondingly reduced. To this end Olesha employs a number of devices of depersonalization. Firstly, there are two cases, in consecutive sentences, where personal pronouns are omitted, shifting the emphasis away from the human agent: "Finely sliced potatoes were being fried in the kitchen *(zharili melko narezannuyu kartoshku)*. The primus stove was being lit *(Zazhigali primus)*" (141).

This process is taken a stage further in two other instances where the nominalization of verbs removes even the implicit reference to an agent: "All sort of moving and knocking started up around the stove *(nachinalos' raznokharakternoe shevelenie i potryoskivanie)*. There was singing *(Razdavalos' penie)*" (141). The first example is particularly striking, as the form of expression disguises the fact that the noise around the cooker is caused by the people preparing their evening meal. It is only by extrapolation that we conclude the involvement of a human agent here at all. Finally, the use of the general "people" *(lyudi)*, and of the highly impersonal, even official, phrase "one lodger" *(odin zhilets)*, together with the almost total absence of proper names, serves further to reduce the status of human beings. In the kitchen description man is not the centre of the world but merely a part of it, and not, perhaps, the most significant part at that.

Point of view here is best defined not as impersonal, but rather as apersonal. By creating a vision of the world in which the "normal" human perspective is destroyed, Olesha establishes a unique sense of distance between the reader, who is allowed to share this privileged viewpoint, and the characters of the story, who are not.[16] Different though these three characters are, each is seen ultimately as being in this important respect "human, all too human."

Before we examine point of view as it functions in the bedroom passage, we should note one further aspect of the kitchen description, namely, the two sentences dealing with the primus stove: "The life of the primus began magnificently when the orange flame shot ceiling-high. It died in meek blue flame" (141). This extract is strongly marked stylistically by the concentration of abstract vocabulary, which, moreover, divides into semantically contrasting pairs: life/died *(zhizn'/umiral),* magnificent/meek *(pyshno/krotkim).* As the story progresses this passage takes on a symbolic significance; the primus stove becomes a metaphor for man himself, whose life passes from the "magnificent flare" of youth to the "meek blue flame" of old age.

The fourth paragraph marks a gradual transition from the apersonal, physical world of the kitchen to the anthropocentric, psychic world of Ponomaryov. Stylistically, this paragraph is of a piece with the preceding three: the syntax is still simple in the extreme, and the vocabulary concrete. But this stylistic unity masks a radical difference, for here the description is decidedly anthropomorphic in the manner of the Turgenev passage quoted earlier. No longer does the itemization of objects give the impression of randomness; each item is of interest for what it tells us of the room's sickly occupant; the physical environment is no more than an extension of the human personality and its condition.

The fourth paragraph, then, prepares us for the following six, in which we become immersed in the egocentric and idiosyncratic psychic world of Ponomaryov. Strictly speaking, we should talk here of Ponomaryov's psychic *worlds,* as we witness him first in a state of delirium, then in a condition of consciousness. In each case the objects of the real world recede from view as they are supplanted, first by the free associations of Ponomaryov's unconscious mind, and then by the abstractions created by his intellect. Olesha is careful to distinguish between these two states. This is done most obviously at the level of style: the short, simple sentences of paragraph 6 (delirium) contrast with the complex syntax of paragraphs 8 and 10 (consciousness).[17] The time-scale is also quite different. If the time element does not enter at all into the delirious state, the conscious state is characterized by a dominant sequentiality, with events ordered in relation to a fixed moment, the moment that Ponomaryov realized that he was dying.

Leaving aside for the present the further implications of Ponomaryov's delirium, I will concentrate here on the account of his conscious state only. Just as the temporal element is highly egocentric, so also is the spatial perspective. Crucial here is the clause: "Then the depletion drew closer to the centre, reaching deeper and deeper, toward the courtyard, the house, the corridor, the room, his heart" (192). Ponomaryov *is* the centre of this world. The passage is saturated with references to him,[18] a significant number of which deal with spatial relations:

> The sick man was surrounded by a few things … *(Bol'nogo okruzhali...)*
>> … close thing … irrevocably remote … far away from him …
>> …parallel with him … to retreat from him … close by, at his side …
>>> … under his very eyes … on the way to him … (192)

The mobile, apersonal viewpoint employed in the kitchen description is here replaced by a point of view which is both highly personal and static.

The contrast is emphasized also at the level of lexis. Here, in marked distinction from the earlier passage, vocabulary is predominantly abstract. The word "thing" *(veshch')* and its derivatives or substitutes, for example, appears no less than fifteen times,[19] which is in fact exactly the same figure as for concrete nouns. What is more, the references to specific physical objects or actions occur almost invariably as illustrations to an abstract generalization. This is a dominant motif:

> With each day the quantity of things decreased. Such a close thing as a railway ticket had already become irrevocably distant to him... he was really hurt to realize that even the things moving parallel with his course were growing more remote. In a single day he was abandoned by the street, his job, the mail, horses. Then the disappearances began to occur at a mad rate, right there, alongside him: already the corridor had slipped out of reach and, in his very room, his coat, the door key, his shoes lost all significance. Death was destroying things on its way to him. Death had left him only a few things, from an infinite number; things he would never have permitted in his house by choice. He had things forced on him. He had the frightening visits and looks of people he knew. (142)

This structural feature contrasts strangely with the semantic level of the passage: whilst Ponomaryov has come to accept that the physical world is beyond his control, his language reflects a perverse tenacity in subordinating concrete objects to the abstract constructs of his intellect. This contradiction is essential to an understanding of Ponomaryov's character, as we shall see.

The key concept throughout the passage under discussion is *power,* which is reflected in a recurrent semantic motif:

> …how few of them remained in his power (v iego vlasti)
>> …slipped from his power
>> …had it been in his power
>> He saw he had no chance of defending himself …
>> … he would never have permitted in his house. (142)

In Ponomaryov's world things exist in order to be controlled by man, to be transformed into language, the emblem of man's evolutionary superiority. It is precisely the loss of this power that causes Ponomaryov such anguish. Significantly, his mortal illness is seen by him ultimately as a threat to the power of language: "… his coat, the door key, his shoes lost all significance" (192). Death is feared not because it signals the end of physical existence, but because its approach suddenly challenges Ponomaryov's entire view of the world, which is based on his faith in man's supremacy.

The opening of "Liompa," then, establishes a network of polar oppositions which may be summarized under the headings: kitchen/bedroom, physical world/psychic world, world of objects/world of language, apersonal viewpoint/personal viewpoint. All of these may be subsumed under the more fundamental opposition of life and death.

It might be tempting to add to our list one further antithetical pair, at the level of character: Aleksandr/Ponomaryov. Certainly, Aleksandr's youth and vigor contrast sharply with the debility of the dying Ponomaryov. The opposition is also suggested by the structural prominence given to each of the characters at the beginning of the two sections:

> The boy Aleksandr was making a model plane. (143)
>> In the room adjoining the kitchen lay the seriously ill Ponomaryov. (141)

The two stand, as it were, at the threshold of their separate, symbolic realms. Olesha suggests an almost physical bond between Aleksandr and his environment by means of an interesting detail of language. The "golden, edible crusts" *(zolotistye, s'iedobnye korki)* which form on the cuts on the boy's hands are echoed in the last sentence of the kitchen passage, where we encounter the "yellow light" *(zhyoltyi svet)* and the "grocery store" *(s'iestnaia lavka),* The connection in the latter case is especially marked in Russian, being lexical as well as semantic.

The opposition of Aleksandr and Ponomaryov, although evident, is only superficial. Moreover, the beginning of the second section of the story (paragraphs 11 and 12) causes us to view the two characters in a radically different way, as it is the similarities between them which now come to the fore. The parallels are both formal and thematic. Perhaps most obvious is the stylistic unity of paragraph 12, where Aleksandr's thoughts are revealed, and those earlier paragraphs dealing with Ponomaryov's intellectual world. Here, too, sentences tend to be comparatively long,[20] the syntax complex, and the vocabulary predominantly abstract. As in the preceding passage also, there is an obviously human logic at work; the entire piece is a syllogism which cogently argues the boy's claim to be considered an adult.

Most important at the thematic level is the seriousness with which both characters view their ability to control their environment. For Ponomaryov, as we have seen, the prospect of imminent death is disturbing because it has caused him to doubt his supremacy over the physical world. In Aleksandr's case it is his capacity to shape objects in accordance with his will that is the very essence of his claim to adulthood. It should be noted that this capacity is explicitly linked with the boy's command of the laws of science, a point to which I shall return later. Adulthood, therefore, takes on a limited and rather specialized connotation in this context, being measured not so much in terms of years lived, but rather in terms of the individual's ability to rationalize the flux of his experience, and to use this ability to control the physical world.

Olesha also stresses the similarity between Aleksandr and Ponomaryov in his use of point of view. In both cases the presentation is non-dramatic (with the brief exception of Ponomaryov's delirium). The omniscient narrator is obtrusive, telling rather than showing, and emphasizing the general condition rather than the specific state. It is as if the narrator has taken on the role of spokesman for Aleksandr and Ponomaryov whilst the characters themselves remain in mute passivity. The unity of the narrative voice serves both to emphasize the similarities between the two characters, and also to play down their differences. Had a more dramatic mode of characterization been employed, the obvious signs of Aleksandr's youth (his lack of linguistic and intellectual sophistication, for example) would certainly have been more conspicuous. As it is, Aleksandr emerges not so much as a child, but rather as a young adult, ready to follow in Ponomaryov's footsteps, the difference in their age being ultimately less important than their similarity in outlook.

The proximity of Ponomaryov and Aleksandr is foregrounded again later by a parallel in their behavior towards the "rubber" boy. On separate occasions the "rubber" boy approaches both Aleksandr and Ponomaryov, unwittingly antagonizes them both, and prompts an aggressive response. The fact that the "rubber" boy is repulsed by both characters in this way suggests a new pattern of opposition: Aleksandr – Ponomaryov – "rubber" boy. Such an interpretation is not without foundation; the inner world of the "rubber" boy differs quite markedly from those of the other two characters. His is a world comprised almost entirely of specific sense impressions. The child's mind simply records without comprehension his visual sensations of the parquet tiles, of the dust under the skirting-board, and of the cracks in the plaster – a far cry, indeed, from the intellectual world of Ponomaryov and the engineer's mentality of Aleksandr. The charm of the passage is guaranteed not only by the naivety of the "rubber" boy's perception, but also by the dramatic immediacy of the description.

We should not, however, press this argument too far. Different though the inner world of the 'rubber" boy is, the distance is not so great as it might first seem. Highly significant in this respect is the presence of the ubiquitous omniscient narrator who intrudes on a number of occasions with explanatory comments:

> In the corridor was a bicycle leaning with its pedal against the wall. The pedal had scratched the paint, and the bicycle seemed to be supported against the wall by the scratch. (143)
>
> Sometimes a wonderful pattern of light appeared. The child started rushing toward it, but before he had even taken a full step, the change of distance killed the illusion. The child looked up, back, behind the stove, searching for it and moving his hands in bewilderment. (144)

By explaining in this way the aberrations and insufficiencies of the "rubber" boy's view of the world the narrator consistently undermines the magic of the passage. We are not allowed to escape entirely the rational, scientific explanation of phenomena. What is more, the perception of the "rubber" boy is not itself completely free of a rational element. The narrator explains: "The boy had only entered (*vstupil*) into the cognition of things. He did not yet know how to distinguish temporal differences in their existence" (143). The use of the perfective aspect *vstupil* makes it clear that the "rubber" boy's initiation into rational thinking has already taken place, and the adverbial phrase "not yet" insists that the development of these intellectual faculties is inevitable. In the course of the passage we even witness the child's tentative efforts to order his perceptions in a rational manner, to encompass them within a framework of causality: "The spider vanished at the boy's mere desire to touch it with his hand" (144). Although the causal relationship indicated here is clearly unsatisfactory from the scientific viewpoint, its very presence is a sign of the "rubber" boy's endeavor to organize his experiences rationally.

The revelation of character in the central, second section of "Liompa" displays, therefore, a discernible pattern, whereby an initial opposition (Aleksandr – Ponomaryov, Aleksandr – Ponomaryov – "rubber" boy) masks a more profound level of similarity, indicating that the differences between the three characters are of degree, rather than kind. If the "rubber" boy and Ponomaryov stand at opposite poles of experience, they are, nevertheless, part of a continuum in which Aleksandr occupies a middle position. Together they represent three ages in the life of man, the development from childhood to old age being presented as a gradual and inevitable process of alienation from the phenomena of the real world, and a corresponding retreat into the abstractions constructed by the human intellect. The reverse order of character presentation achieves an ironic effect. Because we are taken first into the mind of the dying Ponomaryov, who has suddenly come to learn the transience and fragility of his power to control the world, Aleksandr's natural pride in his engineering prowess seems tragically misplaced, whilst the "corruption" of the "rubber" boy invests the entire process of human life with a sense of inescapable circularity.

Aleksandr and the "rubber" boy are little more than ciphers, whose "character" extends no further than their function in Olesha's schematic life of man. Ponomaryov, however, has a more important role. Unlike the two boys, he is individualized in a number of ways, and it is his crisis of consciousness which provides "Liompa" with the high dramatic climax of the third part.

Before examining in detail the story's climax, we should consider what we learn of Ponomaryov's character prior to this event. Explicit information about him is very sketchy indeed: we know nothing, for example, of his age, his occupation, or of the nature of his fatal illness. The sum of our factual knowledge derives from the single sentence: "Countries disappeared, America, then the possibilities: being handsome, rich, having a family (he was single)" (142). Insufficient though these details are, they shed considerable light upon Ponomaryov's character, as they enable the reader to interpret the associations cast up by his unconscious mind during his delirium:

> In the evening he became delirious. The medicine bottle
> was staring at him. The prescription was like the train of a
> wedding dress. The bottle was a duchess on her wedding day.
> The bottle was called 'Name-day' (tezoimenitstvo). (142)

The process of association comprises two main strands. Firstly, there are the sexual connotations of the item of female clothing, which are reinforced by the concept of marriage and the overt sensuality of the scent-bottle association.[21] Secondly, each image also alludes to nobility, wealth, and prestige. These implications also become progressively more explicit: the train of the dress suggests merely a lady of wealth and glamour; in the second association she is transformed into a person of specifically noble extraction (a duchess); the word *tezoimenitstvo* has similar overtones, being a term reserved for the saint's day of those of noble birth, including the Tsar and his immediate family. These images of wealth, status, and sexuality, which rise unsolicited from Ponomaryov's unconscious, would seem, therefore, to indicate the presence of unfulfilled desires which have been suppressed by his conscious mind.

Ponomaryov's poverty may be understood both literally and metaphorically. Deprived of life's blessings, he has retreated into a world of intellectual activity, which offers a surrogate of the power and fulfillment denied him in real life. Intellectual endeavor has become the sum of Ponomaryov's life; hence, it is hardly surprising that his death-bed thoughts on the limitations of his intellect should lead to a profound crisis. The cynical remark he makes to his visitors is transparently an act of mock bravado. Equally comprehensible is his resentment of the "rubber" boy, who stands at the threshold of life, and has at least the prospect of true fulfillment. Ponomaryov's attempt to frighten the young boy is preceded by the following passage:

> Ponomaryov watched the child with melancholy (*s toskoi*). The child walked about. Things rushed to meet him. He smiled at them, not knowing any of them by name. He left the room and a magnificent train of things fought its way after him. (144)

The metaphor "magnificent train" (*pyshnyi shleif*) is richly suggestive. Both parts of the phrase have occurred separately earlier in the story. The train of the dress was, of course, one of the images cast up by Ponomaryov's unconscious in delirium. The adjective "magnificent" (*pyshnyi*) appeared as an adverb in the description of the primus stove: "The life of the primus began magnificently when the orange flame shot ceiling-high" (141). The collocation "magnificent train of things" (*pyshnyi shleif veshchei*) therefore, draws together the notions of life, sexuality, and the physical world, all of which are now beyond the old man's reach.

The entire section of "Liompa" dealing with Ponomaryov's final crisis (paragraphs 19 to 26) is highly dramatic. The omniscient narrator almost ceases to function as commentator, and direct speech and inner monologue feature prominently for the only time in the story. Summary is absent: we are confronted by a chain of specific events. The dramatic immediacy is created also by the syntax. Consider, in particular, the climax of the passage:

> He knew that at any costs he must stop thinking about the rat's name. Nevertheless he kept searching for it, knowing that at the precise moment when he found that meaningless, horrifying name, he would die.
>
> "Liompa" he shouted suddenly in a terrifying voice. (145)

The long sentence, with its staccato syntax, conveys vividly Ponomaryov's breathless tension, which is finally released in the act of naming. The sense of release is all the greater as this is the moment too when the reader's curiosity about the name "Liompa" is at last satisfied.

If the dramatic impact of this scene is apparent, even on a first reading, its function is not so immediately obvious. Here, it seems, two questions should be posed. First, what is the nature of Ponomaryov's crisis? Second, how are we to understand his behavior?

The first question may be answered quite simply by quoting directly from Ponomaryov's thoughts:

> 'I thought there was no outside world, he mused. 'I thought that things were governed by my eye and my ear; I thought the world would cease to exist when I ceased to exist. Now I see everything turning its back on me though I am still alive. But I do still exist! So why don't the things? I thought they got their shape, weight, their color form my brain. But they have left me, leaving behind only useless names, names that pester the brain. (144)

This is the moment of supreme revelation. Ponomaryov has become totally conscious of the fact that his intellectual mode of existence has led to bankruptcy, to a ridiculously extreme solipsism. His reliance on intellect has caused him to reverse the natural order, seeing the world as a product of man, and the phenomena of physical reality as the product of language.

In order to answer the second question we should, perhaps, take account of the Russian literary tradition, and, in particular, the precedent of Tolstoy's "Smert' Ivana Il'icha." Ponomaryov's predicament is, in essence, very similar to that of Tolstoy's character. The resolution, however, is quite different. In the Tolstoy story, the moment of revelation is followed by repentance and then redemption: at the very last moment, Ivan Il'ich accedes to a new state of grace. Olesha resists the Tolstoyan example. In "Liompa" the moment of revelation gives way to no feeling of repentance on the part of Ponomaryov; instead, it breeds a crude resentment which he directs against the innocent "rubber" boy. Natural though this reaction is, it is quite paradoxical, for Ponomaryov now tries to frighten the "rubber" boy with the very same solipsistic notions he had just come to reject. This irony is the source of pathos rather than antipathy to Ponomaryov, the pathos being guaranteed by the fact that the old man's words are powerless to harm the child, who has already left the room.

Ponomaryov's tragic duality, his inability to abandon his discredited philosophy, reaches its climax in the 'Liompa' scene. The problem of language, as we have seen, is central to Ponomaryov's moment of revelation, which ends with his awareness of the "useless names" which "swarm in his brain."

Yet the process of naming is deeply rooted in Ponomaryov's mentality; it is an automatic reflex, the first stage in bringing the data of the real world under the control of the intellect. The entire 'Liompa' scene is a grotesque parody of the process of naming. The very absurdity of giving a rat a proper name is patent enough, yet this absurdity is compounded by the fact that the rat has not been directly *observed* by Ponomaryov. The old man, in fact, merely *assumes* the presence of the rat in the kitchen on the basis of his past experience; most of the sounds that he hears are usually caused by rats. Thus he is naming not a rat, which is absurd enough, but an intellectual abstraction. This is not all. The ultimate irony is that Ponomaryov is distinctly aware, despite, or perhaps even because of his delirium, of the utter absurdity of his futile act. Yet the force of habit is too strong: Ponomaryov's awareness of the truth is unable to prevent him from perpetuating his conceit.

The naming of the rat is an unconscious attempt by Ponomaryov to reassert a mastery whose illusiveness he fully understands. As before, the notion of power is firmly embedded in the language: "Ponomaryov listened: the rat was doing the chores *(khoziaynichaiet),* rattling the plates, opening the tap, making scraping sounds in the bucket" (194). The verb *khoziaynichaiet* is quite untranslatable into English, as its literal meaning "engaged in household chores" is complicated by its overtone of resentment, which is perhaps best conveyed by the idiom "to throw one's weight around." Apparent here, as in Ponomaryov's subsequent thought, "Aha, it's doing the dishes" *(Ege, ona sudomoika),* is a grudging respect for the supposed *power* of the rat. This fixation with power is evident a little earlier too, where the same lexical motif appears in the old man's thoughts of 'useless names which have lost their *masters'(bespoleznye imena, poteriavshie khoziaev).* Try as he may, Ponomaryov is unable to accept the idea of a world in which he does not wield absolute power; this is the barrier to his salvation.

At the end of the story Ponomaryov is reduced to the pathetic condition of endlessly repeating his futile gesture of self-assertion. The sense of anticlimax is almost palpable. Once again Olesha delights in thwarting our expectations. Ponomaryov's certainty that he will die once the word "Liompa" is pronounced proves unfounded; he lives on for several hours after this event. After the excitement of the passage culminating in the desperate cry the following extract seems undramatic in the extreme:

> The house was asleep. It was very early morning, just after five.
> The boy Aleksandr was awake. The kitchen door giving onto

the courtyard was open. The sun was still down somewhere. The dying man was wandering about in the kitchen. He was bent forward, arms extended, wrists hanging limp. He was collecting things to take away with him.

Aleksandr dashed across the courtyard. The model plane flew ahead of him ran through the yard. It was the last thing Ponomaryov saw. (145)

The utter impersonality of the narrative, which verges on the callous in the use of the depersonalizing "the dying man" *(umiraiushchii)*, contrasts strikingly with the highly dramatic "Liompa" scene. We observe Ponomaryov's final sad attempt to bring things under his control with a detachment which is akin to cynicism. The anticlimax points up the very superfluity of his actions, and makes the actual moment of his death seem quite immaterial; for us he is already dead, trapped in the strait-jacket of his own intellectuality. Hence, the final words of the "rubber" boy (who understands neither the significance of the word 'coffin', nor the function of its objective referent) inject a note both of wry humor and of condemnation; it is as if life itself were passing final judgment on the follies of the old man.

. . .

"Liompa" is an extreme and unambiguous statement of Olesha's critique of pure reason and of the conventional modes of thinking which derive from the modern scientific tradition extending back to Newton. The connection is made explicitly in the following passage, which, significantly, immediately precedes Ponomaryov's moment of enlightenment:

There was an apple in the world. It glistened amidst the leaves; it seized little bits of the day and gently twirled them round: the green of the garden, the outline of the window. The law of gravity was lying in wait it under the tree, on the black earth, on the knolls. Beady ants scampered around the knolls. Newton sat in the garden. There were many causes hidden inside the apple, causes that could determine a multitude of effects. (144)

This extract is marked off from the rest of the narrative by virtue of its uncertain motivation (are these Ponomaryov's thoughts, or is this a digression by the narrator?), and constitutes a self-sufficient parable that encapsulates Olesha's argument against scientific thought.

The presence of fruit in Olesha's works, as E. K. Beaujour has pointed out, is normally associated with a state of 'blessedness', often in the form of consummated love (for example, the pears in "Love", or the cherries in "Cherry Pit."[22] Of the present passage the same author writes: 'The apple in "Liompa" symbolically holds all the richness of the world.'[23] The apple is both the food which sustains life, and the beauty and mystery which give it meaning. Its glossy, rounded surface captures the light and transforms the surrounding world into strange, distorted reflections. The "law of gravity" which "lies in wait" beneath the tree injects a sinister note into the description. The verb *podzhidal* has connotations of stealth and predation, whilst, in a metaphorical sense, the law of gravity is a predator which threatens to rob the apple of everything but its potential to illustrate this basic principle of physics.

Somewhat unexpected here, perhaps, is the detail of the "minute ants" which swarm amongst the tussocks under the tree. This is the third in a series of references to invertebrates in "Liompa". The first is to the insects which walk over the stone whilst Aleksandr builds his model (paragraph 13), and the second, of course, is to the spider that so captivates the attention of the "rubber" boy. These are all part of the minute texture of life that normally escapes detection. In addition, the ants in this passage suggest one of the multitude of possible alternative consequences of the apple falling from the tree. As the apple lies on the ground it would be devoured by the ants and other small creatures, hence becoming part of the complex chain of life. This is precisely what Newton's formula disregards.

The apple is also popularly regarded as a biblical symbol, being generally held to have been the fruit which was both the source of man's knowledge, and the cause of his fall from grace. That Newton's apple, transformed here into the symbol of modern scientific thought, has had consequences equally disastrous for the history of mankind is a conclusion which seems central to an understanding of "Liompa".

This critique of science is a recurrent theme in Olesha's work, and a number of specific details from "Liompa" may be discerned in others of his stories. The figure of Newton, for example, appears also in "Love." The theme of gravity also recurs elsewhere. In "Spectacles" (*Zrelishcha*)

Olesha explains the fascination of "wall-of-death" motorcycling in the following terms:

> The secret is that in the spectacle of a man moving in the vertical plane there is an element of the most intense fantasy that is accessible to our consciousness. This is the fantasy that is created in those cases when before our earthly perception some event occurs which has as its cause the failure to obey the laws of gravity. These events constitute the limit of fantasy. They are the more unusual for our earthly perception because, when they occur, a picture of some non-existent world with physical laws contrary to our own appears before us for a second. (276)

Here Olesha's delight in the spectacle derives directly from the power of the act to destroy, or at least to suspend, the influence of our scientific knowledge upon our manner of perception.

Despite these and other similarities "Liompa" differs in one most significant respect from Olesha's other works. In "Spectacles" and "In the Circus" there is the possibility of escaping the thralldom of scientific rationalism in the circus, which is the realm of unfettered fantasy. In "Love" the young Marxist, Shuvalov, is delivered from his narrow materialism by the experience of love, which allows him even to defy the laws of gravity (in the famous scene where he 'flies on the wings of love'). In "Cherry Pit" the dry logic of the planner, Avel', contrasts with the rich imagination and acute powers of observation cultivated by the narrator.

Leaving aside the important questions of how this conflict is presented and resolved in these and other works, we should note that they share a common feature. In each case a new manner of perception is, however temporarily, attainable by man, whether by the force of circumstance (the experience of love, for example), or by positive volition. In "Cherry Pit," the narrator even affects to teach the reader himself how to rediscover his lost powers of perception:

> The land of attentiveness begins by the bed head, on the chair which you moved close to the bed when you were getting undressed before retiring. You wake up early in the morning, the house is still asleep, the room is filled with sun. Silence.

Don't move, so as not to destroy the immobility of the lighting. Socks lie on the chair. They are brown. But – in the immobility and brightness of the lighting – you suddenly notice in the brown material individual multi-colored threads curling in the air: crimson, blue, orange . . . (219)

In "Liompa" this possibility is denied to man. The magic and freshness of perception described above belong only to the very young child, and even here this state of innocence is displayed in all its fragile impermanence. The very process of human development and education renders the loss of this innocence inevitable, and, once lost, like all innocence, it is unrecoverable.

"Liompa" draws on ideas which were common currency in the Russia of Olesha's day. N. A. Nilsson has indicated the connection between Olesha's thinking and the philosophy of Henri Bergson on the one hand and the ideology of the Russian Futurist movement on the other.[24] Like these contemporaries, Olesha directed his critique of science not against the physical products of new technology (indeed, his delight in the inventions of science, especially the airplane, is well known), but rather against the effects of scientific endeavor upon the human mind. The pressure of rational thinking always threatens to reduce the potential richness of human experience to standard formulas, and to stifle imagination and inventiveness. It is the role of the artist, Olesha insisted, to counteract this harmful tendency, and to destroy the barriers imposed by conventional modes of thinking. For Olesha this entailed a totally new vision of man and his importance in the world. In "Liompa" he reveals the precariousness, and the ultimate absurdity, of man's imagined grasp of his physical environment, and raises it to the level of tragedy. Here again, the words of Robbe-Grillet seem uncannily appropriate:

> *Tragedy* may here be defined as an attempt to reclaim the distance that exists between man and things, and give it a new kind of value, so that in effect it becomes an ordeal where victory consists in being vanquished.[25]

ENDNOTES

[1] In the Soviet Union "Liompa" has tended to escape detailed critical attention. For Olesha's contemporaries the story was overshadowed by the controversy surrounding *Envy* (*Zavist'*). Quite recently, however, V. Pertsov has expressed the opinion that "Liompa" is the 'most perfect and tragic of Yury Olesha's stories'. V. Pertsov, *My zhivyom vpervye. O tvorchestve Yuriya Oleshi* (Moscow, 1976), 181.

[2] E.K. Beaujour, *The Invisible Land: A Study of the Artistic Imagination of Iurii Olesha* (New York: Columbia University Press, 1970), 24-30; William E. Harkins, "The Philosophical Tales of Jurij Oleša," *Orbis Scriptus. Dmitrij Tschtieoskij zum 70. Geburtstag,* edited by Dietrich Gerhardt and others (Munich, 1966), 349-54.

[3] Here "meaning" is understood in the broadest sense, as the aggregate of intellectual, moral, emotional, and aesthetic responses to the text.

[4] L. M. O'Toole, "Structure and Style in the Short Story: Dostoevskij's *A Gentle Spirit,*" Tijdschrift voor Slavische Taal – en Letterkunde, 1 (1972): 84-65.

[5] Roger Fowler, "Language and the Reader: Shakespeare's Sonnet 73," *Style and Structure in Literature. Essays in the New Stylistic,* ed. Roger Fowler (Ithaca, NY: Cornell University Press, 1975), 79-122.

[6] Jonathan Culler cites the example of *Middlemarch,* which would come under this same heading, in *Structuralist Poetics. Structuralism, Linguistics and the Study of Literature* (London: Routledge and Kegan Paul, 1975), 211.

[7] The first variant of the story bore the subtitle "Things" (*Veshchi*), which was subsequently removed in later revisions. Yury Olesha, *Izbrannoe* (Moscow, 1974). English translation by Andrew R. MacAndrew is in Yuri Oleha, *Envy and Other Works*, New York: Anchor Books, 1967, 141-145. All page references in the text are to this translation; some passages are slightly modified.

[8] Yury Lotman, *Analysis of the Poetic Text,* ed. and trans. D. Barton Johnson (Ann Arbor: Ardis, 1976), 37. Ann Shukman makes the same point somewhat more intelligibly when she writes: "In the case of a narrative text which tells us about a sequence of events, it is the plot, the ordering of the narrative events, which is the main unifying factor." Ann Shukman, "Ten Russian Short Stories: Theory, Analysis, Interpretation," *Essays in Poetics,* II: 2 (1977): 74.

[9] O'Toole, 83.

[10] Alain Robbe-Grillet, "Time and Description in Modern Narrative," *Snapshots & Towards a New Novel,* trans. Barbara Wright (London: Calder and

Boyars, 1965), 143.

[11] I. S. Turgenev, *Sobranie sochinenii v 12-i tomakh,* III (Moscow, 1954), 229.

[12] M.Yu. Lermontov, *Sobranie sochinenii v 4-kh tomakh* (Moscow, 1958), IV, 9.

[13] I use the term "humanist" in the sense implied by Robbe-Grillet in his article "Nature, Humanism, and Tragedy" (75-95). The article is a militant restatement of the "pathetic fallacy," in which the author passionately defends his own practice of ridding description of anthropomorphic elements.

[14] The concreteness of the passage is reflected in the high density of nouns. Of the fifty-six nouns in the first three paragraphs no less than fifty refer to concrete objects or to people. There are only three adverbs. Adjectives, too, are little in evidence, and are mostly concrete. Of the fifteen adjectives, two may be discounted, as they appear in fixed combination with nouns *(sornyi iashchik, s'iestnaya lavka),* four relate to color, and five only are conceptual *(poslednii, s'iedobnyi, raznokharakternyi, krotkii, prekrasnyi).* Significantly, only the last two are evaluative.

[15] The twenty two sentences comprising the first three paragraphs have an average length of 6.5 words. None is complex: the longest (sentence 3) is, in fact, a chain of simple clauses. Subordination is totally absent, and conjunction rare, with no cases of hypertaxis, and only two of parataxis.

[16] The privileged nature of the apersonal point of view is especially apparent in the following short piece of description, where the narrator is blessed with a vision which allows him to contemplate the universe and the microscopic world of insects in successive moments: "the boy was surrounded by rubber bands, coils of wire, sheets of plywood, silk, light pale yellow silk fabric and the smell of glue. Above him the sky glistened. Under his feet, insects crawled over the stones, and a stone had a little petrified shell embedded in it" (143).

[17] Average sentence lengths are as follows – paragraph 6: 3.9 words; paragraph 8: 14.3 words; paragraph 10: 17.3 words.

[18] Altogether in this passage there are twenty-six specific references to Ponomaryov, either by name, by the word *bol'noi,* by the personal pronoun, by the possessive, or by the reflexive *svoi.* There are, in addition, three cases of ellipsis, where the person of Ponomaryov is implied.

[19] This figure includes the personal pronoun *oni,* and the possessive *ikh,* where these refer to *veshchi.*

[20] The seven sentences have an average length of 13.7 words.

[21] The association of the final image with scent is suggested by Richard Newnham: "It may be conjectured that among the images conjured up in the

delirious Ponomaryov's mind is that of a bottle of scent so named." *Soviet Short Stories,* edited by Richard Newnham (London, 1963), 220.

[22] Beaujour, *The Invisible Land,* 18.

[23] Ibid., 65.

[24] Nib Ake Nilsson, "Through the Wrong End of Binoculars: An Introduction to Jurij Olesha," *Major Soviet Writers,* ed. E.J. Brown (New York, 1973), 269-71.

[25] Robbe-Grillet, "Time and Description in Modern Narrative," 83.

VI

Nabokov's Art of Memory: Recollected Emotion in "Spring in Fialta" (1936-1947).

JOHN BURT FOSTER, JR.

"Spring in Fialta" was published in both Russian and English versions from the 1930s to the 1950s, and though changes in wording do occur, they are relatively minor when compared to the fluctuating text of "Mademoiselle O."[1] This discussion will follow the English version that took shape in the early 1940s, which usually adds helpful clarifications, but significant Russian variations will also be mentioned. The "Fialta" of the title refers to an invented town on the Adriatic, originally a fishing village with a vaguely Slavic background that is now becoming an international resort. In the early 1930s Nabokov's narrator, a Russian émigré with a management position at a German film studio, decides to stop there for a break in a business trip. Victor (Vasen'ka in Russian versions) is alone and, though happily married, is pleasantly surprised when he runs into Nina, another Russian whom he first met before the revolution and at intervals ever since in Europe. She is also married, to a writer named Ferdinand, a "Franco-Hungarian" with a reputation in Paris; but she has a warm, even promiscuous nature, and Victor has been one of her many lovers.

Their chance meeting in Fialta causes Victor to remember their past together; sometime later, as a result of Nina's death that same day in a car accident, he decides to commemorate his whole relationship with her, with the story we read as the result. Victor's memoir shuttles between an account of their reunion in Fialta, itself a memory by the time he writes it down, and all the memories of their previous encounters released by that meeting. Indeed, the complex historical identity of Fialta becomes an emblem for this free movement among several distinct layers of time, consisting as the town does of an old and a new quarter which relate in such a way that "the new and old were interwoven . . . and in certain places struggle with each other."[2]

But memory, as it creates similar transactions and collisions in people's minds, can vary widely in quality, and Nabokov opens the story by stressing this point. At issue are two contrasting kinds of images, the lifeless ones that do not attend to the particularity of past experience and are therefore inert stereotypes, and the vivid ones created by an awakened perception that drinks in concrete sensations. Hence the initial juxtaposition of Fialta's tourist-trade souvenirs with the narrator's ability, despite his inexperience as a writer, to recover precise impressions of his visit. Picture postcards of Mount Saint George, a local landmark, have never been updated since 1910. But Victor, who has arrived with "all my senses wide open," can remember the mountain with a pictorial intensity that crosses over to humanizing metaphor: it appears in "a watery vista between the jagged edges of pale bluish houses, which have tottered up from their knees to climb the slope" (SF 413). This contrast between lively personal memories and cliché-ridden public souvenirs will return later in the story, where it helps to clarify the narrator's quarrel with Ferdinand about what art and memory might mean for a writer.

In Ferdinand's view, as Victor describes it in his hostile account, actual experience has nothing to do with art, which should depend on verbal invention alone. His praise of artifice seems to align him with Nabokov's pronouncements in the 1960s; but actually, as Nabokov was learning from his ongoing work on "Mademoiselle O," imagination and memory were intricately interrelated. Indeed, when the narrator sums up Ferdinand's works by referring to "the stained glass of his prodigious prose," he echoes a key detail from the crucial veranda image presented in the memoir.[3] But there is a key difference, for if Ferdinand's tinted windows once revealed "some human landscape, some old garden, some dream-familiar disposition of trees," now they are opaque; and behind their bright colors the narrator suspects "a perfectly black void" (SF 420). The balance between color and transparency that marked the tinted windows in "Mademoiselle O" has vanished from Ferdinand's empty and lifeless art.

His misuse of experience is confirmed by one of his stories. Victor notices a woman character whose "friendly smile . . . was always ready to change into an ardent kiss" (SF 424), and immediately recognizes Nina. But because this passage portrays Ferdinand's wife "in spite of the artist's intention," it reveals his blindness to the role of deliberate memory in the creative process. Even Ferdinand's vaunted inventiveness boils down to a facility with elevated clichés. Cleverly mimicking current intellectual trends in France (Nabokov might be thinking of the shift from Maritain's neo-orthodoxy to Malraux's activism), Ferdinand has moved from "a brief period of fashionable religious conversion" to a phase of political engagement in which he "turned his dull eyes toward barbarous Moscow" (*SF* 427).

This description of Ferdinand may seem obviously biased, but Nabokov does not simply leave the reader with a conflict between two subjective viewpoints. Here, as at the beginning of the story, Mount Saint George functions as the litmus test. Ferdinand is a sardonic lover of *Kitsch* who thrives on Fialta's souvenirs, and when he triumphantly buys "a dreadful marble imitation of Mount St. George showing a black tunnel at its base, which turned out to be the mouth of an inkwell, and with a compartment for pens in the semblance of railroad tracks" (*SF* 423), he has judged himself. At the level of mass culture, this grotesque artifact embodies both the stereotypical attitudes and the remoteness from experience that also define Ferdinand's highbrow art of pure invention. Hence, though his success as a Hungarian in France might suggest that he is a model of cultural mobility, he has rightly been termed a "decoy character" whose likeness to Nabokov is more apparent than real.[4]

Rebelling against this barren inventiveness, the narrator declares his faith in an art of memory. Thus he bluntly tells Ferdinand that "were I a writer, I should allow only my heart to have imagination, and for the rest rely upon memory, that long-drawn sunset shadow of one's personal truth" (*SF* 420).[5] Paradoxically, of course, this statement occurs in a work that the reader knows is fictitious, but the implicit devaluation of imagination in favor of memory aligns Victor with the author of "Mademoiselle O," and thus identifies him as a fictive autobiographer. The text itself of "Spring in Fialta" bears witness to his literary views, for as Victor writes he learns to remember his meetings with Nina in loving detail. We shall soon see how this process works, but for now it should be noted that Victor has thereby realized his first response to seeing Nina in Fialta, the impulse to go "back into the past, back into the past" (*SF* 415). As the repetition suggests, his retrospective impulse is not a simple one, but double. It results in a narrative that describes two pasts simultaneously – the one-day "drama" of Victor's and Nina's reunion in Fialta and the more diffuse "chronicle" covering the series of their prior meetings. To be sure, Nabokov does limit his manipulation of time: both drama and chronicle are largely told in chronological order, nor do jagged breaks disturb the portrayal of individual episodes. But because Victor tells the two stories side by side, his narrative does jump back and forth between widely separated levels of time on eight occasions.[6] Through these shifts between the recent drama and more distant chronicle, Nabokov produces that "intertwining of the retrospective romance" which he modestly described as "rather neat" to Edmund Wilson.[7]

More than just the manipulation of time, however, is at stake in Victor's art. Indeed, in presenting this aspect of memory, "Spring in Fialta" may seem less daring than stream-of-consciousness fiction. Rather than rapidly juxtaposing past and present in the mind of a single character, the story clearly indicates the transitions between layers of time while offering leisurely "vignettes" of each layer – the pictorial term is Victor's and indicates the extent to which he shares Nabokov's interest in mnemonic images (*SF* 415).[8] But Victor has another goal beyond simply imitating the play of memory through a moderately quickened use of flashbacks; in fact, in the later, English version of the story he even condemns "a ripple of stream of consciousness" as a trite literary fad (*SF* 427).[9] Memory's great value lies elsewhere, in its power to crystallize feelings that were latent in experience but can become conscious only in retrospect, if at all. Hence the key point with which Victor begins his defense of memory to Ferdinand, when he insists that a writer's real subject is the "heart." Memory only enters later as the "long-drawn sunset shadow of one's personal truth," as the faculty that preserves the heart's commitments in the wake of immediate emotion. Though Victor speaks somewhat elliptically, clearly he expects an art of memory to provide emotional insight. Beyond the complex movements of consciousness back and forth in time, such an art should try to show the strong affective currents from the past that, when captured by memory and rendered in an image, can sustain the present.

A convenient emblem for Victor's view of memory would be the Roman letter Z, an abrupt diagonal of emotional connection between two distinct levels of time. It is therefore fitting that he twice associates this very letter with Nina, the main subject of his memories.[10] In fact the economy and precision of Nabokov's writing are such that these two moments do more than offer a generalized diagram for the whole story. Each incident features a specific instance of emotional insight triggered by memory, while both of them, taken together, involve the reader in an analogous process of recollection.

Early in his relationship with Nina, Victor once saw her in Berlin, comfortably sprawled on a sofa with her body in a Z-shape (*SF* 418). She has broken off her engagement with a well-bred guardsman, and greets him warmly, as if they had been more intimate than they actually were. Victor realizes that she has forgotten the actual circumstances of their first meeting – a party on a snowy night in Russia, a general movement outdoors, two stragglers in the dark, and a sudden impulse of tenderness leading to a kiss. But if the details are cloudy in Nina's mind, her greeting does hark back to her emotions at that time. Thus Victor can remark that although "the whole cast of our relationship was fraudulently based upon an imaginary amity," he must concede that this error "had nothing to do with her random good will" (*SF* 418). As a comment on Nina's character, the phrase "random good will" is somewhat misleading. For it trivializes Victor's sense of the kiss as "a wonderful sunburst of kindness" or as "spring water containing salubrious salts" (*SF* 416). It also misrepresents the corresponding Russian passage, which in speaking of Nina's "careless, generous, friendly amorousness" suggested that it might be "a real virtue" (*VF* 15). Still, even as "random good will," it is clear that Nina's generous feelings have persisted, and, despite her forgetfulness of the actual situation, this warmth of character has bridged the gap that revolution and emigration have opened between their meetings.

Years later, when Victor is beginning to sense the waste of their brief, scattered encounters, he sees Nina in the same posture at a party in Paris (*SF* 428). Victor does not specifically say that he recalls the earlier moment, but because Nina is smoking in the same way and makes the same exclamation in recognizing him, readers undoubtedly do remember. As a result they can experience Victor's unspoken shock of recognition, while the sudden juxtaposition of then and now allows them to identify with his otherwise mysterious feelings of heartbreak. Not only has the sudden Z-flash of memory cast more light on the narrator's attitude toward Nina, but Nabokov has constructed the story in such a way that the reader participates in the same process.

Later in this scene Victor experiences a more obscure memory that reaches still further into his life with Nina. As he circulates among the guests, he overhears a chance remark that deepens his sadness: "Funny, how they all smell alike, burnt leaf through whatever perfume they use, those angular dark-haired girls" (*SF* 428). There is no explanation for why the image of burned leaves should affect him so strongly, but careful attention to sensory details in the text suggests that it joins two of Victor's best moments with Nina. At the time of their first kiss they may have gone outside to see a distant fire (hence the impact of "burnt"), while after their first lovemaking Victor went out on a balcony and breathed "a combined smell of dry maple leaves and gasoline" (*SF* 419-20). The implied comparison between these promising beginnings and the relatively hopeless present has sparked Victor's sudden melancholy. As with Nina earlier, so with Victor here: even though he cannot identify the specific details, he does sense a relevant current of emotion.

In the memories considered so far, the feelings released in Nina and Victor have been strong but relatively undefined. Such vagueness is essential to the story, which Victor began by confessing his failure "to find the precise term" to describe his relationship with Nina (*SF* 414).[11] In three key scenes, however, memory shows its power to focus the emotions and give them new significance. Each scene involves a convergence of past and present at a different level of time, first in the period before the meeting in Fialta, then during the encounter itself, and finally while Victor is writing down his memories. These varied scenes lay the groundwork for the story's grand finale, the elaborately crafted concluding sentence that makes no fewer than three Z-strokes through time on its way to defining Victor's ultimate attitude toward Nina.

Before Fialta, Victor's single most revealing meeting with Nina took place by chance on a Berlin railroad platform. She is on her way to Paris to marry Ferdinand, and Victor begins to sense a pattern of missed opportunities in his encounters with her. His mood crystallizes once her train has left, when, after a blank interval, he suddenly recalls a passionate love song that a maiden aunt used to sing with "a powerful, ecstatically full voice" (*SF* 419). The intensity of romantic feeling may be somewhat dated, but these words "from the music box of memory" continue to obsess Victor for hours. Not only does he recall his aunt's exact voice with an image-like specificity, but the song's subject marks his first oblique acknowledgment of love in his elusive feelings for Nina. Since the song is a form of art, moreover, it also suggests his dawning awareness of an art of memory that would link the heart with the imagination by recollecting sharply focused portions of the past.

The second key scene occurs in Fialta itself, near the end of their last reunion, when the narrator and Nina climb to a deserted terrace. It is a special moment, marked as such by a superb view of Mount Saint George, and Nina suddenly kisses him. Victor remembers their first kiss on that snowy evening in Russia, all their other encounters revive as well, and — retrospectively likening this fullness of memory to the triumph of a "circumnavigator, enriched all around" — he blurts out the awkward emotional insight: "Look here — what if I love you?" (*SF* 429). This is a climactic moment of perception, since until now neither of them has ever pronounced the word "love."

But Nina reacts enigmatically to Victor's words: "something like a bat passed swiftly across her face, a quick, queer, almost ugly expression." This odd image highlights our uncertainties about Nina's character, for it could register her disenchantment with marriage to "her eclectic husband" (*SF* 425); or perhaps her own promiscuity makes her uncomfortable with a sincere declaration of love. Perhaps, too, the image simply expresses Nina's inability to remember, apparent in her vague memories of their first kiss in Russia and seen in later meetings as well. And yet, though Nina does not acknowledge Victor's question, and though he quickly says he was only joking, the scene ends on an affirmative note. There is a gap in Victor's narrative — "From somewhere a firm bouquet of small dark, unselfishly smelling violets appeared in her hands" (*SF* 429) — and the reader recognizes Nina's affinity with the "unselfishness" of these flowers. This awareness in some measure counteracts Victor's stated mood of helplessness, for even if their love remains elusive, at least an atmosphere of generous feeling does surround their relationship.

Finally, at a third level of time after the meeting in Fialta, where Victor is author of the story, the very act of writing can create new fusions of memory and emotion. This level of the text becomes particularly evident during the fuller portrayal of Ferdinand midway through the story. Victor breaks off his account of the past when he gets to his character, protesting, "I would rather not dwell upon him at all"; yet his desire to keep silent is overcome by his reawakened disgust: "I cannot help it — he is surging up from under my pen" (*SF* 420). A less obvious suspension of time due to strong emotion has occurred as the story opens, where the effect is at once more subtle and more revealing of the writer's character. Though Victor normally uses the past tense in "Spring in Fialta," he gives his first impressions of the town in the present. As a result, the reader is placed in an ambiguous position, between the actual scene and Victor's viewpoint as author, and this chronological slippage underlines the temporal ambiguity of memory itself, which acts in the present to bring back vivid fragments of the past.

Only on a second reading, however, is the emotional charge of these opening comments released. Between the actual experience of Nina's violets, told at the end, and the decision to write about his last meeting with her, which motivates Victor here, he has had a chance to reflect on what the flowers mean. And so, as he celebrates his delight with Fialta, time circles again, as it had when he used the circumnavigator metaphor. The name of the town triggers a subliminal verbal association that might normally be considered a symbolic anticipation of the ending, but that in this fictive autobiography suggests emotion matured by memory: "I feel in the hollow of those violaceous syllables the sweet dark dampness of the most rumpled of small flowers" (*SF* 413). As Nina's last gesture reappears before him while he writes, Victor shows that he senses as never before the value of her generous spirit. Indeed, when he remarks "I am fond of Fialta," the name's associations with the past mean that this rather ordinary statement amounts to a renewed declaration of his love for Nina, a refusal to endorse his decision at the time to treat it as a joke.[12]

These varied transactions between different levels of the past culminate with the story's elaborate and highly original final sentence. Not only does it shift suddenly to the authorial plane and reveal new depths in Victor's feelings, thus showing how memories evoked while writing have sharpened his perceptions; but it also dramatizes two distinct shocks of retrospective insight at earlier levels of time. As the sentence begins, Victor and Nina are still standing together on the terrace. He notices the warmth of the stone parapet and realizes the explanation for some chance details glimpsed earlier – a glint of tinfoil (*SF* 423), a shining glass of liqueur (*SF* 426), or the sparkle of waves (*SF* 429). The cloudy day has gradually become sunny, but this emblem of hope (which may reflect the younger Nabokov's interest in anticipatory memory) is soon dispelled. For when Victor looks up, he discovers an essentially ambiguous resolution to his Fialta experiences: the sky's "brimming white radiance grew broader and broader, all dissolved in it, all vanished, all passed . . ." (*SF* 429). The burst of sunlight, still quite straightforward while it grows "broader and broader," has become problematic with "dissolved." By the end of the phrase it suggests a remote realm of uncertain truth, somewhat like the distant sky seen by Tolstoy's Prince Andrew Bolkonsky after the battle of Austerlitz.[13] For the radiance that began by spreading light also has the power to make things dissolve, while "passed" transfers this image to time, whose onward flow gives memory its perspective but also erodes the basis for its insights.

The sentence then turns to a second discovery in retrospect, occasioned by news of Nina's death, which occurred when her car crashed into a circus wagon just outside town. This tragedy naturally absorbs Victor's attention, but for the reader it gains added meaning as the final realization of all the scattered hints of an approaching circus throughout the story, particularly of the circus posters that the characters keep seeing all over town.[14] Yet, although Nabokov also pointed out "the crescendo of the circus theme" to Wilson (*NWL* 64), it brings no retrospective insight to Victor. But the juxtaposition of sun and circus has undermined the openness of futurity in a gesture that anticipates the temporal reversal at the end of John Shade's "Pale Fire," when the poet envisions a tomorrow that never comes. And the implicit presence of fatal omens alongside an explicit recognition of ambiguity obviously intensifies the bittersweet closing of "Spring in Fialta." As discussed in the next section, however, the manner of Nina's death also makes sense on an intertextual level, as a signpost marking Nabokov's repudiation of myth-oriented versions of modernism.

Even more pointed than these retrospective insights linked with sun or circus is the abruptness with which the narrative shifts from the terrace to Victor's discovery of Nina's death. The phrase cited above continues as follows: "all vanished, all passed, and I stood on the station platform at Mlech with a freshly bought newspaper." It is this paper that tells Victor what happened. As we have seen, temporal blanks and gaps accompanied earlier revelations, but here the startling elision of an entire day reaffirms the narrator's presence as author. For in this passage past and present fuse, with Victor's memories of Fialta becoming so vivid that the remembered sun dazzles his mind now as much as it did his eyesight then, producing a hiatus in the narrative. This authorial level of time remains effective for the rest of the sentence, which reports the emotional insights stirred in Victor by the crash. First, as he looks back at Ferdinand and his dubious sidekick Segur, his aversions, which had abruptly punctured his story when he first portrayed Ferdinand, now rise to a mythic intensity that is rare for Nabokov. Because both of them have survived the crash, Victor denounces them as "those salamanders of fate, those basilisks of good fortune" for having given the ambiguous portents surrounding Nina their permanent bias.

In his final thoughts, however, Victor gains new, more profound insights into his feelings for Nina. Over the years those feelings were sapped by two growing fears, that their relationship was corrupt because it accepted "the lies, the futility, the gibberish" of Nina's environment and thus squandered "something lovely, delicate, and unrepeatable" (*SF* 425), and that it was frivolous because it pretended to exist in "another, lighter time-medium" apart from ordinary life *(SF* 425). But Nina's death allays these fears. Not only does it rescue her from her "faithful, long-standing imitation" of her sordid companions; but since, in the story's last words, she has "turned out after all to be mortal," she also reaffirms her common humanity. For Victor, meanwhile, as he looks back at this tragic moment, his feelings undergo one final sharpening of focus. His last word "mortal" conveys his anguish at the precariousness of all things subject to time, yet it also voices a definite pride. In a world of constant transience, Nina's kindness and generosity were worthwhile, had even been a gallant retort to time's voraciousness. With this final insight into the value of her love, Victor has decisively surpassed Ganin, from Nabokov's first novel *Mary*. Despite the perplexity he shares with this earlier character at the irretrievable pastness of his memories, he can still find meaning in them.

For readers intrigued by Nabokov's cross-cultural, multilingual career, "Spring in Fialta" offers a rich distillation of his European sympathies, doubts, and disagreements just before he abandons Russian for English. Through a variety of allusions and adaptations, it creates a cultural field defined along three major axes: a strong orientation toward France rather than Germany, an equally strong preference for modernism over the avant-garde, and a more ambivalent oscillation between Western Europe and Russia. Both Russia and the avant-garde confront Victor with cultural situations that help illuminate Nabokov's sense of European modernism by going beyond its boundaries. But the German-French opposition, which is much more specific than Nabokov's early fiction in expressing his preferences among several competing accounts of memory, focuses on a conflict within European modernism itself.

Two vivid images that surface when Victor discovers his art of memory have strong polemical overtones directed at central European innovators in psychology and literature. Ferdinand's mountain-shaped penholder, with its "black tunnel" for dipping the pens, is obviously Freudian, so much so that it can only be meant to mislead the unwary. Its real point is to demote psychoanalytic readings of experience to the level of *Kitsch,* with the text suggesting two main motives for the attack. The Nabokovian preference for precise mnemonic images over deconcretized symbols reappears in the contrast between this grotesquely sexualized memento of the natural scene and Victor's careful description of Mount Saint George as he remembers it.

Even more profoundly, Ferdinand's weird souvenir evokes the primal scene, that ultimate mark of the past in Freudian psychology, which Nabokov would take pains to attack at the beginning of *Speak, Memory*. Lurking behind the two layers of memory, both recent and childish, this persistent trace of infantile experience can enter consciousness only as a distorted displacement. Nabokov, by contrast, emphasizes a more direct reading of the past, for if the narrator's love for Nina is also scattered across recent and more remote levels of time, reassembling this love never requires that he combat stubborn mechanisms of repression, as in Freud. Hence Victor's lyrical tribute to Mount Saint George at the beginning of "Spring in Fialta" can function as an undisputed given. Though Nabokov would concede that such a memory was partly constructed (as the humanizing metaphor at the end of Victor's image makes clear), he rejects the Freudian theory that even the most concrete mnemonic image serves to screen one experience, in the last analysis always the same, which is buried in the unconscious.

Nabokov's other quarrel with central European modernism involves Thomas Mann, whose *Magic Mountain* was the target of a passing squib as early as 1928, when Nabokov still lived in Berlin.[15] In the 1940s, while struggling to publish the English version of "Spring in Fialta," Nabokov continued to dispute Mann's stature, this time in the context of an American perspective on modernist fiction. "How *could* you name that quack Mann in one breath with P. and J.?" (*NWL* 148), he protests to Edmund Wilson, where the initials show his own determination to save Proust and Joyce from a similar guilt by association. Later, in *Strong Opinions,* his criticisms would center on *Death in Venice,* which held a special place among his literary dislikes. Not only does Nabokov compare it directly with *Ulysses, The Metamorphosis, Petersburg,* and Proust's *Recherche,* only to dismiss it as "asinine" alongside these modernist masterpieces; but he also singles it out as a culminating example of *poshlost',* the evocative Russian word he tried to Americanize in his Gogol book. When applied to Mann, its most relevant connotations would seem to be "bogus profundity" and a loosely German penchant for the "poetically antique and mythological."[16] Nabokov thus associates *Death in Venice* with intellectual pretentiousness and with what Habermas would call the archaistic element in aesthetic modernity.

Given these attitudes, it is significant that the basic situation of "Spring in Fialta" recalls *Death in Venice* in its combination of an Adriatic setting, Slavic characters (Poles as well as Russians in Mann), and illicit love. Victor's story might plausibly have been called "Death in Fialta"; and before Mann's hero

Aschenbach goes to Venice, he stays briefly at a resort where the wet weather and the inhabitants "speaking an outlandish tongue" suggest Nabokov's invented town. And both stories deploy a pattern of interlocking motifs, or "themes" in Nabokov's terminology, which foreshadow Aschenbach's and Nina's fates. Thus the circus posters that fail to warn anyone about the impending car crash correspond to the series of impudent strangers whose full import Mann's hero fails to grasp as they lead him to his death.

Nabokov's polemic concentrates on Mann's motif of the strangers, who are at once avatars of Dionysus and figures from a medieval dance of death. In these roles they contribute to the explicitly mythic art of *Death in Venice,* as that story seeks to reawaken the spirit of "poetic legends from the beginning of time."[17] Nabokov's rejection of this kind of collective cultural memory explains the absence of mythic glamour in his story, most notably in the circus, which consists merely of "thoroughly fooled elephants" (*SF* 414) and "mediocre Indians" (*SF* 428). By taking this position, he apparently misses Mann's irony, which makes *Death in Venice* a critique as well as an enactment of myth. Nonetheless, the story does display enough hankering for the antique to support Nabokov's attack. The full significance of Nabokov's revisionary gesture will emerge in *Speak, Memory,* where he reworks the circus motif to make it an emblem for his own art.[18] As his anecdote in that book of the rearranged circus fence suggests, he conceives of cultural memory not as a mythic reawakening of some distant past but as an intertextual confrontation with immediate predecessors.

Mann's Dionysian strangers are mythic in another sense as well, for they herald a "metaphysical" world of mystic significances and dreamlike distortions of reality. Nabokov himself has a genuine interest in creating a sense of "other worlds" in his fiction, but he rejects this rather literalistic, unselfconscious way of doing so. In his story, though it may be disquieting to remember all the circus posters once the car crash has occurred, there is nothing necessarily uncanny about repeatedly spotting advertisements for a public spectacle. The one genuinely occult event in "Spring in Fialta" happens elsewhere, with the episodic character of an English traveler. Victor notices that he has his eye on Nina and then, quite late in the story, the man is shown capturing a moth. Since moths and butterflies are emblems for the soul, both in Nabokov and other writers, this act could be seen as deciding her fate. But it is clear that Nabokov's traveler differs markedly from Mann's strangers. Rather than invoking the collective realm of Greek myth, this character refers back to Nabokov himself in his singular roles of lepidopterist and Anglophile. He thus serves as an authorial signature within the text, as a self-conscious acknowledgment of the writer's role, at a level of reality beyond the fiction, in determining Nina's fate. Nabokov reveals a metaphysical dimension through an individualistic self-consciousness about the artifice of narrative, rather than through a direct appeal to mythic motifs.

French modernism tellingly asserts its priority over both Mann and Freud during Victor's chance encounter with Nina in the Berlin train station. Since she is leaving for Paris, her departure echoes Ganin's projected trip to France at the end of *Mary,* except that here the cultural issues have become much more precise. Only the English version of the story evokes the peculiarly vivid mood in the station, "where everything is something trembling on the brink of something else" (*SF* 418), a comment on novelty and transience that strongly suggests the sense of modernity expressed in Baudelaire's "The Painter of Modern Life." Both English and Russian versions, however, do spotlight the actual moment of Nina's departure, when "all was slipping away with beautiful smoothness" (*SF* 419), until Victor recalls his great-aunt's song. Here he experiences the full problematic of modernity beset by resurgent memory. So marked is the French orientation at this moment that when Victor remembers the song, which is doubtlessly part of that "Franco-Russian" culture Nabokov discussed in "Mademoiselle O," he actually slips into French. Moreover, though there is nothing specifically Proustian about this moment, the identification of the song with "some Parisian drama of love" from the previous century momentarily places Victor in the position of Proust's narrator as he looks back to Swann's love for Odette in the 1870s. In a more general sense, certainly, as a fictive autobiographer who finds literary inspiration in his own past, Victor does recall Proust's Marcel.

In fact, Nina is a Nabokovian version of Odette, but one that diverges from its source in one key respect even as it pays homage to it. To understand her relationship to Proust, we need to distinguish two levels of reception on Nabokov's part. From one perspective, Nina's careless promiscuity might suggest a direct continuation of the Proustian inferno of romantic love and jealousy portrayed in *Kamera Obskura.*[19] Victor briefly glimpses this possibility when he rejects the notion of leaving his wife for Nina. Such a life would be too painful, he reflects, for "it would be penetrated . . . with a passionate, intolerable bitterness" that recalls a Proustian drama of memory and reinterpretation in its sense of "a past, teeming with protean partners" (*SF* 425). But as we have seen, Victor subordinates this side of Nina to a very different image of her character, which overlooks her easy virtue to celebrate her capacity for "woman's love" (*SF* 416). It is this underlying generosity and warmth that leads him to make his declaration on the terrace and to renew this affirmation of love while he writes. We might want to debate Victor's assumption that these qualities are specifically feminine. But in the terms set by "Spring in Fialta" the issue is moot, since the point of Victor's art of memory is to awaken the same "feminine" emotions in him, thereby dissolving his conventional gender distinctions. For Victor, the art dealer's Proustian jealousy in *Kamera Obskura* yields to those values that he associates with the "heart," values that his meetings with Nina have encouraged in himself.

At the same time, however, Nabokov is responding to a deeper current of Proustian inspiration, which now enters his writing for the first time. Beyond the drama of reinterpretation and the question of involuntary memory, and alongside the oscillation of narrative between fiction and autobiography or of the image between concrete sensations and tropes, he also identified Proust as the analyst of that very conjunction of memory with emotional insight that concerns Victor. Hence in his Cornell lectures on the *Recherche* he could define Proust's achievement in the following terms: "The transmutation of sensation into sentiment, the ebb and tide of memory, waves of emotion such as desire, jealousy, and artistic euphoria – this is the material of the enormous yet singularly light and translucid work."[20] The first two parts of this statement apply directly to Victor's relationship with Nina, except that they merely list points whose interconnection is shown much more forcefully in the story. Certain sensations given in direct experience acquire a new power of sentiment *only when* enhanced by memory, whose "ebb and tide" implies a selective emphasis on certain details while others are elided. The reference to "waves of emotion" in the third part of the statement returns to the main issue that separated Nabokov from Proust in "Spring in Fialta." Not that this formula fails to cover Victor's reliance as a writer on deferred emotional insight, but the specific emotions he emphasizes are quite different. Instead of the cycle of desire and jealousy presented in both *Swann in Love* and *Kamera Obskura,* "Spring in Fialta" looks ahead to the basic project of *Speak, Memory* – the creation of images that would crystallize feelings of tenderness and love dispersed through the past and threatened by the harshness of history.

On a second cultural axis that reaches beyond this Franco-German opposition within modernism, "Spring in Fialta" at once broadens and sharpens the polemics in *Kamera Obskura* that defended the "innovators" against rival modes of modern writing. In the 1936 Russian version of the story, Victor's intensely private Proustian memories of Nina contrast with Ferdinand's vogue in advanced artistic circles, which are made to seem cliquish, superficial, and lacking in any real commitment to art. When Ferdinand is first spotted among a crowd of mediocre disciples, he suggests a nightmarish caricature of *The Last Supper* (*VF* 20-22), and he cynically caters to the revolutionary myth of the 1930s by identifying antitraditional art with radical politics (*VF* 30-31). In the English version, Nabokov adds more details on the French context for this polemic. Ferdinand is said to frequent Montparnasse, one of his disciples paints vaguely cubist "eye-and-guitar canvases," and another is a businessman who finances "surrealist ventures" (*SF* 421). And the tendency to link innovative art and left-wing politics is now diagnosed as a tactic of "ultramodern literature" (*SF* 427). Nabokov had already rehearsed this attack on the avant-garde in *The Real Life of Sebastian Knight* (1941), where the Proustian novelist Knight had joined the Russian futurist Alexis Pan on an improbable junket. Like Ferdinand, Pan was accused of exploiting "the queer notion (based mainly on a muddle of terms) that there is a natural connection between extreme politics and extreme art."[21] Owing to this hasty equation of all radicalisms along with a vaguely Freudian fascination with the "submental," he was dismissed as an instance of the "super-modern" fallacy (*SK* 28).

Nabokov's polemic with the avant-garde proceeds on two distinct levels as he moves from the Russian to the English version of "Spring in Fialta." Explicitly he is concerned with the much-discussed topic of literary tendency and political allegiance, which bedeviled so many writers on the left at that time, from Brecht and Benjamin in Germany and Auden in England to the surrealists in France. Nabokov was better informed than most about the basically antimodern tastes of Russian radicals, but otherwise he has little to add to this debate. His second, implicit point is more interesting, for his choice of polemical terms indicates that he is thinking about the relationship between the modernist and the avant-garde consciousness of time. Hence neither of his pejorative labels, neither "super-modern" nor "ultra-modern," rules out an honorific use of "modern."[22] Nabokov cannot object to the basic project of trying to outdo past art, only to an exaggerated one-sidedness in pursuing that project. For one thing, as suggested by Victor's and Ferdinand's contrasting attitudes in writing about their personal pasts, such one-sidedness would exclude the countermovement of memory. Another result would be the loss of all historical context, a denial of the past that ultimately destroys the sense of modernity itself; for without some knowledge of what has been surpassed, it is impossible to assess the newness of the new. When Victor says of Ferdinand that "The fame of his likes circulates briskly but soon grows heavy and stale; and as for history it will limit his life story to the dash between two dates" (*SF* 420), this fate is merely a logical extension of the avant-garde's willful blindness to the past. Nabokov would make a related point to Wilson in describing Pushkin as an innovator while he worked on the English version of "Spring in Fialta." He remarks, "Pushkin never broke the skeleton of tradition, – he merely rearranged its inner organs, – with less showy but more vital results" (*NWL* 67). The essentially modernist pursuit of the new against the old requires a surgical lightness of touch that differs strikingly from the heavy-handed interventions of the avant-garde.

Along a third cultural axis that contrasts Western Europe with Russia, "Spring in Fialta" suggests Nabokov's divided loyalties during a time of major changes in his literary identity. The town itself reflects this ambivalence, for its division into two parts suggests more than the purely temporal opposition of past and present. The new town, with its express trains and Riviera atmosphere, belongs to Europe, but a certain Slavic flavor persists in the old town, with its fading mosaics, Dalmatian natives, and Yalta-like name. At one point, when Nabokov mentions how the two towns, though thoroughly interwoven, still struggle "either to disentangle themselves or to thrust each other out" (*SF* 426), the difficulty of cultural synthesis is made explicit.

This unresolved duality reappears in Victor's impressions of Nina herself, which are summed up in two composite images with divergent cultural implications. The special quality of these images must be distinguished from the concrete sense impressions – the smell of burnt leaf, the bouquet of violets, Nina's Z-shaped posture, or her batlike grimace – that normally punctuate Victor's double narrative. Rather than aiming at documentary accuracy, they are more general; and, by joining many experiences in a single verbal picture, they propose an overview of Nina's life. The first of these images comes quite early in the story, when Victor pauses to describe "her average pose." In another situation that echoes *Death in Venice,* he imagines Nina at the counter of a Cook's travel agency, "left calf crossing right shin, left toe tapping floor," intent on making a train reservation (*SF* 417).[23] But later he replaces this dominant "European" image with a covert one attuned to a "Russian" experience of emigration and exile. At the end of some quick vignettes of random meetings, Victor reports a dream that mingles recent impressions of Nina with something he may have glimpsed during his own flight from Russia: "I saw lying on a trunk, a roll of burlap under her head, pale-lipped and wrapped in a woolen kerchief, Nina fast asleep, as miserable refugees sleep in godforsaken railway stations" (*SF* 425). This visionary traveler, so different from the affluent tourists who patronize the new Fialta, deepens the rift between the story's fading Russian past and its insistently European present.

This rift is never really closed. Both composite images do convey Nina's restless life of moves and trips, and by emphasizing the disorientation of exile give added value to her capacity for generosity and love. But otherwise their authority is problematic. Since neither comes as directly from "experience" as the story's mnemonic images, it is hard to decide which one gives more insight into Nina's life, the imagined "average pose" or the scrambled dream vision. And if placement in the story gives a certain climactic punch to the dream, temporal perspective favors the pose, which occurs to Victor in the course of writing. In one sense, however, these uncertainties are themselves meaningful, for the oscillation between a European and a Russian Nina corresponds to the dilemma Nabokov then faced in his literary identity. Even the writing itself, with its two languages and the Parisian dateline given in some versions of the story,[24] reflects the tension between maintaining a Russian literary vocation and deepening his involvement in European modernity. A similar tension will reappear in *The Gift*, Nabokov's other major fictive autobiography of the 1930s, but in this account of an émigré writer's young manhood and literary apprenticeship, the cultural hierarchy implied by Nina's image is reversed. Russia becomes the dominant presence while in the interstices of the text Nabokov's European interests continue to lead a hidden existence. Only later, as he writes *Speak, Memory* in America, will Nabokov attempt a more thorough Russo-European synthesis.

ENDNOTES

[1] For details on "Mademoiselle O," which eventually became Chapter 5 in Nabokov's autobiography, *Speak, Memory*, see John Burt Foster, Jr., *Nabokov's Art of Memory and European Modernism* (Princeton: Princeton Univ. Press, 1993), 110-29.

[2] Vladimir Nabokov, "Spring in Fialta," *The Collected Stories* (New York: Knopf, 1995), p. 32. Henceforth cited parenthetically as *SF*.

[3] See *Nabokov's Art of Memory*, 121-24.

[4] The term is Andrew Field's in *VN: The Life and Art of Vladimir Nabokov* (New York: Crown, 1986), 164.

[5] In the original Russian version, this sentence is somewhat longer; though it omits the reference to personal truth, it ends with a phrase that emphasizes irrationalism and intuition: "were I a writer, I should only allow my heart to have imagination, and for the rest rely upon memory, that long evening shadow of the truth, but on no account would I haul reason along to masquerades." See Vladimir Nabokov, *Vesna v Fialte* (Ann Arbor: Ardis, 1978), 19. Hereafter cited parenthetically as *VF*.

[6] The temporal structure of the story, as it shuttles between drama and chronicle, may be schematized as follows:

Drama	*Chronicle*
Meeting Nina in Fialta, 413-15	First Meeting in Russia, 415-16
Shopping in Fialta, 417	Encounters in Russia and Paris, 417-22
Joining Ferdinand and Segur, 422-23	Quick Vignettes of Later Meetings, 423-25
The Car and Lunch, 426-28	Last Meeting in Paris, 428
On the Terrace, 428-29	

[7] *The Nabokov-Wilson Letters, 1940-71,* Simon Karlinsky, ed. (New York: Harper & Row, 1979), 64. Hereafter cited parenthetically as *NWL*.

[8] In context, the term appears in the following passage: ". . . I could not have celebrated the occasion with greater art, could not have adorned with brighter vignettes the list of fate's former services, even if I had known that this was to be the last one . . ."

[9] Nabokov should not be understood as making a blanket condemnation of Joyce here. He thought the portrayal of Leopold Bloom in *Ulysses* was superb, but cautioned that the stream-of-consciousness technique was an illusion in that it implied that the main vehicle of thought was words rather than images. As an explanation for this particular alteration in the original Russian text, we might speculate that on the Continent in the 1930s, stream-of-consciousness fiction did not have the same leading position that it held in Anglo-American fiction of the 1940s, after Joyce, Woolf, and Faulkner. We can thus see a transition here from the French to the Anglo-American side of Nabokov's mobile cultural identity.

[10] The Russian version of the story is careful to specify the Roman Z or *zet*; the Cyrillic Z has an entirely different shape.

[11] The Russian version is more specific on this point, since it has Victor hesitate between "friendship" and "romantic love" (*VF* 10).

[12] This linkage with the past is particularly clear in the Russian version, where Victor's declaration to Nina, "*A chto, esli ia vas liubliu*" (*VF* 34), is echoed in his opening statement about Fialta, "*Ia etot gorodok liubliu*" (*VF* 8).

[13] See LeoTolstoy, *War and Peace*, trans. Richard Pevear and LarissaVolokhonsky (New York: Knopf, 2007), 281 (Part III, chapter 16).

[14] There are at least six of these sightings, at *SF* 413, 414, 417, 423, 426, and 428.

[15] The early comment on *The Magic Mountain* occurs in "*Podlets*," in *Vozvrashchenie Chorba* (1929; rpt. Ann Arbor MI: Ardis, 1976), 122, translated as "An Affair of Honor," in Vladimir Nabokov, *The Collected Stories*, 211.

[16] On *Death in Venice*, see *Strong Opinions* (NewYork: McGraw-Hill, 1973), 57, 101. On *poshlost'* and a "German" penchant for myth, see *Nikolai Gogol* (Norfolk CT: New Directions, 1944), 66.

[17] Thomas Mann, *Death in Venice*, ed. and trans. Clayton Koelb (New York: Norton, 1994), 28. Hereafter cited as *DV*.

[18] I have in mind Nabokov's self-critical account of the derivative nature of his first poem, in *Speak, Memory*, 221.

[19] This 1932 Russian novel of Nabokov's was later translated and revised to become *Laughter in the Dark* (1938). In the process the allusions to Proust are submerged.

[20] *Lectures on Literature*, ed. by Fredson Bowers, introd. by John Updike, introd. (NewYork: Harcourt Brace Jovanovich, 1980), 207.

[21] *The Real Life of Sebastian Knight* (New York: New Directions, 1941), 30. Hereafter cited as *SK*.

[22] For more on Nabokov's vocabulary of modernity in *The Real Life of Sebastian*

Knight, see *Nabokov's Art of Memory*, 167-70.

[23] Compare these motifs with Aschenbach's decision to consult the English travel agent (*DV* 53), and with the crossed legs of several of the strangers, including Tadzio, that cross his path (4, 49).

[24] The dateline "Paris, 1938" appears at the end of the version of "Spring in Fialta" that was published in *Nabokov's Dozen* (New York: Doubleday, 1958), 38.

VII

Child Perspective: Tradition and Experiment. An Analysis of "The Childhood of Luvers" by Boris Pasternak.

FIONA BJÖRLING

The dividing line between childhood and adulthood is a matter not merely of physiology, but also of culture. Like the distinction between man and woman, it provides for individuals within a social community a means of defining values and establishing an identity. The criteria according to which we distinguish child from adult vary from culture to culture, from age to age. The criteria of Western civilization today were founded in the middle of the eighteenth century by Rousseau and his followers. Before that time the concept of the child as a human being with specific perceptive, cognitive and emotional patterns was not a widespread cultural phenomenon; the child was measured and evaluated according to how far he could function as an adult. The new attitude to the child, initiated in the thinking of Rousseau, consisted in appreciating and taking account of that which is peculiar to the child, particularly in matters pertaining to education. Since that time Western civilization has frequently resorted to the opposite extreme, that is established childhood as an absolute and desirable state, and measured the adult according to his adherence to the child. Then we have what George Boas has named and decried, that is a cult of childhood.[1] Between ignoring the specifically childlike on the one hand, and adulating it on the other, lies a more dialectical approach. This dialectical thinking, which has revolved around questions of innocence and experience, has become a constant cultural concern expressed throughout the nineteenth and twentieth centuries, both in treaties on education and in works of art.

A starting point for the present study is the idea that, in pursuing in their literature the common cultural theme of the child, the nineteenth and twentieth centuries respectively are concerned with two distinct aspects of childhood.

Discussing the problems which arose in connection with the industrial revolution during the late eighteenth and the nineteenth century, Peter Coveney writes:

> In this context of isolation, alienation, doubt and intellectual conflict, it is not difficult to see the attraction of the child as a literary theme. The child could serve as a symbol of the artist's dissatisfaction with the society which was in process of such harsh development about him. In a world given increasingly to utilitarian values and the Machine, the child could become the symbol of Imagination and Sensibility, a symbol of Nature set against the forces abroad in society actively denaturing humanity. Through the child could be expressed the artist's awareness of human Innocence against the accumulative pressures of social Experience.[2]

The artist turns to the theme of the child in order to establish a system of values, Good and Evil, according to which he as an adult can guide his life. He is searching for ethical norms which will be relevant for society as a whole. These norms may be of a metaphysical order, emanating from the concept of "original innocence," an idea prevalent among the romantic poets[3]; or they may be of a humanist order, concerned with the improvement of society, such as those values which inform the progressive intent of critical realism. Both metaphysical and humanist ethical values are invested in Dostoevsky's frequent concern with the child.[4] As an example of the first we can quote Alesha Karamazov in *The Brothers Karamazov* and Myshkin in *The Idiot*. Not only are these two characters in themselves childlike and innocent, but also they are liked and trusted by children. In *The Idiot* this theme culminates in the story told by Myshkin of the group of children in Switzerland who adored and cared for the socially ostracized Marie. Innocent, childlike adults as well as children themselves are presented in Dostoevsky's works as being closer to the essence of what is good. Humanist values are by implication advocated in the many heartrending descriptions of children cruelly abused by poverty, sickness and drunkenness, as for example the Marmeladov family in *Crime and Punishment*. In Dostoevsky's works, as in other literary works from the nineteenth century, interest in the child is motivated not by a desire to probe the child's mind from within, but rather by the need to use the child as a measuring rod by which to judge the ethical values appropriate to the adult world.

While the ethical concern with childhood has continued into the twentieth century,[5] we can at the same time distinguish a radically new approach differently motivated. This is the approach associated with modernist art, most striking at the beginning of the century in such movements as cubism, futurism, surrealism, dadaism etc. These movements give expression to the acute, post-positivist sense of alienation which characterized European culture at this time. All hitherto established norms – metaphysical, ethical and aesthetic – were felt to lack objective reality. The artist, facing the consequences of his absolute skepticism, had to reject any value which had been handed down; he possessed only his own mind and his medium. He had to create himself the substance to be expressed in his form. In this situation of supposed cultural nakedness, it was not surprising that the artist should draw an analogy between himself and primitive man on the one hand and the child on the other. The analogy was one not only of nakedness but also of potential. For it was recognized that both primitive man and the child, in expressing themselves, manifest a vigor and energy which is creative. By aligning himself with the primitive and the child, the twentieth century artist could turn the despair of existential skepticism into a potential for creation and belief. Searching for a primary experience of life and the world, the artist taps the child's mind through its expression in pictures and words: like the newborn child, the disillusioned artist must learn from scratch. He aligns himself with the child whose vital business is to see, to hear and to understand for the first time. Ethics has little place in this world of primary experience: how can the artist evaluate what he has not yet learnt to see? His concern is not with moral innocence but with perceptive and cognitive innocence. The nineteenth century interest in the child as a beacon to illuminate human morality gives way in early twentieth century art to an interest in the working of the child's mind per se. Instead of approaching the child as an object, victim or redeemer of a corrupt society, the modernist artist approaches him as a subject, source and generator of a new vision.

It is not difficult to establish frequent manifestation of this tendency in the Russian art of the early twentieth century. In his book, *Russian Futurism,* Vladimir Markov alludes continually both to the concern with children's art and to imitations of the same as manifest by the Russian futurists.[6] But the fact remains that children's genuinely naive art and the modernists' sophisticated attempts at imitating the same are crucially different. Whereas critics of visual art make allowances for this difference, critics of verbal art allude diffusely to "infantile" tendencies without defining the same. In his book *Grown-up Narrator and Childlike Hero,* A. F. Zweers assumes certain perceptions and certain linguistic expressions to be typical or untypical of a child. Discussing the drawing which Nikolenka in Tolstoy's *Childhood* attempts to draw with recourse to a single blue crayon, Zweers concludes: "On the other hand, the child's world is evoked because blue hares can only exist in a child's world." Further: "The child's feelings are expressed, but the grown-up narrator is responsible for the choice of words. A ten-year old boy would not use an expression such as *iz'iavit' radost'* (to express joy) or a construction such as *ravnoe, esli ne bol'shee* (equal to if not exceeding that which).[7] As for blue hares, are they not as much at home in an artist's world as they are in the child's? The point is that we as adults have no adequate criteria according to which we can ascertain what is and what is not typical for a child's way of seeing and expressing what he sees. Do we really know what a ten-year-old boy might or might not say? And do we know how his verbal expression corresponds to what he means to express? It is difficult to fall off a bicycle once you have learnt to ride it, and it is impossible for an adult to regain his childhood innocence once he has lost it. This means that when we adults interpret the expressions of a child, we cannot but relate them to our adult habits of seeing and expressing things. When a child says: "Allgone sticky"[8] it sounds to us comic or quaint whereas for the child it is not marked in any such way. Similarly a child's utterance may appear to the adult to incur metaphorical substitution, whereas to the child the utterance is literal since he makes no choice and therefore cannot be said to substitute one word for another. Frequently when adults describe a work of art as being "naive" or "infantile," they mean not that it in actual fact corresponds to the way a child perceives and conceives, but rather that it corresponds to the way in which an adult envisages child perception.

It is this point of view which is relevant in Elena Guro's frequent recourse to the theme of the child. Markov says of Guro: "In her efforts to achieve freshness and closeness to nature, Guro is particularly attracted to the theme of childhood. Often things are presented as perceived or imagined by a child ... Children are able not only to see things as if for the first time, but to hear words in their original freshness."[9] I suggest that

Guro's language is not so much a reconstruction of a child's way of thinking and speaking as a recourse to the language which adults conventionally use in addressing young children. What it expresses is not so much the child's world in and of itself as the adult longing for the child's world. Thus in the poem "A children's little barrel-organ" we note an abundance of diminutives, as for example: little sparks of little icicles (*sosulek iskorki*); the dust of little snowflakes (*snezhinok pyl'*); the little barrel-organ plays a dear little cheerful quadrille (*a sharmanochka igraet veselen'kuiu kadril'*).[10] The diminutives suggest a poem, song or fairy tale written not by but for children. There is no evidence to show that children choose spontaneously to express themselves with the use of diminutives, as though their own smallness should cause them to experience the world a size smaller. Should the opposite not be the case? It is of course adults, addressing children in baby language, who allow the size of the child to infect the names of the objects surrounding the child; children merely repeat the words they have learnt from adults. Likewise the motifs of barrel-organ, Christmas tree and pantomime are motifs commonly and fondly associated with childhood, fostered as it were by nostalgia in an adult world. Naturally this is not a defect on Guro's part; on the contrary a semantic charge lies precisely in the fact that the would-be child language does not emancipate itself from the confines of adult articulation. The pathos in Guro's resort to the theme of childhood in both *The Hurdy-Gurdy* (*Sharmanka*) and *Baby Camels of the Sky* lies in the attempt to conjure up a world which does not really exist.

This leads us to a fundamental difference between the real child and the modernist artist as a would-be child. A child, from the moment he is born, is set on a path of continual development. Child perception and cognition is of itself dynamic: at no point is the child content with yesterday's knowledge, for his basic impulse is to perceive, understand and finally communicate with the world around him. Ironically enough, the modernist artist is trying to divest himself of those very ways and norms of understanding and communication to the acquisition of which the child expends his energy. The modernist artist then has a static view of childhood since he is interested in the moment of epiphany, of dawning understanding, in and of itself, but not as part of a continuing chain of greater understanding. Speaking figuratively we may say that the child and the artist meet head-on on opposite journeys: the child is traveling from innocence to experience, from ignorance to knowledge, while the artist is traveling from experience to innocence. At the point where they meet there may be a superficial similarity of expression, but this expression means something different in each case.

Rudolf Arnheim distinguishes genuine naiveté from modernist naiveté in comparing a child's drawing of a glass of water with a drawing of a saucepan by Picasso: "In a child's drawing of a glass of water (...), the combination of side view and top view in a symmetrical pattern expresses the solid completeness of a trustworthy reality, whereas in Picasso's rendering of a saucepan (...), front view and side view, roundness and angularity, left tilt and right tilt, all coincide in a clashing contradiction."[11] Analysis of pseudo-naiveté in verbal art presents greater difficulties. Children draw pictures long before they learn to write, and those pictures once drawn receive the status of canonical texts and are called "children's art" although they were certainly not created as "art" but merely as what Arnheim calls "visual statements." Studies of children's language concentrate on the acquisition of normal, communicative language.[12] Children's utterances are studied from the points of view of linguistic conformity and contextual adequacy. The creativity of the child learning to speak is of course stressed, but it is treated as a mechanism for acquiring a common code, that is, from the utilitarian point of view. While children's drawings may be pinned up around the house for aesthetic appreciation, their utterances do not appear to attract attention from the aesthetic point of view. This is merely to say that the analogy between children's art and modernist art on the one hand, and children's language and modernist poetry on the other is lopsided.

The use of language as a means of exposing and investigating the child's mind seems in fact to be a double-edged tool. On the one hand language is better suited than all other means of communication to an elaboration in other terms of a complex, synthetic experience. Language can articulate synthetic experience by so to speak dismantling it, analyzing it at different levels – intellectual, sensual, emotional. But on the other hand, in so doing language does not recreate the original experience, it merely transcribes the same in its own terms. A verbal account of a dream for example will at best give an approximation of the actual dream. For the significance of a dream resides in an elusive atmosphere where various levels converge: space or time may become semanticized in a way which is impossible to articulate in normal analytical language. The dream related over the breakfast table often fails to communicate the burning significance which it holds in the form of a powerful but non-verbalizable sensation for the dreamer.

The modernist artist who tries to probe the mind of the not yet articulate child, lying in ambush for the moment of epiphany, of seeing for the first time, finds himself in a paradoxical situation. He wishes to give expression to that which is not yet expressible. He resorts to the all-powerful medium of articulation, human language, in order to express that which by definition is non-verbalizable. Were he to succeed in articulating the non-articulate he would destroy precisely that which he wished to present.

It is possible to distinguish two ways of attempting to realize an expression of inarticulate experience. On the one hand the artist tries to imitate the inarticulate child, imagining the words the child would have spoken if he had possessed them; on the other he bypasses the child's own means of articulation and turns directly to his own, offering his own poetic discourse – not as imitation but as equivalent of the child's experience. In both cases there is a gap between the experience itself and its verbal articulation: this gap is bridged by the artist's imagination.

Pasternak's "The Childhood of Luvers"[13] has a special place in the spectrum of Russian nineteenth and twentieth century literary presentations of child and childhood in that it seems to activate both tendencies discussed above: on the one hand it is motivated by a metaphysical interest in the child as an object (the relationship between the child and "nature" or "life"); and on the other it manifests the modernist attempt to convey the workings of the child's mind per se, from within. Concerning the metaphysical exposition of childhood and its significance, one must stress that the author gives emphasis to the organic rather than to the social, ethical. There is almost no concern with education: Zhenia's education is in fact defective and her contact with the adult world minimal and painful. Nevertheless, under cover of an unhappy childhood, Nature works her mysterious ways, all to the good, as the narrator specifically says:

> These were the circumstances of the children's education. They did not perceive this; for there are few, even among grown-ups, who understand what it is that forms, creates and binds them together. Life rarely tells what she is going to do with them. She loves her purpose too well, and even when she speaks of her work, it is only to those who wish her success and admire her tools. No one can help her; anyone can throw her into confusion. How? In this way. If you entrusted a tree with the care of its own growth, it would become all branch or disappear wholly into its roots or squander itself on a single

leaf, forgetting that the universe must be taken as a model; and after producing one thing in a thousand, it would begin to reproduce one thing a thousand times.

So that there shall be no dead branches in the soul, so that its growth shall not be retarded, so that man shall be incapable of mingling his narrow mind with the creation of his immortal essence, there exists a number of things to turn his vulgar curiosity away from life, which does not wish to work in his presence and in every way avoids him. ... Hence all respectable religions, all generalisations, all prejudices and the most amusing and brilliant of them all – psychology. (164)

This metaphysical slant is a clear manifestation of the essentially romantic import of Pasternak's work; it marks a move away from the more socially orientated childhood descriptions otherwise prevalent in Russia from the middle of the nineteenth century.[14] Interesting to note is the fact that even Zhenia's understanding of the fundamental ethical precept "Love thy neighbor as thyself" comes to her from within, inevitably, without the intervention of social guidance.[15] It is a question not of moral education, but of natural development.

The modernist interest in the inner workings of the child's mind is revealed above all in the wealth of figurative language, poetic tropes, motivated by the need to suggest through equivalence how Zhenia, in a state of sensitive innocence, experienced her life, how she came to understand firstly the nature of her own womanhood, and secondly her involvement with her neighbor in the Christian sense. The breaking away from the nineteenth century tradition is seen too in the composition of the story by Pasternak, in its lack of descriptive exposition, in its fragmentary nature. Further we may note that not only has the author chosen a girl for the subject of his "childhood," but also that he has chosen to stress the physical side of female adolescence, namely menstruation (cf. the moral torture which Tolstoy elaborates in the adolescent stage of his trilogy). It might at first seem unwarranted to consider Pasternak's "The Childhood of Luvers" within the tradition of Russian literary childhood portraits which begins with Tolstoy's *Childhood* (1852) and continues into the twentieth century with A. N. Tolstoy's *Nikita's Childhood* (1920) and P. Romanov's *Childhood* (1920).[16] Clearly, a tradition is established in Russia by use of the actual reference to childhood in the title. These works constitute through their similar titles a specific genre, and Pasternak's "The Childhood of Luvers" likewise aligns itself with that genre through its title. Notwithstanding the experimental (modernist) aspects of Pasternak's story we are thereby justified in considering it as part of a tradition. Modernism for Pasternak is always experiment within and not away from tradition.

Were it not for the title, "The Childhood of Luvers," we should not be challenged to compare the story with Tolstoy's *Childhood*. For in fact the stories are hardly comparable other than in name. The overriding difference between Pasternak's work and all the other "childhood" stories lies in the relationship between the narrator and the object of the narration. From Tolstoy to Romanov we see that literary childhoods are either autobiographical or biographical. In these works, regardless of whether they are written in first or third person, and whether or not the child is given a fictitious name, the relationship between the narrator and hero is such that it undermines the tenor of fiction. That is to say that whether or not the relationship between narrator and hero is formally fictionalized, the narrator has complete access to the life and mind of the child as though he had experienced it himself. The narrator's business is to recall and expose the development from childhood through adolescence to adulthood, following the hero from stage to stage of his life, describing a succession of stages as well as specific incidents. In all cases of the tradition, the narrator and hero are of the same sex. We can talk then of a diachronic identity between narrator and child hero: they are one and the same person at different moments in time. Interestingly, this diachronic identity does not lead to a confusion of perspective: typical for these (auto)biographies is that the child and the adult perspectives are distinct. The narrator possesses his past and is able to present it from the perspective of one looking back, seeing the past for what it is; from the raw material of his past the narrator selects and presents in orderly, organized fashion. The difference between autobiography and fiction proper is not a question of adherence to fact or resort to fantasy, but rather of genre, or narratorial pose. In autobiography the axis of the narrative is memory, in fiction it is imagination. In the former authenticity is given from the start, while in the second it has to be built up within the narrative itself.

Possessing the past, the narrator in Tolstoy's trilogy is at liberty to organize it and present it as best he will. He does not need to present the Child's mind from within since he has absorbed the mental processes of his child self, alternatively his hero, as he moved into maturity. Presumably the motivation in recalling one's past is to bring that past into alignment with the mature self, and accordingly the natural angle of perspective is one of looking back from the position of "how it seems from here and now." The interest of autobiography consists precisely in setting against each other the stuff of childhood and the mature perspective on the same. Thus the memories of Nikolenka Irtenev are organized as a series of portraits, each one elaborated conventionally in expositional style. Each chapter is devoted to a portrait complete in itself; it may be the description of a certain stage of childhood, of a specific person figuring in childhood, or of a specific and colorful, significant event. Each chapter is to a certain extent self-contained, while between them the chapters alternate in a rhythm of recurring themes.

In order to create the feeling of the past Tolstoy has recourse to metonymy. By metonymy I mean the use of a single detail to convey the feeling of a larger slice of childhood, it may be the feeling of a single day or an entire period. Metonymy or synecdoche is a trope for one who has perspective on the narrated events: only when the narrator possesses the whole, can he select from that whole the details which are representative, which convey its essence. Tolstoy's representative details have an extraordinary intensity and have led to his reputation as a modern artist who illustrates the formalist principle of "making strange" (*ostranenie*). These details convey to a certain extent the "fresh" vision of a child. But the detail has been stored in the adult memory since childhood. Let us look at the description of Sonechka:

> On her little white neck lay a black velvet ribbon; her little head was covered in brown curls which from the front suited her sweet little face, and from the back her dear little naked shoulder so well that nobody, not even Karl Ivanych himself, could ever have believed that the reason for their curling that way was that they had been wound up in small pieces of the Moscow News all morning and then cauterized with hot iron tongs. It seemed that she must have been born with that dear little curly head.[17]

We note here not only the fact that the narrator's adult knowledge is superimposed on the child's perception (the child Nikolenka did not realize that Sonechka's curls were artificially created), but more strikingly the fact that the child has so consistently absorbed details that the adult narrator is able to describe each person and scene down to the most minute wisps of hair and involuntary gestures. In fact this is not undiluted memory; the conventions of autobiography allow for a collecting and elaborating of detail which amounts to a recreation, the filling out of a scene only diffusely remembered. This kind of manipulation is only possible when the narrator is in complete possession of his past, when his authority and authenticity is beyond question.

Turning from the narrative perspective to the import of childhood in Tolstoy's trilogy, we find some but not all the characteristics of the typical "Bildungsroman."[18] Conspicuous is the lack of basic conflict between the child and the world around him. Certainly Tolstoy's trilogy manifests sets of opposing values: infinitely loving mother, victim of early death/charming but inadequate, living father; country/town; the homely, German Karl Ivanych/the dandy, French St.-Jérome etc. The child/adolescent is super-sensitive and in comparison with his elder brother he feels himself to be apart, less of a worldly success. But this does not amount to an absolute rejection of society and its values. On the contrary, those values are taken for granted; neither is there any protest by the mature narrator on behalf of a hardly-done-by younger self. Other childhood portraits, for example Gorky's, mobilize through a description of childhood sensibility and susceptibility a dominant note of social protest

The adult Nikolenka Irtenev accepts his lot: he recalls with warmth and tolerance, for better for worse, the people who populated his childhood; he relates with indulgent amusement the foibles of his childhood, and bewails the curse of analytical moralizing which beset his adolescence. This acceptance is consistent with Tolstoy's humanistic belief: believing in man's ability to make himself Good, to live under the guidance of his reasoning conscience, Tolstoy must necessarily believe in the necessity and desirability of passing from the charms of an idyllic childhood to the moral responsibility of adulthood. If conscience is the guiding strength of the righteous man, then adolescence, as the time of life when confrontation with the world at large provokes and activates conscience, is a time of chance and potential. Conflict exists not between the hero and society around him, but within the hero. By calling his books *Childhood, Boyhood* and *Youth* Tolstoy stresses the universality of what he expresses (cf. a specific childhood: *Tema's Childhood,* "The Childhood of Luvers," *Nikita's Childhood*). But the point of his appraisal of childhood is to present its historical relevance in the life of each individual; childhood does not incarnate the essence of life, it is merely the starting point from which human beings must move on.[19]

The title of Pasternak's "The Childhood of Luvers" provokes two questions: firstly how does it relate to the tradition of Russian childhood portraits, and secondly how does it relate to the story itself? Indeed Pasternak's story is hardly about childhood at all. After one page of narrative we read the following: "And that morning she ceased to be the child she had been the previous night. Years passed" (161). The story in fact concentrates on Zhenia's puberty, that is on her exit from childhood; it sketches in barest outline the time leading up to Zhenia's first menstruation.

Further, the title of the story refers to Zhenia by her surname, Luvers. This is particularly disorientating since the name is not Russian and is not declined. The title does not intimate the sex of the subject. The only other reference to Zhenia as Luvers occurs in the first sentence: "Luvers was born and grew up in Perm" (160). Thereafter Zhenia is referred to by her Christian name and alternatively as "the girl" (*devochka*). The significance of the story will be found to lie in the fact that Zhenia grows up, that she ceases to be a child; furthermore she becomes not merely an adult but a woman. Both her age beyond infancy and her femininity are so to speak the point, what is important in this apparent childhood description. The title, on the contrary, is unmarked and unspecific. It suggests not what is to be accomplished within the story, but merely the starting point. Whereas Tolstoy's narration in *Childhood* is carefully organized towards straightforward exposition, Pasternak's "The Childhood of Luvers" is fragmentary, erratic, its inner coherence not immediately available. This applies both to the composition as a whole and to the narrative development of each section. Tolstoy's trilogy is divided into books, and the books into chapters. Each chapter has a heading and is internally coherent with a theme of its own. "The Childhood of Luvers" is divided into two parts of which the first, "The Long Days," functions like a biography, a recording of how Zhenia's early years were, while the second, "The Stranger," develops into something like a short story with a plot connecting its different characters and a proper narrative incident. In fact the two parts of the story are intricately and ingeniously connected but the connection is hidden between the apparent distinction: biography/fiction.

Tolstoy presents each area of childhood in the form of an individual portrait, introducing and elaborating the people, the stages and the significant incidents of Nikolenka's childhood. Pasternak's narrative on the other hand moves in fits and starts and never sustains purely expositional discourse for more than a sentence. This tendency is manifest from the first sentence: "Luvers was born and grew up in Perm. As once her boats and dolls, so later her memories were seeped in the shaggy bearskins of which the house was full" (160). The first sentence exposes the outward circumstances of Zhenia's childhood in traditional, narrative exposition – albeit somewhat cryptically. But straightaway the narrative is distracted by a concrete image, leading into a figurative comparison. The bearskins introduce immediately one of the images which the author uses throughout the story, through it connecting associations of childhood which would otherwise remain disparate. Here in the first paragraph he mentions briefly their origin and once again "digresses" with a further simile: "The white she-bear in the child's room was like an immense chrysanthemum shedding its petals" (160). Thus the tenor of memory which was suggested in the second sentence ("her memories") gives way to a lyrical, figurative mode of discourse. So while Tolstoy's recollections were given expression in metonymically representative details, Pasternak's narrative resorts continually to figurative expression. We have here the situation elaborated above; the artist attempts to render the inner workings of the child's mind through his own poetic medium, that is on a principle not of imitation but of equivalence. Exposition is kept at a minimum since the author is not interested in Zhenia's childhood per se. He is interested in those crucial moments which reveal sudden change, epiphanies of her understanding.

One of the most revealing areas of crucial moments in Zhenia's passage from child to woman is her relationship towards language. Language is not only the means by which the author conveys the inner workings of Zhenia's mind, it is also the specific object of her experience. Throughout the story there exists a tension for Zhenia between the word and the reality to which that word refers. This tension is the condition for her potential "poeticness" or creativity. Like the poet, as conceived within modernism, the child is potentially poetic because she has not yet understood, because the moment of understanding, the moment of giving reality a name for the first time, still lies ahead. What is interesting to note is the fact that according to "The Childhood of Luvers," the very young infant is not creative or poetic. The creative stage of childhood comes later as the child moves out of the parental sphere and into independence. The much-quoted incident revolving around the sight and name of the place Motovilikha marks the end of infancy. This stage when the word has the ability to reassure the child like a talisman is not interesting to Pasternak.[20] But from the moment when Zhenia refrains from questioning her father about "factories," she is on her own; from now on she will not allow anyone else to fit names to realities, she will do this herself, painstakingly, by means of trial and error.

References to Zhenia's concern with words are numerous and each one is revealing. Here are a few examples:

i) Zhenia attempts to fit the graphical word to the reality in the most literal sense: "Why, in the word 'useful' must you write one sort of 'e' rather than another? And she worked hard over the answer, only because all her strength was concentrated in the effort of imagining the unfavorable reasons which would compel the word 'useful' with the wrong 'e' (so shaggy and wild when it is written in this way) to arise" (185). A note by the translator explains that "in the old Russian orthography there were three letters for the sound expressed by the English 'e.'"

ii) Zhenia tests her hardly-won knowledge of pregnancy by hazarding a "mature" inquiry as to whether Aksinia is again pregnant. Her question betrays the inadequacy of her knowledge and, hearing the raucous laughter which she has provoked, Zhenia admits her failure (208).

iii) Zhenia tests her mother's pregnancy by asking her to repeat the words "Decollation of John the Baptist." Zhenia perceives her mother's physically swollen figure as coarseness of speech. The proof of pregnancy will lie in her mother pronouncing her words vulgarly, like the maid Aksinia who is also pregnant (210).

iv) When Zhenia first sees the Urals, she feels her way towards the name. She has identified both the reality and the name, but the two do not come together automatically: "Zhenia held her breath, and at once perceived the speed of that limitless and forgetful air, and at once realized that the huge cloud was some country, some place bearing a sonorous and mountainous name, rolling along like a thunderstorm flung into the valley, with rocks and with sand; and the hazel trees did nothing but whisper it and whisper it; here, there, and away over there; nothing else. "Is it the 'Urals?' she asked of the whole compartment, leaning forward" (176).[21]

v) The Belgian visitors provide a unique occasion for laughter in Zhenia's home. In particular their attempts to utter Russian sounds and trace Russian letters cause explosive mirth. The Belgians, like Zhenia, are learning to utter sounds for the first time (184-185).[22]

But language is not automatically creative. To accept language from the adult world, to inherit the connection between word and reality rather than to forge it oneself, is to go the other way. In "The Childhood of Luvers" two children stand in contrast to Zhenia, in that their acquisition of language is not creative. The first is Sergei, Zhenia's brother; Sergei labels reality quickly and swiftly, slotting together words and reality efficiently and painlessly: "The journey was a novelty for them both, and already he knew and loved those words: depot, loco, siding, through-carriage, and the marriage of sounds: 'class' had a sour-sweet taste in his mouth. His sister was also enthusiastic in all this, but in her own way, without the boyish love of method which characterized the enthusiasm of her brother" (173).

The other child is Lisa, a child who does not share Zhenia's sensitivity. We might say of "The Childhood of Luvers" that the entire story consists in Zhenia's achievement in learning, on her own, to understand the words: "Mother is pregnant." For to be able to say these words, Zhenia must penetrate the meaning of "pregnancy," not only the word but also the reality. And in order to understand the reality she has first to feel herself as a woman. It is the ingenuity of Pasternak's story that his basic analogy between poet and woman is manifest in the way in which Zhenia's struggle to name for the first time is transposed into her struggle to understand what being a woman means. The contrast to Lisa is quite explicit:

> She knew much more about it than Zhenia; she knew everything; as children know things, learning from strange words … Once in a corner, Lisa was told in a whisper about different terrors and uglinesses. She did not choke at what she had heard, but bore everything in her brain along the street and brought it with her to the house. On the way she lost nothing of what was said to her and she took care to preserve all the foulness. She knew everything. Her organism did not burst into flame, her heart did not begin to beat alarm and her soul did not strike blows on her mind, because it dared to recognize something apart from her, not from her own lips, without asking her permission." (223-224)[23]

Intimately connected with the concept of "other people's words" is the idea of "other people's ideas," second-hand initiation into the facts of life. When Zhenia grows up she finds that things are "declared" to her, that she has no part in forging her own destiny. Thus it is announced to Zhenia that she will enter the gymnasium: "There were pleasant things too, like her approaching entry into the school. But all this was *declared* to her. Life ceased to be a poetical caprice; it fermented around her like a harsh and evil-colored fable – in so far as it became prose and was transformed into fact" (182-183). The word "declared" denotes Zhenia's initiation into life by another person's verbal act, an act which encroaches on her integrity. This leads us to another area of Zhenia's innocence. Zhenia is in all senses an unenlightened if not neglected child. The following paragraph is in fact self-contradictory, since it implies that Zhenia's sense of guilt was inevitable, organic, and at the same time a result of her parents' treatment of her:

> In the same way as the girl suffered years of suspicion and loneliness, of a sense of guilt and of what I would like to call[24] christianisme, because it is impossible to call it Christianity, so it sometimes seemed to her that nothing would or could improve, because of her depravity and impenitence; that it was all deserved. Meanwhile – but this never reached the consciousness of the children – meanwhile, on the contrary, their whole beings quivered and fermented, bewildered by the attitude of their parents towards them when their mother and father were at home; when they entered the house rather than returned home. (162)

> Just as linguistic innocence is the prerequisite for Zhenia's creativity in naming for the first time, so her non-comprehension of the world and its ways, her general fog of misunderstanding, seems to be the prerequisite for her "poetic," her synthetic and associative way of experiencing the world. For example, at the end of the second long day, that is the second day of the bleeding which Zhenia does not understand, the narrator conveys her state of mind in a description of the slowly maturing spring and the sick light of the lamps lit before full darkness:

> The lamps only stressed the insipidity of the evening air. They gave no light but swelled from within, like diseased fruit, from the clear and lustreless dropsy which dilated their swollen shade. They were absent. (165 – 166)

This detail, an equivalent of the synthetic state of Zhenia's mind, is poetic in the sense that it connects two things – Zhenia's dawning puberty and the outward circumstances of the day when she became aware of it. It is a striking image, but it is an image which is only born thanks to the fact that Zhenia had been kept in ignorance of knowledge to which other cultures would consider she was entitled. It is an image which expresses a feeling of sickness and deformity. What is difficult for the modern reader to stomach is the narrator's direct justification of Zhenia's painful ignorance in the passage quoted above. Now it seems that it is not childhood or infant innocence which is potentially "poetic," but on the contrary, unjustified adolescent ignorance. What causes Zhenia to be creative is not that she sees the world for the first time, but that she sees the world through a glass darkly. The alternatives are as follows: either the girl creates her own understanding entirely on her own, painfully but poetically as does Zhenia; or she receives knowledge from without at second hand, painlessly but fruitlessly too, without inner understanding, as is the case with Lisa.

The difference between an experience "for the first time" and one "in ignorance" is illustrated by the "estranged" viewpoint from which Zhenia first observes the group of figures which includes a lame man (189). From her position she misinterprets the occupation of the group. This is a question of a visually estranged viewpoint and serves as a classic example of the "making strange" associated with modernist art in particular. But the perception gains further significance: Zhenia cannot forget the lame man and comes finally to feel that she has incurred his catastrophe by noticing him. This is no longer a question of visual estrangement, but has been transposed to the moral plane, to the guilty confusion which Zhenia's adolescence and ignorance cause her. For it is on this very afternoon, directly after observing the lame man, that Zhenia enters the house, observes the medicine bottle and begins – through intuition and association – to grope her way to an understanding of her mother's pregnancy. Thereafter there is always a connection between her seeing the lame man and her mother's pregnancy. The two are woven together in the theme of the story as well as in Zhenia's mind, so that finally, when understanding is penetrated, it results in her comprehending her own ability to have children and her awareness of the Other – in one fell swoop. On the level of plot it is the death of the lame man which causes Madame Luvers to miscarry.

On one occasion there is an adult who is concerned to explain to Zhenia what he is talking about, namely the Belgian, Negarat. In fact the Belgians are special: their jokes are comprehensible to the children and their presence causes relaxation in the Luvers household. Talking about his forthcoming military service Negarat explains the details to Zhenia who appears to be mesmerized by such treatment: "'Yes, yes. I understand. Yes. I understand. Of course I do', Zhenia repeated mechanically and gratefully" (197). After which Zhenia asks a question, straining to express herself as adequately as possible. But her parents are impatient, thinking that the Belgian is merely stuffing her head with unnecessary details. Then we come to a noteworthy passage:

> So well did he explain it to her. No one had explained it to her in that way. A veil of indifference, the hypnotic veil of perception was removed from the vision of white tents: regiments faded away and transformed themselves into a group of separate individuals in military uniform, and she began to be sorry for them at the same moment that their significance brought them into life and exalted them, brought them closer to her and discoloured them. (197)

As Zhenia comes to understand, as she applies Negarat's explanation to the soldiers billeted near her home, so she comes to appreciate their human significance. But at the same time, the color, the brightness of the visual impression which they had created for her fades. They gain a soul but they lose their color, their "estrangement."[25] This implies again that Zhenia's vivid imagination, her poetic associative powers, are in inverse proportion to her real understanding.

It is not possible therefore to read Pasternak's "The Childhood of Luvers" merely as a typical modernist preoccupation with the unspoilt infantile mind. Pasternak's attitude is more complex, more metaphysical. It has to do with his special concern with Woman, with the place which Woman occupies in his metaphysics. Pasternak draws an analogy between Woman and Poet at the same time consigning to them different roles. The analogy is developed in *Doctor Zhivago* and given explicit expression in the following description of Lara:

> For a moment she rediscovered the purpose of her life. She was here on earth to grasp the meaning of its wild enchantment and to call each thing by its right name, or, if this were not within her power, to give birth out of love for life to successors who would do it in her place.[26]

Adolescence is the watershed within which creativity flourishes or founders. Few become poets but for women there is the chance of channeling creativity into child-bearing fertility. The creativity of giving names and the creativity of giving birth in the literal sense are intimately connected. This interconnection is given ingenious expression in "The Childhood of Luvers," in that Zhenia's preoccupation with the relationship between the word and reality is successively channeled into her attempt to understand her mother's pregnancy. She starts as it were from nothing – the smell of weeds in the courtyard, the sight of a medicine bottle, an association to Aksinia's coarseness of figure and speech; and at the end she is able to say to herself: "Mother is pregnant," and to question the doctor on the death of her little brother. No one has told Zhenia anything, she has worked it out for herself, in the associative power of her fertile imagination. Zhenia is destined to become not poet but woman. Therefore it is part of the plan that she ceases to see the soldiers as visual brightness and learns to see them as individuals. Zhenia's involvement with language is a stage on the way to her becoming a woman: once she has achieved both language and understanding, then she has reached the beginning of her destiny as a woman. But the point is that her path towards insight was in itself a poetic path, the path of forging her own understanding. At the end of the story everyone notices the change in Zhenia, not least her tutor Dikikh who wonders both over her involvement with another person and over her new commanding voice as she tells him to wait for her in the class-room. Zhenia's achievement has been to take herself out of her own childhood and to transform herself from a human being of indiscriminate sex (Luvers) into a woman. It is against the neutrality expressed in the title of the story that Zhenia's creativity is illuminated.

One of the paradoxes of Pasternak's poetry in general lies in the fact that that to which he desires to give expression is, by definition, inexpressible. Pasternak is fascinated by powerful, synthetic experiences of Life, Nature and Love; their power is dependent on the fact that they remain unanalyzed.[27] It is not therefore surprising that the theme of adolescence should have attracted him, adolescence rather than childhood proper. We might say that in adolescence the tension between complex synthetic experience and lack of communication of the same is at a maximum. If the infant's perceptive powers are naive, then the adolescent's are sophisticated; all his powers – intellectual, sensual and emotional – are about to reach full maturity, but they are as yet inarticulate, in a state of turmoil, what Piaget calls "the inextricable chaos of adolescent thought."[28] It is at this point of maximum experience and maximum confusion that the poet enters the mind of his inarticulate heroine and tries in the medium of his poetry to render its inner workings. How does he achieve it, if indeed he does achieve it?

Whereas the narrator in Tolstoy's trilogy possessed his past as a whole and could therefore present it metonymically with representative and significant detail, the narrator in "The Childhood of Luvers" does not and cannot possess his heroine's world as a whole. He is forced to bridge the gap between his mind and his heroine's by means of imagination and he does this with recourse to figurative language. The leap of imagination incurred in figurative language, that is between the literal and its figurative substitute, reflects the leap of imagination between narrator and adolescent heroine. Like all of Pasternak's works, "The Childhood of Luvers" is saturated with metaphorical substitutions, these frequently taking the form of simile. It is through positing likenesses that the narrator hopes to suggest, by means of an equivalent, the associative workings of Zhenia's imagination. In merely positing likeness we can say that the simile is adequate to the task; the simile is not categorical, it does not actually substitute but merely suggests a possible association. By way of example, let us examine the following:

> Their faces resembled cakes of fresh soap, unbroken, from the wrapper, sweet-scented and cold ...When they spoke, it was as though they were spilling water on the tablecloth: noisily, freshly, immediately, sometimes to one side where no one expected it, with the long-lingering trails of their jokes and their anecdotes, always understood by the children, always quenching their thirst and clean. (183)

The subject of the description is the Belgians of whom Zhenia knows not even their names; they appear in the house as friends and business colleagues of her father and — in accordance with the children's upbringing — are not presented to her. She perceives them immediately in their sensual aura, through no prism of prior knowledge. The general tenor of the similes is of something new, fresh and satisfying to the needs of the children. In fact together these two similes touch on a wide area of sensual and emotional experience: smell ("sweet-scented"), touch ("cold"), sound ("noisily"), movement ("spilling"), sense of time ("immediately"), sense of expecta-tion ("where no one expected it"), humor ("jokes"), understanding ("always understood by the children") and satisfaction ("quenching their thirst") as well as the more diffuse mixed sensations stimulated by "unbroken", "freshly", "clean". The narrator has threaded these different sensations together by means of the comparison of faces to new pieces of soap, and speech to spilled water. By means of a verbal simile he attempts to collect together the different aspects of a synthetic sensation. The use of the figure, the simile, prevents the use of language from emerging into its analytical tenor and thereby the poet maintains the synthetic aspect of the experience notwithstanding the fact that he has articulated it in words. The use of the explicit comparative terms ("resembled" and "as though") provides a safety-catch. The narrator has not abused his position of authority, but has left a loophole according to which we cannot be sure whether the comparison was actually present in Zhenia's mind, or whether it was merely supplied by the narrator as a corollary to the multiplex but not quite articulated associations which Zhenia actually experienced.

We have touched on a crucial question, namely the relationship between the narrator and his heroine, and it is this relationship which will finally provide a clear indication as to the distinction between the "childhood" tradition and Pasternak's "The Childhood of Luvers." A relevant question is: according to what principle of authenticity is the adult, surely male, narrator able to enter the mind of an adolescent girl?

Of Tolstoy's trilogy we said that there existed a diachronic identity between narrator and hero, they were one and the same person but at different moments in time. This identity guaranteed the authenticity of the narration. The (auto)biographical tenor is however missing in "The Childhood of Luvers," where apart from the second sentence of the narrative, there is no activation of the axis of memory. Instead the narrative implies a synchronic identification between narrator and heroine: the narrator is close to Zhenia, at the moment of her present; he is not the same person as she is, but he is sympathetic to her, in tune with her. This relationship is of course far more complicated than the autobiographical identity. In itself it appears to be paradoxical – an impossibility – relying entirely on the fictional convention that narrators enter the minds of fictional characters. What is particular in this case is that the narrator purports to communicate a state of mind which by its very nature must remain closed to him.

We saw above in the analysis of the simile how the narrator attempts to bridge the gap between his mind and the mind of his heroine. The two enter so to speak a kind of partnership whereby the experience is Zhenia's and the expression the narrator's. By pivoting the expression on the uncertain point of a simile the narrator just manages to express without expressing, to articulate without destroying the innate inarticulateness of the experience. In fact, whereas the perspective in Tolstoy's *Childhood* is always clear, that is we always know whether or not the vantage point is the child's or the adult's, in "The Childhood of Luvers" the opposite holds true: it is virtually impossible to extricate the two vantage points and to say that an image arose in Zhenia's mind or, on the contrary, that the image was provided by the narrator. Whose point of view is expressed in the following passage?

> Strange, as though it had become warmer in the street, as though it had turned into spring, when men ran cheering, with bent backs, down the street and their felt shoes and primitive stockings flashed as they ran. The pigeons were not afraid of the crowd. They flew along the road in search of food. Millet seed, oats and dung-seed were spread on the pavement in the snow. A cake-stall shone with grease and warmth. And this heat and polish fell into mouths rinsed with corn-brandy. The grease inflamed their throats. Afterwards it escaped by way of their palpitating chests. Perhaps it was this that warmed the street. (225)

The narrator is describing how Zhenia experienced her time at the Defendovs, and presumably the point of view, including the diffuse feeling that the street has been heated, is hers. Yet the image of "mouths rinsed with corn-brandy" seems to be a digression on the part of the narrator away from Zhenia's consciousness.

The fact is that much of the imagery in "The Childhood of Luvers" is reminiscent of Pasternak's imagery on the whole; sometimes the images are authentically suited to articulating Zhenia's thoughts, but sometimes they lose that special orientation and appear familiar from Pasternak's other works, e.g.: "She did not call the tutor into the schoolroom, where the sunny colors clung so closely to the color-wash walls that in the evening the adhesive day could only be torn off with bloodshed" (182).[29] At these times the narrator exceeds his role as Zhenia's interpreter and becomes a poet in his own right, that is to say he no longer confines himself to articulating the way Zhenia sees things, but steps in to perceive them directly. The lack of clarity in the identification between narrator and Zhenia can be explained by the fact that in some real sense the two are alike, in that both are poets. At no point is it said of Zhenia that she is like a poet. Nevertheless the comparison between adolescent child and poet lies just beneath the surface, a result of the lack of a clear dividing line between Zhenia's point of view and that of her narrator. The two are alike in that both are struggling to put words and realities together, to name that which has not yet been named. In this attempt Pasternak complies with the twentieth century interest in the creative potential of the new mind and his story has little in common with the Russian "childhood" tradition.

But on occasion the narrator takes upon himself another role altogether. This role is more than that of the omniscient narrator who has so far been discussed, omniscient in that he enters Zhenia's mind. At several moments in the story the narrator takes the position of Nature's or Life's spokesman and pronounces over the inevitable path which Zhenia's destiny is to follow. Now instead of presenting Zhenia's point of view, the narrator discusses her and her destiny from without, e.g.: "And that morning she ceased to be the child she had been the previous night" (161); "…there are few, even among grown-ups, who understand what it is that forms, creates and binds them together. Life rarely tells what she is going to do with them. She loves her purpose too well." These passages, and there are many more, are – with their metaphysical credo – hardly to be considered a typical expression of modernist skepticism. While in comparison to the humanist or socialist ideas expressed in the tradition of childhood portraits in Russian literature, they appear outdated, the legacy of romantic rather than realist tradition.

ENDNOTES

[1] George Boas, *The Cult of Childhood* (London: Warburgh Institute: University of London, 1966). See also Peter Coveney, *Poor Monkey. The Child in Literature* (London: Rockliff, 1957), particularly chapter 10.

[2] Coveney, *Poor Monkey*, xi.

[3] Ibid, xii.

[4] Cf. William Woodin Rowe, *Dostoevsky: Child and Man in his Works* (New York-London: New York University Press, 1968).

[5] The final chapter of Coveney's book is devoted to modernist works, discussed from this the philosophical point of view. *Poor Monkey,* 250-281.

[6] Vladimir Markov, *Russian Futurism* (Berkeley and Los Angeles: University of California Press, 1968), 36, passim. See also Barbara Lonnqvist, *Xlebnikov and Carnival* (= Stockholm Studies in Russian Literature 9). (Stockholm: Almqvist & Wiksell International, 1979), 22-23, passim. For a study on the child in Symbolist literature, see Stanley J. Rabinowitz, *Sologub's Literary Children: Keys to a Symbolist's Prose (*Columbus, Ohio: Slavica publishers, 1980).

[7] A. F. Zweers, *Grown-up Narrator and Childlike Hero* (The Hague-Paris: Mouton, 1971), 76-77.

[8] Example quoted after M. D. S. Braine in Dan I. Slobin, *Psycholinguistics* (Glenview, Illinois-London: Scott, Foresman & Co, (1971) 1974), 43.

[9] Markov, *Russian Futurism,* 16. Cf. 19 and 36.

[10] Elena Guro, *Sochineniia,* compiled by G.K. Perkins (Oakland, California: Berkeley Slavic Specialties, 1996), 101. In Russian the first four lines read: "*S ledianykh sosulek iskorki, / I snezhinok pyl' . . . / a sharmanochka igraet / veselen'kuiu kadril'.*"

[11] Rudolf Arnheim, *Art and Visual Perception* (new version) (Berkeley-Los Angeles-London: University of California Press, 1974), 132-3. Cf. B. A. Uspenskij, et. al., "Theses on the Semiotic Study of Cultures," *Structure of Texts and Semiotics of Culture,* ed. Jan van der Eng and Mojmír Grygar (The Hague-Paris: Mouton 1973), 4-5.

[12] E.g., Jean Piaget, *The Language and Thought of the Child* (New York: Meridian Books, (1955) 1973); Slobin, *Psycholinguistics*; Philip S. Dale, *Language Development. Structure and Function* (New York: Holt, Rinehart and Winston, (1972) 1976).

[13] *The Childhood of Luvers* was written in 1918. The text is quoted from Boris Pasternak, *Safe Conduct. An Autobiography and Other Writings* (New York: New Directions, 1958), 160-230. Translation by Robert Payne.

[14] For example, N. Garin-Mikhailovskii, *Tema's Childhood* (1892) and A. M. Gorky, *Childhood* (1913).

[15] It is not uncommon to interpret *The Childhood of Luvers* as having a Christian message. Cf. Angela Livingstone, "The Childhood of Luvers. An Early Story of Pasternak's," *Southern Review* 1 (1963), 83.

[16] See Zweers, *Grown-up Narrator,* chapter III, "Other Childhoods in Russian Literature," in particular p. 113. In discussing Tolstoy's "childhood" portrayal, I allude also to the later parts of the trilogy, *Boyhood* and *Youth.*

[17] My translation from L. N. Tolstoy, *Sobranie sochnenii v dvadcati tomax, Tom pervyi* (Moscow: *Gosudarstvennoe izdatel'stvo khudozhestvennoi literatury*, 1960), 85-86.

[18] See for example the characterization of "Bildungsroman" in Jerome Hamilton Buckley, *Season of Youth. The Bildungsroman from Dickens to Golding* (Cambridge, Mass.: Harvard University Press, 1974), 17.

[19] Tolstoy manifests the exact opposite of the Peter Pan syndrome so common in late nineteenth century in England. See Coveney, *Poor Monkey,* chapter 10.

[20] This much-quoted passage is not fully clear: apparently Zhenia formulates her fear by asking about the unknown lights and her father answers: "It was – Motovilikha ..." But the reason for Zhenia's fear was more complex, probably she could not formulate it adequately: "it had no name, no clearly defined color or sharp outline: in its motions it was familiar and dear to her and was not the nightmare, it was not that which rumbled and rolled in clouds of tobacco smoke, throwing fresh and wind strewn shadows on the reddish beams of the gallery. Zhenia began to cry" (161). Note that the unnamed lights are "dear and familiar" while the named "they were playing cards" is described as "a nightmare". Most critics ignore this paradox.

[21] On another occasion Zhenia perceives reality via a diffuse verbal association: "They wore black, like the word 'nun' in the song" (*Oni chernelis', kak slovo 'zatvornitsa' v pesne*) (189).

[22] References to language, the word and speech are innumerable and they are not limited to Zhenia's own speech acts, cf. the description of Lisa's father: "He spoke in a clear, level voice, as though he formed his conversation not with sounds, but composed his words from the alphabet, and he pronounced everything, including the accents" (219-220).

[23] The creativity as opposed to the sterility of language is an important theme in *Doctor Zhivago* where the poet's desire to give birth to words is contrasted to sterile post-revolutionary dogma, the sterility of its language emphasized by meaningless phrases (e.g. chapter 15, 7).

[24] There is no first person narrative ("what I would like to call") in the Russian which uses instead an impersonal statement [*khochetsia nazvat'*].

[25] Compare an earlier perception of a soldier: "The August sun bored through the wooden leaves and took root in a soldier's hind-quarters. Reddening, the sun embedded itself on his uniform and like turpentine greedily soaked into him" (187).

[26] Boris Pasternak, *Doctor Zhivago,* trans. Max Hayward and Manya Harari (New York: Pantheon Books, 1958), 66.

[27] Tension between Life itself and its verbal description is a constant theme in Pasternak's poetry, cf. the title of his poetic cycle "My sister life" (*Sestra moia – zhizn'*). See Fiona Björling, "Aspects of Poetic Syntax. Analysis of the Poem "*Sestra moja – zizn' i segodnja v razlive'* by Boris Pasternak", *Boris Pasternak. Essays,* ed. Nils Ake Nilsson (= Stockholm Studies in Russian Literature 7) (Stockholm: Almqvist & Wiksell International 1976), 176.

[28] Jean Piaget, *The Language and Thought of the Child,* 65. Piaget's conception of two distinct kinds of thought, non-communicable and communicable, is potentially extremely interesting in connection with my present argument. Since the former non-communicable (individual, autistic) thought "works chiefly by images, and in order to express itself, has recourse to indirect methods, evoking by means of symbols and myths the feeling by which it is led" (63), it would seem to encompass both the non-articulate mind of the adolescent Zhenia and Pasternak's poetic, figurative language to describe the same. In this case poetic language as an 'equivalent' to unarticulate thought would prove more adequate than I have assumed. In fact Piaget's distinctions concerning what he calls egocentric logic might well apply to Pasternak's poetics in general: "1° Ego-centric logic is more intuitive, more 'syncretistic' than deductive, i.e., its reasoning is not made explicit. The mind leaps from premise to conclusion at a single bound, without stopping on the way. 2° Little value is attached to proving, or even checking propositions. The vision of the whole brings about a state of belief and a feeling of security far more rapidly than if each step in the argument were made explicit. 3° Personal schemas of analogy are made use of, likewise memories of earlier reasoning, which control the present course of reasoning without openly manifesting their influence. 4° Visual schemas also play an important part, and can even take the place of proof in supporting the deduction that is made. 5° Finally, judgments of value have far more influence on ego-centric than on communicable thought" (66).

[29] I have modified the printed translation of this passage.

VIII

Andrei Platonov and the Inadmissibility of Desire

ERIC NAIMAN

> But the more passionately
> fragrant life became,
>   And the more tender was
> beauty in the world,
>   The more greedily did death
> seek her out
>   And still her singing lips...[1]

> ...such images, in which the
> author employs physiology in
> order to lay bare the idea of his
> work, are probably not to every
> reader's liking...[2]

Throughout the second decade of his career, Andrei Platonov struggled with the necessity of his characters' accepting the consequences of physical desire as they moved beyond the apocalyptic spirit of the Revolution. Years after he began to portray the ideal society in an ambiguous light, Platonov still strove in his writings to reconcile himself to the normality of sexual relations and to a world no longer founded upon absolute principles. The dual nature of his difficulty is not surprising, for Platonov had always depicted the Utopia as a community built upon the negation, or nonrecognition, of sexual urges. In Platonov's fiction, the sacrifice of sexuality often *appears* to be a price necessarily paid for the hero's admission to and continued residence in the Utopia. A close look at the author's work, however, and in particular at the

1936 story "The River Potudan" (Reka Potudan')[3] discloses that the rapport between sexuality and Platonov's Utopia is more ambivalent and complex than
a superficial reading would suggest. The suspicion arises that the Utopian goal
itself has been established to justify the elimination of desire from the surface
of the text, that the espoused ideal is a passionately conceived and fervently
maintained excuse for a libidinal purging which, moreover, may be only
superficial. If Platonov is repeatedly compelled to excise sexuality from his
Utopia, it is only because sexuality is implicitly, essentially present within it.
For Platonov, utopianism and sexual desire are painfully and contradictorily
knotted together; each is necessary – and antipathetical – to the other.

In the decade which followed the Revolution, Soviet society as a whole
struggled with "the problem of sex," the question of the place sexuality
would occupy in the Communist society of the future as well as during
the transitional phase of the New Economic Policy. Doctors, statesmen,
educators and writers all participated in this debate.[4] Sexuality was portrayed
alternatively as a liberating, elemental force, as a healthy proletarian urge
not to be restrained by the repressive demands of bourgeois morality, and
as a parasitical hindrance to the building of socialism. Platonov continued to
wrestle with sexuality's role in the ideal society long after other authors had
abandoned the topic, and the tracing of sexuality's path through his work
illuminates the clash of the competitive, contradictory factors that interact
to produce his texts.

As several studies have demonstrated, a distinctive feature of Platonov's
Utopia is its association with a return to the womb.[5] While Platonov's characters often speak of the resurrection of the dead as their aim, the author's
language and imagery frequently indicate that return to the uterus is an
equally desired end. Digging is a perpetual motif, reaching its extreme in
The Foundation Pit, which deals with the never ending excavation of a gigantic
and "uterine" (matochnyi) foundation pit, and in Juvenile Sea (Iuvenal'noe more),
in which the protagonists have as their chief goal the extraction of "maternal
water" (materinskaia voda) from the earth's depths. Catteau writes that for
Platonov Utopia is often

> la descente vers l'enfance et les retrouvailles avec le liquide
> amniotique. Cette régression s'exprime fortement ... par la
> descente verticale, le puits ou l'on s'enfonce pour retrouver
> 'l'eau maternelle' ou la chaleur confortable et sécurisante des
> entrailles.[6]

The fetal paradise, however, has an uncanny way of becoming a grave. Death can also be seen as a return to the womb, similarly a state of non-being.[7] In Chevengur this slippage between paradise and death even reaches ironic, metaliterary proportions. In the "humorous" description of the forest supervisor we read:

> [His] father used to compare bad books to stillborn children who had perished in their mother's womb from the lack of correspondence between their own excessively tender bodies and the coarseness of the world, which penetrated even a mother's womb.[8]

As Teskey, Geller, and Tolstaia-Segal have demonstrated, *Chevengur* bears the mark of Nikolai Fedorov, an influential philosopher of the late nineteenth century. Blending Christianity and what now seems like science fiction, Fedorov's project for the human race calls upon man to overcome the repressive forces of nature through the physical resurrection of the dead. According to Fedorov, resurrection can be accomplished through technological development and through the replacement of sexual by filial love.

Fedorov views sexuality as a destructive force which symbolizes man's subjugation to nature. Sexuality's "necessary companion" is death; those engaging in reproduction are inevitably destroyed by the physical decay inherent in the creation of progeny.[9] For Fedorov, "the question of the power which forces the two sexes to unite in one flesh for their conversion into a third being by means of birth is a question of death"; he inveighs against "this exclusive adherence to women, which causes the forgetting of fathers."[10] He advocates the elimination of all sexual urges and an institution of marriage founded upon "the knowledge of fathers," the perfection of which will be "the transformation of birth into resurrection."[11] The word "chastity" (*tselomudrie*) appears often in Fedorov's work; it is a sort of categorical imperative, essential for the overcoming of death.

In her summary of Fedorov's theory, Teskey writes:

> Fyodorov's assertions would seem to have a great deal in common with Freudian theories on sexuality, in particular that of the 'Oedipus Complex', but while Freud saw the displacement of the 'Father' by the 'Son' as a natural development – sexual

> deviance or mental problems would result if this normal
> process failed to take place – Fyodorov adopted the view that
> this process was in itself unnatural and ultimately destructive.[12]

What should be added is the rather obvious statement that Fedorov's fervent desire to overcome sexual urges is based upon an implicit acknowledgement of and horror at their strength. Sexuality is a "blind force," "powerful and terrifying."[13] Part of Fedorov's appeal depends upon potential adherents recognizing and attempting to suppress elements of their own sexuality.

In his works of the 1920s, Platonov in many respects envisions his Utopia along the lines of Fedorov's philosophy. Accordingly, it is not surprising that sexuality is almost always viewed with hostility and that in *Chevengur* the introduction of women precedes the eternal city's destruction. There is, however, one striking departure from Fedorov's philosophy in Platonov's treatment of sex: the position of importance openly accorded to the mother. Although Fedorov speaks of the resurrection of "prior generations," the father is the worshipped parent. Resurrection is "the task of man, of the mortal, of the son of dead fathers."[14] Fedorov does not glorify maternity. Resurrection depends on women developing a sense of "daughterliness" (*dochernost'*); maternal feeling, like sexual desire, is an animal emotion.[15] Mothers belong to that class of women who are "base, sensual and intolerant"; the ideal woman, a prototype for whom Fedorov finds in Mary Magdalene, Cordelia and Antigone, is capable of great suffering and sacrifice for fathers and brothers. In Platonov's work mothers are glorified, their memories openly held in reverence. His stories and novels are replete with idealized visions of maternity; at times his positive heroes themselves acquire traits of idealized maternity, becoming "maternal Prometheans" who give birth to the new world. Mother worship naturally coincides with Platonov's vision of the Utopia as a womb, but both these elements inject a certain degree of danger and instability into the repressive structure of Fedorov's philosophy. By feminizing the Utopian goal, Platonov reintroduces the possibility of sexual desire.

The mid-1930s mark a fundamental shift in Platonov's career. In the first half of the decade the author was virtually silenced. He published only three short fictional works and one article between 1930 and 1935.[16] In 1936, when he began to regain his public voice, the focus of his works started to change. Most noticeably, there was a drift away from Utopian themes and toward the depiction of everyday existence. In part, this change was due to external pressure; as Geller remarks, Utopias were no longer welcome in Soviet literature.[17] There was an internal change, though, as well: a rising, tormented hostility towards the Utopian ideal. A comparison of *The Foundation Pit* and *Juvenile Sea* with *Chevengur* shows that as early as 1929 Platonov had begun to portray the Utopian quest in tones more grotesque than lyrical, endowing the brutal dreamers of the new world with much less pathos and charm. In *The Foundation Pit* utopian efforts become nightmarish, even in *Juvenile Sea,* a novel written in accordance with many rules of the prevailing official canon,[18] we witness an unprecedented disintegration of language and a frenzied effort to repress desire.

In "The River Potudan" Platonov also experiments with the themes of mourning and desire, but here the figure of the mother recedes into the background; more evident is mourning for the Utopian ideal – her repressive substitute. This substitution allows Platonov to deal much more explicitly than ever before with the theme of the hero's sexual desire. For the first time, sexual desire is valorized positively and accepted; simultaneously the painful process in which Platonov has been engaged for years becomes the central subject of his tale, as the writer openly tries to exorcise the Utopian demon which has haunted him for so long.

The plot of "The River Potudan" is as follows. The hero, Nikita Firsov, returns to his village after the Civil War. There he lives with his aged father and renews his acquaintance with Liuba, whom he knew as a child. Eventually, he and Liuba wed, but Nikita is unable to consummate the marriage. After a short time he leaves the village and goes to the town of Kantemirovka, where he cleans outhouses, stops talking and loses his sense of personal, individual existence. His father meets him by chance and tells him that Liuba has tried to kill herself by jumping into the Potudan River. Nikita returns and has intercourse with Liuba, making possible mutual happiness based upon the "poor but necessary pleasure" (*bednoe, no neobkhodimoe naslazhdenie*),[19] inherent in the fulfillment of sexual desire.

The name Firsov carries great significance and serves as a cathecting lightning rod for several of the story's sexual currents. To the reader versed in Russian literature, it evokes memories of Firs, the old servant in *Cherry Orchard,* who is trapped at the end of the play in the former nursery which becomes his symbolic tomb. This, however, is only the most superficial of several layers of meaning. Etymologically, the name is derived from the Greek "thyrsos", the pine cone tipped staff associated with Dionysus.[20] A trace of this extremely phallic object is found in "Fro," where the heroine listens to a song about the cones on a fir tree. In "The Potudan River," though, the staff of desire is not a tangential but an implicit part of the hero's identity. The story chronicles Firsov's effort to activate the etymology of his name through his contact with love.[21]

Returning from the Civil War, Firsov finds himself in the plight of the author, who has turned away from Utopian concerns and must focus on a smaller theme – not the world's reconstruction but that of familial life. On his way home, Firsov lies down "beside a small stream that flowed from its source along the bottom of a gully and down into the Potudan." Here, in this uterine landscape, Nikita has a terrifying dream:

> Suddenly Firsov sat up, breathing heavily and in fear, as though he were on fire (zapalilsia), winded from some invisible race and struggle. He had a terrifying dream – that a small, plump animal was suffocating him with its hot fur, some sort of field creature (polevogo zver'ka) grown fat from eating pure wheat. Soaking with sweat from its efforts and greed, this creature had got into the sleeper's mouth, into his throat, trying to burrow with its tenacious little paws into the very center of his soul, in order to burn up his breath. Firsov had chocked in his sleep and had wanted to cry out and run away, but the small feature had torn itself out of him of its own accord, blind, pitiful, itself terrified and trembling, and had vanished in the darkness of its night. (214)

This is a remarkable passage of sexual terror, all the more startling because motifs of castration and cannibalistic fellatio which for years have been appearing in Platonov's work with apparent impassivity, as if inconsequential, now demand a much more conscious reading. The beast, which Platonov refuses to name (it is *"vrode,"* "like" or "sort of" a field animal), represents both the female genitals ("the hot fur" – *goriachaia sherst'*) on account of his longing for which the hero may be castrated, and the hero's own phallus, threatening and endangered, which in this story he will openly be forced to confront. In effect, Firsov is raped and impregnated with his own, hitherto repressed desire. The result is a terrifying identification with the animal that both consumes him and is consumed by him. Once devoured, the creature is no longer merely terrifying but is also pitiful; it ceases to be a distinctly foreign object and merges with the figure of the hero who is entirely a phallus and without a phallus, a "blind [and] pitiful" (*slepoi, zhalkii*) beast.[22] Indeed, the reference to "*its* night" (*svoia noch'*) creates an even broader identification, merging the creature with the narrative environment surrounding the hero, as if the text itself were being generated by this terrifying and pitiful embodiment of desire.

The dream serves as the centerpiece of the tale. Firsov never again feels such terror, but when motifs or words contained in this passage reappear, they sexualize the narrative. Most obvious in this respect is the adjective "*polevoi*" (field), which resonates with "*polovoi*" (sexual, floor [adj.]). When Firsov learns that Liuba is ready to marry him, he goes to her, walking through a "the wind from the fields" (*polevoi veter*, 232). The morning after the first night together, Nikita says to Liuba, "Let me scrub the floor, it doesn't look clean" (*Dai ia pol vymoiu, a to u nas griazno*). He promptly sets to work washing the "floor boards" (*polovye doski*, 234). Nikita and Liuba often sit on the floor (*na polu*) in front of the stove, a repressive substitution for bodily warmth and sexual heat.

Images of heat carry special significance, as in Firsov's dream when his body seems to be on fire ("*zapalilsia*"). The story traces Firsov's effort to transform Promethean, Utopian heat into sexual body heat and his simultaneous struggle against this transformation. Firsov is continually lighting Liuba's stove rather than making love to Liuba: "At her house his usual occupation was keeping the fire going and waiting for Liuba to say something to him ..." (224). Various forms of the verb "*topit'*" (to heat) are used with reference to Nikita seven times. The Utopian, non-sexual side of Nikita's nature is emphasized also by his making little figures out of clay instead of real children. This activity, performed on the floor, recalls the myth of Prometheus' creation of man from clay.

It is not surprising that the field animal crawls into Nikita's mouth. Elsewhere in Platonov's oeuvre the oral cavity has been compared to the genitals, the center of desire and pain.[23] Sound and sexuality are accorded the same locus, and the denial of one becomes the denial of both. Throughout "The River Potudan" mouths and throats are sexualized. Nikita's departure from Liuba occurs soon after she kisses his throat; after she tries to drown herself blood flows frequently from her mouth.

In Kantemirovka the impotent Nikita becomes known as "the mute" (*nemoi*). This identification functions on symptomatic, hagiographic and symbolic levels. The inability to communicate is a traditional symptom of profound depression, along with fatigue, apathy, impotence and, in general, a regression to a relatively infantile level of functioning.[24] Platonov describes Nikita's gradual withdrawal from the world, his frequent crying episodes, and low self esteem. Firsov has difficulty devoting himself to a task: "There was nothing, no task, that could wear out his grief and Nikita was afraid, just as in childhood, of the approaching night" (237). Nikita's regression to childhood – a gradual retreat to the womb if there ever was one – is foreshadowed in his relationship with Liuba, which centers around the basic activities of feeding and the provision of heat.[25] His stay in Kantemirovka, where all his activities focus on feces and food, represents an acceleration of this regressive process.[26] The desired uterine "*uezd*" of Chevengur has become the "*otkhozhee mesto*" in which Nikita is cast by the conflict between sexual and Utopian pressure. Firsov loses consciousness of all but the most basic realities, and in his preoccupation with excretion he seeks to purge himself of his torment.[27]

On a hagiographic level, Nikita's resort to muteness as a defense against sexual attraction recalls the life of Saint Nikita Muchenik (The Sufferer), who defies his father by accepting Christianity after seeing the Virgin in a dream. One of the more inventive tortures devised by the Saint's father to shatter the appeal of this divine vision consists in tying Nikita to several logs and placing him on top of a beautiful, corrupt girl "so that he might cleave to her and make sacrifice to the idol gods."[28] Nikita's salvation is horrifyingly ingenious: he bites off his tongue. "The foul girl, seeing his mouth filled with his blood, felt disdain and did not devote herself to his sin." This legend is linked to Platonov's story not only by the thematics of temptation and Oedipal conflict but also by the repeated use of the word "to suffer" (*muchit'sia*) used in the story seven times.[29] In addition, the Saint's life helps explain the odd image of the tree root that Nikita fashions from clay "gnawing itself and tormenting itself" (236). Platonov's story, however, does not use the legend simply as an exemplary subtext; rather, it employs the Life of Nikita Muchenik as a repressive model against which it must struggle. The legend is refracted, as Nikita tries symbolically to reenact it while Liuba attempts to revert it, to take the suffering upon herself while telling Nikita "You mustn't be so unhappy while I am still alive" (227) and pressing him to her breast so that he might "forget his own torment" (*svoe muchenie*, 229); by the tale's end it is her throat that will have been bloodied and he who, having overcome his horror, will have learned not to repress his arousal.

Nikita's muteness is also significant on a purely symbolic level, since for the genitalized body, words are the equivalent of sperm; and the Utopian drive is the movement toward the elimination of both. In "The River Potudan" the disintegration of language distinguishing *The Foundation Pit* and *Juvenile Sea* reaches its logical conclusion – the absence of speech. In neither the womb nor the tomb is language present, both are marked by the "silence of the deserted place" in which Nikita sleeps and dreams. In *total* muteness the subject virtually disappears, effacing himself in the depths of a self-negation that allows him to encompass the rest of the world. For Platonov, the Utopia, that all embracing emptiness into which the human universe can fraternally fit, is "ulogic," a place where his heroes die and where even his profession will cease to exist. As early as 1922, Platonov, following Plato, informed his readers that there would be no poets in the shining future; the narrator of "Descendants of the Sun" (*Potomki solntsa*) declares: "We now have not a single poet, not a single lover, and not a single person who does not understand, and in this lies the greatness of our epoch."[30] For Platonov, writing had always been nearly as problematic as sexuality, representing a potentially dangerous split between mind and body, thought and deed. Not universal speech (Esperanto), then, but non-speech is the signifier of the ideal. Utopia connotes a "withering away" not only of the state and of the phallus but of the tongue and pen as well.[31]

Immediately after the paragraph describing Nikita's dream, Platonov writes: "Firsov washed in the stream and rinsed out his mouth, then quickly walked on; his father's house was not far away and he could get there by evening" (214-15). In this short paragraph, consisting of only one sentence, the dream has led directly to a reference to Nikita's father. The figure of the father, repressed and threatening in earlier works, here is explicitly linked to the hero's repressed sexuality; the father's emergence into the narrative parallels the surfacing of the hero's desire. For the first time, the father-son relationship is openly admitted to be competitive. The father secretly imagines himself marrying Liuba, and Nikita takes comfort in the fact that his salary will soon be larger than his father's. Nikita courts Liuba successfully; earlier, his father found himself incapable of courting her mother.

Having found his son at the bazaar, Nikita's father says, "We thought you were dead and gone long ago. So you are all right? (*tsel*, literally "whole") (243). The symbolic nature of this meeting at the bazaar is crucially important. Nikita arrived there after following a beggar who was carrying a "full bag" (*polnaia suma*, 239) Nikita recognizes his father after the latter steps out of a latrine "with an empty sack under his arm" (*s pustym meshkom*, 105). The substitutional link between feces and semen in this story is quite apparent; the empty sack symbolizes both the discharge and the absence of a paternal threat.[32] Nikita embraces his "thin, bowed father" (243) then returns to Liuba. The weakness of this paternal vision has enabled Nikita to abandon his father for Liuba, an action that shows how far Platonov has drifted from the explicit dictates of Fedorov.

Furthermore, Firsov masters his longing for his mother, becoming the first of Platonov's heroes successfully to resolve an Oedipal crisis. Earlier in the story, Liuba comes to him when he is feverish and lying in his mother's bed. This is the same bed in which Nikita was born. It is the bed that his parents shared: "the pillow seemed to carry the smell of his mother's breath" (228). The bed is as close to a return to the womb as Nikita, with his whole body "burning" can realistically come, but he leaves it in order to go home with Liuba.

Significantly, Liuba's removal of Nikita from the maternal bed is described as a rescue at sea:

> He reached out and grasped the pocket of her coat – the coat
> that had been sewn from his Red Army greatcoat – and clung
> onto it like an exhausted swimmer clinging to a sheer rock, half
> drowning, half saved. (228)

The images of drowning are not accidental: Nikita considers drowning in the Potudan' River; Liuba throws herself in but is dragged out alive. Neither is permitted to follow Dvanov's path in *Chevengur*. Throughout the story there is a play on forms of the verbs "*topit'[sia]*" (to heat or to drown), which appear in various prefixed forms no fewer than fourteen times. In the past, the Promethean task has indeed been equivalent to self-inflicted death. But Nikita and Liuba do not drown because the author has them accept the consequences of their desire. Over the alluring and repressive depths of the river Platonov for the first time erects what Foucault calls "the contradictory thinness of a transparent and unbreakable partition" – language that protects from death.[33] In effect, through his own folk etymology Platonov infuses new meaning into the concept of drowning, for only in "utopiia" (u-topia) can one "utopit'sia". The couple are beyond Utopia and beyond death. They make love and speak so as not to die in the ideal; the river will not accept them.

Tolstaja-Segal, in her comments on the river's name, points out its resonance with "*potustoronnost'*" (otherworldliness).[34] Platonov was surely appreciative of this association, but there was another factor behind his choice of this river, which does in fact flow through the Voronez oblast', for his story's and his collection's title. Here a metathetic reading is required. Nikita and Liuba resist immersion; they are indeed "*nad utop*" (above utop[ia]). The homonymic link of the title's first word with an Old Russian form of the present active participle of the verb "to speak" (*reka*) reinforces the story's function as a reaffirmation of professional and personal character. Platonov here recovers from political and sexual repression. We find him accepting the distasteful realities of everyday existence and, therefore, "saying" "*Potudan'*."

In the story's final scene, after Nikita and Liuba have made love, Liuba asks him to light the stove. For the first time, there is no wood. This lack of a source of artificial heat, like Nikita's success in providing sexual heat, signals a break with the past. Nikita chops two boards into kindling and feeds them to the stove. Potentially this is another image of castration, but Platonov emphasizes that talismans are no longer needed, that the demonstration of sexual potency has rendered the fear of castration impotent. By accepting the "cruel, pitiful strength" of sexuality, Firsov exorcises the repressive fear which motivated the terror of his dream. Nikita and his creator have completed an extremely painful maturing process. They are, to use the story's four last words, "in the cool half dark of late time" (246), but the absence of the womb's warmth now allows a measured, moderated form of survival in which existence is no longer conditioned upon a powerful drive towards the self's infinite expansion and obliteration. Instead, the final words signal an affirmation and acceptance of reality and temporality. The story, which began with an acknowledgement of Utopian timelessness ("the grass, which there had not been time to see before" (213)), does not conclude joyously, but it does end with the conquest of a meager yet still self-sustaining power — the ability to survive the cold emptiness of 'real', non-utopian life.

One final observation is warranted. Immediately before describing Nikita's first encounter with his father, Platonov writes:

> That night the father of Nikita Firsov was sleeping as usual, from
> necessity and because he was tired. A cricket had lived for years
> in the earth ledge outside the house and it used to sing there
> in the evenings: it was either the same cricket as the summer
> before last or else its grandson. (215)

In the description of the cricket the paternal generation is omitted and a link is established between grandfather and grandson.[35] This effacing of the father in the paragraph following the one which introduced him is founded upon an intimate connection between the author and his hero. Andrei Platonovic Klimentov, who adopted his father's Christian name (Platon) as his *nom de plume* (Platonov), in "The River Potudan" builds his hero's last name upon the first name of his paternal grandfather (Firs), a name he was to use as the basis of a pseudonym for several critical articles in the following year (A. Firsov). Platonov's selection of his grandfather's name for this hero who marks the author's break with the past is highly significant, for at the very moment when the paternal threat is defused, when the son at last competes successfully with his father by transferring their contest away from the Oedipal arena of "Mother" and "Utopia," the son's link with his male parent is reaffirmed and maintained through a reversal of their roles. By identifying with the figure of the grandfather, the son plunges into temporality and, by aging himself, puts an end to his father's parental control.

Platonov's use of the cricket as the bearer of the encoded information serves as a reference to the young Puskin's name in the literary society Arzamas – "Cricket" (*Sverchok*). In 1937, the one hundredth anniversary of Pushkin's death, Platonov wrote two articles about Pushkin and began to envision a play about the poet's youth.[36] The uniting of Pushkin and the theme of filial conquest in the image of the cricket reinforces the son's triumph as a matter of personal and professional self-definition, for Platonov viewed Pushkin as a writer who had tried, albeit from a historical viewpoint prematurely, to reconcile the builder of Utopia (Peter) with the principle of love (Evgeny/Parasha), the father (Gasub) with the son (Tazit).[37] Indeed, reconciliation is the pedal note for all of "The Potudan River," as the liberation from the unlimited demands of Utopia necessitates the acceptance of the limited demands, humble and humbling, of moderation and routine. Paradoxically, at the very time when his country was moving ever deeper into the malevolent paternal shadow of Stalin, Platonov was conquering the forces of repression within him as he simultaneously sought to adapt his works to his nation's repressive demands. The publication of the *The Potudan River* collection and of his critical articles was the result. The *story* "The River Potudan" represents a painful, necessary step along the varied planes of this reconciliatory process. It is a work of mourning carried through to a successful conclusion, a lament which both grieves for and celebrates the renunciation of Utopia, the recovery of a professional, public voice, and the authorial admission of desire.

ENDNOTES

[1] Andrei Platonov, *"Zhivia glavnoi zhizn'iu," Volga* 9 (1975), 173.

[2] Vladimir Vasil'ev, *Andrei Platonov* (Moscow: Sovremennik, 1982), 156.

[3] *"Reka Potudan'"* first appeared in collection *Reka Potudan'*, which was published in 1937. The final draft was submitted to the printer on December 16, 1936 – *Reka Potudan'* (Moscow, 1937).

[4] See, inter alia, A. L. Berkovich, *"Voprosy polovoi zhizni pri svete sotsial'noi gigieny," Molodaia gvardiia* 6 (1923); E. Iaroslavsky, *"Moral' i byt proletariata v perekhodnom periode," Molodaia gvardiia* 5 (1926); A. Kollontai, *"Dorogu krylatomu Erosu," Molodaia gvardiia* 5 (1923); S. Smidovich, *"O liubvi," Pravda,* March 24, 1925; E. Troshchenko, *"Vuzovaia molodezh'," Molodaia gvardiia* 4 (1927); A. B. Zalkind, *"Polovaia zhizn' i sovremennaia molodezh'," Molodaia gvardiia* 6 (1923).

[5] See Ayleen Teskey, *Platonov and Fyodorov: the Influence of Christian Philosophy on a Soviet Writer* (Wiltshire, Eng: Avebury, 1982), 92-108: J. Catteau, "De la Métaphorique des utopies dans la littérature Russe et de son Traitement chez Andrej Platonov," *Revue des Études Slaves* 56 : 1 (1984) : 47-50; Erik Naiman, "The Thematic Mythology of Andrej Platonov," *Russian Literature* XXI: 2 (1987): 210-213.

[6] Catteau, "De la Métaphorique des utopies," 47.

[7] Naiman, "The Thematic Mythology of Andrej Platonov," 210.

[8] A. Platonov, *Chevengur,* trans. Anthony Olcott (Ann Arbor: Ardis, 1978), 101.

[9] Nikolai Fedorov, *Teoriia obshchego dela,* vol. I (Vernyi, 1906), 321, 345.

[10] Ibid., 9.

[11] Ibid., 321.

[12] Teskey, *Platonov and Fyodorov,* 17.

[13] Fedorov, *Teoriia,* 314.

[14] Ibid., 317, 346

[15] Ibid., 323.

[16] V. Maramzin, *"Biobibliograficheskii ukazatel'," Echo* 7 (1980): 149.

[17] Michail Geller, *Andrei Platonov v poiskach shchast'ia* (Paris: YMCA-Press, 1982), 298-300.

[18] Ibid., 310.

[19] Andrei Platonov, *Soul and Other Stories,* trans. Robert and Elizabeth Chandler et al. (New York: New York Review Books, 2008), 245. All quotations from *"Reka Potudan'"* are from this edition. The original version of the article provided quotations in Russian.

[20] A. V. Petrovsky, *Slovar' russkikh licnykh imen* (Moscow: *Russkie slovari*, 1980), 224.

[21] Firsov has a precursor in Platonov's work, the beggar Firs who makes a brief appearance in Chevengur. The landscape out of which Firs appears is one in which "the earth slept bare and tormented, like a mother whose blankets have slipped to the floor." Firs is drawn towards Chevengur because he has heard that "a free place had been opened out in the steppe, where passers-by lived and everybody got fed what they produced." Firs does not reach the maternal paradise, because he finds its equivalent in a nearby stream:

> He liked flowing water. It aroused him, demanded something of him. Firs though did not know what the water needed and why he needed it. He just picked out spots where the water was thickened with earth and dipped his sandals in that direction. At night he wrung out his foot cloths for a long time, in order to test the water with his fingers and once again see its weakened flow. When near brooks and riffles he would sit and listen to the living currents until he became totally calm, ready himself to lie down in the part and become part of the nameless meadow brook. The night before he had slept on the shore of a river channel, listening all night to the singing water, and then in the morning he had crawled down and lowered his body to the enticing dampness, thus achieving peace before reaching Chevengur. (*Chevengur*, trans. Anthony Olcott, 158)

"The River Potudan" recounts Firsov's struggle to dispel the fatal attraction of the maternal, Utopian siren, to break the tie which binds him to Firs.

Another possible literary allusion is Trediakovsky's *Ezda v ostrov liubvi* (1730). The hero of this novel has the conventional Arcadian shepard's name of Tirsis and wins the love of the beautiful Aminta after a battle between the personified characters of "*Zhalost'*" and "*Zhestokost'*."

[22] As Korchagina points out, in "The River Potudan" the word "*zhalko*" (pitiful) almost always serves to fuse the narrative with Firsov's thoughts (E. P. Korchagina, "*O nekotorykh osobennostiakh skazovoi formy v rasskaze 'Reka Potudan',*" in *Tvorchestvo A. Platonova* (Voronezh, 1970), 111.

[23] The throat in particular often serves as a symbol for sexual suffering, with pain being inflicted upon it as a price for arousal (See, e.g., the story "Takyr"). Guttural sounds are quite often associated by Platonov with pain and desire. In

the early 1930s screenplay *Father-Mother* (*Otec-mat'*), a couple, soon to be married, hear a "long, guttural voice of a man in torment, similar to a baby's cry" coming from a venereal clinic. A doctor's voice is heard, reminding the patient: "Did you enjoy the loving and the kissing? Was it good? Now sing, go on, sing" (A. Platonov, "*Iz zapisnykh knizhek*," *Literaturnaia gazeta*, 48 (November 29, 1967): 122).

[24] For discussions of depressive symptoms, see Myer Mendelson, *Psychoanalytic Concepts of Depression* (Flushing: Spectrum Publications, 1974), 195-200, 206; and Edith Jacobson, *Depression: Comparative Studies of Normal, Neurotic, and Psychotic Conditions* (New York: International Universities Press, 1971), 172.

[25] The centrality of food in their relationship recalls the ingestion of the "field creature grown fat from eating pure wheat" in the dream. Platonov repeatedly highlights this sexual contextualization. On one of Nikita's first visits the following dialogue occurs, replete with the sexualized themes of food, cruelty, pity and guilt:

> 'Have you got any paraffin?' asked Nikita.
> 'No, I've been given some firewood. We [Liuba and Zhenia, her studying companion] light the little stove – then we sit on the floor. We can see by the flame.'
> Liuba smiled hopelessly, with shame, as if some cruel, sad thought had entered her mind.
> 'I expect her elder brother hasn't fallen asleep,' she said. 'He's just a lad. He doesn't like his sister feeding me, he begrudges it. But it isn't my fault! I am really not all that fond of eating. It's not me – it's my head. It starts aching and thinking about bread, it stops me from thinking about anything else' (221-22).

Like the field creature, Liuba both devours and is to be devoured. Jokingly, she tells Nikita:

> 'I am not such a tasty morsel. You only think I am' (230).

It should be noted that Nikita's feeding of Liuba is closely connected by Platonov to Nikita's relationship with his father:

> "Once the old man noticed that his son had got hold of two white rolls. But Nikita immediately wrapped them up in a piece of paper and did not offer his father anything. Then he put on his

army cap as usual and was off, probably till midnight, taking both the bread rolls.

'Nikit, take me with you!' the father begged. 'I won't say anything. I'll just look. It must be interesting there, you must be going somewhere really outstanding!' (225)

'How are you?" Liuba asked quietly.

'My father and I are all right, we are alive,' said Nikita. 'I've got something here for you. Please eat it,' he begged' (223).

[26] The name "Kantemirovka" itself signifies a regression – a reference to the literature of the eighteenth century.

[27] In his rather rigidly ordered scheme of libidinal development, Abraham suggests that a relationship exists between anality and depression, and that a preoccupation with feces signifies ambivalence about retention and rejection of the lost love object (Karl Abraham, "A Short Study of the Development of the Libido, Viewed in the Light of Mental Disorders" [1924], in *Selected Papers of Karl Abraham* (London, 1965), 418-453).

[28] Grigory Kuselev-Bezborodko, *Pamiatniki starinnoi russkoi literatury* (Sankt-Peterburg, 1861), 147.

[29] In prefixed and non-reflexive forms the verb appears an additional three times (87,97,103). The word "*muchen'e*" is used twice (80, 84). "Muchenie" is a theme which appears throughout Platonov's work, often signifying a character's emotional, nearly intuitive perception of the gap between the real and the ideal.

[30] A. Platonov, *Starik i starukha* (Munich, 1984), 40.

[31] Platonov's attitude towards writing and, more generally, towards art, merits treatment in a separate study. His statements on art's function and utility vary greatly. Compare:

> "[Poetry] is as much a human need and a human function as sweating, in other words, a most ordinary one. Because of this every person is a poet" ([1920] – Quoted in E. Inozemtseva, "Platonov v Voronezhe," Pod'em 2 (1971): 93 [emphasis in original]),

> and

> "But how boring it is to write about the suffering millions when one can take action and feed them. A hungry man is not touched by

big words, whereas the sight of bread will move him to tears, as if it were music, which will never move him to tears again" ([1921] Quoted in V. Verin, "Andrei Platonov – publitsist," Literaturnaia Gazeta 2 (January 7, 1987): 5).

In his early work, at least, Platonov was capable of considering art as a positive phenomenon only when he shifted his view from the individual creative act and from the specific implement of paper to art as a universal theme with unifying capabilities:

"Proletarian Art reflects all mankind in its best aspirations, and it is created by all mankind, by the whole harmonious organized collective... Individual, personal creation produces only 'artificial art,' and not art itself: it [art] is the lot of mankind, not of an individual" ([1919] 1986:92).

A notebook entry of much later (but uncertain) date shows Platonov continuing to predicate an appreciation for art on its unifying powers:

"A working man has to have a deep understanding of the fact that one can make a great number of buckets and locomotives, while one cannot make song or excitement. No object is dearer than song; it brings people together. And this is the most difficult and most important thing" (1967b:7).

[32] The figure of the hero's old, ineffectual father appears in much of Platonov's work of this period ("Fro," "The Switchman" (*Strelochnik*), "The Third Son" (*Tretii syn*), replacing the absent, threatening father of the years before. Platonov is preparing to bury the paternal threat along with the maternal Utopia. "The Third Son" concludes with the following words:

in the morning the six sons lifted the coffin onto their shoulders and carried it out to be buried, while the old man took his granddaughter in his arms and followed them; by now he was used to missing the old woman, and he was pleased and proud that he too would be buried by these six powerful men – and buried no less properly" (Andrei Platonov, Soul and Other Stories, 153-54)

[33] Michel Foucault, "Language to Infinity," in his *Language, Counter-Memory, Practice* (Ithaca: Cornell University Press, 1977), 60.

[34] Elena Tolstaja-Segal, "*O sviazi nizshikh urovnei teksta s vysshimi: proza Andreia Platonova,*" *Slavica Hierosolymitana* 2 (1978): 197-198.

[35] The two quoted sentences also appear, with one minor difference ("*v pozaproshlom godu*") in one of Platonov's notebook entries. No date is provided for the entry in the published excerpts in which it has been included (A. Platonov, "*Iz zapisnykh knizhek,*" *Literaturnaia Gazeta* 48 (November 29 (1967): 6). It seems more probable that Platonov wrote the sentence in the notebook first (for later inclusion in the story) rather than that he copied an already published phrase into what he referred to as his "raw material" (*syr'e*).

[36] "*Puskin – nash tovarishch,*" *Literaturny kritik* 1 (1937); "*Pushkin i Gorky,*" *Literaturny kritik* 6 (1937); "*Uchenik Litseia,*" *Nash sovremennik* 6 (1974). In the play *Uchenik Litseia*, Pushkin's uncle says: "in any house of the Pushkins, every cricket is a poet" (*vsiakiy sverchok poet*) (75).

[37] A. Platonov, *Razmyshleniia chitatelia* (Moscow: *Sovremennik*, 1980), 13-16.

IX

"This Could Have Been Foreseen": Kharms's The Old Woman (Starukha) Revisited. A Collective Analysis

ROBIN MILNER-GULLAND

The Old Woman is the longest and most complex of the prose works of Daniil Kharms (pseudonym of D. I. Iuvachyov, 1905-42), and was written towards the end of his too-short life, in May-June 1939. Together with the cycle of thirty brief pieces gathered together in the same year under the title *Sluchai* (*Incidences, Happenings* or *Events*), it stands in most estimates as the summit of his idiosyncratic achievement in literature. Unusually, he subtitled it *povest'* (tale). Apart from writings for children, none of Kharms's works appeared in print from the late 1920s till the Soviet Thaw period of the 1960s. Thereafter his almost-forgotten legacy was revived both outside and inside Russia, and he has been justly re-evaluated as one of the most original and arresting of the Russian (indeed European) modernists. Much has been written in the last quarter century about him and his associates (particularly in the group called OBERIU, which he largely organized), about his life, his eccentricities, his sad fate and his special genius; while individual works have been closely examined by literary specialists.[1]

The Old Woman, naturally, has not escaped their scrutiny. It has attracted an astonishing variety of critical approaches and interpretations, unlike his brief "minimalist" prose-pieces which have mostly been regarded as exercises in absurdity, defamiliarization, or deconstruction of literary tradition. For A. S. Nakhimovsky, its idea "is a simple and traditional one: acknowledgement of the presence of God." For several critics, led by Ellen Chances, the story's significance depends on a mass of intertextual and parodic echoes of past literature (notably Pushkin's *The Queen of Spades* (*Pikovaia dama*) and Dostoevsky's *Crime and Punishment* (*Prestuplenie i nakazanie*), works of Gogol, Chekhov, Meyrinck, and Hamsun, from the last of whom the story's epigraph comes). For A. Aleksandrov, it "conveys the anguish, fears, torments of isolation and anonymity which many Soviet intellectuals shared with its hero." For Neil Carrick, author of both the longest and (to date) most recent study of the tale, the intertextual elements represent unwelcome "insurgent narratives," ultimately conveying the bleak "idea that human beings believe themselves to be free, but that their belief is a mere delusion." For Rosanna Giaquinta, it is an example of "the modern grotesque, which is both destructive and without hope," where "the irrational is treated as if it were real." For Graham Roberts, by contrast, the tale represents an "exploration" in search of tested truth by a "deceptively wise man." This is merely a sample of critical approaches and responses to the story, but sufficient to indicate how varied they have been; so much so that we can already say something with assurance about *The Old Woman,* that it comes into the interesting category of works whose "unfinalized" and multivalent quality ensures that they serve as a touchstone for criticism itself, revealing the critics' deeply-held feelings about what might constitute a satisfactory interpretation or interpretative strategy. We shall explore these matters more systematically below.

Much of what has already been written about *The Old Woman* tends indeed in the direction of global interpretation or "unriddling" of the tale. My aim in this paper is more humble: not to challenge any of these large-scale interpretations, or to choose between them, still less to put forward any all-embracing interpretation of my own (though I shall not hide some of my preferences), but having considered the range of interpretative strategies on offer, to examine the structure of the story at the sort of textual level that the interpreters have generally neglected. To give one example: the narrative of the story shifts frequently and unpredictably (eighteen times, by my count) between past and present tenses. Any attentive reader will notice this feature on first acquaintance with *The Old Woman,* and may well wonder what semantic significance it carries, yet so far as I know it has never previously been mentioned in print.

When at the Neo-Formalist conference in September 1995 the participants devoted an evening session to a "collective analysis" of *The Old Woman,* it was not with the aim of challenging the previous interpreters on their own ground by substituting yet another new reading of the tale; rather, by subjecting the text to close scrutiny and measuring various interpretative strategies against this, to help the reader find ways of balancing up their value. Members of the group responded fruitfully to the challenge (and several people unable to be present sent helpful contributions on paper); this study – or notes towards a reading of *The Old Woman* – is in part a summing-up of the session. I am most grateful to all who took part, some of whom will (even when not acknowledged by name) recognize points they made.[2] No particular commitment to a Formalist or even "Neo-Formalist" methodology was expected, though it had been suggested beforehand that the schema put forward by Michael O'Toole – a senior member of our group – in his book on *Structure, Style and Interpretation in the Russian Short Story* – might provide a suitable framework for structural analysis.[3]

Any attempt to summarize the plot of *The Old Woman* will be unsuccessful and probably misleading: the story is replete with small plot-elements, often of the most throw-away kind, that pick up significance (or, sometimes, fail to realize their expected significance) as the tale proceeds, and a summary that did justice to all such details would no longer be a summary, but a re-telling. Nevertheless it may be useful to indicate the main structural divisions into which it can be seen to fall.

1. The narrator has an unsettling encounter with an old woman carrying a clock without hands. He goes with a friend, Sakerdon Mikhailovich, to a pub, thence returns home to turn off his electric stove. There he is inspired to write a story about a miracle-worker who declines to perform miracles, but in his excitement can write only one sentence: "The miracle-worker was tall."

2. The old woman comes to the narrator's room, orders him to kneel and then lie on the floor. The narrator loses consciousness, and when he comes round realizes the old woman is sitting dead in his armchair. He dozes, and dreams of a clay Sakerdon Mikhailovich. On waking he finds the dead old woman is on the floor and kicks her on the chin.

3. Hungry, the narrator goes to the shops to buy sausages and bread. In the queue he converses with a "nice little lady" who offers to buy his bread for him. He gets some vodka, but cannot take her home because of the presence of the old woman. He escapes by tram and goes to share his meal with Sakerdon Mikhailovich.

4. The central (and longest) section describes the narrator's meal and conversation with Sakerdon Mikhailovich, during which he suddenly asks the latter if he believes in God and in immortality. The narrator leaves and in a final paragraph Sakerdon Mikhailovich is described from an "external" viewpoint.

5. The narrator makes his way home, has various encounters, and on entering his room sees the old woman crawling towards him.

6. Escaping in terror to the corridor, he has a ghoulish "conversation" about corpses with his own thoughts. He reenters, finds the old woman lying peacefully, and agonizes over what to do. He decides to sink the corpse in a marsh outside the city, shifts it into a suitcase and borrows thirty rubles from his neighbor, an engine-driver.

7. He takes the heavy suitcase to the station, on the way glimpsing the "nice little lady." In the suburban train he is seized by stomach cramps; returning from the toilet, he finds the suitcase has disappeared (as have his companions in the carriage). At his destination, Lisii Nos, he goes to a wood, hides behind juniper bushes, drops to his knees, touches a green caterpillar and speaks the words, "In the name of the Father and of the Son and of the Holy Ghost, for ever and ever, Amen."Two and a half ruled lines and a coda follow: "At this point I temporarily end my manuscript, considering that it is already sufficiently long-drawn-out in any case."

It should be noted that this division of the story into what I discern as seven parts is made simply for convenience. Kharms (judging by the text of the story as edited by V. Glotser in *Novyi Mir*, 4, 1988, and reproduced by Aizlewood) indicated only one division in the text, a line's space between my parts (4) and (5), until the row of dots separating out the last sentence. Aleksandrov *(Sky Flight [Polet v nebesa])* leaves another line's space in my part (2) immediately after the narrator lies down on the floor. The reliability of such apparently minor, but in fact not insignificant editorial decisions could only be established by consulting the surviving Kharms MS of *The OldWoman* (which is in private hands; it deserves, as I have proposed elsewhere, to be published in facsimile).[4]

Since, as has been suggested already, *The Old Woman* (for all its apparent reliance on traditional short-story elements) does not yield up any transparent meaning, it has given rise to a striking range of critical approaches. It may be worthwhile to summarize these, which in their sheer variety seem to me to provide a small anthology of hermeneutics. It goes without saying that they sometimes overlap and can be combined. I distinguish a dozen different – often very different – such approaches, some of them capable of further sub-division.

1. Intertextual. Is it a commentary on, pastiche, or parody of Pushkin (*Queen of Spades*), Dostoyevsky (*Crime and Punishment, Notes from Underground* [*Zapiski iz podpol'ia*], *Raw Youth* [*Podrostok*]), Gogol, Chekhov, Meyrinck, Hamsun? Quite detailed verbal and situational parallels have been pointed out, notably by Chances. For Carrick this is a "classic St. Petersburg tale." But for Roberts, Kharms had "debunked the St. Petersburg tradition" already ten years before in his *Comedies of the City of Petersburg (Komedii goroda Peterburga)* and by implication here too. Such intertextuality must have been employed purposefully, so in this case there will be further explaining to do. Intertextual criticism is obviously favored by literary specialists who by way of their work can pick up such echoes more readily than the general reader. Maybe situational similarities are the most interesting. I shall add three observations of my own to the growing file on intertextuality in *The Old Woman*.

> **1.1** "There are only those who wish to believe and those who wish not to believe" – an echo of Pechorin's question towards the end of Lermontov's *Hero of our Time (Geroi nashego vremeni):* "Who knows if he believes a thing or not?"
>
> **1.2** "At this point I temporarily end my manuscript...": clearly, as I and others have previously pointed out, a blatant imitation of the "deflationary" ending of *Notes from Underground*, yet also a reminiscence of the moment at which the main narrative of *Eugene Onegin (Evgenii Onegin)* is abruptly cut short at a "difficult moment" for the hero.
>
> **1.3** The glimpse of the "nice young lady" as the hero travels on his fraught journey would seem to be an echo of the glimpse of Fraulein Burstner as Joseph is led to his execution in the last chapter of Kafka's *The Trial*, a work with which *The Old Woman* anyhow has a certain thematic similarity. Yet there is virtually no possibility that Kharms had ever read a word of Kafka (despite multiple situational coincidences in their work overall). Intertextuality can lead one down false paths (which may actually be more interesting than broad highways).

2. Psychological. Is it a "case study" in the pathology of a deluded or paranoid narrator, again in the tradition of *Hero of our Time, Notes from Underground* and *Queen of Spades*? The narrator's disintegrating personality recalls the Romantic and Dostoevskian psychological theme of "the double."

3. Grotesque. Is it essentially a fantastical or horrific story in the tradition of "literature to make our flesh creep" that goes back to the early nineteenth century (basically the approach taken by Giaquinta; of course there are distinctions that can be made between grotesquerie, fantasy, horror and related modes)?

4. Religious. The last page of *The Old Woman*, together with the strange intrusion into two of its dialogues of the question of belief in God, encourages an approach that would see it as fundamentally the bearer of religious meaning. Kharms's own (if idiosyncratic) religious belief and occasional religious writings support this. Its religious message might be on a generalized spiritual or moral plane, or specifically Christian. Perhaps the whole work is some kind of religious allegory (see 9 below).

5. Mythic. Kharms's late works, particularly *Happenings* (*Sluchai*), include many examples of what could generically be called "urban myths," a modern form with roots in the St Petersburg literary tradition (as well as e.g. the Paris of Baudelaire or London of Dickens). Two contributors to the collective analysis independently pointed to the curious similarity of *The Old Woman*'s plot with the well-known English urban myth of the "dead granny concealed in a carpet or trunk stolen from a vehicle." Yet the story may be rooted in more ancient and pervasive Russian folk mythology related to the "unquiet dead" (though commentators seem so far to have ignored this; I shall return to it later).

6. Biographical. Some commentators (Aleksandrov, Aizlewood) have tellingly drawn attention to the echoes of Kharms's own life-circumstances in the late 1930s in the narrator's personality, the action and setting of *The Old Woman*, his hunger, his frequent lassitude and loss of inspiration (which he called "ignavia"), his animosity towards children etc.[5] There is a remarkable clue in the fact (reported by Aleksandrov) that "Sakerdon Mikhailovich" was a name that replaced the original "Nikolai Makarovich" in the story's draft – the first name and patronymic of Kharms's close friend, the journalist and poet N. M.

Oleinikov (who had incidentally been arrested in 1937).

7. Social. Cassedy seems to have been the first to point out how saturated with Soviet *realia* the story is: he tellingly evokes the atmosphere in Russia after the promulgation of the 1936 law-code, when an ostensibly secure and just legal system had a shadowy counterpart in unspoken prohibitions and arbitrary arrests of the guiltless. A contributor to the collective analysis mentioned how close (though in lighter vein) the world of Zoshchenko is to that of late Kharms – of course they were both Leningrad writers and probably knew each other (Grubisic – see note 1 – points out several parallels). One commentator (A. Anemone) takes the story's social message further, close to the point of allegory: he reads it as Kharms's repudiation of his youthful OBERIU nihilism of ten to twelve years before and an acceptance of responsibility for its social consequences.

8. Philosophical. Much in Kharms's writing has its origin in a continual explicit or implicit dialogue with his philosopher friend Druskin (as Aizlewood convincingly pointed out in a written contribution to our analysis); both the "burden" of the old woman and the story's concern with time, its nature and apprehension, can be seen as philosophical themes in fictional form. I shall add another: the obsessive self-questioning of the narrator, on first discovering the dead old woman is no longer in his chair, as to whether his earlier perceptions were dreams (and if so, how far back they stretched) echoes famous self-doubts in Descartes's *Meditations* and *Discourse* as to how he can know if he is awake or dreaming.

9. Allegorical. Maybe (as has been mentioned above) the story should be read as a coherent allegory: of Kharms's society and times, of his own life-circumstances, of the unsought burdens of the human condition. In notes sent in advance of the collective analysis, McBurney suggested a more remarkable hidden reading still: of *The Old Woman* as an allegory of the Passion according to St John (Kharms knew the works of J. S. Bach intimately), on the basis of parallels in the time-scale and sequence of events. (Are the thirty rubles the narrator borrows in some way a reminiscence of Judas's thirty pieces of silver, I wonder?)

10. Bakhtinian. Readings based on the theories of Mikhail Bakhtin can be powerfully argued. Indeed the Bakhtinian approaches should be subdivided, since at least three of his concepts can be separately applied.

10.1 Dialogism. The epigraph to the whole tale ("And between them the following conversation takes place" – from Hamsun's *Mysteries)* alerts us to the exceptional importance of dialogue – worthy of Dostoevsky himself – in the tale. We shall return to this point. But as Aizlewood has suggested there is an overarching dialogue, between the author and Druskin, at work in *The Old Woman* too; Carrick suggests a "dialogue" between Kharms and the earlier writers he echoes.

10.2 Chronotope. A chronotope-based study of *The Old Woman* is rewarding. One participant in the collective analysis (Cornwell) proposed, partly on the suggestion of one of his students, a "psychological-chronotopic" reading, based on the opposition "interiority/the room/self" against "externality/the street/the other." Another (O'Toole), citing Toporov, emphasized the chronotopic liminality (threshold situations) so characteristic too of Dostoevsky: "the focus on liminal spaces of stairways, landings, streets, queues, stations, tram-platform, toilet on the train, even the bushes on the edge of the wood" and "most of all the liminal mental states of dream, daydream, introspection, imagining, phobia, etc."

10.3 *Carnivalization.* To the ordinary reader, *The Old Woman* may hardly seem "carnivalistic" in spirit, but it has much about it that accords with Bakhtin's special sense of this term, and Roberts has produced an eloquent reading of the text in the light of the carnival-associated genre of "Menippea" or "Menippic satire." Brandist has extended the menippean reading by linking it with the mediaeval grotesque and with what Likhachev and Panchenko famously termed "the laughter world of Old Russia." We shall return to these points.

11. Metafictional. Kharms was much concerned – often satirically – with the nature of the literary process and status of the writer (he "mocks the very notion of "Literature" as "high art"," as Roberts has put it). Such metafictional concerns are characteristic of much early Soviet writing, as Shepherd in particular has shown.[6] The narrator of *The Old Woman* is evidently an ineffective and self-aggrandizing denizen of the literary fringes. We are given two of his products as "inserted narratives": his one-sentence story about the miracle worker (repeated near the end), and part of his dialogue with the "nice little lady," presented in the format of a ludicrously naive playlet. This episode, portentously introduced with a version of the Hamsun epigraph to the work as a whole ("And between us the following conversation takes place") subverts the general first-person viewpoint of the tale, as does the strange paragraph describing Sakerdon Mikhailovich from a "god's-eye view" when the narrator leaves his flat. The narrator models his plan of action on "detective novels and newspaper reports." These and several other features of *The Old Woman* – notably the author's comment on the length of his own narrative in the last sentence – point up the metafictional dimension of the text.

12. Ironical. Maybe the whole story is intended as "a wicked irony," as Briggs and Barratt have suggested (quoting Lermontov's words) of *A Hero of Our Time*. I think I am the only commentator to have suggested this, and no more than semi-seriously at that, but the possibility should not be instantly dismissed. It depends on the last sentence, imitating the end of *Notes from Underground* and retrospectively ironizing, in similar fashion, what has gone before. If so, we are left with the unpalatable possibility that the affecting episode immediately before the end – where the narrator kneels and pronounces a blessing – is not to be taken seriously (Roberts has suggested as much, regarding the scene as an expression of the narrator's gratitude at the "miracle" of having lost his burdensome suitcase while in the train's toilet).

This list of approaches to *The Old Woman* is of course provisional and to some extent arbitrary; I am aware different labels might be attached to some of them. Some are no more than just that: approaches, facilitating the next step towards one or another full-scale interpretation; others necessarily involve such an interpretation.

It may be noted that, despite Kharms's common reputation as an "absurdist," I have not suggested an "absurdist" reading of *The Old Woman:* I have not seen such an approach to this story put forward,[8] and have indeed many doubts about the validity of the term "absurd" in relation to any of his work save perhaps that intended for children. I have not suggested a separate "symbolic" reading, either. The identification and elucidation of symbolic motifs is implicit in most of the approaches already listed, and if sufficiently consistent may lead to an allegorical interpretation. Any interpretative strategy is going to have to take account of the many events, objects and personalities in the story that may or may not suggest a symbolic explanation of some kind. But all such strategies should also take account of matters of structure, tone, narrative manner, linguistic register etc., to which we now turn our attention.

The method effectively employed by Michael O'Toole for the structural analysis of short stories involves a scheme of six levels of analysis to define a story's distinctive features.[9] He groups these in pairs, thus:

> Narrative structure – Point of view
> Plot – Fable
> Setting – Character

He privileges the first pair, considering the others essentially secondary. It is worth noting that O'Toole himself emphasizes that such dissective analysis should be followed by synthesis, thus returning us to the problems of overall interpretation. Some remarks on each of the six levels follow.

Narrative structure. This is "the dramatic trajectory of the story's action...[via] a *peripeteia*...to a closing situation,"[10] that which gives dynamic and syntactic form to an underlying meaning. O'Toole himself sent a most useful note on this to the collective analysis:

> If I were to apply my Narrative Structure model to the story, I think I would note a sort of counterpoint between the clear linear narrative (peripeteia: the disappearance of the body) and a much more fugue-like musical structure whereby motifs get introduced, worked over, then dropped, only to be recapitulated later: mocking boys, the false teeth, Sakerdon's enamel saucepan, the little lady etc. Each time I read the story I found the tension between this musical (or poetic) circularity and the linearity of the plot more powerful.

Musicality and musical structures were indeed of great interest to Kharms. There are other significant recapitulations: the shadow falling across the narrator's face as he writes his "story," and again as he leaves his room with the suitcase (it is almost unavoidable that we should read this symbolically!), for example; one of the most pervasive recurrent motifs is that of the meal (also "non-meal") – from the dream of the of the knife-and-fork clockface, the visit to the pub, the aborted meal and drink with the "nice little lady," the central "feast" with Sakerdon Mikhailovich and its grotesque excretory consequences. These recapitulations, or "fugal" elements, seem to counteract the throw-away briskness of the developing narrative line.

Point of View. The ostensibly authoritative, straightforward first-person narrative voice soon reveals itself as problematic. We suspect the narrator is paranoid and doubtless unreliable: as often in stories of the fantastic we cannot tell if the scene where the dead old woman crawls towards him is being presented to us as "authentically" supernatural or as a by-product of his disordered imagination (the parallel with *The Queen of Spades* is close). Particularly disruptive of an ordered point of view are the two third-person episodes that were mentioned above: the "playlet" with the little lady and the view of Sakerdon Mikhailovich, after the narrator has left, sitting on the floor with this hands behind his back "and they could not be seen" (by whom?!). The "coda" consisting of the final sentence seems to imply a new first-person viewpoint, extrinsic to the rest of the tale.

Plot and Fable. For O'Toole these are to be taken to designate respectively the causal and the temporal relations within the story. As far as "plot" in this sense is concerned, *The Old Woman* seems a well-plotted tale, like the detective thrillers or newspaper report to which the narrator compares his plan of action. Yet causality is curiously weak or somehow unfocused: the plot episodes often seem disconnected, the conversations not quite coherent. There are "false leads" when plot events are left hanging in the air, unresolved: for example when the narrator, returning home, is informed by his neighbor Mariia Vasil'evna that an "old man"(!) has been asking for him but cannot provide further information. The parallel with the atmosphere of Kafka's stories is remarkable: here too an ostensibly realistic plot reveals itself as closer to dream-logic or even insane logic than to common sense. The reader has no choice but to be plunged into the narrator's nightmarish world: the action is launched *in medias res* with no "preparation." The ending too turns out to be a "pseudo-resolution," leaving everything uncertain.

As for "fable" in O'Toole's sense, we note a remarkable fixation on time of day, on telling the time and temporal imagery, from the story's memorable opening (even, maybe, its title, pinpointing "age") onwards. We veer between obsessive temporal exactitude and vagueness (the narrator loses all track of time after the old woman first appears in his room, and is unaware even whether it is daytime or a "white night"). The narrator (a writer without regular working hours) is dislocated from the ordinary social ordering of life: for him and for us as his readers "time is out of joint" (Chances). The fable sets up a tension between temporality and eternity, between the narrator's first utterance, the question "What's the time?" (whence, it may be thought, the whole action flows) and his last: "...for ever and ever, amen" (literally "now and forever and unto ages of ages"). But this final image of eternity is undermined by the down-to-earth coda: "At this I *temporarily* [my emphasis] end my manuscript..." This unresolved tussle between the temporal and the eternal is a counterpoint to the narrator's consuming concern with death and immortality.

Character. How do we "read" the personality of the narrator – with whom we have the involuntarily close, teasing relationship that comes (as in *Notes from Underground*) from not being informed of his name? Are we being presented with the satirical portrait of an idle, lying, sadistic, cowardly, schizophrenic or paranoid self-deceiver – as full of *mauvaise foi* as Kafka's Josef K. or any Sartrean villain; or by contrast with a truth-seeker who "merely feigns stupidity" (Roberts); with the oppressed victim of the ever-tightening noose of Stalinism; the "little man" at the mercy of huge impersonal forces; an Everyman on a blind spiritual quest or undergoing an almost Christ-like passion? Answers do not come easily, and may depend on the sort of interpretative strategy we favor. The other major character has by contrast a first name full of meaning – the strange *Sakerdon* (presumably from Latin *sacerdos,* priest, cognate with "sacred"). He is just as elusive as the narrator. Do we read him as the latter's *alter ego?* If we are to assume a connection with the real-life Nikolai Makarovich Oleinikov – mathematician, writer and biting wit, whom I believe Kharms encoded into many of his works[11] – that adds another and perhaps irrecoverable layer of extrinsically-derived meaning to Sakerdon's enigmatic character. The "little lady" scarcely has character – she is rather a two-dimensional parody-figure, as her diction indicates – but insofar as the tale is modeled on *Crime and Punishment* she could represent a "mock-Sonia." The one normal and good-hearted character in the entire story, ironically enough, is the narrator's neighbor Matvei Filippovich, a straightforward Soviet workman who lends the narrator thirty rubles without demur. As for the old woman, insofar as she reveals herself at all, she seems more of an "anti-character," a malign force of nature or fate. She issues commands to the narrator in the intimate second person singular (he responds in the polite plural).

Setting. This is of continual significance, and I have already mentioned several relevant aspects of it: the frequent liminal locations in which the narrator finds himself (see above, Chronotopes), the alternation between "private" (closed) and "public" (open) locations and the unwelcome intrusions of each into the other. The rather squalid Leningrad setting (though the city itself is not mentioned by name) carries its own associated baggage. But not the whole story unrolls in the great spectral city: the last few paragraphs transfer its setting to the country. Iurii Lotman has referred to the "universal theme of opposition of 'home' to 'forest' – a place of temporary death." It can hardly be accidental that the setting for the last curious rite that the tale describes takes place behind a screen of juniper-bushes, which have had connotations of deathliness for writers from Boratynsky to Zabolotsky.

The six structural levels that O'Toole distinguishes should be supplemented by an examination of the grammar, linguistic register and narrative manner that underpin them and can themselves have structural significance. They are characterized by remarkable simplicity (if not always lucidity). Often the sentence structure is as uncomplicated as anything in Zoshchenko – indeed one may feel the influence of Zoshchenko (another Leningrad writer, after all!) not only in narrative manner, but in setting and subject-matter: "the same trivial incidents filling the little man's horizon...a naive, helpless and very self-conscious, even paranoid anti-hero, browbeaten by women and at the mercy of bystanders, neighbors, officialdom, holding to a tenuous reality through the most ordinary everyday objects" as O'Toole aptly puts it in his contribution to the collective analysis. But there are none of the colorful dialect, slang and heightened *skaz* effects that enrich much of Zoshchenko, save for Mariia Vasilevna's lisping. O'Toole goes on to point out that it seems a characteristic of absurd writers that "their language is more or less uncolored (or deliberately colorless?) literary language. The effect of this is, curiously, to heighten the surrealism and incipient threat which would be diluted or deflected by dialect or gothic stylization." One of the chief grammatical characteristics of *The Old Woman* is the paucity of modal forms and constructions – something that heightens the "no-nonsense," straightforward tone of the narrative register. Such modality as we find is on the everyday level of (e.g.) the narrator's self-questionings and wishes: "Yes, could it really be doubted?... this could have been foreseen!"; "Good God! Surely miracles can happen?" (*Neuzheli chudes ne byvaet?*) The narrative adopts a relaxed, modern, conversational register of language, avoiding complex constructions or out-of-the-ordinary vocabulary. In one episode, the conversation (partly in "playlet" form) with the "little lady," this is taken to a ridiculous extreme: in Aizlewood's words "this is uncomfortably – and funnily – close to a textbook situational dialogue"; he notes a "repetitive quality bordering on the mechanical," particularly in the verbs of communication ("I said," "I ask" etc.). This "mechanical" quality of the story-telling not only sets its surrealistic elements in relief, but helps to create a constant undercurrent of black humor that not all commentators seem to have taken into consideration.[12] One further grammatical characteristic was noted during the collective analysis (by Polukhina): the considerable importance of negative forms, from the clock with no hands, through the narrator's (and Sakerdon's) non-writing, his inability to cover the corpse with a newspaper, and many further significant textual details until the final self-concealment in a place where no-one could see him. We are reminded of the notorious "negative descriptions" in the brief "incidence" known as "The Red-Haired Man."

The most striking grammatical characteristic of the narrative manner, however, is one that was mentioned in the introductory section of this article: the frequent shifts in the tense of the main narrative – at least eighteen – between present and past (usually but not always perfective). The story both begins and ends in the present, but more of the total text is in the past, including nearly all of the long middle section in Sakerdon

Mikhailovich's room. We know of course that the narrative (or "historical") present tense "is more alive in Russian than it is in English," as in the oral narrative of many languages (O'Toole), but the past/present switches in parts of *The Old Woman* take on the air of a nervous tic. It is not obvious why these switches happen at a given moment, so they seem to instill a surreptitious sense of unease into the narrative. But it is clear that the present tense can lend a particular immediacy to several short passages of free indirect discourse (thoughts and feelings presented in the narrator's language as if narrative events, thus: "The day had begun so well, and now here's the first mishap already"; "Burst into the room and shatter the old woman's skull. That's what needs to be done!"). The past-present switches, as indeed the features we have already mentioned at each of the six main levels of analysis, serve to give *The Old Woman* a particularly unsettled, unfinalized, ambiguous quality, that the narrator's rather desperate attempt to produce an "unmarked," styleless register of language cannot hope to allay: serves in fact to emphasize.

As we try to draw disparate threads together and come to whatever conclusions we can in our analysis of *The Old Woman*, it remains to make a few observations about the story's symbolic system and generic qualities. There are many persons, things and events that can with greater or lesser plausibility be read symbolically (according to one's preferred interpretative strategy) in the tale, but it is particularly worth mentioning the presence of several characteristic "mythologemes," furnishings of the private writing-world of Kharms and such close colleagues as Vvedensky, Zabolotsky and Oleinikov, and thus indefinable or multivalent when treated as symbols. Such are *clock/clockface, cupboard, trunk/suitcase, insect* (and various individual species of insect), even *old woman*. One day, perhaps, a concordance to these writers may put us in the position of assessing the semantic weight such mythologemes carry in various contexts. Here I shall draw attention to three instances where awareness of this world of mythologemes helps to cast light on *The Old Woman*.

1. Clock and clockface are central images in the remarkable poem *Time* (*Vremia*, 1933) by Zabolotsky, which as I have shown elsewhere[13] is a lightly-encoded, if no doubt fantastical, reflection of the meetings and feasts held by members of the "Club of Semi-Literate Scholars" (*Klub malogramotnykh uchenykh*) in the early 1930s – in this case four of

them, the host Lipavsky, Oleinikov, Kharms and Zabolotsky himself. The poem (which among its furniture features a coffin-like trunk) ends dramatically when the character Lev, representing Kharms, metaphorically "destroys Time" by shooting the clockface (thus burying "human reason," as the poet concludes).

2. The trunk or suitcase as a liminal mythologeme representing a link between life and death appears in a remarkable Kharms's "Incidence" (the ninth), in which a man shuts himself into a trunk to carry out an experiment as to which side will win (as he suffocates) in the battle between life and death. His conclusion – zhizn' pobedila smert' – is (as Kharms later pointed out) fully ambiguous, and untranslatable, since it can mean equally "life has conquered death" or its opposite.

3. Insects appear repeatedly in the works of the writers mentioned (particularly the poems of Oleinikov). They are ambiguous: both miniature illustrations of Nature's miraculous handiwork and a grubby threat to civilization, both a metaphor for human soullessness and pitiful victims of human destructiveness (there are Dostoevskian motifs here). An insect in the form of a green caterpillar plays a significant part in The Old Woman: at the denouement behind the juniper bushes at Lisii Nos the narrator kneels down and touches it, whereupon it twists this way and that. Maybe the point of this is that the browbeaten narrator, plaything of malign fate, can actually affect the life of another being. We may also have here a comic intertextual echo of Lewis Carroll, whom Kharms revered – the earlier, rather arbitrary, appearance of a croquet-mallet may derive from the same source (as Burnett pointed out at the collective analysis). But it would seem likely that in the tense circumstances of the last page of the story Kharms was calling upon weightier symbolic meanings: those associated with the earthbound caterpillar's metamorphosis into a butterfly, ancient symbol of the soul and of immortality – the goal of the narrator's quest. Maybe it is not irrelevant too that the butterfly can symbolize the Great Goddess, and a white butterfly the spirit of the dead.[14] But touching the caterpillar is even more fundamentally, perhaps, a signal of the narrator's renewed contact with Nature, in opposition to the unnaturalness and topsy-turveydom of city life, a humble gesture of self-abasement.

There are also less specific Kharmsian mythologemes to be identified in the tale, for example the breaking loose and independent existence of parts of the body (here, particularly exemplified by the old woman's false teeth): clearly a Gogolian motif. Hands too play strange roles in the story: Sakerdon places his so that no-one can see them, while in the narrator's dream his arms are turned into the knife and fork (for Polukhina, hinting at hammer and sickle!) that he had earlier witnessed, and been repelled by, as clock hands. There is much flaccidity, decay and bodily dissolution in the story (Tronenko made the comparison with Dali, for whom "there is no such thing as the confident body"), leading up to the nightmare-epiphany of the narrator's attack of diarrhoea on the suburban train, no doubt symbolically "evacuating" the old woman from his life. But perhaps the most pervasive element in the symbolic structuring of *The Old Woman* is the oppositional doublet seeing/non-seeing: from the story's opening scene ("'Look' says the old woman to me. I look and see...I go on, not looking round") to its end point ("I look round. No one sees me."), via the sinister observation that "some things need to be done alone, without witnesses" and the world-weary "this could have been foreseen." The relation between "seeing and believing" is an important subtext, while (as Aizlewood has pointed out) the opposition "videnie-nevidenie" is a central element of Druskin's thought.

Beyond specific mythologemes and symbols, however, it would seem there is a mythic patterning to the whole story, into which (at least to my mind) its evident Christian aspects are subsumed. Modernist and urbanist as he may have been, Kharms was by no means unresponsive to elements of Russian folk-belief – a belief system too archaic to be ruled by such concepts as guilt or conscience, faith or redemption. The hubristic narrator ignores warning omens – the old woman's shouted remark, the shadow settling on his face, the passing crow, the man with the mechanical leg – and encounters his nemesis not just in literary impotence (maybe what he wrote was all that it was necessary to write) but in the most appropriate of retributions for querying the nature of time, the unsought burden of the "unquiet dead." Corpses become for him (he cannot but generalize his experience!), in a memorable, flesh-creeping neologism, "*bespokoiniki,*" "the restless [dead] ones." Even the motifs of the "biting corpse" and "corpse poisoning" have folk analogues.[15] The "auto-destruction" of the old woman brings her into the category of the most feared of the restless dead to folk-belief – the suicides. As Brandist aptly puts it, "with her entry the sealed-off nature of the everyday world is breached and the fantastic, shadowy realms are made coterminous with the mundane." The strange little rite of self-abasement the old woman makes the narrator perform when she irrupts into his personal space has its necessary counterpart at the end of the tale when the narrator, again on his knees, furtively (among the trees that are the equivalent in the folk-belief to a church) utters the blessing that may be the only way to consign the corpse to oblivion. Several commentators have described this blessing as a prayer, but that carries wrong implications: it seems rather to be a truncated funeral rite, intended to lay the ghost of the "restless one" who wrought such mayhem on the narrator's life and integrity.

How, finally, can we categorize *The Old Woman* as a story? Our answer may have considerable bearing on what we perceive as its meaningfulness. The various Bakhtinian approaches are very helpful here, I believe. That dialogue is a keystone of the tale's structure is unmistakably suggested by the author in its epigraph: "And between them the following conversation takes place." Of course the tale contains many conversations, but three stand out: first the curious, almost mechanical dialogue with the "little lady," where with hilarious inappropriateness (just after they have agreed to have a vodka-drinking session together) the narrator asks if she believes in God; then the long conversation with Sakerdon Mikhailovich, which comes round to the question of belief in immortality; then the bizarre, alarming "conversation" the split-minded narrator holds with his own thoughts, raising the vision of the "unquiet dead." Each conversation, trivial at its outset, moves on in its own odd way to "ultimate things." But perhaps there is "dialogism" on a larger scale at work in *The Old Woman*: the "conversation" in which, as Aizlewood has noted, Kharms's later work continually engages with his philosopher-friend Druskin; also the dialogue with the ghosts of the earlier writers with whose intertextual echoes the story so resounds (perhaps some of Kharms's contemporaries – Zoshchenko, Oleinikov, Zabolotsky – are to be heard too). Maybe this is the best way to regard the "insurgent narratives" that Carrick sees essentially as tokens of human unfreedom, changing the narrator from being author of his narrative to a mere character within it.

Bakhtin understood playful yet philosophically-imbued dialogue as Socratic in origin, and the late-antique and subsequent successor-genre to "socratic dialogue" as being the Menippic Satire or "menippea." Indeed he traces the menippic tradition, through numerous metamorphoses, as an uncanonical and often subversive current of European literature (via Rabelais, Swift, Diderot etc.) to Dostoevsky. He relates its spirit to the "carnivalism" mentioned earlier. To see how closely *The Old Woman* fits the menippic type, we need only mention the fourteen characteristics of the menippea as Bakhtin lists them in *Problems of Dostoyevsky's Poetics* (*Problemy poetiki Dostoevskogo*).[16] In summary, they are:

1. The comic element (often "reduced laughter");

2. Freedom of invention (in plot and in philosophy);

3. Extraordinary situations to provoke and test an idea;

4. "Underworld" naturalism (often with obscene or blasphemous elements);

5. Concern with "ultimate questions";

6. Liminal (threshold) situations;

7. Experimental fantasticality;

8. Interest in abnormal states (including "doubles");

9. Scandalous scenes and incongruities;

10. Odd, oxymoronic combinations;

11. Social-utopian elements (often in dreams or journeys);

12. Use of inserted genres or narratives;

13. Variety of tone or style;

14. Topical or publicistic qualities (*Diary of a Writer*).

It will be seen at once that it is not only a matter of some general tendency towards the menippea, but that every one of these points is characteristic, often centrally characteristic, of *The Old Woman*. Probably the least-obviously applicable are the "social-utopian elements," but they are implicitly supplied by the Soviet setting itself. Several of the major features of the "carnivalism" that Bakhtin associates with menippea are equally apparent: the concern with death and rebirth, with the lower bodily functions, with parody, with human positions as roles fated to be played out, and Roberts has ingeniously read the inspiration and subsequent deflation of the writer-narrator in terms of carnivalistic "crowning and uncrowning," while Brandist has supplemented this by pointing out the role of carnivalistic "holy-foolishness" in the late work of Kharms generally. The recurrent plot-element of "hungering-feasting-excreting" has a Rabelaisian, hence Bakhtinian ring to it. It is also worth mentioning that a further major Bakhtinian concept, that of "chronotope" (the time/space matrix within which a story or some part of it unfolds), on which a brief comment was made earlier, may also assist our understanding of the meaningful structure of the tale. The constricted and private spaces (always vulnerable to unwelcome invasion from without) in which most of the tale is set give way at the end to a spatial opening out, where the narrator can make symbolic contact with both lowest things (earth and caterpillar) and highest (heaven). Temporally, the story moves through a world of extremes; from the finicky clock-watching of the everyday world, through the disordered limbo of the narrator's "working" life, the bewitched, disorientating timelessness induced by the old woman's irruption onto the scene, to apprehensions of immortality and at last eternity. The overall setting is Leningrad/ Petersburg at the season of the "white nights," a supremely carnivalistic chronotope, when night becomes day, when (to quote Gogol) "all is deceit, all is not that which it seems."

The Old Woman, then, fits remarkably well into the category of menippea (so well that I wonder if Bakhtin – who lived in Leningrad in the years preceding his exile in 1929 – ever discussed his concepts with Kharms: they probably met, but we cannot be sure[17]). To say this is to say much: in particular, that a central theme of the story will be the quest for, and testing of, a truth, through exceptional and apparently incongruous or shocking means. But it is not to say everything. We cannot, for example, even be sure what truth or truths might be here subject to such a test: immortality; the nature of belief; divine (or diabolical) power; our position in the cosmic (or social) scheme of things; fate versus free will; the limits of sanity; more mundanely, but no less urgently for Kharms, the status and authority of the writer (as Roberts argues)? To quote Carrick, "the principal riddle seems to be to know what riddle could possibly require so many disparate clues to solve."[18]

It must also be understood that as a generic category the menippea does not exclude other genres. Like all Bakhtin's preferred discourse, it is by its nature unfinalized. A menippea might well also stand as an allegory, a comic spoof, a pastiche, a horror story, a fantasy, an autobiography or whatever. The reader alone can decide what mix of generic elements is present and what additional interpretative weight they can ultimately carry. To my mind, *The Old Woman* belongs also to the specifically Kharmsian genre of "*sluchai*," "incidence" or "happen-ing." Like the components of the cycle of "incidences" he was compiling at the same period, *The Old Woman* is a "what if...?" story (Cornwell's phrase), a testing of the categories of eventuality and causality. He also tests the "lower limits" of fictionality – the extent to which circumstantial and explanatory trappings can be stripped away from the minimal units of narrative. Viewed in this light, the whole of *The Old Woman* might emerge as an ironic view of the "creative laboratory" within which the narrator fashions his four-word tale, the ultimate example of Kharmsian minimalism.

ENDNOTES

[1] Of the many Kharms publications, the selection that best gives an all-round view of his work is *Polet v nebesa*, ed. by A. Aleksandrov (Leningrad, 1988); it contains both "*Sluchai*" and "*Starukha*." The best translation into English of his selected prose is *Incidences,* ed. and trans. N. Cornwell (London: Serpent's Tale, 1993). An up-to-date edition of *Starukha* with annotations by R. Aizlewood has been published by Bristol Classical Press, 1995.

Several studies of Kharms with relevance to *Starukha*, of both Russian and non-Russian origin, have been published in *Daniil Kharms and the Poetics of the Absurd: Essays and Materials*, ed. N. Cornwell (London: Macmillan, 1991) — henceforth referred to as "Cornwell ed."

Publications on Kharms to which particular reference is made in this article:

R. Aizlewood, "Guilt without Guilt," *Scottish Slavonic Review* 14 (1990): 199-217.

A. Anemone, "The Anti-World of Daniil Kharms," in Cornwell *ed.*, 71-96.

N. Carrick, "A Familiar Story; Insurgent Narratives and Generic Refugees in "Daniil Kharms's *The Old Woman*," *Modern Language Review* 3 (1995): 707-21.

S. Cassedy, "Daniil Kharms's Parody of Dostoevskii: Anti-Tragedy as Political Comment," *Canadian-American Slavic Studies* 18 (1984): 268-84.

E. Chances, "Daniil Charms' *Old Woman* Climbs her Family Tree," *Russian Literature* 17 (1985): 353-66.

Ia. Druskin, "On Daniil Kharms," in Cornwell *ed.*, 22-31.

A. Gerasimova, "OBERIU (Problema smeshnogo)," *Voprocy literatury* 4 (1988): 48-79.

R. Giaquinta, "Elements of the Fantastic in Daniil Kharms's *Starukha*," in Cornwell *ed.*, 132-48.

L. Grubisic, "Laughing at the Void: a Structural Analysis of Kharms's *The Old Woman*," in *Oregon Studies in Chinese and Russian Literature*, ed. by A. Leong (1990), 221-36.

R. Milner-Gulland, "Beyond the Turning-Point," in Cornwell *ed.*, 243-67.

A. S. Nakhimovsky, *Laughter in the Void* (Vienna, 1982).

G. Roberts, "A Matter of (Dis)course. Metafiction in the Works of Daniil Kharms," in *New Directions in Soviet Literature*, ed. S. D. Graham (London: Macmillan, 1992), 138-63.

[2] Among those who were present at the collective analysis and made comments that have been reflected or quoted in this article were Robin

Aizlewood, Joe Andrew, Leon Burnett, Neil Cornwell, Andre van Holk, Valentina Polukhina, Robert Reid, Gerry Smith, Sasha Smith, Natalia Tronenko: my apologies if I have left anyone out. Some of these kindly gave me comments in writing, as did Craig Brandist, Gerard McBurney, Michael O'Toole and Graham Roberts, who could not be present. (Aizlewood's, Brandist's and Roberts's contributions were substantial extracts from forthcoming publications.) I am also grateful to my Sussex final-year students of modern Russian literature (Autumn 1995) for fruitful discussions.

[3] L. Michael O'Toole, *Structure, Style and Interpretation in the Russian Short Story* (New Haven: Yale University Press, 1982).

[4] My informant on the manuscript is Gerard McBurney, who saw it in 1994. The ms, and hence the story, seems to be a "finished" product: it is written in a tiny hand (with corrections in colored inks) on only six sides of paper. McBurney distinguished the obliterated text of the Lord's Prayer before the blessing on the last page, of which at least four versions were made. Printed editions replace the two-and-a-half ruled lines of the manuscript with a row of dots.

[5] Kharms could also "intertextualize" his own work: there is a poem of 1933 called *Starukha*, whose last two lines read: "*Bezhi, starukha, v roshchu sosen/ I v zemliu lbom lozhis' i tlei*" ("Run, old woman, to the grove of fir-trees/ And push your forehead into the earth and decay"). See the D. Kharms, *Sobranie sochinenii*, ed. M. Meilakh and V. Erl (Bremen: K-Presse, 1978), 19.

[6] Kharms's pose of hostility towards children should not be taken as his normal real-life attitude: Nikita Zabolotsky (a child in the 1930s, when Kharms often visited the Zabolotsky household) affirms his genuine warmth.

[7] D. Shepherd, *Beyond Metafiction: Self-Consciousness in Soviet Literature* (Oxford: Oxford University Press, 1992).

[8] A. Anemone's article in Cornwell *ed.* (see note 1), though beginning as a discussion of "the absurd," soon takes a very different turn.

[9] L. M. O'Toole, *Structure, Style and Interpretation*, 3.

[10] Ibid., 5.

[11] R. Milner-Gulland, "Beyond the Turning-Point," in Cornwell *ed.*, 252-4. See also R. Milner-Gulland, "Grandsons of Kozma Prutkov," in *Russian and Slavic Literatures*, ed. R. Freeborn et al. (Columbus, OH.: Slavica, 1976), 313-27.

[12] But see Gerasimova, "OBERIU (Problema smeshnogo)," though not specifically on this story.

[13] R. Milner-Gulland, "Zabolotsky's *Vremya*," in *Essays in Poetics* 1 (1981): 86-98.

[14] Brandist however sees more sinister connotations — with a serpent, or a worm at the heart of an apple. In complete contrast, Jaccard (in the course

of some interesting reflections on Kharms's concept of the "sublime" and the role of "miracle" (*chudo*) within it) rather surprisingly equates the caterpillar with God: "Here is the miracle awaited since the very beginning of the tale: mankind is created in the image and likeness of God, whereas God appears in this instance only as a caterpillar, twisting about on the earth in expectation of redemption (maybe indeed only in the form of a butterfly!)". Zh. F. Zhakhar, "*Vozvyshennoe v tvorchestve Daniilla Kharmsa*," in *Sbornik materialov*, ed. V. Sashin (*Kharmsizdat/Arsis*: St. Petersburg, 1995), 16. (my translation). See also J. C. Cooper, *Illustrated Encyclopedia of Traditional Symbols* (London, 1978), 27-8.

[15] L. Ivanits, "Suicide and Folk Belief in *Crime and Punishment*," in *The Golden Age of Russian Literature and Thought*, ed. D. Offord (New York: St Martins Press, 1992),140.

[16] M. Bakhtin, *Problems of Dostoyevsky's Poetics*, trans. R.W. Rotsel (Ardis, 1973), Ch. 4, particularly 93-7.

[17] M. Holquist's "Bakhtin," in *Handbook of Russian Literature*, ed. V. Terras (New Haven: Yale, University Press, 1985), 34, implies they knew each other personally. Note however that the discussion of menippea was included only in the second, expanded edition (1963) of *Problems of Dostoevsky's Poetics*.

[18] N. Carrick, "A Familiar Story."

X

Testimony as Art: Varlam Shalamov's "Condensed Milk."

LEONA TOKER

In a 1973 discussion of the artistic accomplishments of Solzhenitsyn's Gulag fiction, Victor Erlich echoed Irving Howe's remark on problems with registering a "purely" literary response to material that presents "the belated revelation of a long-denied nightmare."[1] At issue was "respect for the autonomy of literary criteria" and a recognition that it was impossible to separate the literary analysis of ethically-oriented fiction from its moral-philosophical consideration. Though Erlich concludes that it would be wrong to inhibit one's literary response and to underestimate the heroic writer's actual effectiveness "out of an excessive distrust of our own motives," the examination of one's motives is as relevant as that of the structural and stylistic "effectiveness" of the works discussed.[2] Studies of the literature of atrocities must involve ethical self-reflexivity, though not necessarily explicit breast-beating. This is particularly true in the case of the literary critical examination of documentary prose – memoirs, autobiographies, and related genres.

The story that I shall discuss here can be *used* as historical evidence and as testimony for the history of ideas. Yet it can also be read for its own sake – that is, for the sake of its artistic achievement.[3] The tools used for the analysis of this achievement must, however, take into account the multifunctionality of concentration-camp literature, in particular its ethical orientation.

The theory of works of art as multifunction objects has been developed by Jan Mukarovský (of the Prague Linguistic circle); one of its central points is that the different functions, such as the communicative and the aesthetic, become marked at different stages of reception.[4] While the Gulag still existed and consciousness-raising testimonies about it sought to enlist public opinion in the struggle against forced-labor camps, a sustained literary analysis of such testimonies would, indeed, have appeared callous. Now the situation has changed: the Gulag is no longer news, and the whole complex of issues it raised is now the concern of scholars rather than journalists. After the communicative contents of the memoirs of a particular atrocity have been studied by historians, economists, and sociologists, their artistic merit can become the subject of a literary scholar's uninhibited discourse.

The features that underlie the aesthetic and the consciousness-raising functions of Gulag testimonies are closely interrelated: one cannot do full justice to the communicative significance of documentary prose works without proper attention to their formal traits – nor can one account for the relative artistic merit of these works without taking into account their ethical stance. It has by now become recognized that the form of a literary work has an ethical aspect,[5] as well as that the content of ethically oriented writings may be intrinsically "implicated in their literary structure."[6] The ethics of literary form is to a large extent a matter of the textual features (such as focalization, ironies, collocations and temporal deployment of motifs, intertextual links, etc.) that create the conditions for a certain kind of reader response; and such etiology of reader response is the province of intradisciplinary literary-critical analysis to be performed against an interdisciplinary data background.

The specific features of reader response to survivor memoirs are associated with the specific bi-functionality of documentary prose. One usually turns to such memoirs in quest of facts, of knowledge in "gift-wrapping,"[7] knowledge as "amenity,"[8] even if this knowledge is of the kind that generally we would rather do without. If we are then struck by the literary merit of these texts, we still hesitate whether to regard them as art or just as well written testimony. This hesitation is, to some extent, a variant of the "suspicion of fraudulence" that is an integral aesthetic effect of modernist art: is the artist pulling our leg? is this, anyway, art at all?[9] Yet in the case of the literature of atrocities, the terms of such hesitation also involve an anxiety of the kind that stimulated Adorno's provocative remark that it may be barbarous to write poetry after Auschwitz[10]: perhaps aesthetic experience – or any positive reference to it – is inadmissible in the case of accounts of terrible human suffering. However this may be, an initial downplaying of the aesthetic function of such works under the weight of the communicative function is a necessary part of reader response.

Reading works of documentary prose as transparent vehicles for factual evidence amounts to treating them as interchangeable means to an end. The end may be a sociological or historical study, such as, for instance, *Forced Labor in Soviet Russia* by Dallin and Nikolaevsky, or the invaluable books by Robert Conquest. I would not cast aspersions on such a *use* of primary materials. On the contrary, the need for the *use* of survivor memoirs as primary materials has never been as evident as in the days when many KGB archival materials have become available: one may critique the factual reliability of the limited and subjective first-hand reports and wax enthusiastic over archival statistics but only so long as one bears in mind that he human realities behind the archival documents are incomprehensible without survivors' narratives – or rather much less comprehensible than camp realities usually remain for those who have not experienced them at first hand.

Another end for which survivor memoirs can be legitimately *used* is exemplified by Terence Des Pres' *The Survivor* (1976), a study of the structure of survival in the camps in those limited cases when survival depended on the prisoner's own strategies and powers of endurance and was not blankly canceled by external circumstances. Twenty years after Des Pres, Tzvetan Todorov's *Facing the Extreme* reexamined concentration camp testimonies in an attempt to draw ethical conclusions, refine distinctions, evaluate responses, and qualify statements on guilt and suffering. Both these books were obviously written in response to the authors' urgent ethical need to reach some level of the understanding of the world in which genocide and concentration camps (Nazi and Soviet) were possible. Both the authors were self-conscious – Des Pres about the para-religious language of his discourse, Todorov about the intuitive character of his distinctions as well as about memories of his young days under a totalitarian regime. Though written by literary scholars, these two books belong not to the field of literary study but to that of the history of ideas.

Towards the very end of *Facing the Extreme*, Todorov does, however, offer us three sections of ethically oriented literary criticism – he discusses Primo Levi's heritage, Claude Lanzmann's film *Shoah*, and Gitta Sereni's *Into That Darkness*. He repeatedly emphasizes that these are not merely documentary works but also works of art. The same statement could, in fact, have been made about a number of other materials to which Todorov turns for testimony, prominently including the work of Varlam Shalamov, author of *Kolyma Tales*.[11] In fact, my case about the bifunctionality of documentary prose is to some extent weakened by my choice of example. It would have been a greater challenge to discuss the bifunctionality of works written by people who were not such conscious artists as this writer, whose stature in Russian is now almost canonical – even though his literary achievement has still not received the recognition it deserves.

Shalamov survived almost two decades of the Gulag. On his release, he explored his camp experience mainly in the genre of the short story. Some of his stories are emphatically autobiographical; others are quite obviously fictional; still others occupy a borderline area between the two. Powerful documentary prose often contains areas of hesitation between what can and what cannot be subject to the procedures of public verification. There is no way of knowing whether Shalamov's "Condensed Milk" is strictly factual, autobiographical, or whether it presents a fictionalized individual version of what was a typical war-time situation in Soviet hard-labor camps. As a result, the reader has to treat its material as historical testimony but also ask of it the kind of questions that are usually asked of representational art. This two-fold attitude of the reader reflects the double function of the story as a document and as a literary text.

In "Condensed Milk" a stool pigeon, a geologist by the name of Shestakov, who holds a soft job in a camp office instead of working in the gold mines like most prisoners, organizes a group escape attempt and then leads the fugitives into a prearranged ambush: some of the fugitives are killed, the others are captured and given new prison sentences. The first-person protagonist, who first pretends to accept but ultimately declines the offer to take part in the escape attempt, eventually meets Shestakov in another camp: the agent-provocateur has given state evidence and remained unharmed.

The presence of what is obviously American lend-lease tins of meat and fruit preserves in the camp store (which the protagonist has neither the means nor the permission to use) – sets the story in the early forties, when the Soviet Union was at war with Nazi Germany. At the time, police and camp-guard officers were liable to be sent to the front lines; therefore, in order to prove that they were badly needed in their safe berths in the rear, some of them arranged frame-ups that led to new charges against camp inmates and newly extended sentences. As a work of historical testimony, the story presents the mechanics of one provocation of this kind.

Yet it can also be read as testimony to the history of ideas. Indeed, Shalamov's blanket condemnation of the quality of moral life in the camps contrasts with Solzhenitsyn's leaning towards the illusion that whatever does not kill you can, in principle, ennoble you. Shalamov belonged to those thinkers who rejected the redemptive view of suffering. In tune with the Aristotelian belief that a person's character deteriorates as a result of adversity, Shalamov repeatedly states that camp experience generally changed people for the worse.[12] Left at large, Shestakov might have remained an inoffensive geologist and have never turned into a provocateur; and the protagonist might have remained an active and caring intellectual instead of dwindling into a half-extinguished soul incapable of selfless exertion.

Yet Shalamov preempts our reducing the story to these types of exemplification. The ironies of his narrative qualify categorical positions and call into question the sweeping diagnoses of what is "good" or "bad." One of the most salient techniques that pull the interpretive ground from under our feet is his characteristic ambivalent punchline. Shalamov usually began composing his stories with the first and the last sentences.[13] In "Condensed Milk" these sentences shift the focus from the villainy of the outer circumstance to the inner moral predicament of the protagonist: it is the protagonist, more even than Shestakov, who is put on the spot.

The protagonist (or rather what Gérard Genette would call the "focus" in contradistinction to its more reflective narrative "voice"[14]), a rank-and-file political prisoner, is the narrator's former self – for brevity I shall refer to him as "Shalamov." The fact that the "I" is never referred to by name leaves it unclear whether the story is representative or directly autobiographical. The first sentence indicates "Shalamov's" physical and mental condition: "Envy, like all our feelings, had been dulled and weakened by hunger" (80).[15] This is what Primo Levi referred to as "the prescribed hunger,"[16] the chronic calorie deficit that was an integral part of the camp authorities' *deliberate* policies. According to the specifically Gulagian reasoning, if a hungry man's rations are further cut for his failure to meet the production quotas, food becomes an incentive for making greater efforts at the work site – thus the Communist state contravened the Marxist analysis of slave labor as economically inefficient because of lack of incentive.[17] According to the insights shared also by the Nazis, chronic starvation produces exactly the kind of personality changes described in the story – all emotions are dulled, intellectual activity impeded, and the prisoner's ability to stand up to the authorities is practically canceled. In *Facing the Extreme* Todorov refuses to deal with the moral condition of people who have already crossed a certain threshold of suffering[18]; the greatness of Shalamov lies in his leading us beyond that threshold. The experience of people who have reached an advanced stage of dystrophy is different from anything familiar to healthy organisms; hence it can hardly be explained in a discursive manner. It is only the total artistic effect of the text, not the discursive comments and explanations, that can convey, at least in part, the quality of the moral predicament involved. The physical symptoms of this condition are the scurvy sores on "Shalamov's" legs: his body has already shed all its fats, and has started burning its protein. The brain has been affected as well. In the course of the story, trying to persuade the narrator to flee, Shestakov spouts the famous slogan of the Spanish communist leader Dolores Ibaruri:

> 'Better to die on your feet than live on your knees.' Shestakov pronounced that sentence with an air of pomp. 'Who said that?'
>
> It was a familiar sentence. I tried, but lacked the strength to remember who had said those words and when. All that smacked of books was forgotten. No one believed in books. (82)

The protagonist's failure to place the quotation known to every Soviet schoolchild is a symptom that his brain has already disembarrassed itself of what is the least necessary for everyday functioning, namely general memory. Yet the brain is still tenacious of the logistics of survival: the irreversible stage of hunger dementia is not far behind but has not yet set in. Thinking is a physical effort but not yet an impossible one: "It was hard to think. For the first time I could visualize the material nature of our psyche in all its palpability. It was painful to think, but necessary" (83). "Shalamov" understands not only that the escape attempt is a provocation but also that some benefit may be reaped from it: he intimates that he will join in if Shestakov first gets him some food to help muster his strength. They settle on condensed milk.

At night "Shalamov" dreams of the treat, for once raising his eyes, as it were, beyond the grim line of the mining-site horizon:

> I fell asleep and in my ragged hungry dreams I saw Shestakov's can of condensed milk, a monstrous can with a sky blue label. Enormous and blue as the night sky, the can had a thousand holes punched in it, and the milk seeped out and flowed in a stream as broad as the Milky Way. My hands easily reached the sky and I drank the thick, sweet, starry milk. (83)

Almost in tune with Bruno Bettelheim's theory that camp inmates tend to regress to infantilism, "Shalamov" is for a moment an infant of the universe, feeding on stellar milk, scooping it with his hands, like snow. Contrary to the traditional associations of night and blackness, the night sky is blue – probably because the action is set in the polar summer. Infantilism is associated with innocence, and stars with dreams, fate, and lofty aims, yet all such connotations are placed in an ironic perspective by the grotesque ("monstrous") blow-up of the blue-labeled can.

In the evening of the following day, having returned from work, "Shalamov" eats his two cans of condensed milk. Like his fellow prisoners, we watch him do so. We watch sympathetically, though he does not share the treat with anyone.

One must note here that the portions of text that are mainly accountable for the pleasure we derive from Gulag prose, whether disinterested aesthetic or vicarious pleasure, are usually those dealing not with suffering but with times of reprieve. It would be interesting to obtain the proportion of the amount of text that these works devote to downright evil, agony, and despair as opposed to recuperation, vitality, attempts to endow endurance with meaning, attempts also, in Nietzsche's terms, to turn "nauseous thoughts about the horror and absurdity of existence into notions with which one can live: . . . the *sublime* as the artistic taming of the horrible, and the comic as the artistic discharge of nausea of absurdity."[19] Unlike Holocaust testimonies, Gulag testimonies are rather densely punctuated with accounts of reprieves, as well as with comic plunges and with moments of the sublime. One of the most prominent features of this body of literature is its "pulsation" method: memoirists do not dwell on hardships uninterruptedly.[20] The literature of atrocities runs the risk of inuring its readers and blunting their emotional response, thus making them re-enact the very callousness its authors attack. To counter the risk of defeating their own purposes, some writers arrange their accounts of atrocities in an escalating sequence, yet the escalation usually ends by producing a cumulatively blunting effect.[21] Most Gulag authors avoid escalation; in their narratives the accounts of suffering alternate with those of reprieves or with informative or analytic passages that act as a foil to the new shocks to come.[22]

Writers have practically no resources for an adequate presentation of the interminable hours of hard, monotonous, and humiliating slave labor. It is therefore very difficult to imagine what it was like for a starving and sore organism to have to fell trees or load carts for over twelve hours a day, often in the rain, frost, or amid vicious gnats. Literature is more effective with shorter intensities. Thus, in an attempt to convey the sense of hard work at Buna, Primo Levi chooses the day when he has to carry heavy beams which make his whole body ache and which, when thrown off the shoulder, produce the "ephemeral and negative ecstasy of the cessation of pain."[23] Very little human communication can take place during hard work; which is one more reason why in Gulag literature much textual space is allotted to lucky respites, smoking or meal breaks, days off, and after hours. The action of "Condensed Milk" takes place entirely in after hours, and at its center is an all-too-condensed reprieve: "Shalamov's" staving off the oncoming hunger dementia with the help of a maximally prolonged yet still shortlived treat.

Having finished the milk, "Shalamov" turns the tables on Shestakov:

> 'You know,' I said, carefully licking the spoon, 'I changed my mind. Go without me.'
>
> Shestakov comprehended immediately and left without saying a word to me. (84)

"Shalamov" must then face the ethical significance of his conduct:

> It was, of course, a weak, worthless act of vengeance just like all my feelings. But what else could I do? Warn the others? I didn't know them. But they needed a warning. Shestakov managed to convince five people. They made their escape the next week; two were killed at Black Springs and the other three stood trial a month later. Shestakov's case was considered separately ["for legal considerations"].[24] He was taken away, and I met him again at a different mine six months later. He wasn't given any extra sentence for the escape attempt; the authorities played the game honestly with him even though they could have acted quite differently.

Then comes the punchline:

> He was working in the prospecting group, was shaved and well fed, and his checkered socks were in one piece. He didn't say hallo to me, [though why not? Two cans of condensed milk are not, after all, such a big deal...].[25] (84-85)

Though the bulk of the story has been working up to the near-orgasmic pleasure of eating condensed milk, the punchline reminds us, among other things, that two cans of condensed milk, blown out of proportion in "Shalamov's" dream, are, after all, not "such a big deal." In a sense, the story is here "untold," just as the benefit of the extra calories will soon be burnt up. The ironic deflation of the protagonist's minor victory in the struggle for survival places his concerns into perspective. Shalamov frequently pits his own authorial comments against the action of his stories – as if both to express his opinions and to refrain from imposing them upon the reader: his stories test both the attitudes that the reader brings to the text and the ideas that he himself is at times impelled to formulate.[26] The material and structure of the stories amend his authorial diagnoses of the human condition in the camps.

Let us return to reader response. On being told that after the event Shestakov would not greet Shalamov, the reader may think for a moment that Shestakov wishes to avoid the witness of his shameful act. Yet the punchline, "two cans of milk are, after all, not such a big deal," suggests that Shestakov may be free from shame or remorse; he may just be holding a grudge against "Shalamov" for double-crossing him. All feelings of guilt and all the need for self justification that come into play are exclusively "Shalamov's."[27] He has led on Shestakov and obtained some food on false pretense; whereas, as the penultimate paragraph tells us with a kind of melancholy sarcasm, the authorities have played fair in this case—they could have used Shestakov and then shot him to cover their tracks.[28]

The ultimate ironic belittling of the two cans of condensed milk reflects "Shalamov's" residual hankering for a *prima-facie* morality. He has, after all, broken a contract, thus making the will of the other serve the will of his own body. One may counter this by saying that Shestakov was about to use fraud to make "Shalamov's" will serve his own. In Schopenhauer's ethical system, Shalamov's breaking the contract would be considered legitimate self-defense[29]; yet in Kant's system his breaking of an implicit promise would be *prima-facie* immoral.

Obviously, however, the central *prima-facie* issue lies elsewhere. The real cause of "Shalamov's" remorse lies in his failure to prevent Shestakov's deception of five other people – though, all things considered, in his dystrophic condition he had no strength to seek them out. Gilbert Harman notes that, according to contemporary moral conventions, failing to help someone is less bad than deliberately hurting someone.[30] Yet such a convention is hardly acceptable to a person who had been educated in the spirit of supererogation cherished by generations of Russian intelligentsia. One may call to mind how in Dostoevsky's *Crime and Punishment* the conscientious doctor Zosimov, who never fails to come to the sick Raskolnikov and treat him *gratis*, is, from Razumikhin's point of view, a comfort-loving swine – perhaps because he would not give up his last shirt to a friend, only the last but one. The very fact that under the conditions of chronic starvation in the camp extra food is not shared with others suggests that the moral universe in question is radically different from the one created by traditional humanistic education, especially in its Russian versions. Sharing a spoonful of condensed milk would require as superhuman an effort as summoning the residue of a goner's energy to seek out and warn the prospective victims of provocation.

The fact that on meeting Shestakov in the epilogue of the story, "Shalamov" is not averse to greeting him presents a challenge to the reader's semiotic activity. We can infer that he does not expect this stool-pigeon to try to destroy him for having, though tacitly, blown his cover. Shalamov would probably have agreed with Solzhenitsyn that the line separating good and evil runs through each human soul[31]: most of his stories raise the question of the precise location of this line. Shestakov is taking good care of himself: this is made clear by his still possessing his checkered socks and not being reduced to wearing the common camp footrags. After the Black Springs adventure, his socks are still in one piece. The reference to the socks is a realistic part of camp semiotics, but it may also be a submerged allusion to *Crime and Punishment*: when Razumikhin finds Raskolnikov feverish and broke, he brings him a whole second-hand outfit – with the exception of socks. Socks, he says, he could not get. Which means that, up to his change into prison garb, Raskolnikov will be wearing a sock soaked in the murdered old woman's blood: he will be literally treading on blood. In his bid for self-preservation, Shestakov likewise walks over corpses, in checkered socks. Yet Shalamov feels that there is a line that even Shestakov is not prepared to cross: he will not deliberately seek to destroy another person on his own initiative. In ethical theory this is called the principle of the "double effect": it is bad enough to hurt someone while seeking other goals; but it is still worse to actually aim to injure the other.[32] Thus the acts of both Shestakov, the instrument of the victimizers, and "Shalamov," the victim, are describable in terms of bad and worse, or bad and less bad. The two have drawn the lines across their souls at different distances from the poles of total saintliness and total evil. And though the dialectical principle of the leap from quantity to quality is here quite obviously effective, the story questions the easy division of people into *us* and *them*.

Some further light on Shalamov's willingness to acknowledge Shestakov despite the latter's treason can be shed by the diametrically opposite circumstances described in the story "The Chess Set of Doctor Kuzmenko."[33] "Shalamov" and Dr. Kuzmenko, formerly a camp surgeon, are about to play chess using a uniquely elaborate set fashioned out of the prison-ration bread that has been chewed and brought to a moldable condition by the prisoners' saliva. This chess set, whose figures represent historical personages from the Times of Trouble, the period of political turmoil following the death of Tsar Boris Godunov, was made by the sculptor Kulagin. Two pieces are missing: the black Queen, now lying headless in Dr. Kuzmenko's drawer, and the white rook. Driven to the irreversibly lethal stage of dystrophy and dementia, Kulagin started eating his chessmen. It was too late – he should have started earlier; he died after having swallowed the rook and bitten off the head of the Queen. At this point the surgeon makes the following remark:

> 'I did not give the order to get the rook out of his stomach. It could have been done at the post-mortem. Also the head of the Queen…Therefore this game, this match, is two figures short. Your turn, maestro.'
>
> 'No,' I said. 'I somehow don't feel like it any more.' (458-59, my translation)

Why? Obviously not because of tactile squeamishness at the thought of the clay from which the chessmen have been made. "Shalamov's" nausea here is, I believe, caused by the sudden realization that there is a moral gulf between him and the intellectual with whom he has just been engaged in a highly meaningful conversation about historical documentation, unsolved mysteries, and prisoners' fates, the person whose attitudes had seemed to be so close to his own. As Bernard Williams notes in *Ethics and the Limits of Philosophy*, one may sense that a person is morally alien to oneself if that person is able to so much as *consider* certain things as *options*. Surgeons and pathologists are known to be hardened, and, after all, Dr. Kuzmenko did not commit the sacrilege of having the missing chess pieces extracted from the corpse, but the way he speaks about it suggests that he must have *considered the option* of doing so.[34] Which makes it impossible for "Shalamov" to play chess with him, at least not with this particular set. Here the discovery of the qualitative difference in the moral make-up of the two men on the same side of the barricade starkly contrasts with the reluctant discovery of the quantitative nature of the difference between "Shalamov" and the traitor Shestakov. Ethics and psychology are usually at odds with each other, but they converge in the complex attitudes conveyed by the endings of "The Chess Set of Dr. Kuzmenko" and "Condensed Milk."

In an article on Paul de Man, Geoffrey Hartman wrote that "it is impossible to see either fascism or anti Semitism as belonging simply to the history of ideas: they belong to the history of murder."[35] The same may be said of Soviet totalitarianism and the Gulag as its notable achievement. The important word in Hartman's remark is "simply": the atrocities belong both to the history of ideas and to the history of murder. But they are, in addition, associated with a third kind of history, namely the history of individual – or representative – attitudes. The main communicative function of documentary prose is to provide evidence for the history of crime. Its aesthetic function involves "staging" human experience,[36] and the aesthetic merit of such staging, in its complexity, is associated with the creation of intellectual constructs that test ideas – ideas that led to the crimes, or failed to prevent them, or were enlisted in the drawing of lessons, or in denying them. The rhetorical facet of the staging of experience involves calls for processing and shaping our attitudes to the material. Attitudes are units of spiritual life that blend psychological drives and moral-ideological commitments. They are one of the few aspects of life in concentration camps that can be understood and re-enacted by outsiders. They precede the formation of ideas, exceed ideas in complexity, and lag behind them in their degree of crystallization. They are therefore more amenable to adjustment, to perfectibility; they are more fluid, and more liable to fall between the conceptual frameworks of philosophical disciplines. Processing and transforming our own attitudes is what makes reading literature, including the best works of documentary prose, an ethical as well as an aesthetic experience, ethical in the narrower, evaluative meaning of the word.

— *The Hebrew University of Jerusalem*

ENDNOTES

[1] Irving Howe, "Predicaments of Soviet Writing," *The New Republic* (May 11, 1963): 19.

[2] Victor Erlich, "The Writer as Witness: The Achievement of Aleksandr Solzhenitsyn," in *Aleksandr Solzhenitsyn: Critical Essays and Documentary Materials*, ed. B. Dunlop et al. (New York: Collier Macmillan, 1973), 16-17.

[3] Arthur Schopenhauer wryly remarked that Kant's practical imperative – to treat people not as means only but as ends in themselves – is "very suitable for those who like to have a formula that relieves them from all further thinking": indeed, it does not provide all the answers; *The World as Will and Representation*, trans. E. F. J. Payne (New York, Dover, 1969), I: 349. Tzvetan Todorov has noted that "at times individuals must inevitably be treated as a means," yet they should "not be considered solely that." *Facing the Extreme: Moral Life in the Concentration Camps*, trans. Arthur Denner and Abigail Pollak (New York: Holt, 1996), 158. If we replace "individuals" by "individual texts" in this formulation, we shall say that literary texts may perform varied functions for different interpretive communities and for individual readers, but they should also be granted individual attention for their own sake.

[4] See Jan Mukarovský, *Aesthetic Function, Norm and Value as Social Facts*, trans. Mark E. Suino (Ann Arbor: University of Michigan, 1970), 1-9. For a more detailed application of this theory to documentary prose, see my article "Toward a Poetics of Documentary Prose – from the Perspective of Gulag Testimonies," *Poetics Today* 18 (1997): 187-222.

[5] See, in particular, Wayne Booth, *The Company We Keep: An Ethics of Fiction* (Berkeley: University of California Press, 1988); Martha Nussbaum, *The Fragility of Goodness: Luck and Ethics in Greek Tragedy and Philosophy* (Cambridge: Cambridge University Press, 1986), and Cora Diamond, *The Realistic Spirit: Wittgenstein, Philosophy, and the Mind* (Cambridge: The MIT Press, 1991), 367-81.

[6] Berel Lang, *Act and Idea in the Nazi Genocide* (Chicago: University of Chicago Press, 1990), 120. On verbal responses to the accounts of atrocity as (second- or third-degree) testimony to one's own response to the testimony of others, see Shoshana Felman and Dori Laub, *Testimony: Crises of Witnessing in Literature, Psychoanalysis, and History* (New York: Routledge, 1992).

[7] Heather Dubrow, "The Status of Evidence," *PMLA* 111 (1996): 16.

[8] Bernard Harrison, *Inconvenient Fictions: Literature and the Limits of Theory* (New Haven: Yale University Press, 1991), 1-8.

[9] Stanley Cavell, *Must We Mean What We Say? A Book of Essays* (Cambridge: Cambridge University Press, 1976), 188-9.

[10] See T. W. Adorno, Noten zur Literatur III (Frankfurt/Main: Suhrkampf, 1965), 125.

[11] *Kolyma Tales* (*Kolymskie rasskazy*) were first published, in Mikhail Heller's edition, by Overseas Publications Interchange, London, in 1978; they were then reprinted, twice in Paris, by the YMCA Press. These editions, based on the materials (mainly Samizdat) smuggled out of the Soviet Union, unfortunately place stories that were to be part of later collections amidst the first three cycles, "Kolyma Tales" (which Heller refers to as "The First Death"), "The Artist of the Spade," and "The Left Bank." Definitive editions were put together by Shalamov's literary heir, I. P. Sirotinskaia, and published in Moscow after the perestroika had gained momentum. Particularly useful of these edition is *Sobranie sochinenii v chetyrekh tomakh* [Collected Works in Four Volumes] (Moscow: *Khudozhestvennaia literatura/Vagrius*, 1998).

[12] See Todorov, *Facing the Extreme*, 32-43; V. Yakubov, "*V kruge poslednem:Varlam Shalamov i Aleksandr Solzhenitsyn*" ("In the last circle: Varlam Shalamov and Aleksandr Solzhenitsyn"), *Vestnik Russkogo Khristianskogo Dvizheniya*, 137 (1987): 156-61; and Anna Shur, "*V.T. Shalamov i A.I. Solzhenitsyn: Sravnitel'nyj analiz nekotorykh proizvedenii*" [V. T. Shalamov and A. I. Solzhenitsyn: A comparative analysis of some works], *Novyi zhurnal* (*The New Review*, New York) 155 (1984): 92 101.

[13] See Varlam Shalamov, "*O moei proze*" ("On my prose"), *Novyi mir* 12 (1989): 62.

[14] Gérard Genette, *Narrative Discourse: An Essay in Method*, trans. Jane E. Lewin (Ithaca: Cornell University Press, 1980), 186 – 99.

[15] The page numbers refer to the English version of "Condensed Milk" in Varlam Shalamov, *Kolyma Tales*, trans. John Glad (Harmondsworth: Penguin, 1994), 80-85.

[16] Primo Levi, *If This is a Man / The Truce*, trans. Stuart Woolf (London: Abacus, 1990), 42.

[17] See Robert Conquest, *The Great Terror: A Reassessment* (Oxford: Oxford University Press, 1990), 332.

[18] See Todorov, *Facing the Extreme*, 38-39.

[19] Friedrich Nietzsche, "The Birth of Tragedy," in *Basic Writings of Nietzsche*, trans. and ed. Walter Kaufman (New York: The Modern Library, 1968), 60.

[20] Cf. Alexander Wat: "Let's go back to the cell. If I keep launching into digressions and often needless rationalizations, it's not only the result of my bad habits or my literary failings, but also because it's not easy in the least to return to prison voluntarily. To return to prison after twenty five years by the

faithful exercise of memory involves my entire being and is almost a physical act; it requires the greatest concentration I am capable of, and I'm already so much older now, so much more devastated." *My Century: The Odyssey of a Polish Intellectual*, trans. Richard Lourie (New York: Norton, 1990), 200-201.

²¹ Precisely this effect is explored, through the use of escalation, in Kosinski's *The Painted Bird*.

²² See also Leona Toker, *Return from the Archipelago: Narratives of Gulag Survivors* (Bloomington: Indiana University Press, 2000), 87-9.

²³ Levi, *If This Is a Man*, 73.

²⁴ Amended translation. I am grateful to Gennady Barabtarlo for help with the meaning of this passage.

²⁵ Amended translation.

²⁶ On literature as a testing ground for ideas cf. Wolfgang Iser, *The Act of Reading: A Theory of Aesthetic Response* (Baltimore: Johns Hopkins University Press, 1974), 68-79; and Bernard Harrison, *Inconvenient Fictions*, 1-8.

²⁷ Some writers on camp life consider it a moral universe with its own specific semiotics; others regard it as a field in which tendencies at work in the society as a whole reach a kind of diabolical crystallization. Shalamov explicitly leaned to the latter position and made a number of on-record comments on the shift in the scales: explicitly, indeed, he speaks of his feelings as more or less "normal" in quality though weaker in intensity. The punchline, however, suggests the opposite: the shift has occurred not only in the quantitative specificity of the emotion but also in the quality of the attitude: the tinge of remorse has been redirected from the failure to seek out and warn the victims of the provocation to the double-crossing of the agent provocateur (himself a double-crosser *ex officio*).

²⁸ Shestakov is the namesake of the author of Stalinist high-school history books. His name may have been chosen in order to evoke the covering up of the past, the massive rewriting of history, and the falsification of records – but for all we know the name may also be authentic.

²⁹ See Schopenhauer, *The World as Will and Representation* I: 334-50.

³⁰ See Gilbert Harman, *The Nature of Morality: An Introduction to Ethics* (New York: Oxford University Press, 1977), 111.

³¹ See Aleksandr Solzhenitsyn, *The Gulag Archipelago: An Experiment in Literary Investigation*, trans. Thomas P. Whitney (New York: Harper and Row, 1975), 615-6.

³² See Gilbert Harman, *The Nature of Morality*, 58.

³³ Varlam Shalamov, *Kolymskie rasskazy*, ed. I. P. Sirotinskaya. Moscow: Sovremennik, 1991), 456-9.

³⁴ Williams notes that in order for people to be able to rely "on not being

killed or used as a resource, and on having some space and objects and relations with other people they can count as their own," certain motivations must be encouraged, "and one form of this is to instill a disposition to give the relevant considerations a high deliberative priority in the most serious of these matters, a virtually absolute priority, so that certain courses of action must come first, while others are ruled out from the beginning. An effective way for actions to be ruled out is that they never come into thought at all, and this is often the best way. One does not feel easy with the man who in the course of a discussion of how to deal with political of business rivals says, 'Of course, we could have them killed, but we should lay that aside right from the beginning.' It should never have come into his hands to be laid aside." *Ethics and the Limits of Philosophy* (Cambridge, MA: Harvard University Press, 1985), 185.

[35] Geoffrey Hartman, *Minor Prophesies: The Literary Essay in the Culture Wars* (Cambridge, MA: Harvard University Press, 1991), 131.

[36] Wolfgang Iser, *The Fictive and the Imaginary: Charting Literary Anthropology* (Baltimore: Johns Hopkins University Press, 1993), 296–303.

[37] Cf. Martha Nussbaum *The Fragility of Goodness*, 13, 32 and *Love's Knowledge: Essays on Philosophy and Literature* (New York: Oxford University Press, 1990), 143 – 5.

XI

The Writer as Criminal: Abram Tertz's "**Pkhents.**"

CATHARINE THEIMER NEPOMNYASHCHY

At the end of the day there's still another theme concerning the Suprematist quadrilateral (more exactly, the square). It's worthwhile dwelling on the question of who it is and what it contains. Nobody has given any thought to this.

And I, too, am peering into its mysterious black space – one which is becoming a kind of form of the new face of the Suprematist world, its external appearance and its spirit. Perhaps you consider my ideas excessively audacious.

Oh, no. I see in it what people at one time used to see before the face of God.

-Kazimír Malevich, *Letter to Pavel Ettinger*, 1920

In his closing speech at his trial, Siniavsky, deploring the impulse to categorize everyone different as an enemy, invoked his story "Pkhents" as an example of alterity that eluded the binary opposition of "for" and "against": "In my unpublished story 'Pkhents' there is a sentence that I consider autobiographical: 'You think that if I simply am different, you must immediately curse me …' So there it is: I am different. But I do not regard myself as an enemy, and my works are not hostile works."[1] His two earliest "fantastic stories,"[2] "At the Circus" and "Pkhents," are constructed around metaphors that cast the text as a "criminal" body in order to explore the origins of art's alterity.

As Siniavsky acknowledged at his trial, there are obvious autobiographical allusions in "Pkhents."[3] The first-person narrator of the story claims to be a creature from another planet. Assuming the story to have been written in 1957, the alien's arrival on earth thirty-two years earlier corresponds with Siniavsky's own birth date.[4] His adopted earth-name, Andrei Kazimirovich Sushinsky, clearly echoes Andrei Donatovich Siniavsky, just as his supposed half-Russian, half-Polish ancestry mimics Siniavsky's own background.[5] Moreover, the extraterrestrial's dual identity, fear of exposure, and recording of his secret in writing parallel Siniavsky's own status at the time of the story's conception as a pseudonymous underground writer. These references to Siniavsky's own biography in "Pkhents" underscore the problem of the relationship between author and text, between the self and its representation, addressed by the story.

The status of these references to Siniavsky's autobiography is rendered ambiguous by the complex interplay of names in the story.[6] First of all, the narrator in essence remains nameless throughout, since his "true name" is lost to the reader. This lacuna throws into doubt the very possibility of naming the author of the text. His "pseudonym," moreover, articulates a complex problematic of construction of the self. Siniavsky, after all, endows his fictional character with his own proper name – *Andrei* – only, so to speak, provisionally, since it is *not* that character's real name, but only a marker for his "forged" identity. Similarly, the alien's adopted surname, *Sushinsky*, does not simply echo *Siniavsky*. It also contains the Russian root *sush-*, which denotes dryness. This signals an essential disparity between the name and the named, since the extraterrestrial, who resembles a cactus, lives on water. The name contains the possibility of the destruction or negation of what it names, since dehydration is the greatest threat to the creature's survival. *Sushinsky* also suggests a conflation of *Siniavsky* and *Pushkin*. This assertion of parentage contains an acknowledgment of the cultural burden borne by the self that intrinsically calls into doubt the integrity both of the proper name and of the boundaries of the self. This play with Pushkin's name also extends to the narrator's "double," the hunchback Leopold Sergeevich, who not only bears Pushkin's patronymic, but is described by his neighbors by analogy with Pushkin – an analogy that originates in an expression of his difference: "See, Leopold Sergeevich's brother . . .""No, you're mistaken. Next to him our hunchback is the spitting image of Pushkin" (240). Pushkin's name thus becomes a marker for the interplay among shifting borders of similarity and difference out of which the text and the alien's assumed identity are composed. Coupled with the text's allusion by name to Tolstoy and its invocation of Gogol in the specter of a burned manuscript, the buried reference to Pushkin in the narrator's pseudonym marks the alien's plight as not simply an autobiographical representation of the dilemma of the underground writer Andrei Siniavsky, but a metaphorical dramatization of the existential predicament of all writers – who are trapped in language, while the ability of language to mean, to express the self, is called into doubt.

Other names in "Pkhents" appear to allude directly to the problem of representation. The narrator's Polish patronymic, *Kazimirovich*, most obviously serves as a marker of foreignness, signaling the otherness of the being it purports to name, and of the difference within – connoted by his "legal" description as half-Russian and half-Polish – that renders the self resistant to simple, unambiguous labeling. The name would also seem to allude, however, to the painter Kazimir Malevich, constituting yet another claim to cultural parentage – a genealogy in which the writer figure at the center of "Pkhents" has been "fathered" by the early twentieth-century avant-garde. This name again is problematized by its simultaneous pseudonymity and illegality; its authenticity rests on the alien's faked documents. Moreover, the evocation of Malevich, taken together with the name of the narrator's neighbor and would-be mistress, Veronica, introduces the central problem of representation posed in the story. According to legend, St. Veronica, on the way to the Crucifixion, gave her veil to the suffering Christ to wipe his face, and his image was miraculously transferred to the veil. Veronica's veil thus came to signify the representation of the divine "not made by hands" (*nerukotvornyi*), untainted by human agency.[7] The allusion therefore both raises the question of the possibility of human representation of the divine and postulates the authenticity of art as a function of direct contact with the body. Malevich, who, for the first public display of his painting *Black Square*, had it hung "diagonally across one of the upper corners of the exhibition space" (the equivalent of the icon corner [*krasnyi ugol*] in a Russian peasant hut) and who claimed that in looking at the "Suprematist quadrilateral" he saw "what people at one time used to see before the face of God," aspired to attain the authenticity of the image "not made by hands," to represent the divinity of the self "made in the image of God" through nonmimetic, objectless painting.[8] As we shall see, Tertz broaches the same issue in "Pkhents."

The references to Malevich and to St. Veronica in the names of the characters thus provide a cultural context for the primary concern enacted in the narrative and epitomized in the story's title. Just as critics have recognized the echo of Siniavsky's name in his protagonist's terrestrial name, so have they also noted the acoustic similarity between *Tertz* and *Pkhents*.[9] This reflection of the duality between Tertz and Siniavsky in the duality of Pkhents and Sushinsky reverses the "real-life" roles of the two hypostases, casting Siniavsky/Sushinsky as mask. Tertz/Pkhents thus becomes an embodiment of the "true" self, as opposed to the "legal" identity. While it has been suggested that the invented word is the name of the alien's home planet,[10] we cannot in fact know from the information given in the text what it denotes. All we are told is that it is "*indescribably* beautiful" (245, my emphasis) and that it is a "sacred name" (241) that serves in the text, as we shall see below, as a sign of recognition of true identity. The point lies precisely in the fact that *Pkhents* is a signifier loosed from its signified; only the narrator remembers the language in which it is a meaningful word, and it is untranslatable into human language. The name thus becomes a metaphor for the impossibility of the text itself, which struggles vainly to explain the meaning of the word and fails because of the inadequacy of human language to convey the concept.

The proper names in the text of "Pkhents" thus chart a map of a text that calls into question the very possibility of "mapping," of representing reality. The narrator, imagining himself trying to explain to earthlings who he is, writes:

> You can see for yourself – a creature from another world. Not from Africa, not from India, not even from Mars or your Venus, but even farther, even more unattainable. You don't even have such names, and I myself – if you were to lay out before me all the astronomical maps and plans there are available – I would not be able to find, honestly, I would not be able to find that magnificent point where I was born.
>
> First of all, I am not a specialist in astronomy. I went where I was taken. Secondly, it's a completely different picture, and I couldn't recognize my native sky in your books and papers. Even now – I go out on the street at night, raise my head and see: again it's not right! And I also don't know in which direction to grieve. Perhaps, from here it is impossible to see not only my earth, but even my sun. Perhaps it is registered on the other side of the galaxy. It's impossible to figure out! (243)

The narrator's dilemma challenges the possibility of all representation by positing the relativity of the defining center – the sun – and of all perception to the extent that it is a function of visual perspective determined by bodily location. It therefore articulates the basic problematic of body, perception, and representation around which the story revolves.

The narrator's body serves as both the origin and the gauge of his otherness.

Trying to situate himself in relation to a human system of reference, the narrator maintains: "I am neither human nor beast, and, if you please, I tend most nearly – out of that which you have – to the vegetable kingdom" (244). As he views human reality from the point of view of a plant, he radically dislocates basic coordinates of orientation. His "reading" of human cooking practices provides a most unsettling example of this estrangement:

> I have always been struck by the sadism of cookery. Future chicks are eaten in liquid form. The innards of pigs are stuffed with their own meat. An intestine that has swallowed itself and been covered by the foetuses of chickens – that is what an omelette with sausage is in fact.
>
> They treat wheat even more mercilessly: they cut it,[11] beat it, grind it into dust. Is that not why flour and torture [muká i muka] differ only in stress? (235)

He then imagines the same operations performed on a human being:

> And what if a human being were prepared by the same procedure? If an engineer or writer were larded with his own brain and a violet stuck into his roasted nostril – and given to his coworkers for dinner? No, the torments of Christ, of Jan Hus, and Stenka Razin are a veritable trifle next to the torments of a fish pulled out of water on a hook. They at least knew – for what. (235)

These two fantasies locate the origin of estrangement in the narrator's dual perspective, as a being caught in two worlds between which he must translate. Representation thus becomes the dislocation of taxonomy effected by the writer's looking on from a vantage point of alterity.

The narrator's discovery of his own difference is enacted in the narrative in his confrontations with Veronica and Leopold Sergeevich, confrontations that explore the interplay between body and sight, on the one hand, and language and representation, on the other. The episode with Veronica plays out the disruption of a binary opposition by difference within one term of that opposition. The narrator is disturbed that Veronica's amorous interest in him will undermine their union against their "common enemies" (234), the other tenants in the communal apartment. He most fears that Veronica will declare her love and thereby force a recognition of the difference between them: "Was it worth spoiling our military alliance against the evil neighbors?" (236). When Veronica does speak, she attempts to authenticate her words by exhibiting her naked body, which she exposes to the narrator's estranging vision. The narrator has previously studied the human body in an anatomy textbook and observed little boys swimming in the park. Now, however, he views the female of the species in the flesh for the first time. Long disturbed by the "problem of sex," he directs his gaze at the genital region:

> And now, overcoming my confusion, I decided to seize the opportunity and glanced there where – as was written in the textbook – the genital apparatus was located, which, like a catapult, shot out already-finished infants.

> I caught a glimpse there of something that looked like the face of a human being. Only it was, it seemed to me, not a woman's but a man's face, elderly, unshaven, with teeth bared.
> A hungry, ill-tempered [zloi] man dwelled between her legs. Probably he snored at night and used foul language out of boredom. It must be from there that the duality [dvulichie] of woman's nature comes, about which the poet Lermontov aptly wrote: 'as beautiful as a heavenly angel, as perfidious and evil as a demon.' (238)

The body, as perceived by the narrator, reveals its difference not only from the narrator, but from itself. On it is inscribed an essential duality – between feminine and masculine, good and evil, human and divine. The narrator is relegated to the status of a voyeur, viewing without allowing himself to be viewed, recognizing difference without revealing his own difference. The narrator's vegetable, and therefore transgendered, body precludes sexual intercourse and true dialogue. He rejects both Veronica's words and her body.

The destabilization of one bipolar categorization – his "alliance" with Veronica against their hostile neighbors – leads the narrator to seek to construct another bipolarity by finding his like: "At least one – the same (odinakovyi)." (239). The story in fact begins with the narrator observing another hunchback leaving his dirty linen at the laundry. As we later learn, the narrator believes the hunchback to be a creature from his world, like himself masquerading as a deformed human. After fleeing Veronica, the narrator seeks out the home of the hunchback, whose address he has discovered on a laundry receipt. When the two are alone, he immediately tries to elicit an admission of common origin, of kinship: " 'I recognized you at first glance. You and I are from the same place. Relatives so to speak. PKHENTS! PKHENTS!' I recalled to him in a whisper the name that for both of us was sacred" (241). When Leopold Sergeevich claims not to understand, the narrator persists, finally taking him by the shoulders. It is this contact with the body, rather than Leopold Sergeevich's words, that convinces him of the hunchback's difference, that authenticates his words: "Suddenly through his wool jacket warmth – which came from an unknown source – reached me. His shoulders became hotter and hotter, just as hot as Veronica's hands, like thousands of other hot hands, which I preferred not to shake" (242). Leopold Sergeevich is not a fellow being from his home planet, but "a human being, the most normal human being, although humpbacked" (243).[12] As in the encounter with Veronica, the evidence of the body here frustrates the narrator's attempts to find an ally, someone like him. In this instance, the difference between bodies is even more directly linked with a failure of language: because his body is different, because he is not an extraterrestrial being like the narrator, Leopold Sergeevich cannot understand the word *Pkhents*.

Forced to acknowledge his difference from others, his uniqueness, the narrator considers revealing his alterity: "Why shouldn't I, after all, legalize my position? Why for thirty-two years, like a criminal, have I pretended to be someone else?" (243). His difference from others thus leads him to focus on his difference from himself, to a juxtaposition of his official identity as Andrei Kazimirovich Sushinsky with the story of how he came to earth, to a confrontation between legal language and fantastic narrative. He relates how, en route to a resort, the spaceship in which he was traveling was hit by a meteorite and fell to earth. The only survivor of the crash, he was soon forced by the inclement environment to take refuge with a tribe of nearby Yakuts (identifying his landing place as eastern Siberia). Initially fearing that they would eat him, he disguised himself in "some rags": "that was my first theft, excusable given the situation" (244). Because he required central heating to sustain the temperature necessary to his plant-like body, he made his way to Moscow, where he has remained, under his assumed identity, ever since. Aware of the disparity between his legal identity, authenticated by official words, and his story, inscribed in his body, the narrator foresees three equally unpalatable outcomes, each defined by the relationship between language, body, and society. The first alternative is that his story, divorced from his body, will simply not be believed:

> Tell this sad story [*povest'*] to whomever you like, in the most
> popular form there is – they won't believe it, they won't believe
> it for anything. If I could at least cry as I told my story [*rasskaz*],
> but while I have more or less learned how to laugh, I don't know
> how to cry. They will consider me a madman, a fantast, and
> moreover they could place me on trial [*k sudebnoi otvetstvennosti
> mogut privlech'*]: a false passport, forgery of signatures and seals,
> and other illegal acts. (245)

The apparent paradox embodied in the narrator's vision of being both
disbelieved and branded a criminal for forging a false identity dramatizes
Tertz's vision of literature. The writer's crime resides precisely in the
noncorrespondence between his "legal" identity and his story. The figure of
the narrator's body here becomes a marker for the unabashed fictionality
of the text: the body cannot be produced to validate the narrator's story
because it has no material reality, it is a figment of the writer's imagination.
This fantastic body, which ultimately will be equated with the text itself,
stands outside the law, has no legal status but to undermine the narrator's
claim to a lawful identity, to brand him a criminal.

It would, however, be "even worse," the narrator imagines, if he were
to be believed:

> Academicians from all the academies would come together from
> all over – astronomers, agronomists, physicists, economists,
> geologists, philologists, psychologists, biologists, microbiologists,
> chemists, biochemists – to study me to the last little spot; they
> would forget nothing. And they would do nothing but ask
> questions, investigate, examine, elicit.
>
> Millions of copies of dissertations, movies, and poems about
> me would be sold out. Ladies would begin to paint their lips
> with green lipstick and order hats in the shape of cactuses, or at
> least ficuses. And all hunchbacks – for a few years – would enjoy
> colossal success with women.
>
> They would call by the name of my homeland models of
> automobiles, hundreds of newborn infants – not even to mention
> streets, and dogs. I would become as famous as Lev Tolstoy, as
> Gulliver and Hercules. And Galileo Galilei. (245)

Recognition turns the writer and his writing into parodies of themselves. Canonization transforms the writer from a representing subject into an object of representation; the line between reality, fiction, and myth – Tolstoy, Gulliver, and Hercules – is erased. People remake their physical appearance and trade on their likeness to the fetishized body. The word is detached from its referent and is used to name what has no relation to it. The writer may attempt, like Galileo, to redefine the center, but he cannot communicate its essence:

> But despite all this general attention to my humble person, no one would understand anything. How can they understand me when I myself in their language can in no way express my unhuman essence. I do nothing but dodge all over the place and make do with metaphors, but as soon as it comes to what is most important – I fall silent. And I only see the solid, low GOGRY, I hear the swift VZGLYAGU, and the indescribably beautiful PKHENTS overshadows my trunk. Ever fewer and fewer of these words remain in my fading memory. The sounds of human speech can only approximately convey their construction. And if linguists were to crowd around and ask what it means, I would say only GOGRY TUZHEROSKIP and make a helpless gesture. (245)

Metaphor thus becomes the writer's tool of final resort, the closest he can come to conveying his experience, his self. "What is most important," however, reduces him to silence.

The third alternative faced by the narrator is a logical extension of the second, of his reduction to silence. If revealing his "true" identity will lead either to being branded a criminal or to being reduced to a fetish, it is better, he decides, to "drag out his solitary incognito" (245). This course, however, will inevitably end in his death and the discovery of his body, which, wordless, will be made into a display in a zoological museum, put "into an acid bath, into a glass crypt, into history; for the edification of future generations – for all eternity – they will submerge me – a monster, the most important monster of the Earth" (248). Envisaging the visitors viewing his preserved body, the narrator foresees that his corpse will be perceived as threatening, as ugly precisely because it is a "hybrid": "And filing past, they will begin to tremble from fear and, in order to buck themselves up, will start to laugh insolently, to stick out their squeamish lips: 'Oh, what an abnormal, what an ugly mongrel [*ublyudok*].'" (245).[13]

The body, transformed from a speaking subject into a mute object, comes to represent the opposite of what the narrator himself sees in it. The corpse thus suggests an image of the writer, divorced from his self, transformed into the body of the text. His viewers, or "readers," kill the body by seeking in it some "educational" value. Attempting to find some use in it, they "misread," seeing in the corpse only an exemplification of impure and ugly heterogeneity. Art, reduced to didactic aims, becomes dead art.[14] The narrator, on the other hand, finds in his body the epitome of harmonious beauty. This discovery is prompted by his stay on earth, by his juxtaposition with the other: "Perhaps if I had not lived in foreign parts for thirty-two years, it would never have entered my head to admire my own exterior. But here I am the only exemplar of that lost harmonious beauty that is called my native land. What is there for me to do on earth but delight in myself?" (247). This disparity in vision articulates two incompatible views of art: the ideal of beauty as an end in itself, versus the practice of subordinating artistic creation to a didactic end. This discrepancy is rooted in the impossibility of viewing the other as subject rather than object. The alien's disguise impairs his ability to see the human beings around him: his multiple eyes are concealed and damaged by the human clothing with which he must cover them.[15] Alone, his limbs freed from their disguise, he is able to look at himself through all the eyes in his "arms and legs, on the top and back of the head" (246):

> But I turned my head, not limiting myself to a semicircle – the pitiful one-hundred-and-eighty-degree norm allotted to the human neck – I began to blink all of my eyes that remained intact, dispelling fatigue and darkness, and I succeeded in seeing myself from all sides – simultaneously in several perspectives. How captivating is this spectacle, unfortunately accessible to me now only in rare hours of the night. All you have to do is lift up your hand and you see yourself from the ceiling, so to speak, rising and hanging over yourself. And at the very same time – with your remaining eyes – not losing sight of the bottom, the rear, and the front – all your branching and forking body. (247)

In viewing his own body, the narrator is vouchsafed a transcendent vision. He is able to see himself from outside, from multiple perspectives. He therefore sees beauty and harmony where others, looking on from a single angle of vision, can discern only a monstrous crossbreed.

Rejecting the three fates that would seem to await him upon discovery, the narrator decides on a fourth path: to abandon human society, to find the hole left when his spaceship crashed, and, freeing himself of human disguise and human language, to live out a final summer before immolating himself when the weather turns cold in the autumn. This retreat into a "private" language, however, is problematized by its negation of the very nature of language as a social institution, reiterating the question of meaning posed by the story's title. The narrator's recognition of signs of assimilation in himself, moreover, calls into doubt the possibility that he can abandon human language: "Strange desires at times visit me. Sometimes I long to go to the movies. Sometimes I feel like playing checkers with Veronica Grigorevna's husband" (249). The narrator, as he becomes more "human," is thus drawn to forms of representation and play, a development that he views as threatening to his very nature and that he seeks to flee. The possibility of flight, however, is finally challenged by the ending of the narrative itself, which degenerates into a mishmash of foreign expressions, animal sounds, and nonsense words:

> "O motherland! PKHENTS! GOGRY TUZHEROSKIP! I am coming to you! GOGRY! GOGRY! TUZHEROSKIP! TU-ZHEROSKIP! BONJOUR! GUTENABEND! TUZHEROSKIP! BU-BU-BU!
>
>   MIAOW-MIAOW!
>
>   PKHENTS!" (250)

Even with no one to speak to, the narrator cannot return to a perfect language. Instead, as he tries to express himself in words, language itself fragments him into competing stances. The attempt to translate the beautiful harmony of the self into language is defeated by the medium itself.[16]

While enacting in his text language's inability to represent, however, Tertz does not negate the possibility of literature, but rather affirms it in terms of paradox: the impossibility of representation becomes the ontological condition of the text. Key here are the biblical references that underlie the narrative of "Pkhents." The images of water and water deprivation are clearly allusions to baptism and to Christ's suffering from dehydration on the Cross, just as the narrator's decision to burn himself in his thirty-third year echoes the Crucifixion.[17] The narrator's situation thus can be read as a metaphor for the dual nature of Christ, simultaneously human and divine, caught between heaven and earth. At the same time it has been recognized that the "fall" of the narrator's spacecraft

—"we fell [*padaem*], deprived of support, not knowing where, we fell for seven and a half months" (244) – echoes the fall of humanity, thus casting the narrator as an image of the soul trapped in a fallen world.[18] Like the narrator's equation of his true self with the sacred Pkhents, this implied equivalence between the soul and the divinity of Christ has some correspondence with the Russian Orthodox belief in the purity of the true self created "in the image of God." The problem of the representation of the true self, the soul, thus becomes the same as the problem of embodying the divine: the impossibility of representing the transcendent in the "fallen" substance of human words.

The narrator's "irregular diary," in which he records his attempts to define himself in relation to and preserve himself against the alien world into which he has "fallen," is his attempt to convey in human language what he himself has recognized the impossibility of translating: the totality of meaning and therefore absolute meaninglessness betokened by the name *Pkhents*. The problem is figured in the distortion of the legend of Veronica's veil out of which his text, in a sense, arises.[19] The narrator borrows ink from Veronica to write his diary. As a metonymy for the words he will write with it, the ink simultaneously recalls the episode of the veil and diverges from it. While the representation of Christ's image on the veil draws its authenticity from direct contact with the divine body, the narrator's writing is marked as a failure of contact and its authenticity therefore called into question.

The central issue addressed in the text thus hinges on the correlation between the narrator's body, as an emblem of his otherness and "the only exemplar of that lost harmonious beauty that is called my native land," and his diary, in which he attempts to "embody" it. Both will be burned in the end. The text we are reading, moreover, is clearly the very same text that the narrator says he will burn. We are therefore reading a text that ostensibly has been destroyed. Thus, the narrator's fantastic body – which asserts its own fictionality, its status as a sign with no referent, no body with which to authenticate its story, which exists only in the text – and the text that exists despite the impossibility of its existence merge. Mimicking metaphorically the identity of body and representation postulated as the source of legitimacy in the legend of Veronica's veil, the text places in question the issue of authenticity. Like the alien being, the text has no "legal" status. Its criminality inheres in its simultaneous denial that language can contain the self and its assertion of the priority of the imaginary over the real.

ENDNOTES

[1] Aleksandr Ginzburg, ed., *Belaya kniga po delu A. Sinyavskogo i Yu. Danielya* (Frankfurt am Main: Posev, 1967), 306.

[2] The first Russian-language publication of Tertz writings under this title included five of the six stories generally grouped together under the heading "fantastic stories," as well as *The Trial Begins*. Like *The Trial Begins* and *What Is Socialist Realism*, it was issued by the house that published the journal *Kultura* in the series *Kultura Library* (see Abram Terts, *Fantasticheskie povesti* (Paris: Instytut literacki, 1961). "Pkhents" was placed together with the other stories under the heading "fantastic stories" only in a later edition entitled *Fantasticheskii mir Abrama Tertsa*. Margaret Dalton maintains that "the title of the collection clearly points to E. T. A. Hoffmann ("*Fantasiestuecke in Callots Manier*," 1814-15)" (Margaret Dalton, *Andrei Siniavskii and Julii Daniel': Two Soviet "Heretical" Writers* (Wurzburg: Jal-Verlag, 1973), 49). Andrew Field also traces the title to Hoffmann (Andrew Field, "Abram Tertz's Ordeal by Mirror," in Abram Terts, *Mysli vrasplokh* (New York: Rausen Publisher, 1966), 10).

Aside from Dalton and Field, a number of other critics have written about the fantastic stories within the context of Tertz's writings. See, e.g., Richard Lourie, *Letters to the Future: An Approach to Siniavsky-Tertz* (Ithaca: Cornell University Press, 1975), 124-54; Michel Aucouturier, "Writer and Text in the Works of Abram Terc (An Ontology of Writing and A Poetics of Prose)," trans. Alexandre Guerard, in *Fiction and Drama in Eastern and Southeastern Europe: Evolution and Experiment in the Postwar Period,* ed. Henrik Birnbaum and Thomas Eekman (Columbus, Ohio: Slavica, 1980); Deming Brown, "Art of Andrei Siniavsky," in idem, *Soviet Russian Literature since Stalin* (Cambridge: Cambridge University Press, 1978); Edward J. Brown, "Exodus into Samizdat and Tamizdat: Siniavsky," in idem, *Russian Literature since the Revolution* (Cambridge, Mass: Harvard University Press, 1982), 238-50. However, only Andrew Durkin, in what remains one of the finest studies of Tertz's writings, has examined the stories as a unified whole: "The *Fantastic Tales* are not merely a random collection – they are interrelated by similarities in narrative situation and structure, by their concern with certain basic devices, and by their thematic affinities, in particular each protagonist's search for a way out of an existential impasse. In an intricate system of echoes, each story responds to and develops, in a new way, devices and themes suggested by one or more of its companions; the *Fantastic Tales* represent a set of variations on a limited number of motifs. In this sense the stories are recursive and centripetal, each one enhancing and illuminating our understanding of the others" (133) (Andrew Durkin, "Narrator, Metaphor, and Theme in Sinjavskji's *Fantastic Tales*," *Slavic and East European Journal* 24: 2 (1980): 133-44).

[3] For articles specifically on "Pkhents," see Walter Kolonosky, "Inherent and Ulterior Design in Sinjavskji's "Pxenc," *Slavic and East European Journal* 26:3 (1982): 329-37; and Ronald E. Peterson, "Writer as Alien in Sinjavskji's "Pxenc," *Weiner Slawisticher Almanach* 12 (1983): 47-53. I have found a number of points made by Kolonosky in his suggestive article particularly helpful in developing my own argument.

[4] Early critics had difficulty placing "Pkhents" chronologically in relation to Tertz's other fantastic stories, because it was published only after Siniavsky's trial. According to Siniavsky, he had shown it to Sergei Khmelnitsky, who later appeared as a witness against him at the trial and who served as the prototype for the character called alternately S. and Sergei in *Goodnight*. Siniavsky delayed publication of the story because he feared that Khmelnitsky would give away his identity if the story appeared under the Tertz pseudonym in the West. "Pkhents" is accurately dated 1957 in the two-volume edition of Abram Tertz's writings published in Russian in 1992. It is worth noting that even the season of the year in which the alien arrives on earth seems to correspond to Siniavsky's birthday. Siniavsky was born in October, and it appears to be autumn when the spaceship crashes: "Besides, I felt a growing cold in the atmosphere" (Terts, *Sobranie sochinenii, 1:244.*) Page numbers from this edition will henceforth be given in parentheses in the text. [The English translation can be found in Clarence Brown, ed. *Portable Twentieth-Century Russian Reader* (New York: Penguin Books, 1985), 465-490. (ed.)]

[5] Siniavsky is in fact one-quarter Polish.

[6] Kolonosky points to the significance of naming in the story: "To examine the semantic field of names in 'Pxenc' is to discover the first clues to an underlying discourse about difference involving the alien, the author, and Soviet society" (Kolonosky, "Inherent and Ulterior Design," 331).

[7] For a history of the evolution of the legend, including a provocative discussion of its sexual implications, see Ewa Kuryluk, *Veronica and Her Cloth: History, Symbolism and Structure of a "True" Image* (Cambridge: Basil Blackwell, 1991).

[8] Quotes are from Sherwin W. Simmons, *Malevich's Black Square and the Genesis of Supermatism, 1907-1915* (New York: Garland, 1981), 233. For an excellent discussion of the theoretical background of Malevich's conception of the Supermatist quadrilateral, see the chapter "The Icon Unmasked: 1915," in ibid., 224-53.

[9] For example, Kolonosky points out: "The alias of the alien, Andrej Kazimirovic Susinskij, is a rather bold counterpoint of the name of the author, Andrej Donatovic Sinjavskij, who, like the alien, has also adopted another name" (Kolonosky, "Inherent and Ulterior Design:" 331). Lourie remarks that "the word 'pkhentz,' which the hero remembers from his native tongue, sounds suspiciously like 'Tertz' " (Lourie, *Letters to the Future*, 154), and Olga Matich observes: "Tertz's alienation was much more extreme, as expressed in the image of the extraterrestrial outsider in the short story 'Pkhents: whose title is reminiscent of the sound combination Tertz'" (Olga Matich, "Russian Literature in Emigration: A Historical Perception on the 1970s," in *The Third Wave: Russian Literature in Emigration,* ed. Olga Matich and Michael Haim (Ann Arbor, Mich.: Ardis, 1984), 17).

[10] Kolonosky and Field make this assumption (Kolonosky, "Inherent and Ulterior Design:" 332; Field, "Abram Tertz's Ordeal by Mirror," 34).

[11] *Rezhut* here also has the connotation of slitting someone's throat.

[12] Leopold Sergeevich as double who physically "mirrors" the narrator, suggests a subtle subversion of realism. While the narrator's body becomes a figure of the fantastic text, of that which has no referent in reality, Leopold Sergeevich, who has the ability to mimic human beings, to play the "classic role of the humpback" (240) and who turns out to be none other than what he appears to be, suggests an image of the realist text. We should also note that Veronica, spurned by the narrator, marries an actor from the Stanislavsky Theater.

[13] I would like to thank Shawn Vietor for having pointed out the image of the preserved corpse past which viewers file may be read as a parodic allusion to Lenin's mummified body preserved in a mausoleum on Red Square. Benjamin Cramer also suggested that the image recalls Peter the Great's collection of human organs, rarities, and monsters in the Kunkstkammer in Petersburg. When I relayed these observations to Siniavsky in May 1994, he pointed out that, as he writes in *Soviet Civilization*, Lenin's brain was preserved in alcohol (see the brain in Globov's dream in *Trial Begins*).

[14] I am grateful to Richard Borden for having suggested this observation to me.

[15] The narrator also laments that one of his eyes was damaged in 1934. Kolonosky and Peterson have recognized this as a reference to the first Congress of Soviet Writers at which Socialist Realism was proclaimed the official method of Soviet literature (Kolonosky, "Inherent and Design; 337; Peterson, "Writer as Alien," 9).

[16] Aucouturier sees the title and conclusion of "Pkhents" as examples of what he terms "'Tercian' *zaum*," which, he argues, is the extreme manifestation

of "the notion of 'the text as an object'" and gives "the effect of 'transmental language,' devoid of external reference" (Aucouturier, "Writer and Text," 6). Although he does not discuss the concept of the image not "made by hands" in relation to "Pkhentz," Aucouturier does pose it as the possible ideal to which "the poetics of the text as material object, independent of any external reference" (3) manifested in Tertz's works aspires. Durkin's reading of the ending complements Aucouturier's by implicitly seeing in it an image of "the death of the author (Durkin, "Narrator, Metaphor, and Theme," 135).

[17] See Kolonosky's reading of the alien as "a Christ-figure" ("Inherent and Ulterior Design," 333-34).

[18] Lourie writes of "Pkhents" that "the story is really a portrait of man after the Fall, the Expulsion" *(Letters to the Future,* 151). Boris Filippov suggests a Neo-Platonic reading of the story: ''The Platonic teaching about the soul-psyche, which flew into our corporeal world and is imprisoned in the prison of the flesh, is vividly incarnated in this small story" (19) (Boris Filippov, *"Priroda i tyur'ma,"* in Tertz, *Fantasticheskii mir Abrama Tertza* (New York: Inter-language literary Associates, 1967), 5-23.

[19] The first mention of the diary comes when the narrator "penetrates" her room to borrow the ink. The episode both plays on the parallel with Christ, in the absence of physical contact, and simultaneously marks a "failure" in relation to the postulation of an equation between body and material inscribed in the legend of the veil.

XII

Vasilii Shukshin's "Cut Down to Size" (Srezal) and the Question of Transition.

DIANE NEMEC IGNASHEV

Transition, mobility between realms, is a key theme of Vasily Shukshin's fiction, and of its interpretation. For the most part the material of cultural historians and literary sociologists, Shukshin's prose has been evaluated primarily as a chronicle of Soviet society. "Transition" from this critical viewpoint is considered a disadvantageous state, a function of the instability and conflict latent in Soviet life. As Geoffrey Hosking has noted, Shukshin's "heroes are the uprooted, who have left one milieu and never quite settled in another. . . ."They are "the children of the Soviet Union's whirlwind years of social change," whose fistfights, arguments with shopkeepers, suicides, "result from their failure to secure a definite position in ever-changing Soviet society."[1] Shukshin related his protagonists' instability to his own:

> And so, here, on the verge of forty, it turns out I'm not completely an urbanite, nor any longer a villager. It's an awfully uncomfortable position. It's not even like being between two chairs, rather like having one leg on the shore and the other in the boat. You can't remain in that position for long, I know, you'll fall. I'm not afraid of falling (falling? from where?), it's just quite uncomfortable.[2]

Despite its high cost, though, Shukshin also saw advantages to transitional status. The insecurity of belonging to neither realm is offset by the added perspective mobility lends the artist. "But this situation of mine has its 'gains' (I almost wrote 'pains'). From comparisons, from my various 'here to there's' and 'there to here's' involuntarily come thoughts not only about the 'village' and about the 'city,' but about Russia."[3]

Just how Shukshin the artist employed mobility between realms, here fictional and immanent reality, can be seen through analysis of the tale of one of his most "pained" heroes, Gleb Kapustin of "Cut Down to Size."

Published in 1970, in his last cycle of stories to appear in *Novyi mir* (*New World*), "Cut Down to Size" is among Shukshin's most provocative stories. It recounts the return of a certain *kandidat filologicheskikh nauk* (candidate for the degree of doctor of philology), Konstantin Zhuravlev, to his native village, Novaia, after many years' absence. Zhuravlev is a model of successful upward social mobility. Since leaving the village he has obtained a degree in philology, married another *kandidat* (doctoral candidate) and begun a family, and acquired sufficient affluence to ride from the station to the village in a taxi. In the process he has also so alienated himself from the life of his native village that he brings as presents an electric samovar, a flowered housecoat, and wooden spoons: souvenir-store kitsch. Zhuravlev's arrival sends the *muzhiki* (village men), his former friends and schoolmates, scurrying to Gleb Kapustin. Whenever a *znatnyi* (eminent) visitor arrives, the peasants ask Gleb (not a native of the village) *srezat'* (to cut down to size) the guest. Gleb and the peasants march to Zhuravlev's. The reunion warms and Gleb is almost forgotten, when suddenly he makes his move. He asks Zhuravlev three questions. Unable to answer them, Zhuravlev instead tries to impugn Gleb's intelligence (and sanity) with abusive remarks and a pregnant glance to his wife. The glance propels Gleb into a two-page tirade on the wrongs of judging people by their outward appearances. Gleb then exits dramatically, followed by the peasants, who simultaneously marvel at Gleb's ability and pity Zhuravlev. It is at this point that the narrator intrudes, concluding that despite their admiration, the peasants do not love Gleb, because he is *zhestok* (cruel). The next day at work, he tells us, Gleb will inquire about the Zhuravlevs. His victory confirmed, Gleb will pronounce the story's concluding lines: "Never mind," Gleb will note magnanimously. "It'll do him good. Let him think about it in his spare time. Otherwise they take on more than they can handle."[4]

Gleb's words have occupied the spare time of many philologists. He is typical of the spiteful aggressors who evolved in Shukshin's work of the late 1960s from the *chudiki* (romantic dreamers and harmless eccentrics) of his earlier prose. The appearance of Gleb and his pugnacious ilk brought immediate consternation to Shukshin's conservative promoters, confusion still evident in Soviet criticism after the author's death in 1974. Gleb is a socialist realist headache. On the one hand, he is beyond doubt the story's "hero." Only he merits description in narrator discourse and is called by name. (Zhuravlev is referred to as "the doctoral candidate"; the peasants are anonymous.) To him the narrator relinquishes more than half of the story's discourse. No matter how vicious Gleb turns, Zhuravlev with his taxi, suitcases, useless presents, and glances to his wife deserves the slap. On the other hand, Gleb's victory over Zhuravlev is pyrrhic, his questions unfair. One technically is not a grammatical question and the remaining two so jumble battered terms and concepts – *strategicheskaia filosofiia* (strategic philosophy), *global'nyi vopros* (global issue), *Luna delo ruk razuma, razumnye sushchestva . . . vylezut k nam navstrechu* (the moon as the creation of reason, rational beings . . . will slither out to meet us) – that any philosopher (as Gleb assumes Zhuravlev to be) or philologist would have difficulty understanding them.[5] No one, including the critics, loves Gleb, and the predominating response to "Cut Down to Size" has been to accept Gleb and his kind as anti-heroes, negative examples of pseudo-enlightenment deserving of the author's (and our) repudiation:

> It is possible that Gleb Kapustin is close to the truth (*istina*). But the 'fruits of enlightenment' are most evident in the 'self-righteousness' of the 'critics' themselves. After all, the diatribes of Kniazev in *Shtrikhi k portretu* (Brush Strokes to a Portrait), Kapustin, and Kudriashov in *Psikhopat* (The Psychopath) – fantastic conglomerations of concepts, opinions, names, and facts – are demonstrably absurd. Do our heroes recognize this? No, they remain in complete ignorance, egotistically self-assured of the truthfulness of their knowledge, which 'accumulated' through information sources sent along various channels – by word of mouth and through reading. . . . Immeasurable consumption of pseudo-scientific information has aroused in them self-opiniatedness, cockiness, and a certain maniacal quality, putting these village proselytes in an awkward, tragicomic situation. Shukshin called Gleb Kapustin's verbal tourneys 'cruel'; 'Gleb is cruel and no one anywhere has ever yet loved cruelty.'[6]

Gleb's apologists, an unpopular minority, have also been forced to agree that he and his relations are "aggressive" and "vengeful."[7] Even critics who have tried to avoid value judgments by analyzing rather than interpreting "Cut Down to Size" in the end have found Gleb caught in the linguistic limbo of *ne-iazyk* (non-language), his transitional status (neither villager nor urbanite) ultimately a disadvantage: "Gleb with his pseudo-language loses his right to the main role in this fairy tale about how the crafty peasant out-argued his educated master, and becomes the hero of another – in which lies, in my opinion, the main message of this short story – of the tale of the peasant who lost his language but never learned another."[8]

Though the critics' unanimity on "Cut Down to Size" comes as no surprise, it should be suspect. Rarely has a writer engendered such agreement between Westerners and Soviets. Rarely has interpretation left such basic exegetical lacunae. First, how did Shukshin, advocate of peasant solidarity, arrive at this odd plot wherein the peasants pit a non-native against a fellow countryman, then reject their advocate for his efforts on their behalf? Second, is there not an inherent contradiction in the narrator's condemnation of Gleb? That is, if Gleb has no right to chastise Zhuravlev, by what right does the narrator pass judgment on Gleb? Had not Shukshin, only two years earlier, in "Morality is Truth" (*Nravstvennost' est' pravda*), said that

> . . . honest, courageous art does not set itself the goal of pointing with its finger: this is moral, but this is immoral; it deals with man 'as a whole' and wants to perfect him, man, by speaking the truth about him. One can instruct, but to instruct by the method – this is a 'no-no' but this is 'nice-nice'– well, it's better not to instruct at all. One's students will grow up lazy, sly, and inclined to a parasitic way of life. For there is nothing easier than not having to solve a difficult question by yourself and just copying from the board.[9]

Is "Cut Down to Size" but another object lesson in Shukshinian inconsistency, or in following the narrator and condemning Gleb do we overlook a more deeply embedded lesson? These are the questions explored here.

As implied in the synopsis, the stage for Gleb's confrontation with Zhuravlev is set by tensions between the local peasants and the arrival from the city. But this "urban-rural" conflict requires qualification. Shukshin depicted Soviet society in meticulous linguistic microcosm. His rural dwellers alone form three distinct socio-linguistic categories. Urbanites, from hereditary intellectuals to those like Zhuravlev (rural by birth and urban by education) offer yet another three.[10] "Cut Down to Size" builds on a linguistic and semantic opposition between only two chronologically comparable elements in this broader socio-linguistic spectrum. The *muzhiki* do not represent all Soviet peasants. They are the younger inhabitants of the village *Novaia* (New), a synecdoche for contemporary, modernizing Soviet ruraldom: slow to change and easily intimidated, but fascinated by the new, and better educated than their parents. Their speech correspondingly exhibits none of the phonemic and morphological deformations common to Shukshin's older villagers. Similarly, Zhuravlev embodies not all urban culture, but one generation of post-World War II urban society, its most recent arrivals, those who bought their migration at the expense of traditional language and values. In his actions and speech Zhuravlev is as enthralled by his new urban existence as the peasants are bound to theirs. His linguistic return home, like his ostentatious arrival and useless presents, is entirely inappropriate. Attempting to shift idioms, he overshoots his mark, prematurely switching from *vy* (formal address) to *ty* (familiar) and confusing criminal argot with rural dialect:

> 'That's what you call 'a steamroll," said the doctor. 'You broken off your chain? What's the. . . ?'
>
> 'I don't know, I don't know,' Gleb rushed to interrupt him, 'I don't know what it's called, since I've never been in prison and I've never broken off a chain. What's the point? No one else here,' Gleb scanned the peasants, 'has been in prison either, they won't understand.' (174)

The narrator, like Gleb, employs the village men as a backdrop. Like observers at a tennis match, they sit quietly on the sidelines, their eyes shifting from Gleb to Zhuravlev as each makes his point. Though not without blame, Zhuravlev, too, is little more than a device, an excuse for yet another Kapustin performance. Were Zhuravlev less enamored of academic jargon, he might have stopped Gleb dead in his tracks:

> 'In what field do you distinguish yourself?' asked Gleb.
>
> 'Where do I work, you mean?' The doctoral candidate

didn't understand.

'Yes.'

'In the Philo Department.'

'Philosophy?'

'Not quite. . . . Well, you could call it that.'

'A most indispensable thing.' Gleb needed it to be philosophy (171)

The "urban-rural" conflict in "Cut Down to Size" thus does not pit pre-Revolutionary patriarchy against the old urban intelligentsia, but revolves on differences that have arisen within a single generation.

Gleb, the appointed mediator between these factions, stands apart from both fields physically, socially, and linguistically. He is a villager, but not a native of Novaia. Judging by his use of naval terminology (e.g., *vaterliniia*), he has spent some time beyond the countryside. In his physical mobility he somewhat resembles Zhuravlev. But whereas Zhuravlev is linguistically static, Gleb is still a verbal "bird of passage." Talking with the peasants, he flits from their idiom to a humorous imitation of urban jargon, whose irony the peasants do not acknowledge.

'In what field are the doctoral candidates?' asked Gleb.

'What field of specialization? Hell if I know. . . . Granny told me they're doctoral candidates. He and his wife.'

'There are doctors of technical science and there are doctors of general education, most of whom specialize in blabbology.' (170)

Conversing with Zhuravlev, Gleb imitates literary Russian, this time at its bureaucratic worst, again to humorous ends, as will be demonstrated below. But when he finally "soars like a hawk," and delivers his tirade, Gleb suddenly lights on his own linguistic medium, entirely literate, replete with metaphors, bereft of parody, and accessible to both poles:

We've been listening long enough! We've had, so to speak, the pleasure. Therefore, allow me to point out to you, Mr. Doctoral Candidate, having a degree is not like owning a suit of clothes, which you buy once and wear for a lifetime. For that matter, even a suit needs to be cleaned once in a while.

> While a degree, if we're agreed that it's not a suit, all the more
> so requires upkeep . . . (174)

Other critics have noticed this sudden shift in Gleb's verbal behavior,
but have been at a loss to explain it:

> It is necessary to note that in Gleb's accusatory speech, his
> crowning number, the errors and mixture of foreign elements
> are absent and he expresses himself totally correctly and
> literally. Here, I think, the author departed from these ironic
> negative shadings, with which he had characterized Gleb up
> to this point, because here [Gleb] expresses the true feelings
> of the peasant men and his words acquire true weight. The
> inconsistency in the linguistic characterization is explained
> by the logic of the development of the fundamental conflict
> of the story.[11]

However, Gleb's sudden eloquence seems an inconsistency only if we
view it as an accident and regard his preceding verbal behavior as a constant:
static, pseudo-linguistic nonsense, the garbled results, as Apukhtina saw it,
of "pseudo-enlightenment," of whose ridiculousness Gleb is unaware. In
fact, though, there is nothing accidental or inconsistent about Gleb, neither
his language nor his behavior.

Kapustin, whose surname suggests the satirical skit *kapustnik,* is the
quintessential Shukshinian hero – artist, singer, actor. Narrator remarks
underscore Gleb's thespianism: "Many were dissatisfied by this, but many,
the village men in particular, simply couldn't wait for Gleb Kapustin to
cut another eminence down to size. Not only could they not wait, they
would go to Gleb's house first, and only then, together, head for the guest's
house. They went exactly as if for a performance" (169). "Gleb threw down
the gauntlet. Gleb assumed a seemingly careless pose and waited for the
gauntlet to be picked up. The doctoral candidate picked up the gauntlet"
(171). "Gleb Kapustin got up and bowed with restraint to the woman
doctoral candidate. And blushed" (172). "Gleb smirked and departed
unhurriedly from the hut. He always left the homes of eminences alone"
(175–6). "Tomorrow, when he arrives at work, Gleb Kapustin will ask the
village men, in passing (he'll pretend) . . ." (176).

There is method to the madness of Gleb's assault.[12] Every step is premeditated: "Gleb sat down too. For the time being he kept quiet. But it was apparent that he was drawing himself up to lunge ...he was sizing up Zhuravlev. . . ." "Gleb required that the subject be philosophy. . . ." "[Gleb] probably awaited just this moment." Gleb's timing is precise: he knows exactly when to interrupt Zhuravlev. Except during his final speech, quoted earlier, Gleb remains calm and collected, while Zhuravlev grows increasingly agitated.

Gleb is a particular kind of artist, an actor, a farceur. His performances suggest the *skomorokh* or carnival jester, who turns official, established, concepts upside down and thereby reveals their falseness.[13] His questions have been carefully scripted to his purposes. They are: 1) If, according to "strategic philosophy" (i.e., Marxism-Leninism), matter is primary and spirit secondary, and if philosophy, according to Marxist-Leninist doctrine, interprets nature, how does philosophy interpret the recently discovered phenomenon of weightlessness? 2) How does Zhuravlev feel about "the problem of shamanism in certain regions of the Far North?" 3) How does Zhuravlev relate to the proposition advanced by some scientists that the "Moon is the creation of reason, rational beings?" If the Moon is an artificial satellite, what happens to all calculations of natural trajectories? If there really is intelligent life on other planets, how are we to communicate?

Under their "gibberish" camouflage, Gleb's questions raise sticky issues of Soviet Marxism. They are hardly "absurd," though the same reasons for which some critics would want us to think they are seem to have led editors to modify them.[14] Moreover, they all directly preface the matter of Gleb's concluding speech, that human beings have come to be defined solely by their physical nature (their clothes, their jobs, their places of residence) to the exclusion of their spiritual nature, their souls (the recurring *dusha* [soul] of Shukshin's prose).

Gleb first questions Engels's relegation of spirit (soul, consciousness) as secondary to and derivative of matter. In situations of weightlessness inertial and gravitational forces operate in equal opposition, causing all bodies to experience the same acceleration. In a weightless environment the effects of gravitation are absent. A person in a situation of weightlessness observing an object in the same environment assigns different values to these processes from those assigned by someone outside the situation. The physics of weightlessness denies absolute objectivity. In addition, through the Lorentz transformation, Einstein generalized from the theory of special relativity, of which weightlessness offers one natural proof, that mass and energy are one and the same. Hence, in a condition of weightlessness the dialectic of matter and spirit is proven false.[15] Gleb's question cuts to the core of physics' debate with Soviet philosophy.

Gleb's second question on the persistence of shamanism bridges the first and third question. First, it continues the theme of the primacy of spirit, which shamanism sees in all matter and processes, organic or inorganic. Second, a shamanistic world view maintains that the universe is filled with heavenly bodies peopled by spiritual beings. The notion of the cosmos as a spiritual realm, of dusha, leads into Gleb's third question, an embarrassing example of how Soviet science as ideology's handmaiden has proved to be no more "scientific" or objective than a Neolithic religious system. As Geller explains:

> *The third question* . . . reflects in a crooked mirror the heated debates about outer space, its conquest, and its possible inhabitants, which burned at the time of the first sputniks and other accomplishments of renewed Soviet science and technology. In particular, it brings to mind the once much-publicized hypothesis of astro-physicist I. S. Shklovsky that the satellites of Mars were artificially produced and built by representatives of one of the numerous galactic civilizations (an aside: of late I. S. Shklovsky has been defending a contrary hypothesis on the inequality in space of Earth's civilization). In these discussions the possibilities of contact with inter-planetary beings and in connection with this the variations on the development of intelligent creatures and their societies were always brought up.[16]

Gleb's third question also illuminates through analogy his belligerence towards Zhuravlev and other "eminences":

> 'Let's assume that an intelligent being crawled out onto the surface of the Moon. . . . What would you suggest one do? Bark like a dog? Crow like a rooster?'
>
> The peasants laughed. They shifted in their places. And once again focused on Gleb.
>
> 'Nevertheless we need to understand each other. Right?

How?' Gleb fell into an inquiring silence. He looked at everyone. 'I propose this: draw a diagram of our solar system in the sand and show him that I'm from Earth. That in spite of the fact that I'm dressed in a space suit I also have a head and I'm also an intelligent being. To support this one can point out to him on the diagram where he's from: point to the Moon and then to him. Logical? Thus we've established that we are neighbors. But nothing more. In addition it's required that I explain to him the laws according to which I developed before becoming what I am at the present stage. . . .'

'Well, well.' The doctor shifted and gave a pregnant glance to his wife. 'That's very interesting: what laws were those?' (173–4).

Gleb's hypothetical encounter between earthling and moon-being parallels the encounter between Zhuravlev and the peasants. Zhuravlev comprehends the metaphor. Yet, with "a pregnant glance" he rejects this final offer for a truce. The condescending glance propels Gleb into his uncontrollable tirade, where, among other things, the cosmonaut metaphor continues: "Therefore, my advice to you, comrade doctor: come down to earth a little more often. I swear to God, there's intelligent sense to that. And besides it's less risky: it won't be so painful a fall" (73–4).

Shukshin's reliance on folk humor in Gleb's examination parallels his dependence on folk narrative structure in general. Gleb is the Proppian boundary-crosser of the fairy tale.[17] Though Gleb's aggression obscures this relationship, his linguistic mobility, his stature as con-artist, links him and other spiteful anti-heroes of Shukshin's later fiction with the harmless *chudiki* (gentle eccentrics) of Shukshin's earlier fiction, who too are both literal and metaphorical artists. It simultaneously places him and his tale in the larger syntagmatic structure of all Shukshin's artist/heroes, essentially one and the same character.[18] In Propp's terminology, "Cut Down to Size" contains one "move" of a much larger tale. Gleb's confrontation with Zhuravlev is at once a self-sufficient plot of "deficiency alleviation" (the second in a series of three?) and the unresolved second third of Shukshin's composite hero's proto-quest. "Cut Down to Size" continues the quest at Propp's twenty-third function (fig. 1).

Propp	"Cut Down to Size"
23. The hero arrives unrecognized in another country	Gleb comes to Novaia
24. A flase hero presents unfounded claims.	X makes claims of superiority [*znatnost'*] with his arrival. (Each arrival by a *znatnyi* challenges Gleb's reputation.)
25. A difficult task is proposed to the hero.	The peasants ask Gleb to "cut" X "down to size."
26. The task is resolved.	Gleb succeeds.
27. The hero is recognized.	The peasants praise Gleb.
28. The false hero is exposed.	The peasants recognize X as their own (not Gleb).
29. The hero is given a new appearance (through deception).	Gleb will pretend before the peasants at work.
30. The false hero is punished or recieves a magnanimous pardon.	Gleb magnanimously forgives X.

X = colonel, Zhuravlev, ?

⟶ indicates repetition of the sequence or "move"

Figure 1. Proppian Functions in "Cut Down to Size."[19]

Gleb, whom the narrator compares to a street-fighter, is in the second of the three rounds into which Shukshin divided life: "I regard my entire life as a boxing match of three rounds: youth, maturity, old age. One has to win two of these rounds. I've already lost one."[20] What came before in Gleb's biography is the repeated subject in Shukshin's stories of younger men at earlier stages in their lives. In one way or another all have had their sense of self-worth challenged in encounters with urban culture. (Leaving home in Shukshin's fiction is at once taboo violation and an inevitable stage of adulthood. See, for example, the story of Petr Ivlev, *Tam, vdali* ... [1966].) Gleb, like so many other failed Shukshin heroes (e.g., Egor Prokudin), is engaged in a circular and eventually ill-fated quest to restore his self-worth. The problem is that though he rails against *znatnye*, Gleb himself has replaced *chelovechnost'* (humaneness) or *dushevnost'* (spirituality/heart) with *znatnost'* (eminence). He will continue to struggle against "false heroes," whose *znatnost'* stands as challenge to his own. As Propp explained, "if the hero arrives home, the false claims are presented by his brothers. If he is serving in another kingdom, a general, a water-carrier, or others present them. The brothers pose as capturers of the prize; the general poses as the conqueror of a dragon. These two forms can be considered special cases" (60).

Gleb's previous victim was a colonel. And though not linked biologically, Gleb and Zhuravlev can be regarded as "brothers" or alter-egos. They are approximately the same age, have left their native villages, are talented, and make their reputations through language, Zhuravlev as a professional philologist, Gleb as performer. In Shukshin's fiction (for example, *Ignakha priekhal* ["Ignat's Arrived"], *Zemliaki* ["Countrymen"], *Kak zaika letal na vozdushnykh sharikakh* ["How Bunny-Rabbit Went for a Ride on Balloons"]) contests between brothers, actual or metaphorical, as well as between two aspects of single characters (self-diagnosed schizophrenics as in *Daesh' serdtse!* ["Go for the Heart!"]) are a constant. The titles of his later collections, *Zemliaki, Kharaktery* (*Characters*), and *Brat moi* (*My Brother*), similarly reflect the brother syndrome. Viewed within the context of this metamorphosing paired hero complex, "Cut Down to Size" marks Shukshin's movement away from *derevenshchina* (village romanticism): the village now no longer protects the brother who remains or restores the brother who leaves. If in 1966–67 Petr Ivlev or Chudik could return to the village to lick his wounds and recover, by 1970 Shukshin's hero is beyond the village's influence. The conclusion to Gleb's story, his third round, forms the final chapter to all Shukshin's tales of aspiring, talented, but fatally compromised heroes: death.

Transition, however, is more than a generator of plot for Shukshin; it is the dominant structural principle of his narrative technique. As noted earlier, it is not the peasants but the narrator who rejects Gleb. Employing a device most commonly referred to as represented or shared discourse, Shukshin places the narrator's rejection in discourse that is linguistically (and, correspondingly, psychologically) ambiguous in its source. On the one hand, the remarks highlighted below are properly contained within the narrator's field. On the other hand, they are marked by linguistic features (for example, the past imperfective and/or the present tense, apostrophe, and situational semantics [for example, *tut* (here)]) that signal the narrator's movement into the chronological and perspectival plane of his *dramatis personae*. The effect of this arrangement on reading is, in oversimplified formulation, that we interpret as a character's the narrator's response to Gleb. Through represented discourse the narrator assumes the role of actor within his own story:

> 'He flattened him! . . . What a brain, the dog. How does he know so much about the moon?'
>
> 'Cut him down to size.'
>
> 'How does he do it?'
>
> And the peasants shook their heads in wonder.
>
> 'What a brain, the dog. He put poor Konstantin Ivanich in his place, . . . no? Like a puppy! And what's her name, Valia, she didn't even open her mouth.'
>
> 'What can you say? You can't say anything. He, Kostia, wanted to say something, of course, but for every one word he took five.'
>
> 'What can . . . What a brain, the dog!'
>
> A certain pity for the doctoral candidates, sympathy, could be heard in the voice of the peasants. As always Gleb Kapustin had not failed to surprise, amaze, even delight. But, we'll venture, there wasn't any love for him. No, there wasn't any love. Gleb is cruel, and no one anywhere has ever yet loved cruelty. (176)

Shukshin could easily have avoided ambiguity by placing the narrator's judgment in the peasants' direct discourse. They implicitly possess some knowledge of Gleb's history, at least more than what the narrator tells us. They have a motivation to dislike Gleb, who, after all, treats them no better than he does Zhuravlev. Yet Shukshin chose to place the condemnation in his narrator's mouth.

The narrator's intrusion in "Cut Down to Size" exemplifies the functional mobility of all Shukshin's narrators as they subtly, but persistently, move in and out of the traditional realms of "tellers" and "actors." His movement across planes is but one aspect of his linguistic mobility. L. Geller has characterized narrator discourse in "Cut Down to Size" as homophonic, but stylistically diversified.[21] We would argue that the narrator, like Gleb, moves through several lexical and semantic realms and through his functional and linguistic mobility establishes himself as Gleb's alter ego.

Like Gleb, the narrator of "Cut Down to Size" is not a native of Novaia.

In the story's first paragraph he demonstrates intimate knowledge of the village, yet signals simultaneously that he is not a member:

> Old Agaf'ia Zhuravleva's son, Konstantin Ivanovich, had arrived at her house. With his wife and daughter. For old times' sake, to have a rest. The village of Novaia was a small village, but Konstantin Ivanovich had to drive up in a taxi, and the whole family just had to take a long time hauling the suitcases out of the trunk. . . . Soon the entire village had found out: Agaf'ia's son and his family, the middle one, Kostia, the rich one, the scholar, had arrived. (169)

The repetition of facts and modified references to Zhuravlev and his family are motivated by the presence of two voices, separated by the colon. The stylistic differences between the two are obvious. They complement opposing sets of attitudes towards Zhuravlev. The first expresses a formal relationship to "Konstantin Ivanovich" and his mother and overt disdain for Zhuravlev's display – "but Konstantin Ivanovich had to drive up in a taxi, and the whole family just had to take a long time hauling the suitcases out of the trunk . . ." – while the second expresses both familiarity ("Kostia") and a naive impressionability ("the rich one," "the scholar"). Thus the framing narrator (first voice) is differentiated from any second voice potentially representative of Zhuravlev or the peasants. Having established this difference, Shukshin had no more need for the second voice and dropped it. He devoted the remainder of the story to the relationship between the first voice and his hero.

Introducing both Zhuravlev and Gleb over the next two pages, the narrator in the first voice supplies more information about himself as well as about his subjects. The impression of an outsider inside the village builds up. He draws attention to himself as an "informed" source: "A few words need to be said about Gleb in order to understand why the peasants were waiting for him on the steps and what they were waiting for" (169). But he also reveals the limits of his knowledge: "Somehow it had come to be. . .";"And somehow it came about . . ." (169). As in the first paragraph, the narrator here focuses on the visitors' occupations and their "distinction," the latter presumably by comparison with the villagers' mundaneness. His frequent repetition of the noun *znatnost'* and the adjective *znatnyi* bespeaks a value system not unlike his hero's own.

Throughout the story a curious tension exists between the narrator and Gleb. He casts Gleb as repugnant: "Gleb Kapustin is a thick-lipped, towheaded peasant near forty years old, widely read and cunning" (ibid.). He reiterates Gleb's predatory and spiteful nature: "Gleb smirked. And sort of narrowed his insistent eyes. . . . [Gleb] was drawing himself up to lunge . . ." (170–1). But he also openly admires Gleb's talent: "Last year Gleb cut a colonel down to size . . . with style, beautifully . . ." (169). And, near the conclusion, he ascribes to Gleb a certain humanity: "Gleb even looked at the doctoral candidates with a certain pity" (175). The narrator lacks a sound vantage point outside of Gleb. At times he looks at him from the side: "On the whole, from the side, it appeared that the peasants were escorting Gleb."[22] Then he focuses in on Gleb: "Everyone sat down to table. And Gleb Kapustin sat down. For the time being he was keeping mum. But it was apparent that he was drawing himself up to lunge" (173). Then he abandons him: "He didn't hear how later the peasants, as they were leaving the doctoral candidates' place, said . . ." (176). In scattered moments of represented discourse which foreshadow his eventual repudiation of Gleb, the narrator assumes Gleb's lexicon and semantics. The first example involves a slight lexical adjustment, dropped from all editions except that in *Do tret'ikh petukhov* (*Until the Cock Crows Thrice*), wherein the narrator takes Gleb's condescending view of female academics: "Gleb again smiled graciously. Smiled especially at the wife of the doctoral candidate, also a doctoral candidate, a doctoral candidette, so to speak . . ." (172). The second occurs just as Gleb and Zhuravlev reverse their roles in the middle of the second question. It too has been dropped from other editions: "'But there is no such problem!' The doctor again shot from the hip. There was no point in doing that. He shouldn't have done that" (173). While some have interpreted this as the narrator's assumption of the peasants' discourse and sympathies,[23] we note that the peasants do not refer to Zhuravlev as the "doctoral candidate." To them he is "Kostia." Only Gleb, and the narrator after him, refer to Zhuravlev by his academic rank. In addition to the two moments where the narrator borrows from Gleb, "Cut Down to Size" contains evidence of Gleb's borrowing from the narrator. Describing Zhuravlev's arrival, which he did not witness, Gleb reiterates the narrator's description in the first voice, quoted above: "'We, of course, can be amazed here: driving up to the house in a taxi, hauling five suitcases out of the trunk . . .'" (174). The uneasy intimacy between hero and teller manifests itself further in the narrator's preface to Gleb's tirade. He seems to know how Gleb feels, yet with an otherwise superfluous *naverno* (probably) he distances himself:

That was also pointless, because his pregnant glance was intercepted; Gleb soared upward. . . . And there, from the height of heights, he struck the doctoral candidate. And every time, in conversations with the village's eminences, this moment, when Gleb would soar upward, would arrive. He probably waited for just this moment, was gladdened by it, because from there on everything would happen on its own.

'Are you inviting your wife to smirk?' asked Gleb. Asked calmly, but inside he was probably all atremble. 'Good job. . . . Only don't you think we might first learn how to read the newspapers at least? Huh? What do you think? They say it doesn't hurt doctoral candidates either . . .' (ibid.).

The narrator even proves himself capable of emulating his hero's tactics when, recounting Gleb's strike at the colonel the year before, he omits the answer to Gleb's question (who ordered the burning of Moscow in 1812?) and vicariously tests his readers' knowledge of a much-disputed question of Russian history.

The narrator's proximity to Gleb unquestionably affects his report of the events. Others have noted the structural-semantic opposition Shukshin employed in narrator discourse to underscore the conflict expressed in character discourse.[24] But in addition to heightening the conflict, narrator discourse colors readers' evaluation of the opponents' respective positions. Take, for example, repeated use of the gestures of laughing and smiling. Zhuravlev and Gleb employ these gestures quite differently. When the Zhuravlevs laugh at Gleb's questions, their laughter is perhaps condescending but not malicious. When they laugh, the Zhuravlevs laugh alone, betraying beneath the condescension their discomfort in the peasants' company. Their laughter undermines their position. For Gleb, like Shukshin when he formulated Gleb's questions, laughter plays an offensive, subversive role. Accompanied usually by a self-effacing remark, it is used by Gleb to mislead his opponent into a sense of security. While laughter for Zhuravlev is a function of nervousness, in Gleb's case it signifies control, just another device in his actor's bag of tricks. Here, as throughout the story, the narrator manipulates us (in the same way as Gleb misleads the peasants) into granting Gleb the upper hand. Gleb, after all, has the last laugh. And, of course, the higher he soars, the more resounding will be his crash in the end.

Shukshin's narrator is never omniscient or neutral. Besides representing the events, he plays an active interpretative function, telling us how the *dramatis personae* react to each other and how he reacts to them.[25] He is as much within Gleb as he is outside him. He is Gleb's alter ego, Gleb at an advanced stage of consciousness who has recognized his hero's (and his own) confusion of *znatnost'* with *dushevnost'*. Rejecting Gleb, he rejects a facet of himself, his past. Interpretation of the narrator's condemnation of Gleb as self-criticism removes any logical (or ethical) contradiction.

In "Cut Down to Size" we see how through the mobility offered him by verbal art, Shukshin achieved an uncomfortable, but valuable perspective on himself. As does all his prose, "Cut Down to Size" contains discreet autobiographical allusions. To an extent these have been considered by the critics, though for the most part only superficially.[26] In a literary world where writers can be held personally responsible for the fates of their fictionalized heroes and where biographical information as basic as a natural father's death (Shukshin's died in prison as a *kulak)* and marital status (before Lidia Fedoseeva, Shukshin was married to Viktoriia Sofronova, daughter of the writer Anatoly Sofronov) is guarded as a state secret, the notion that a writer might implicate himself is extremely subversive. But for Shukshin, as for many of his artist heroes, the function of art *(pesnia* [song] in his vocabulary) was to liberate the soul, often (as in Egor Prokudin's case) from years of repressed guilt. "Every true writer, of course, is a psychologist, but he himself is the patient."[27] Like Gleb through his "ridiculous" questions, Shukshin through "Cut Down to Size" turns established interpretations, this time of himself as moralist and chronicler of others' shortcomings, upside down and reveals their falseness.

In the first half of his performance Gleb does not deny philosophy, he only challenges the Marxist concept of matter as primary to spirit. In looking for resemblances between hero and author, readers, too, should keep in mind the primacy of spirit over outward appearances. Notably, in the second half, during his emotional tirade wherein he finds his "language," Gleb offers practical suggestions that echo statements Shukshin himself made in his own non-fiction. For example, Gleb tells Zhuravlev:

> When you're alone, think about it. Think hard and you'll
> understand.' Gleb even looked at the doctoral candidates with
> a certain regret. 'You can repeat the word 'honey' a hundred
> times, but that won't make your mouth any sweeter. You don't

need to pass qualifying exams to understand that, right? You can write the words 'the people' hundreds of times in all your articles, but that's not going to make you any more aware. So, whenever you go out among that self-same 'people,' be a little more collected. Prepared, if you will. Otherwise you may easily find yourself made a fool of. Good-bye. Have a pleasant vacation . . . among 'the people.' (175)

In *Monolog na lestnitse* (Monologue on a Staircase), a virulent attack against urban intellectual condescension towards village culture, Shukshin had advised: "One more consideration: going out into the countryside are future philologists, historians, literati, artists, journalists, lawyers, that is, those who as part of their future work should know folk customs, the special features of dialects, the psychology of the rural dweller. . . . There, in conversation with a peasant, you can learn things no professor in a university knows."[28] Likewise, Gleb's response to Zhuravlev's misuse of prison jargon, quoted earlier, resembles Shukshin's remarks in *Problema iazyka* ("The Problem of Language").[29] And Gleb's complaints about the low quality of television recall Shukshin's story *Kritiki* ("The Critics") as well as repeated remarks in his non-fiction on the dearth of good cultural enrichment programs for rural dwellers.[30] These coincidences in the "spiritual" make-up of author and hero elucidate Gleb's final linguistic switch. There is no contradiction in it. Gleb assumes a more correct idiom, his true voice, only at the moment when he (and the writer through him) no longer pretends, when he is "carried away" by the strength of his convictions and drops his mask.

But if Gleb speaks Shukshin's own words, why, through his narrator, did the writer condemn him? "'Would you like me to explain what makes me tick?' 'I would, explain.' 'I like to flatten noses – no rising over the waterline'" (175). Gleb's words are one thing, his motivations another altogether. In theory Gleb is right, in practice he is wrong. He fails to practice his own beliefs. He prostitutes a noble cause for his own self-promotion. He accomplishes the task of reuniting the peasants with the "eminent guest," but he does so unwittingly and only by devastating the "eminence," as the title emphasizes, by "cutting him down" to the peasants' size. He mediates between the two realms only to advance his own reputation and to avenge his own personal sense of injury. As Shukshin himself explained: "The fellow has decided that he has been overlooked in the distribution of society's wealth, and he has taken it upon himself to avenge [the insult] on the scholars. It is revenge in its purest form, without any coating; well, if it's been coated at all, then only to pull the wool over the eyes of his comrades."[31]

Worst of all, Gleb passes off his personal vendetta as solidarity with the peasants, when in fact he considers himself superior to them. He refuses to speak their language. He uses them only for rhetorical gesture. When he says "We're not philosophers, we don't get the salary. But, if you're interested, I can share with you the direction in which we provincials think," he does so as a preface to his *own,* not to the others', ideas. Stating that shamanism is "not exactly a global issue, but from the point of view of the brethren here, it'd be interesting to know what you think," Gleb realizes fully that the peasants do not care at all about shamanism. All they want is a response which to their untrained ears will sound as good as Gleb's question. Ironically posturing or not, Gleb insults them again when he says to Zhuravlev: "Excuse us, but here, far from the cultural centers, we occasionally get the urge to chat, but you can't really let loose, there's no one talk to." Gleb's alienation from and sense of superiority to the other peasants is alluded to in narrator remarks as well. Gleb comes and goes to work by himself, he walks ahead of the others on the way to Zhuravlev's, and he leaves alone. In short, Gleb *srezaet* (cuts down to size) distinguished visitors to preserve his own *znatnost'*. He is a fraud. That is his cruelty. It is also his punishment: each attack only further alienates him from the peasants as well as from the outside world.

Describing the characteristics of folk humor, Bakhtin noted "that the carnival is far distant from the negative and formal parody of modern times. Folk humor denies, but it revives and renews at the same time. Bare negation is completely alien to folk culture" (Bakhtin, 11). Heretofore critics have focused on the "bare negation" of Shukshin's portrait of Gleb, the hero as a negative example. But Shukshin was no less able *skomorokh* (jester) than his hero, and through the mobility provided by his art offered readers *of "Srezal"* a positive, if somewhat subversive, object lesson in the advantages of life in transition. In this story Shukshin not only portrays the rural advocate and artist-mediator as a negatively charged "other," he simultaneously – through device and subject matter – establishes the anti-hero as an aspect of himself. Hero and author are inextricably bound in a relationship that transcends the boundaries of "historical reality" and "fiction." Recognizing and exploiting his own transitional status as his own hero, Shukshin could repudiate Gleb while sidestepping the trap of accusation that binds Gleb, and many of his critics. Negotiated through mobility between the realms of "fiction" and "reality," the potentially destructive act of accusation becomes an act of creation.

ENDNOTES

[1] Geoffrey Hosking, *Beyond Socialist Realism. Soviet Fiction since Ivan Denisovich* (NewYork: Holmes & Meier Publishers, 1980), 166 ff.

[2] Vasilii Shukshin, *Voprosy samomu sebe* (Moscow: *Molodaia gvardiia*, 1981), 36.

[3] Ibid., 36–37. Shukshin's use of the word *fliusy,* "an abscess under the periosteum caused by a diseased tooth and accompanied by swelling of the cheek" (Volin and Ushkakov), may bear indirect reference to Dostoyevsky's Underground Man, a literary historical source for Gleb and similar protagonists of Shukshin's late fiction worthy of note but beyond elaboration in the present study.

[4] *Srezal (Novyi mir,* 7 [1970]: 55–60); rev. ed., *Kharaktery:* Moscow: *Sovremennik,* 1973; 2nd rev. ed., *Brat moi,* Moscow: Sovremennik, 1975; 3rd rev. ed., *Do tret'ikh petukhov,* 1976. This quotation is cited from *Do tret'ikh petukhov,* 176. Hereafter all citations are from *Do tret'ikh petukhov* unless otherwise noted. English translation can be found in Laura Michael and John Givens, trans., *Stories from a Siberian Village* (DeCalb, Ill: Northern Illinois University Press, 1996) [ed.].

[5] L. Geller, "*Opyt prikladnoi stilistiki. Rasskaz V. Shukshina kak ob'ekt issledovaniia speremennym fokusnym rasstoianiem,*" *Wiener Slawistischer Almanach* 4 (1979): 95-123. Though I depart from Geller's conclusions, I am indebted to his pioneering analysis.

[6] V. A. Apukhtina, *Proza V. Shukshina* (Moscow: *Vysshaia shkola*, 1981), 34.

[7] Lev Anninskii, "*Put' Vasiliia Shukshina.*" In Vasilii Shukshin, *Do tret'ikh petukhov* (Moscow: Izvestiia, 1976), 660. Anninskii's interpretation of Gleb's attack as an act of self-mortification has been heatedly debated. Cf. V. Gusev, "*Imenno zhizn', a ne chto drugoe.*" *Literaturnoe obozrenie* 1 (1974): 52.

[8] Geller, "*Opyt prikladnoi stilistiki,*" 115.

[9] Shukshin, *Voprosy,* 60.

[10] For more on Shukshin's use of socio-linguistics as the foundation for character depiction, see Nemec Ignashev, "Song and Confession in the Short Prose of Vasilij Makarovi Šukšin." Ph.D. diss., University of Chicago, 1984.

[11] Geller, "*Opyt prikladnoi stilistiki,*" 112.

[12] Ibid., 107-10. Geller alludes to a system, but does not elaborate.

[13] M. Bakhtin, *Rabelais and His World,* trans. Helene Iswolsky (Cambridge, MA: MIT Press, 1968).

[14] Besides Geller, who wrote in emigration, the closest any Soviet critic has come to acknowledging substance in Gleb's questions is V. Kantorovich, "*Novye tipy, novyi slovar', novye otnosheniia (o rasskazakh Vasiliia Shukshina).*" *Sibirskie ogni* 7

(1971): 178. On the textology *of Srezal,* see Geller, *"Opyt prikladnoi stilistiki,"* 116–8.

[15] On the implications of the theory of relativity for Soviet philosophy and science, consult Gustav A. Wetter, *Dialectical Materialism. A Historical and Systematic Survey of Philosophy in the Soviet Union,* trans. Peter Hath (New York: Praeger, 1958).

[16] Geller, *"Opyt prikladnoi stilistiki,"* 109.

[17] Vladimir Propp, *Morfologiia skazki* (Leningrad: Academia, 1928). Geller recognizes the significance of fairy-tale morphology for the structure of Shukshin's texts, yet his bias against transition as a healthy state leads him to analyze the morphology of *Srezal* as a tale wherein Zhuravlev, not Gleb, functions as "hero." Proving Shukshin's dependence on traditional structures, he eventually rejects his own morphology, preferring that of the "tale of the peasant who lost his language."

[18] Michael Heller, "Vasily Shukshin: In Search of Freedom," trans., George Gutsche, in Donald M. Fiene, ed., *Vasily Shukshin. Snowball Berry Red and Other Stories* (Ann Arbor, MI: Ardis Publishers, 1979), 215.

[19] Propp *Morfologiia skazki*, 60–5.

[20] Shukshin, *"Iz rabochikh zapisei,"* Voprosy, 249

[21] on *erlebte Rede,* see Lubomir Doležel, *Narrative Modes in Czech Literature* (Toronto: University of Toronto Press, 1973)

[22] Geller, *"Opyt prikladnoi stilistiki,"* 113

[23] The words "from the side" (*so storony*) were dropped from the *Do tret'ikh petukhov* edition.

[24] Geller, *"Opyt prikladnoi stilistiki,"* 112–3.

[25] Ibid., 103–7.

[26] A narrator with strong interpretative responsibilities is characteristic of Shukshin's fiction, though he has eluded the critics. Stephen le Fleming, for example, writes: "Shukshin does not identify with his characters, he withholds comment on them, so we can only guess to what extent he sympathizes with his characters" (Stephen Le Fleming, "Vasily Shukshin, A Contemporary Scythian," in Richard Freeborn, R. R. Milner-Gulland, and Charles A. Ward (eds). *Russian and Slavic Literature. Selected Papers in the Humanities from the First International Slavic Conference. Banff, September 1974,* 449-66 (Cambridge, MA: Slavica Publishers, 1976), 458). See also Geoffrey Hosking, *Beyond Socialist Realism,* 165–6.

[27] Besides Anninskii, the only Soviet critic to posit seriously the possibility that Gleb, Kniazev, Kudriashov et al. are as much fictionalized models of the

writer himself as were the "gentle eccentrics" of his earlier fiction has been Igor'
Dedkov.

[28] Shukshin, *Voprosy*, 250.

[29] Ibid., 45.

[30] "This is most strange: in literature it's become fashionable while in life
it's just not that way. (I'm talking about the degree to which it's necessary to
introduce into the work of art professional jargon, terminology, etc.) A real thief
will never *'po fene botat'* – speaking in thieves' vernacular. Only hooligans, petty
thieves, 'dudes', and students *botayut*" (Ibid., 149).

[31] E.g., in "*Monolog na lestnitse*," and "*Voprosy samomu sebe*" (*Ibid.*, 43, 19).

[32] "*Ia rodom iz derevni. . . ,*" *Ibid.*, 205.

XIII

Carnivalization of the Short Story Genre and the Künstlernovelle: Tatiana Tolstaia's "The Poet and the Muse."

ERIKA GREBER

Tatiana Tolstaia's stories are famous for their fantastic plots and eccentric, grotesque figures. Most commentators concentrated, alongside major feminist issues, on the characters and their narrative presentation since these seemed to be the freshest and most appealing aspect of her texts,[1] and soon critics noted the "aptness of such Bakhtinian concepts as heteroglossia, refraction, orchestration, for a reading of Tolstaia."[2] In the following, the Bakhtinian analysis[3] of the thematic level, of characters and plots – aspects that are most obviously subject to carnivalization – is taken as a starting point for a meta-discussion of the generic, rhetorical-stylistic and aesthetic conceptions that inform Tolstaia's prose. I shall concentrate on a text where the thematic and metatextual levels are most intimately intertwined, namely the metapoetic story about the Poet and the Muse, "*Poet i muza*." The story was published in 1986 and soon translated into English by Jamey Gambrell (1990); her version has since been included in Tolstaia's two prose collections, *Sleepwalker in a Fog* (1992) and *White Walls* (2007).[4]

The story – to quote from Helena Goscilo's basic article – "takes as its point of departure two cultural bromides, which the narrative proceeds to explode through double-voicing, literalized metaphor, 'Homeric' catalogues, and ironic citation of biblical, folkloric, and mythic elements: (1) Woman as an inspirational Muse and (2) everyone's 'right to personal happiness'."[5] In her short analysis of the reversal of gender stereotypes in this story, Goscilo takes the coupling of the gentle poet and the militantly possessive muse as one of Tolstaia's "romantic-sexual liaisons" that "stand out as oxymoronic *mésalliances* cast in a Bakhtinian key" and indicates how such "carnivalized pairings...destabilize dogmatic distinctions and institutionalized hierarchies,"[6] that is, in her argumentation, the institutionalized hierarchies of male and female.

The metatextual reading I am proposing here would interpret the same aspects from a poetological point of view. This involves grasping the ironicized concept of so-called "romantic" love not only as romantic in the melodramatic popular sense, but also as referring to the Romantic in the literary sense, to Romantic aesthetics. This also means that I will treat the effect of carnivalized pairing not only as a critique of sociocultural stereotypes and norms, but also as criticism of aesthetic dogma. This criticism aims, among other things, at accepted generic distinctions – that is, in the given case, the genre of *rasskaz*, the Russian short story. The defamiliarization of typical aspects and distortion of crucial features defining this genre produces a carnivalesque destabilizing of generic and narrative norms (for example, the combination of short story and epilogue discussed below represents a *mésalliance* in terms of generic standards). Therefore when referring to Tolstaia's texts one can speak of carnivalization not only *in*, but *of* the short story.

Headed by the arch-romantic subject "poet and muse," the word "*romantika*" in the third paragraph displays an unmistakeable double meaning: "no romanticism, nothing romantic." However, whether there is indeed no (or no more) literary Romanticism is up to metapoetic interpretation. The key word functions as an indicator of the vocabulary's double-codedness (or rather multi-codedness) in other instances, beginning with the very first sentence, "Nina was a beautiful, ordinary woman." The semantic tension (as if every ordinary woman were beautiful) proves to be a metatextual tension between poetic and nonpoetic, between the discourse of the fairytale and ordinary discourse (*prekrasnaia* /beauteous is the fairytale heroine's standard attribute[7]). Projected more specifically onto the Romantic literary scene, the word connotes the very idea of the beautiful, thus evoking the discussion of the Beautiful and the Sublime in Romantic aesthetic theory. The lofty style was characterized by rich rhetorical ornamentation, and much in the same way the rhetoric of "Poet and Muse"(and of most of Tolstaia's texts) is based on a wealth of rhetorical figures. Thus, the opening expression "a beautiful, ordinary woman" is rearranged at the end of the paragraph as "an ordinary woman, a beautiful woman," the juxtaposed terms being disconnected and inverted

– whereby the figure of inversion may well be taken as a rhetorical symbol of the reversal of stereotypes, of the carnivalistic inversion of canonized values. The motif of beauty recurs throughout the text in various lexical items: *prekrasnyi* and *krasavets* (the beautiful poet Grisha), or *krasivaia* (his beautiful school friend Agniia), or is expressed by the etymologically related expression *krasno* ("red," formerly: "beautiful"). Referring here to the female rival, the artist Lizaveta, "red" is used in a travestying sense, as a negation of beauty, in a so-to-speak anti-Petrarchan description of the "mistress": "her dull hair decked out with an orange ribbon, red-handed, red-faced, sweaty..." (40). The semantically debasing adjectives are morphologically of the composite type (Church Slavonic, modelled on Greco-Byzantian) and belong stylistically to the solemn and elevated style. With words such as *krasnorukaia*, *krasnolitsaia* there eventually emerges from the intricate isotope -*krasn*- another metapoetic or rather metarhetoric idea: the notion of *krasnorechie* – literally: beautiful speech, i.e. eloquence, oratory, the art of rhetoric.

The ornamental rhetoric of Tolstaia's writing, her "sumptuous, spendthrift" style, has invariably been reproached of exaggeration even by well-disposed critics (not to mention other, less favourably disposed ones), and the quantitative argument of "too much" has been turned into the qualitative argument that "Tolstaia's stylistic abundance shifts even to pretentious artificial beauty."[8] Labelling an ornate style *vychurno* has an anti-mannerist undertone; Tolstaia herself ironically uses this label in the passage mentioned, when she comments on the paintings of the "red-handed, red-faced" artist by casual exhibition visitors who would write into "the gallery's luxurious red album...something slobbery, mannered about how sacred and eternal art had supposedly pierced them to the core" (40). Here not only the ancient and Romantic concept of sacred art associated with grand style rhetoric is laughed at through carnivalistic profanation and degradation; implicitly, by metatextual double-coding, the author's own poetic manner(ism) is meant as well. It is as if Tolstaia anticipated that her ornamented style, one of the most distinctive features of her prose, would as well become one of the most controversial.

The ornate verbosity the characters are portrayed with is part of the carnival logic of the text and serves the carnivalistic presentation of the poet as an anti-poet and the muse as an anti-muse. The strange selection of accidental features and their absurd combination form grotesque portraits in the style of Gogol'; this is so not only in the case of Nina, the "beautiful, ordinary woman, doctor," but even more so in that of the poet Grisha and his artist friends and their bohemian circle – a creative union reminiscent of the Romantics' circles of initiates mutually inspiring each other. But in this circle miscommunication and mispairing dominate, whereby the carnivalistic programme of mésalliance is laid bare by contrastive pairings like "all these holy fools, acknowledged and unacknowledged, geniuses and outcasts" (39) or by even openly arbitrary combinations like "girls and freaks, old men and jewellers" (41). A similar device is the enumeration "Grisha, custodian, genius, poet, saint!" (37), an amalgamation where the apparently heterogeneous, if in Soviet reality all too compatible, paradigms of sublime and trivial are combined to familiarize the saintly poet. When Nina first meets him, he is described in a way that plays out the role reversal and thereby ironicizes the classical topoi of male love lyrics. He is lying on the sick-bed, "completely unconscious…under knit blankets, his beard sticking up," a "near-corpse," "mournful shadows on his porcelain brow, darkness around his sunken eyes, and the tender beard, transparent as a springtime forest" (37). These catalogues are not, as Goscilo would have it, "Homeric" catalogues, but transpositions of the Petrarchan beauty catalogue, the *blazon*, and they ironicize Petrarchism and anti-Petrarchism *(contre-blazon)* at the same time.[9] Not only has Nina the active, domineering male role and Grisha the passive, female function of reaction and of being redeemed like Snow White, but this exposure of the "male myth of possession"[10] is expressed in terms of a literary male myth.

The reversal is not a simple role reversal, but it might prove to be multiple, and even in view of the well-known anti- or at least non-feminist statements of Tolstaia (or rather, of Tolstaia's "interview persona," as Goscilo put it[11]), I suspect that there is more to this story than the plain and somewhat misogynist reversal of the classical male/female hierarchy which makes female dominance result in the death of the poet and of poetry and thereby turns the muse into an anti-muse. On the one hand, the poet is indeed a flop, and the muse is really the opposite of a muse as she gradually "destroys the inspiration of the poet she has 'captured',"[12] telling him "Don't you dare write things like that!" and eventually "Will you stop writing!" (41). On the other hand, if the culturally gendered formula *"poet i muza"* presupposes a male poet and a female muse, its inversion could consist in transgendering the pair: woman as poet, man as muse. And indeed, the male hero in Tolstaia's story is not only feminized in terms of role behaviour, but is introduced with standard features of the muse – of course, in carnivalesque distortion. Whereas the classical female muse hides behind a veil (*pokryvalo*), the transgendered muse is covered beneath a blanket (*odeialo*); and the traditional epithet of the feminine veil, transparent (*prozrachno*), a symbol of the unfathomable mystery of inspiration, is transferred to the masculine beard, thereby acquiring the ridiculous meaning of "wispy."[13] Later in the text follows a pun: instead of the expected adored beard (*boroda*) comes a wart (*borodavka*). The formula "the beautiful man's transparent beard" reminds one especially of "the beautiful lady's transparent veil," i.e. the transparent yet unrevealing veil of the beauties of the neo-romantic Silver Age figuring under the labels of *Neznakomka* or The Beautiful Lady – who in their turn belong to the all-European tradition of mystical femininity praised from Dante and Petrarch on through to Novalis, Zhukovsky or Blok, to name the outstanding examples. What Tolstaia eventually presents is a demystifying, defamiliarizing and profanatory variant of the inspirational principle's image. Whether one takes the female or, as I proposed, also the male figure to be the Muse of the story's title, Tolstaia's concept differs from earlier images of the muse by women writers, most notably Akhmatova and Tsvetaeva, for whom the inspirational principle remained feminine (and veiled, cf. Akhmatova's *Muza*, 1924) and divine and who conceived of the relation between poet and muse as a relation between sisters. A possible feminist pre-text for Tolstaia is the carnivalized image of the female muse in the poem *Muza* from the cycle *Secrets of Craft* (*Tainy remesla*) (1960) where Akhmatova makes fun of the concept of poetic frenzy and the sacred inspired word and has her muse utter a most prosaic "*gu-gu.*" For Tolstaia's conception of art in "*Poet i muza*," there exists neither secret nor sacred, neither poetic revelation nor literary craft (or, if any craft, then the craft of a confectioner, as will be outlined).

The hero's claimed position of transgendered male muse (which does not touch on his primary position of poet) would require that the heroine be the inspired poet – which seems to contradict her profession of a doctor and the fact that there is no word about poetic activities whatsoever on her behalf. If there is no word about her poetic production, there is her word itself which is poetic diction, and it is in the same diction, through the double-voiced word of Nina and Grisha and the narrator, not distinguishable from each other, that some of the poet's works are reported. There is a cryptic side to the story and a sense in which it is possible to translate the title "*Poet i muza*" as "The Poet and her Muse" (in a metaphorical way, one could also say that she is a poet, a maker – cf. original Greek *poiein*: to make

— by using him to realize her dreams: he is the "device" of turning her life into an artful design of fantasies, and later on, an art cabinet or museum). The cited pun *boroda / borodavka* belongs to a context in which the object of Nina's desire is again described in the manner of Petrarchan praise of the mistress with the opening topos of inexpressibility and an anti-Petrarchan turn following:

> …Ah, no one can paint [literally: write] the portrait of the
> beloved when, rubbing his sleep-filled blue eyes and freeing a
> young, hairy leg from beneath the blankets, he yawns with all
> his might! Entranced, you gaze at him: everything about him
> is yours, yours! The gap between his teeth, and the bald spot,
> and that marvellous wart! (41)

This passage and the following paragraphs represent the "gaze" of Nina and are formulated from her point of view. They contain a mixture not only of free indirect discourse, but also of interior monologue, that is, direct discourse, and they are clearly the poetic product of the heroine's imagination. As such, they substantiate the claim that she could be taken for a poet, maybe even *the* poet. Another example of her interior monologue is the following extended metaphor:

> Oh, to wrest Grisha from that noxious milieu! To scrape away
> the extraneous women who'd stuck to him like barnacles to
> the bottom of a boat; to pull him from the stormy sea, turn
> him upside down, tar and caulk him and set him in dry dock in
> some calm, quiet place! (40)

If such imagery betrays the egoistic and sadistic traits in Nina's love, the verbal art of such passages attests to her poetic faculty, albeit an ironicized one. This undercover poetess in a carnival mask has no more talent than a banal or even bad prosaic imitator of Petrarchan poetry — but anyway one would expect nothing more from the poetic gift of a poet figuring in a travesty of the Romantic *Künstlernovelle*. The poor talent of the female corresponds to the doubtful gift of the male hero named "the poet" in this story.

While witnessing the artistic frenzy of his friend Lizaveta the painter,[14] the poet is quite literally inspired by a special breath: the scent of sweets.

To the uncomprehending Nina he explains that "this is inspiration, this is the spirit" while "exhaling sweet toffee breath" (39). This is quite close to a mocking literalization of the habitualized metaphor "to devour a book, to devour someone's words."

When the poems of the carnivalized anti-poet are characterized through the imagery of a confectionery, the combination of these remote ideas produces many a conceit:

> Flushed, self-conscious, Grisha read on — thick, significant poems that recalled expensive, custom-made cakes covered with ornamental inscriptions and triumphant meringue towers, poems slathered with sticky linguistic icing [*slovesnym kremom do viazkosti*], poems containing abrupt, nutlike crunches of clustered sounds and excruciating, indigestible caramel confections of rhyme. (38)

This is simultaneously a parody of mannered style and its witty apotheosis. Poetry and sweets are interconnected for a poet or a muse, who, as it were, took all too literal the metaphor of sweet-talk and the according ancient rhetorical concept preserved in expressions like *sladkoglagolivyi propovednik, sladkozvuchnyi pevets, sladkopesnivyi pevets* (to be found in Dal's dictionary).[15]

The two paradigms are probably even more intimately interconnected for an author in whose name the semantic isotopes of literature and fattening food cross, an author who like her famous ancestors bears a telling name with the meaning "fat, thick." This is a sensitive subject to touch on, but it seems that Tolstaia herself, either consciously or subconsciously, provokes it in using the expression *tolstaia* several times[16] and acknowledging by this detail the semantic load of her name.[17] In one instance, when Grisha visits his painter friend and meets her fat daughter who has artistic leanings as a sculptor ("*tolstaia, ispugannaia doch'*," 117), and when he is shuffling about and caressing the fat girl: "*toptalsia poet, gladia tolstuiu Nastiu po golove*" (ibid.), there appears even an anagrammatical congruence and word combination *tolstaia / poet*, with the cryptogrammic message that now a Tolstaia is *poet*, not only a Tolstoy. Thus the poet Grisha may be a carnivalized Alter Ego, and certainly he is a carnivalistic reversal of the writers Tolstoy. Otherness was the starting point for Tolstaia's qualifying as a writer of her own right: there would have been no chance of writing like her namesakes, the one or the other, no possibility of joining any variety of realist poetics without risking the reputation of an epigone or the total disinterest of the literary public and the editors of the so-called "thick journals."[18] Therefore, the "patrilineal justification" virulent in women writers' careers[19] works in Tolstaia's case as an imperative not to imitate precisely the Tolstoyan style, something which for her as a representative of the so-called "other prose," *drugaia proza*, happily combines with opposition to the then mainstream tradition of Socialist realism.[20] Only concerning one idea especially associated with the name of Lev Tolstoy, the concept of *ostranenie* (defamiliarization) with its never-failing potential of renewal, Tolstaia is in line with one of her kinsmen. A favorite device of hers is the defamiliarizing literalization of metaphor, as well as of certain plot situations (equivalent to Tolstoy's famous opera scene, Tolstaia devised a ballet scene in *Fakir*[21]). Thus Tolstaia, who, quite naturally, hates "being discussed as a relative of someone" (as she states in interviews[22]), cannot escape these associations.

"Anxiety of influence" and the "defence of influence" call for the use of apotropaic literary methods and the invention of tropes. Devising the metaphoric correlation of poetry and sweets and their carnivalistic mésalliance in the transgendered anti-poet's work, the writer with the inherited fat literary name found a way to expropriate and yet appropriate this name. Mind and matter combined in a fantasy of logophagia: the act of carnival laughter allows for this ambivalence, for simultaneous "negation and affirmation, ridicule and triumph."[23]

Apart from choosing the literary branch of carnivalized discourse that dissociates Tolstaia from the Tolstoys by way of associating her with the opposite tradition from Gogol' to Bulgakov, she chooses to inscribe herself in the tradition of ornamental, arabesque prose of which again Gogol' is a prominent forerunner.[24] This is why the issue of style is central to Tolstaia's satiric characterization of the artists of her *Künstlernovelle*.

As an act of bohemian resistance[25] to Nina's Philistine, conformist Soviet conception of literature, her subjection to the idea of *zakaz* (commissioned, ideologically conformist work) and to the censorship of a certain "*tovarishch Makushkin*" (an editor with a telling name of the grotesque Gogolian type[26]), the poet refuses to write what they want, refuses to eat and turns to nonverbal ornament reminiscent of Art Nouveau, thus keeping up his former stylistic manner in graphical form. Thereby, the concept of arabesque ornamentation with its non-representational aesthetics is being diametrically opposed to concepts of realist aesthetics.

> ...he didn't want to eat, and he didn't want to write neatly on
> clean paper but, out of habit, kept on picking up scraps...and
> scribbling or else just drawing flourishes and curlicues. (41)

The idea of arabesque ornament, of course, was already present in the metaphoric description of those poem-cakes with their "intricate inscriptions...towers...and verbal icing." There is a special Russian term for the arabesque scripture from medieval Russo-Byzantian book art — *viaz'* — which turns up here in a lexical form estranged by the confectionery imagery, namely: *viazkii*, sticky, glutinous ("*do viazkosti*," 115). The etymological connection between the words seems to motivate the combination of the isotopes of mannered art and glutinous sweets: a *viazkii* tort should naturally be decorated with a *viaz'*, an arabesque ligature of letters. The motif of *viazkii* returns in another passage where the confectionery metaphor represents Nina's slightly malicious view of Grisha's poetry.

> Nina herself would go to see Comrade Makushkin and finally
> resolve the long-drawn-out question of the poetry collection:
> she would ask Comrade Makushkin to look over the material
> carefully, to give his advice, correct a few things, and cut up
> the thick, sticky layer cake [viazkii tort] of Grisha's work into
> edible slices of pastries. (41)

Viaz' and *viazkii*, both words derive from the same root, *viazat'*, which means to bind, knit, or crochet. As I have demonstrated in a book on the relevance of metapoetic textile imagery (especially weaving, braiding, spinning) to structuralist and post-structuralist conceptions of textuality and texture,[27] the motif of *viaz'*[28] in connection with textile motifs and in contexts characterized by intricate, mannered style can be traced back to the Old Russian poetics of *pletenie sloves*, "word-weaving" or "word-braiding."[29] The epoch of *pletenie sloves* was characterized by intense metatextual reflection and a richly ornamented manneristic prose style which can be considered an early variant of what is called, referring to literature of Modernism and after, Ornamental Prose.[30]

Against this background it is now understandable why the poet in Tolstaia's story was transvested in knit blankets, "*pod viazanymi odeialami*" (114): He is a representative of "word-weaving," as is his creator.[31] In the long and inventive history of medieval and modern variations of "word-weaving," Tatiana Tolstaia devised one of its rare amusing variants by transvesting and travestying the craft of word-weaving into a craft of word confectionery.

Towards the end of the story and towards the end of his life, when the poet has totally stopped writing his richly ornamented poems, he also "completely stopped eating, and he kept going up to the mirror and palpating himself" (42). Besides the travesty of female anorexia discernable in this behavior, one could see it as a sign of asceticism closely related to the venerable conception of the poet-prophet (or, regarding the discussed background more specifically, as related to the famous asceticism of the ageing Lev Tolstoy; still another association might be Gogol' who starved himself to death). The correlation of art and food is preserved in its reversed form, changed from abundance and wealth to its negation. Again, there are traces of travesty: whereas authentic asceticism was a means of conquering the corporeal and material principle through the principle of spiritualism, in this story it is nonetheless matter that triumphs over mind. The poet's solution to his creative dilemma is truly carnivalistic and therefore accompanied by the sign of carnival, namely laughter (as opposed to the anti-jovial position of his muse).

> "What are you so cheerful about?" Nina interrogated him. He opened and showed her his identity card where the blue margin was printed with a fat lilac stamp: "Not Subject to Burial." "What does that mean?" asked Nina, frightened. Grisha laughed again and told her that he had sold his skeleton for sixty roubles to the Academy of Sciences, that "his ashes he would outlast, and the worms elude," that he would never lie in the damp ground, as he had feared, but would stand among lots of people in a clean, warm room, laced together and inventoried, and students – a fun crowd – would slap him on the shoulder, flick his forehead, and treat him to cigarettes; he'd figured it all out perfectly. And he wouldn't say another word in answer to Nina's shouts; he simply proposed that they go to bed. But she should keep in mind that from now on she was embracing government property and thus was materially responsible before the law for the sum of sixty roubles and twenty-five kopecks. (42)

This merry vision of the body as a collective body in a public place implies a carnivalistic re-valuation of the material and the corporeal. As if following Bakhtin, who defined the culture of laughter as materialistic, the poet's "answer to the traditional revulsion towards the material and the corporeal…is to propound a celebration of matter and the body that seeks to suspend the dualism of mind and matter and that travesties the "victory" of the mystical and the ascetic over the body."[32] There is a double irony to the skeleton idea in that it reverses the inverted carnival relation between official and unofficial: in order to escape the authoritarian regime of his wife, the poet establishes relations with the Soviet bureaucracy. Thus, the official system acquires the function of opposition and dissidence in regard to the repressive marital order and is therefore able to cooperate with the respectless, familiarizing student crowd.

The concept of immortality not through poetry, but through a material metamorphosis of the body is an ironic revision of the concept of the poet and of poetry as handed down in the Platonic and Neoplatonic traditions. This decidedly materialistic and yet transcendental concept of overcoming death seems to break up traditionally irreconcilable contradictions.

That there are central issues at stake here is confirmed by the crucial expression "tolstoi" which appears in the cited motif of the fat stamp. This inter- and auto-textual marker is succeeded by an unmarked but unmistakeable[33] quotation from Pushkin's immortal verse, actually those verses in which Pushkin declares himself immortal as a poet – "*Ja pamiatnik sebe vozdvig nerukotvornyi*," the sophisticated transposition of the classical Horacian *Exegi monumentum*[34] in which Pushkin also recapitulates the ancient image of the divinely inspiring muse. Tolstaia's slightly defamiliarizing quotation reads, in almost identical words: "his ashes he would outlast, and the worms elude" (42; "*svoi prakh perezhivet i tlen'ia ubezhit*", 119). This is a productive misreading in the Bloomian sense. Of course, Pushkin's unsurpassable apotheosis of "eternal" poetry and creative genius can be responded to only by a profanatory counter-model. Thus the monument Tolstaia's carnival poet now erects for himself is not his eternal poetry, but his mortal body – mortal, yet transsubstantiated to immortality by scientific consecration and certified by the materialized stamp of eternity: "Not Subject to Burial / *Zakhoroneniiu ne podlezhit*." In this way, Tolstaia's story is not only a travesty of the Romantic *Künstlernovelle* (Pushkin, Gogol', Odoevsky, and others) but also parodies a poem that is the very epitome of Romantic metapoetry. Furthermore, "The Poet and the Muse" confirms its affiliation with the poetics of carnivalization by not only displaying "techniques of mixing genres and styles, intercrossing discourses, transgressions against decorum, treatment of extreme themes," but also the "parodistic, travestying orientation towards works of high literature"[35] that is typical of carnivalized texts. Thus, the poet's actual legacy to posterity is the intertextual message not to take Pushkin too seriously (something which also characterized Pushkin's own attitude towards himself). The Pushkin reference was anticipated earlier in the text by the allegedly unmotivated appearance of a mysterious Tungus in the circle of Bohemians ("the Tungus who for unknown reasons kept coming"), something which must refer to the most famous literary Tungus, i.e. the "*nyne dikii* / Tungus" of Pushkin's *exegi-monumentum* poem. Tolstaia's carnivalistic description of absurd nonverbal communication and strange behaviour creates the impression that modern Russia did not bring about the cultural, literary and linguistic "civilization" of Pushkin's "still wild Tungus." This might indicate a criticism of Pushkin's then colonialist Russo-centric perspective as well as a cultural critique of the increasingly barbaric contemporary Russian capital. Another, directly political implication of the corpse motif lies, as Alexandra Smith has added,[36] in its reference to the corpse of Lenin on "eternal" display in the Red Square Mausoleum.

The poet's wife, the bad muse who was only an obstacle to divine inspiration, is a carnival anti-muse. But she is, after all, not an uninspiring muse: her censorship challenged the poet's irrepressible, unsilenceable creativity (as did state censorship in Pushkin's and in Lenin's time) and spurred his ultimate, glorious idea of how to surpass even Pushkin's summit.

The Pushkin quotation, literal in its phrasing and lyric rhythm, differs in two slight, but meaningful points: the omission of the subject *dusha*, the transcendent soul, and the shift from first to third person (instead of Pushkin's "my soul shall outlive my dust and escape corruption," Tolstaia writes: "he shall outlive his dust and escape corruption"). This shift is caused by the change in discourse from poetry to prose and by the accompanying change in genre from poem to short story. At this point, I can take up my initial thesis regarding carnivalization of the short story genre.

The most notable change occurring in Tolstaia's intertextual transformation is the shift from the subjective voice of the Romantic self-centered individual "I" to the multi-voiced narrative of a postmodern, decentered and refracted personality. While Pushkin's poem is polyphonic "only" in the intertextual sense, Tolstaia's story is multi-layered in intertextual and narrative respects. The shifting and elusive point of view is one of the most distinctive characteristics of Tolstaia's narrating and makes it a truly polyphonic, multi-voiced narrative[37] in which the individual voice of the figures and the narrator overlap and occasionally become indistinguishable to a point that irritates readers and evokes a desire for good old quotation marks.[38] Within such a polyphonic frame, the formerly unified position of the Pushkinian poet is refracted in several narrative and semantic positions without definite valorisation but, on the contrary, with ironic ambiguity and ambivalence.

Such a multivocal rendering of poetic creation in Tolstaia's *Künstlernovelle* calls for unusual methods which are partly known from Nabokov's or Vaginov's metafiction but partly wholly original. An example is the following passage in a narrative mode which one could term – in analogy to indirect reported speech – "reported poetry." It is a sort of ironic simulation of the creative process through various stages and types of discourse between verse and prose, containing skilful metaphors and culminating in a realized metaphor.

> He roamed the apartment and muttered that he would soon die, and the earth would be heaped over him in clayey, cemeterial layers, and the slender gold of birch coins would drift over his grave mound like alms, and the wooden cross or pyramid marker...would rot beneath the autumn rains, and everyone would forget him, and no one would visit, only the idle passerby would struggle for a moment to read the four-digit dates, – he strayed from poetry into ponderous free verse as damp as pine kindling, or into rhythmic lugubrious prose, and instead of a pure flame a sort of white, suffocating smoke poured from his malignant lines, so that Nina coughed and hacked [...]. (42)

Tolstaia's fresh style of "reported poetry" is most ingenious in a passage where it is additionally crossed with spoken colloquial language of the *skaz* type.[39] Stylized oral intonation is given in a way that the story occasionally seems to be told by a speaker who addresses his/her listeners within the frame of an oral narrative situation. Usually this storytelling intonation refers to persons and events, but Tolstaia extends it in some instances even to poetry. When markers of *skaz* orality (like *mol, deskat'* or *budto*) occur side by side with sublime motifs from sophisticated Symbolist poetry,[40] this results in a strange, carnivalesque mixture (unfortunately less noticeable in translation).

> ...putting him to bed, she fed him mint-and-lime-blossom tea, infusions of adonis and motherwort, but he, the ungrateful one, whimpered and made up poems that offended Nina, about how motherwort had sprouted in his heart, his garden had gone to seed, the forests had burned to the ground, and some sort of crow was plucking, so to speak, the last star from the now silent horizon, and how he, Grishunya, seemed to be inside some hut, pushing and pushing at the frozen door, but there was no way out, there was only the pounding of red heels in the distance... (41)

This innovative discourse type created by Tolstaia's carnivalesque syncretism might be called "*skaz* verse."

The crucial point of this syncretic discourse is that there is never given the direct word of a first-person poet; by means of narrative focalization the voices of both characters are mingled with the narrator's voice. So one never knows who actually composed the poems ...who is poet and who is muse.

As a consequence of this doubling, the testamentary vision of Grisha's skeleton as an anti-Romantic monument of his creativity is not the only answer to Pushkin's monument. Although the impression might have arisen that the carnival poet triumphs, (t)his is not the last word in this story.

There is another turn in the story, one that reverses the logic and generic structure of the classical short story. The story continues after what would have been a witty twist, a brilliant ending to the story. After the closure-like "skeleton" passage, there is another, if less effective ending:

> And from that moment on, as Nina said later, their love seemed to go awry, because how could she burn with full-fledged passion for public property, or kiss academic inventory? Nothing about him belonged to her anymore. (42)

This second ending, however, turns out to be the opening of a sort of post-story, a pseudo-epilogue in which even a totally new person is mentioned. The story goes on to tell how Nina relates fragments of a parallel case, the story of another widow who made the room of her deceased husband into a Russian-style decorated showroom "with all kinds of peasant shoes, icons, sickles, spinning wheels – that kind of thing" (ibid.). Focusing on this other plot, the story eventually breaks off in typically oral manner without any sign of proper classical closure.[41]

"*Poet i muza*" clearly belongs to the "nonclassical" tradition of Ornamentalism, to a string of "works which are in open rebellion against the traditional genres of the novel and short story"[42] by virtue of fundamental emphasis on the material dimension of the sign and on their richly "woven" textures. Tolstaia's story adds to this tradition a carnival variant which subverts the structural laws of discourse. The careful segmentation of virtual, but cancelled and annihilated, endings foregrounds the transgression of institutionalized genre rules and underlines the unthinkable combination of short story and epilogue, of *rasskaz* and *roman* structures. Thus the irony of narrative style is supplemented by the "Romantic" irony of narrative structure[43]. "*Poet i muza*"seems to be one of those "novels of ten-page length" Tolstaia spoke of in a conversation about the conventional differences between the forms of *rasskaz*, *povest'* and *roman*.[44]

The carnivalesque logic of ambivalence denies "the end" by sublimating death in and through laughter. The idea of the end (the end of life and the end of the text) is central in the intertextual relation between Pushkin's and Tolstaia's metapoetic texts. Pushkin denies the end by resorting to a concept of transcendence and by appealing to an endless intertextual "texte général": the text as eternal monument. Tolstaia's story, while participating in intertextual recycling, has its protagonists offer various versions of negating the end. The carnival poet counters with an inverted materialist transcendency: the body as eternal monument. The carnival muse, surviving, muses on the possibility of a museum with spinning-wheels on display – the spinning-wheels of eternally recurring fantasies and unruly mock epilogues to sort stories.[45]

ENDNOTES

[1] Cf. Natal'ia Ivanova, "Bakhtin's Concept of the Grotesque and the Art of Petrushevskaia and Tolstaia," in *Fruits of Her Plume: Essays on Contemporary Russian Women's Culture*, ed. H. Goscilo (Armonk, NY: Sharpe, 1993), 21-32.

[2] Cf. Helena Goscilo, "Tat'iana Tolstaia's 'Dome of Many-Coloured Glass': The World Refracted through Multiple Perspectives," *Slavic Review* 47, No. 2 (1988): 283, note 11.

[3] As the focus of the present article is on the metatextual reading of Tolstaia's prose in the light of Bakhtin's theories, his concepts themselves are not under discussion here, but serve as tools of interpretation. Among the huge amount of criticism on Bakhtin, I should like to mention the stimulating collection of articles edited by David Shepherd (*Bakhtin. Carnival and Other Subjects* (Amsterdam-Atlanta, GA: Rodopi 1993), see especially part III: Feminism) and one of the classical contributions to theoretical discussion, Renate Lachmann's article on Bakhtin's concept of counter-cultural carnival as deriving from his book on Rabelais and folk culture ("Bakhtin and Carnival: Culture as Counter-Culture," *Cultural Critique* 11 (1988): 115-52).

[4] Considered from the perspective of a metatextual reading, the English translation is not really satisfactory (nor are the two German ones), so that in the following, for the sake of precise argumentation, the English quotes are revised where necessary to correct errors and omissions. Reference is to the first publication: "The Poet and the Muse". *The New Yorker* 15 (1990): 36-42. The original Russian, where necessary, is also from the first publication: "Poét i muza," *Novy mir* 12 (1986): 113-119.

[5] Helena Goscilo, "Monsters Monomaniacal, Marital, and Medical. Tatiana Tolstaya's Regenerative Use of Gender Stereotypes," in *Sexuality and the Body in Russian Culture*, ed. J.T. Costlow and St. Sandler and J.Vowles (Stanford: Stanford University Press, 1993), 210.

[6] Ibid., 330, note 2.

[7] In order to preserve this typically Tolstaian fairytale connotation, the translation should read "beautiful," and not simply "marvellous" like in Gambrell's translation (36).

[8] Cf. Irina Grekova, "*Rastochitel'nost' talanta*," *Novy mir* 1 (1988): 253, 254. Translations are mine.

[9] For a feminist discussion of the *blazon* tradition, cf. Patricia Parker, *Literary Fat Ladies: Rhetoric, Gender, Property* (London/New York: Methuen, 1987).

[10] The quotation in its context reads: "Tolstaya embeds the male myth of possession within the larger narrative of romantic/marital entrapment. Like the heroes of the classic male formula, Nina unilaterally 'chooses' Grisha on the basis of his looks...as the appropriate inhabitant of the doll's house in which she will psychologically incarcerate him. The unresisting Grisha, by contrast,... fulfills the standard feminine role... ...Diminutives in the story *(blazhennenkii, slaben'kii, rovnen'ko)* are applied principally to him." Helena Goscilo, "Monsters Monomaniacal, Marital, and Medical," 212.

[11] Ibid., 218.

[12] K.A. Simmons, "*Zhenskaia proza* and the New Generation of Women Writers," *Slovo. A Journal of Contemporary Soviet and East European Affairs* 3 (1990): 73.

[13] Nevertheless the translation should not be outright "wispy," as in Gambrell's version, but, for sake of the poetological meaning, "transparent." which is polyvalent enough to include the ironic connotation of a wispy beard.

[14] Lizaveta is characterized with all features of eccentricity regarding ecstasy of inspiration as well as scandalizing behaviour at the wedding party, which is conceived of as a Dionysian feast corresponding to carnival rules.

[15] The association of poems and toffees is also to be found in Nabokov's satirical characterization of bad poetry. Apart from Nabokov, who is reported to be Tolstaia's favorite author, the author who probably made the most extensive use of the device of degrading and trivializing characters by gastronomic imagery is Gogol', cf. N.M. Kolb-Seletski, "Gastronomy, Gogol' and His Fiction," *Slavic Review* 29 (1970): 35-57. In "*Poet i muza*," the humorous characterization of Nina's colleague and lover as "egg-shaped" (36) specifically remind one of Gogol'.

[16] Three times in female gender (117, 117, 119), once in masculine gender (119); also occasionally in the other stories in various gender forms.

[17] Asked about the function of details, Tolstaia said: "In short stories...one must discard unnecessary elements, thereby placing much more weight on those that remain. ... That is why I think that if a detail catches the reader's eye, the rest of the text will corroborate the importance of that detail." Tamara Alagova and Nina Efimov, "Interview with Tatyana Tolstaya," *World Literature Today (Books Abroad)* 67 (1993): 52.

[18] The main literary journals are *tolstye zhurnaly* and as such the main source of circulation of new texts, especially short stories. That they "need to publish at least one in every issue, which would otherwise look 'incomplete and unusual' to their readers" shows that "the short story is an indispensable genre in Soviet literature." Henry Gifford, "The Real Thing," *New York Review of Books* 36: 9 (June 1, 1989): 3.

[19] Cf. Robert Strazds, *Contemporary Russian Soviet Women's Fiction 1939-1989* (PhD diss., McGill University, Canada) 1991, 99. Contrary to Strazds' criticism that "many critics writing about Tatiana Tolstaya find it necessary to point out that she is grandniece [sic] of the writer Alexei Tolstoy" (ibid.), it is really necessary – and, as I have argued, even justified by her own texts – to point out her (non-) relatedness to her grandfather.

[20] Stylistic opposition in many cases coincides with a criticism of ideas. For example, the often sarcastic criticism of the idyllic topos of "family happiness" in Tolstaia's prose can be viewed as an opposition to Tolstoyan ideas (as presented in his "Family Happiness") as well as to the Soviet ideal of woman. Cf. Helena Goscilo, "Monsters Monomaniacal, Marital, and Medical," 335, note 29.

[21] "Much as Tolstoy in *War and Peace* shows Natasha Rostova viewing the first act of an opera through the estranged eyes of a naïf uninitiated into the conventions of the genre, so Tolstaya has Galya watch the ballet without the suspension of disbelief essential to any experience of art. ...The atomizing logic of *ostranenie* (estrangement) prevents a submission to art's lure." Helena Goscilo, "Perspective in Tatyana Tolstaya's Wonderland of Art," *World Literature Today (Books Abroad)* 67 (1993): 84.

[22] Interview with Marta Mestrovich, "Tatyana Tolstaya," *Publisher's Weekly* 239 (Jan.1, 1992): 38.

[23] "In the act of carnival laughter, crisis manifests itself as negation and affirmation, as ridicule and triumph." Renate Lachmann, "Bakhtin and Carnival: Culture as Counter-Culture," *Cultural Critique* 11 (1988): 124.

[24] Tolstaia's use of the motif of the tower in particular reminds one of Gogol's conception of arabesque style in literature and in architecture and its relatedness to the idea of the sublime. Cf. Suzi Kotzinger, "*Vozvyshennoe u Gogolja: Vlast' ritoriki i vozvyshennoe iskusstvo*," In *Traditsii i novatorstvo v russkoi klassicheskoi literature (...Gogol'...Dostoevskij...)*, ed. Sergei A. Goncharov (Sankt-Peterburg: Obrazovanie, 1992), 3-24. The tower motif which appears in "*Poet i muza*" in the context of the confectionery tarts takes a central place in *Fakir* in its primary architectural context, referring to the hero's apartment in a tower. Tolstaia's description repeatedly attracted critics because this "poetic, densely instrumented passage...explicitly registers its [the apartment's] esthetic dimension and its fortresslike unassailability... Moreover, the particularized description of the building's torte-like exterior (one of the city's famous Stalin-buildings) highlights emblems of culture, in an occasionally archaic vocabulary ... ornate image of impregnable strength". Helena Goscilo, "Perspective in Tatyana Tolstaya's Wonderland of Art," 82. – When Gogol' describes in his essay

on architecture (1833/34) the sublime architecture of the medieval Christian Gothic in terms such as lace, interweaving, spiderweb and network (VIII, 57), this can be taken as an indication of his affiliation with the tradition of ornamental 'word-weaving' (see below).

[25] The collision of the two totally different life styles and world views was outlined by Goscilo: "Tolstaya throughout stresses the life-denying sterility of Nina's single-minded fixation on control, order, cleanliness, and 'domestic' values. ... This straitjacketed order is systematically placed in diametric opposition to the carefree vitality of the artistic circle that Grisha, Lizaveta, and Agniya typify – in Nina's hygienic eyes, a world of eccentrics and outcasts." Helena Goscilo, "Monsters Monomaniacal, Marital, and Medical," 213f.

[26] *Makushka* means "the back of the head" as well as "summit, top," which suggests here the "summit" of Soviet literature and its censorship system.

[27] Erika Greber, *Textile Texte. Studien zur Tradition des Wortflechtens und der Kombinatorik*, Köln/Weimar/Wien: Böhlau, 2002.

[28] The motif of *viaz'*, originally belonging to the sphere of calligraphy, was transposed to a literary metaphor in Aleksandr Blok's metapoetic poem *Snezhnaia viaz'* from the cycle *Snezhnaia maska*. Cf. ibid., ch. IV.

[29] A comprehensive book on the subject of medieval Slavic word-weaving is by Maurice L. Hébert, *Hesychasm, Word-Weaving, and Slavic Hagiography* (Munich: Sagner, 1992).

The motif of weaving is of mythopoetic origin and appears in many folk tales as a symbol of time and storytelling. The fairy tale *The Feather of Finist the Bright Falcon* which Tolstaia alludes to at the beginning of the story also contains motifs of textile. The magic tools of the beauteous maiden with which she produces "magnificent patterns" are a spinning wheel and golden spindle and a golden lace frame and needle. Incidentally, the tale is used here as a pretext which is characterized by role reversal; whereas most fairy tales deal with the triple trial of a male hero, this tale is about a triple test of the "*krasnaia devitsa*" and thus can be cited as "a heroine's classical feat" (36).

[30] The main characteristics of Ornamentalism, as the following encyclopedia definition shows, likewise apply to the style of word-weaving: "Linguistic textures, stylistic richness and variety ... devices of rhetoric and declamation, word play, striking imagery, musicality – a complex mixture of alliterations, assonances, consonances, repetitions (leitmotifs), and phrase rhythms – are typical, while narration is sometimes fragmentary, a montage of diverse, juxtaposed narrative styles drawn from the nonliterary and oral (skaz), the solemn and philosophical...and so on." Kenneth N. Brostrom,

"Ornamentalism," in *Handbook of Russian Literature*, ed. Victor Terras (New Haven-London: Yale University Press, 1985), 324, with further references to criticism on Ornamental prose.

[31] In view of the proposed relation of Tolstaia's style to "word-weaving," it appears to be not coincidental that some critics (unconsciously?) imitate the criticized (or admired) mannered style and actually use textile metaphors and related imagery of intricate structure, cf. the quotations in the original publication of this article (*Essays in Poetics* 21 (1996): 50-78, notes 9 and 33).

[32] Renate Lachmann, "Bakhtin and Carnival," 125.

[33] The English edition uses quotation marks because in translation, the phrasing loses its exact recognizability, also depending on the chosen version (alternative Pushkin translations would be: "My soul will outlive my flesh and won't decay" or "Safe from the worm, my spirit will survive" etc.)

[34] Cf. Renate Lachmann, "Intertextuality as an Act of Memory: Pushkin's Transposition of Horace" in Renate Lachmann, *Memory and Literature. Intertextuality in Russian Modernism* (Minneapolis, Minn.: Minnesota Press, 1997).

[35] Renate Lachmann, "Bakhtin and Carnival," 142.

[36] While I agree with her taking my interpretation further, it remains unclear in what sense the Lenin reference should be "metapoetic". Cf. Alexandra Smith, "Carnivalising the Canon: The Grotesque and Subversive in Contemporary Russian Women's Prose: Petrushevskaia, Sadur, Tolstaia, Narbikova." In *Russian Literature in Transition*, ed. I. K. Lilly and H. Mondry (Nottingham: Astra, 1999), 35-58, here 45.

[37] "Probably the most distinctive aspect of Tolstaia's writing is its narrative voice, descended from the garrulous storytellers of Laurence Sterne and Nikolai Gogol'. Pulsing with iridescent vitality, rife with contradictions and illogicalities, ellipses, erratic shifts in mood, flaunted lapses of memory side by side with perfect recall of apparently irrelevant and minute detail, this obtrusive narrative voice indulges in digressions, disclaimers, apostrophes, rhetorical questions and exclamations, as it freely mixes colloquialisms with elevated and poetic diction. ... Tolstaia actually orchestrates a multivocal narrative...". Helena Goscilo, "Tat'iana Tolstaia's 'Dome of Many-Coloured Glass': The World Refracted through Multiple Perspectives" *Slavic Review* 47:2 (1988): 283.

[38] From the hypothetical position of a 'corrector tracing the punctuation marks', Nevzgljadova observed that 'there occasionally appears the professional wish to put within quotation marks the speech of the figures that wilfully keeps digging into the narrator's speech, and to cut the latter into dialogues so that

there would distinctly emerge two voices' (Elena Nevzgljadova, "*Eta prekrasnaia zhizn'. O rasskazakh Tat'iany Tolstoi*" *Avrora* 10 (1986): 112).

[39] A state-of-art article on *skaz* is Wolf Schmid, "Skaz." *Russian Literature* 54 (2003): 267-278.

[40] Drawing on organicist imagery of plants and growth, the metaphoric style in both quotations makes use of another motif paradigm rooted in the tradition of 'word-weaving' and, incidentally, not uncommon especially in Symbolist word-weaving, as vegetable motifs are generally prominent in *Fin de siècle* art and literature. The characterization of Lizaveta's paintings earlier in the story may equally refer to Art Nouveau and to such well-known Symbolist poems as Bal'mont's sonnet *Podvodnye rasten'ia / Underwater plants*, and labeling her art line *kogtizm*/nailism functions as an ironic reference: "The style was called 'nailism' – it was a terrible sight to behold. True, there did result images that somehow resembled underwater plants, stars, and castles hanging in the sky, something simultaneously crawling and flying" (39).

[41] The question of finale is crucial to others of Tolstaia's stories, too: "As frequently in Tolstaya's prose, the story's final section further complicates the narration. ... Closure is a particularly fraught issue in 'The Fakir' because the specific genre of Filin's art raises questions about the nature and function of storytelling." Helena Goscilo, "Perspective in Tatyana Tolstaya's Wonderland of Art," 85.

[42] Kenneth N. Brostrom, "Ornamentalism," in *Handbook of Russian Literature*, ed. Victor Terras, 324.

[43] For Pushkin's use of Romantic irony, cf. Monika Greenleaf, "The Sense of Not Ending: Romantic Irony in *Eugene Onegin*." In her *Pushkin and Romantic Fashion: Fragment, Elegy, Orient, Irony* (Stanford: Stanford Univ- Press, 1994), 205-286 and notes 385-393. Of course, the first intertextual source to refer to is Sterne, as is specifically testified by Tolstaia's story *Fakir*. "It is no coincidence that the author who Filin claims to read...is Laurence Sterne, the supreme master of narrative manipulation and of the insatiable narrative drive that defies closure." Helena Goscilo, "Perspective in Tatyana Tolstaya's Wonderland of Art," 86.

[44] "Sometimes it seems to me that I am writing novels – of ten-page length. And sometimes it seems to me that I am writing prose poems." Peter I. Barta, "The Author, the Cultural Tradition and Glasnost: An Interview with Tatyana Tolstaya," *Russian Language Journal* 44 (1990): 277.

[45] As an "epilogue" I would like to refer to Alexandra Smith's feedback to this article in its 1996 first printing. In her resumption of the question of

carnivalization in "The Poet and the Muse," Smith adds the key carnivalistic aspect of festivity (which was irrelevant to the generic problems discussed above but is certainly relevant to carnival poetics as such), cf. Alexandra Smith, "Carnivalising the Canon: The Grotesque and Subversive in Contemporary Russian Women's Prose: Petrushevskaia, Sadur, Tolstaia, Narbikova," 35-58, esp. 42ff.

XIV

Down the Intertextual Lane: Petrushevskaia, Chekhov, Tolstoy.

LYUDMILA PARTS

"...In a writers' cafeteria... Dante, Boccaccio, Buzzati, Tolstoy, Chekhov, Joyce, and Proust sit around tables. And here I ... find myself in this writers' cafeteria, and what if the only available seat is at the table where Tolstoy, Chekhov and Bunin sit together. I'd come near and they would stare at me, Tolstoy would be especially displeased... Not to mention the other two..."

L. Petrushevskaia, "A chance at menippea."

Lyudmila Petrushevskaia's story "The Lady with the Dogs" (*Dama s sobakami*, 1990), a part of the *Requiems* cycle, presents in less than three pages the life and death of a woman who liked to take care of stray dogs and whose only companion was her own dog. Even though the text itself does not establish any obvious connections, the title suggests an intertextual link with Chekhov's story "The Lady with a Dog" (*Dama s sobachkoi*). As a rule, intertextual elements signal the author's intent to respond to an earlier text. The effect of such a linkage is twofold: as the new text encapsulates the older one's themes and images in order to use them for its own starting point, the older text is reread through the prism of the new one. The new text, meanwhile, establishes its place in the tradition, capitalizing on its relationship with those texts already sanctified by cultural memory. This sequence is potentially endless since there is always a possibility of a new voice joining in the exchange. By the same token, the sequence can reach as far back into the past as the chain of texts allows. Thus, Chekhov's story is itself engaged in an intertextual dialogue with Tolstoy's *Anna Karenina*. By 1899, when "The Lady with a Dog" was written, Chekhov had largely rejected Tolstoy's philosophical teachings; nevertheless, he continued the literary dialogue in several of his late stories.

The choice of title for a text is the easiest way for an author to announce intertextual intent and direct the reader toward the source-text or texts. In the last two decades, Russian writers have created a broad variety of intertextual titles, from Vladimir Makanin's *Underground or a Hero of Our Time* (with its clear allusions to Dostoevsky and Lermontov) and Evgenii Popov's (Turgenevian) *On the Eve of Eve*, to Sergey Soloukh's (Chekhovian) *Sergeant Prishibeev's Club of Lonely Hearts*, and many others.[1] In the process of reinterpreting its history, contemporary Russian literature has turned to the classics to gain a new perspective on both this legacy and its own position vis-à-vis this legacy. The reader may therefore not be surprised by the title of "The Lady with the Dogs," but he or she will be hard pressed to find the connection between the story's intertextual title and its protagonist, who is utterly unlike the Chekhovian heroine. A close look at Petrushevskaia's "The Lady with the Dogs" instead reveals some surprising, but definite, parallels not so much with Chekhov's story as with *Anna Karenina*. Although Petrushevskaia is following the line of dialogue started by Chekhov, her objective is even more ambitious than adding another link to the great intertextual chain: by retracing the intertextual links embedded in Chekhov's story she intrudes on the latter's dialogue with Tolstoy. She picks up the main issues addressed by the two masters, relocates their characters by placing them within the reality of end of the twentieth-century Russia and makes a statement of her own. Petrushevskaia's nameless lady with the dogs possesses features of Anna Karenina but is presented under Chekhov's title and accompanied by his heroine's dog, while being subjected by Petrushevskaia to a contemporary version of sexual passion, social decline, divorce and suicide.

Immediate critical reactions to Petrushevskaia's stories in literary journals, invariably touch upon the author's attitude toward the human tragedies she describes. She is generally considered to present an "unfeeling" stance towards the events presented, but opinions vary about the reasons behind it. Opinions are evenly split: either Petrushevskaia's "harshness is saturated with pain" and the reader is forced into cathartic recognition of responsibility for everyone's pain, or this harshness signals a "certain indifference on the part of the author," which eventually results in the reader's "getting used to indifference."[2] The debate may, in my view, be resolved thus: in most Petrushevskaia texts there is a narrator who is clearly an authorial construction. This narrator is not openly contradicted by an authorial voice "correcting" the narrator, or any other voice setting "things right," but it is there. The implied author does not interfere, but her presence is nevertheless felt. Thus, while Petrushevskaia's silent implied author may be seen as remaining within the humanistic tradition of Russian literature, her constructed narrators lack human compassion, crossing over into a sphere of callous indifference to suffering and degradation. Numerous critical discussions of stories such as "Night Time" (*Vremia noch'*), "Our Crowd" (*Svoi krug*), and "Such a Girl" (*Takaia devochka*) address this kind of apparently single-voiced narrative where any compassionate authoritative voice seems absent; and they point to the vital importance of unmasking the narrator as crucial to a proper understanding of the stories.[3] Indeed, a dramatized or unreliable narrator presupposes distance between him or her and the implied author. However, in "The Lady with the Dogs," as in many *Requiem* stories, Petrushevskaia withdraws even further from the authorial position to such a degree that her absence is not only difficult to detect but in fact total. I am suggesting that the effect of this technique is to force the reader to become the missing counterpart to the narrator's voice, to do the job of the implied author, as it were. In the case of "The Lady with the Dogs," the only non-narratorial perspective that the reader gets is the intertextual contextualization of this contemporary story in terms of classic pre-texts. He, or she, is drawn into the literary dialogue of three authors, into three conflicting attitudes toward love, life, and death, each of which reflects a different historical epoch. It is this clash of attitudes that invites the reader to take the stance the author refuses to indicate by any other means, or at least to select one from the alternatives thus suggested – provided the reader has the literary competence, of course.

The Tolstoy – Chekhov dialogue as conducted between *Anna Karenina* and "The Lady with the Dog," has of course been noted repeatedly and critically dealt with many times; what critics of Petrushevskaia's oeuvre have so far failed to see is that she adds a radically new dimension to this dialogue by sharply negating both their positions through the intrusion of a third voice, the voice of her morally indifferent constructed narrator. Judging by the epigraph, Petrushevskaia seems to think that her interference in their dialogue is bound to displease both Tolstoy and Chekhov, but maybe she is exaggerating: in formulating a statement on life in the present through allusions to literature of the past, she creates a juxtaposition of epochs that clearly favors older times without her having to imply this in any "authorial" way; most readers are likely to mourn the keen interest in moral issues that the 19th-century texts demonstrated – in however different ways – and that contemporary reality seems to have lost, substituting moral indifference for earnest engagement. The voices of two classical author substitute for the implied author's voice and provide the missing counterpoint to that of the narrator's voice. As the reader follows Petrushevskaia down the intertextual lane, he or she faces the gap between the narrator's vision of the world and the time-honored humanism of classical Russian literature. Petrushevskaia's vision of her times is indeed dark: the gap separating contemporary Russia from her past seems unbridgeable. If there is a reason indeed for the older writers, especially Tolstoy, to be displeased with Petrushevskaia's story, as she – judging by her statement in the epigraph – imagines they would be, it is because she drags them and their characters into a modern world that would terrify and appall them.

As has been pointed out, Chekhov's portrayal of ordinary people has the effect of "broadening the social side of a given conflict."[4] "The Lady with a Dog" certainly expresses this author's "avowal of independence from traditional treatments" in regard to the adultery theme, juxtaposing his portrayal of an extramarital affair to Tolstoy's and, in effect, challenging Tolstoy's conservative approach to the themes of love, family, morality, and judgment.[5] Chekhov brings Tolstoy's grand tragedy down to earth: in contrast to a strikingly beautiful society lady and a dashing army officer who are led to a tragic end by their fateful passion, his characters are ordinary people facing love as the unexpected outcome of a banal summer affair. Although there are several similarities between the two texts – adulterous love, travel, trains, both Annas' disdain for their husbands, and their desire to experience life – one scene in particular is crucial in sustaining and making obvious the intertextual link between Chekhov's and Tolstoy's texts, as well as the two authors' different stance in regard to adultery: the seduction scene, in which both Annas experience excruciating guilt and sorrow. In this scene Chekhov brings Tolstoy's theme to its culmination and also turns away from Tolstoy in order to concentrate on his own artistic and philosophical goals.

Chekhov's seduction (perhaps it should be called the after-seduction) scene opens the same way as Tolstoy's: resolutely after the fact. The focus is on the characters' reaction to what has happened between them, and it is the similarities and the differences in that reaction, which determine the function of the scene in each text. Before Chekhov's Anna even starts to speak Gurov has been contemplating his past affairs, trying to categorize Anna among his many lovers: as careless, good-natured, hysterical, capricious, cold, etc. He cannot find a category for her, and finally settles on a cultural reference: "Her features lengthened and drooped, and her long hair hung mournfully on either side of her face. She assumed a pose of dismal meditation, like a repentant sinful woman in some old painting."[6] Seeing Anna as a woman in a picture, Gurov frames Anna, just as Tolstoy frames Anna Karenina several times in the course of his novel. Tolstoy repeatedly employs the device of ekphrasis. As Amy Mandelker has pointed out, "framing" the character, Tolstoy emphasizes the problematic nature of the Western tradition of portraying women as the object of male gaze and, in general, of portraiture as a closed and final version of a person.[7] Every description of Anna's portraits in Tolstoy's novel represents someone's vision of her, someone's version of her essence.

Unlike the artists who have "finalized" Anna, Levin leaves her "free." When Levin, just before meeting Anna for the first time, contemplates Anna's portrait, it initializes his spiritual conversion; the scene, in Mandelker's analysis, presents the beginning of his "tolerance for the imperfection of human lives and his resulting compassion."[8] Levin leaves Anna's house feeling pity for her, the feeling that his wife immediately mistakes for love. Kitty may be too hasty in her conclusion that Levin "ha[d] fallen in love with that nasty woman," but she is fundamentally right in linking compassion and love. Significantly, Levin sees Anna's portrait before she enters the room, and he performs an action contrary to Gurov's, an un-framing, so to speak. He sees Anna "stepping out of the [portrait's] frame in a brilliant light," sees "not a painting but a lovely living woman" (VII, IX). Gurov's moment of framing, in contrast, is far from including compassion; it is rather a result of his inability to see a living woman. He puts her in a pictorial and "framing" context to ease and bracket off his own discomfort. He remains a free subject of the gaze that forces Anna Sergeevna into the position of an object of interpretation, the position in which she has no voice. At the end of the story, however, Gurov has learnt the same lesson as Levin did – but by looking at himself, not Anna Sergeevna. He sees himself in a mirror: his gaze is directed back at him and prompts self-examination.[9] He realizes at that moment that he is not a free agent as he thought he was when eating his melon and gazing at his crying mistress, but that both he and Anna are "framed" by circumstances, their situation, encroaching old age, the passage of time – that there is no such thing as classification and objectification, but only a shared human condition. The mirror, the most faithful of portraits, forces Gurov to look inside himself and there he finds compassion and tenderness for another by transferring self-pity to empathy. Looking at and into himself, he accepts that he no longer can bracket off life's challenges. He finally accepts love with all its consequences, which would have been impossible for the Gurov of the beginning of the story.

The trope of framing, however, puts the lady with a dog in the context not only of personal but also of cultural experience. The image of the sinful woman, while referring to the biblical figure, also invokes its literary representations. In Tolstoy's novel, biblical references (starting with the epigraph) are linked to Anna's transformation from a "good wife" into an unrepentant sinner. When Chekhov's character describes a real woman in terms of a portrait, his perception is likewise mediated: his reference is to "the cultural pose of the 'sinful' woman."[10] Coming together with other intertextual links to Tolstoy's novel, and in light of the importance of the pictorial in *Anna Karenina*, Chekhov's technique allows us to read the "classical painting" as a classical novel, that is, as a reference to *the* literary image of a sinning woman – Tolstoy's masterpiece. Thus Chekhov discloses the dialogical thrust of his text, and immediately moves to the point where he parts ways with Tolstoy's novel.

While the two women in their post-seduction scene behave in very similar ways, the men do not. Thomas Winner points out that "unlike Vronsky, Gurov appears cynical. When faced with Anna's shame, he takes her unhappiness lightly and eats watermelon while she weeps."[11] Nabokov singled out this moment as well: for him, the image of Gurov calmly taking a slice of a watermelon is a "realistic detail – another typically Chekhovian technique."[12] I would argue that this detail is the culmination of the Tolstoyan line of the story, and one of the story's most important symbols. Anna's monologue imploring Gurov not to despise her mirrors that of Anna Karenina who "felt herself so criminal and guilty that the only thing left for her was to humble herself and beg forgiveness" (II, XI); Anna Sergeevna cries out: "I am a wicked, fallen woman. I despise myself" (10: 132). Annoyed, Gurov even thinks that she might be playing a part, the part, obviously, of a fallen woman; indeed, if Anna Sergeevna is, subconsciously, following a literary model, the most famous and readily available one would be that of Anna Karenina.

The pathos of this scene, so alien to Chekhov's style, is justified solely by his objective of entering into a dialogue with Tolstoy's novel, and it is consequently undercut in a very Chekhovian manner by Gurov's prosaic gesture of slicing the watermelon. There is more to this detail than realistic effect though: with this gesture Chekhov's story symbolically parts ways with Tolstoy's novel and rejects its message. In *Anna Karenina*, Vronsky becomes "infected" (to use a Tolstoyan term) with Anna's guilt and fear as he is invariably influenced by her emotions throughout the first part of the novel. This time, while Anna is overcome by humiliation and guilt, he feels "what a murderer must feel when he looks at the body he has deprived of life." The equation of adulterous sex with murder refers first of all to Vronsky's feelings and actions:

> But despite all the murderer's horror before the murdered body, he had to cut this body into pieces and hide it, he had to make use of what the murderer had gained by his murder. And as the murderer falls upon this body with animosity, as if with passion, drags it off and cuts it up, so he covered her face and shoulders with kisses. (II, XI; emphasis added)

The twice repeated word "cut" is the detail Chekhov picks up in his story: his character does cut but his cutting is decidedly literal, mundane and practical, without a trace of pathos. Bored with Anna's speech, and seeing a watermelon on the table, "Gurov *cut* a slice for himself and started eating it without hurry" (10: 132). Thus the scene includes both conspicuous similarities with Tolstoy's scene and the no less striking deviation from it. When Tolstoy equates adultery with murder to make his point, he goes to an extreme; when Chekhov shows Gurov becoming bored by Anna's guilt he goes to the opposite extreme: not only is Gurov completely immune to Anna's feelings, but he sees their adulterous encounter as a most ordinary event on a par with the consumption of food. This dramatic difference in the men's reaction to adultery and to the women's expression of guilt highlights the differences between Chekhov's and Tolstoy's artistic and philosophical objectives: unlike Tolstoy, Chekhov underplays the moral aspect of the characters' situation. Just as his setting emphasizes the characters' ordinariness, so his tone shifts from Tolstoy's high moral indignation to the subtle lyricism of the love story that develops after the seduction. Furthermore, Gurov's ultimate response is emblematic of

Chekhov's response to Tolstoy's view of morality. Chekhov renders Tolstoy's moralistic and social message ineffective by assigning inherent value to love; whereas Tolstoy subordinates love to moral and social obligations, Chekhov acknowledges the difficulty of his characters' situation without criminalizing their breaking of conventional moral rules. He operates with a moral code wholly different from Tolstoy's, one according to which marriage for money or convenience, like those of both Annas and Gurov, is truly immoral, more immoral perhaps than adultery that results from such marriages. This view of morality as a private struggle full of compromises is very different from Karenina's and Levin's maximalist demand for complete hold on the world and its truths. With the subtlety that earned him the title of a writer without principles, Chekhov cancels out Tolstoy's moralizing by sidestepping rather than disputing it. Tolstoy recognized this by judging the story "on the other side of good."[13] Chekhov, however, was no more inclined to be influenced by this kind of criticism than Gurov is affected by Anna's pathetic plea.

Thus Chekhov is interested in the development of the characters' relationship and in its effect on them. The relationship is not over at the end of the story and its outcome is difficult to predict. The only definite conclusion of the story is that "love has changed them both." While Anna Karenina's story is unequivocally tragic, the other Anna's often-proclaimed unhappiness is subject to doubt. Karenina's fate is sealed and predicted in the first scene in which she appears. Chekhov's story's ending is famously open. And this is where Petrushevskaia comes in. In contrast to Chekhov's poetics of openness, hers might be called 'the poetics of the end.' The raw material of her texts are dysfunctional families, broken hopes, abandoned children, sick mothers, misery and destitution, all of which produce an effect of unrelieved gloom.[14] This vision of the world allows neither for lyricism nor for moralizing. Nor does it allow for an open ending that at least theoretically offers the possibility of a positive outcome. In this story, she picks up where Chekhov left his story open and provides the ending – but one that does not replicate Tolstoy's either.

Chekhov's story ends with the word "beginning": "the most complicated and difficult part was only just beginning." Vladimir Kataev has commented on the tension between the motifs of "ending" and "beginning" which informs the end of the story in the same way as the tension between "it seemed" and "it turned out" (*kazalos'/okazalos'*) propels its development throughout.[15] Jan van der Eng elaborates on the function of the word "end" in the story: "the whole point of the story is, in fact, centered in the ambiguity with which the word 'end' is echoed through it."[16] He maintains that there are two kinds of "ends" in the story, opposing each other: a positive one, or the end of their predicament, signaling the beginning of a new life, and a negative one or the end of the affair itself. The motifs of end and beginning play against each other, contributing to the story's open-endedness. Petrushevskaia subverts the dynamics of beginnings and endings: she foregrounds and manipulates both the conventional expectations and Chekhov's use of beginnings and endings.

She opens her story about the "lady with the dogs" with a pointed accumulation of the past tense "ended" and the verb denoting the ultimate end – death: "She is dead now, and he is too; their abominable love affair is over. And what's interesting about it is that it was over long before their death (*ona uzhe umerla, i on uzhe umer, konchilsia ikh bezobraznyi roman, i, chto interesno, on konchilsia zadolgo do ikh smerti*)."[17] The sentence starts with the twice-repeated verb "died," goes on to the also repeated "ended," and ends with the noun "death." This semantic overflow of "end" words, coming as it does in the very first sentence of the story clearly manifests the author's intention to set a morbid mood and rigid boundaries to the story. Unlike Chekhov's story, which ends with a beginning, her story has ended before it begins. Petrushevskaia's poetics of the end are in full force here: the character is dead before we learn anything about her; the subsequent portrayal is as finalizing and objectifying as only a posthumous one can be.

The dominant feature of the description of the lady with the dogs is the use of the past tense. The events of the story are doubly removed: she had already died, and what is described happened long before that: "They had already separated long before, about ten years; he was living somewhere or other, while she came and took up residence at the House of Creative Workers, as if for effect – she and a dog" (199). In the following passage, the past tense "was" and the words "memory" and "to recall" indicate the erosion of her social status:

> ... an old memory of her lived on here, of her escapades and
> scandals, of their benders for all the world to see, of the fact
> that she was the wife of an eminent artist – well, she had been.
> At the same time they recalled that she was also the daughter
> of an eminent figure from the old days, and, powerless to do
> anything about it, they allocated an apartment to her, and she
> moved in there with her dog... (199)

The narrator shows remarkable knowledge of the lady's past and present situation although she admits to having heard most of the facts from others, emphasizing that the lady's privileged status and scandalous life have held her at the center of public attention. Like Karenina, who in Dolly's assessment is "the wife of one of the most important personalities in Petersburg and a Petersburg *grande dame*"(I, XIX), she belongs to the highest circles of Soviet society. She is a daughter of a former high-ranked government official and the wife of a famous artist. Her status thus combines the political power of her father and the power of the fame of her artist spouse. The artistic circles form a new, twentieth-century version of the glamorous high society in which Karenina shone a hundred years earlier.

Once the reader retraces that line, to Tolstoy's novel through Chekhov's story, the similarities between the lady with the dogs and Anna Karenina emerge with great clarity: there is in both texts a woman of remarkable beauty, a passionate and public love affair, an estranged child, people's contempt, and finally a suicide attempt. The beauty of the lady with the dogs is described in the past tense also and is contrasted with the condition of "the lady" in her post-glamorous state which the narrator knows best. The details of that description correspond exactly, in negated form, to Tolstoy's description of Anna:

> Since the divorce her outward appearance had changed dramatically; her once voluptuous bust had shrunk, her hands had withered like potato plants, the hair she once wore proudly and erectly she now hid under headscarves, and the one and only thing she had left was her love for baubles. (200)

Compare this description to Anna Karenina's "full shoulders and bosom [...] and her rounded arms with their very small, slender hands"; her "full arms with bracelets on them, firm neck with its string of pearls..."; her "holding herself extremely straight, as always"; "her once proud, gay, but now shame-stricken head"; "her two beautiful hands with their so-familiar rings"; "her beautiful, ring-covered hands."[18] The following details are central to both descriptions: the full body, the thick hair, a proud and very straight posture, and the jewelry. In Petrushevskaia's story, both the beauty and the pride are things of the past, and the jewelry has become symbolically cheap. To Tolstoy, at least two of these details – Anna's body and posture – are crucially important. They symbolize the proud and destructively irresistible power of her beauty. They also serve to juxtapose Anna's inner and outer worlds, which are in harmony before her fall and in discord afterwards. Finally, when she commits adultery, both her inner and outer beauty are destroyed: first her human essence, and in the end her body. In Petrushevskaia's story, the tragedy is toned down, modeled to the reality of the post-Soviet time: the love is gone, the suicide is unsuccessful; the lady's beauty and life are destroyed by time, gossip, and sickness.

Petrushevskaia's reader is denied access to "the lady's" inner world. She remains an object of external description and a hostile, totally finalizing gaze throughout the short narrative. In this manner Petrushevskaia subverts one of the basic realistic techniques – psychologism. Tolstoy's novel is the exemplary model of nineteenth-century psychologism that penetrates into a character's inner world in order to illuminate in detail every motive, however conflicting, behind any and every action. Chekhov does not of course follow Tolstoy's omniscient approach; he nevertheless combines carefully selected details with occasional glimpses into the characters' thoughts to recreate their psychological state. Tolstoy attempts to "tell," and Chekhov to "show" (to use Percy Lubbock's terminology) the psychological state of their respective characters.[19] In both cases, albeit to varying degrees, the reader is allowed into the characters' thoughts and mood. Petrushevskaia's narrator does not gain even a glimpse into her protagonist's soul, and the narrator's authority is further undermined by the fact that gossip is the source of her knowledge. Petrushevskaia's commonly unreliable narrators freely make assumptions about characters' states of mind, motives, and thoughts – here there is not even the slightest attempt to verify even the most unreliable information.

In this story, too, since the narration consistently undermines and ridicules the lady's life story, she remains an object and a victim of the narration. When she does speak, the few words she utters are projected through other people's accounts and interpreted (or misinterpreted) according to the narrator's predetermined objectives. The narrator assigns motives to her actions and behavior, which are hypocritical and mean, even suggesting that the suicide was faked. The only scene presenting the lady's words without such aggressive and deforming interpretation is the passage in which the lady brings back to the Retreat a dirty and hungry dog, one of the many that she takes under her wing. We see her addressing her own "socially conscious" and "proper" dog, who looks embarrassed trotting along with such a lowly creature:

> The lady would rebuke her poodle, saying it didn't have the
> right to persecute this unfortunate wretch, this carrion, if
> they wanted to fatten it up. Everybody had the right to live,
> this Brigitte Bardot would shout (to her it seemed like she
> was telling the dog off quietly), nobody should be persecuted!
> Persecute not, and you shall not be persecuted! (*ne goni, i ne
> gonim budesh'!*)[20]

The lady seems to be advocating pity toward those less fortunate. It is
characteristic, however, that she, the only character to do so in the story,
is presented as crazy, ridiculous, and herself unable to elicit pity or respect
from others. Her gesture is further undermined when in the next paragraph
her love of dogs is juxtaposed to her hatred of children: "Incidentally, she
hated children and also had a scandalous relationship with her fairly adult
child." The dogs serve as a preferable substitute for people because "animals
were the only creatures that had never bawled her out," or in other words,
never talked back.[21] The lady attempts to monologically rule her world
in the same way as the narrator rules the larger world of the story. If the
reader feels inclined to distrust the narrator he or she gets no help from
the implied author: no other information or perspective is offered. In the
absence of authorial directions, the narrator's perspective with its obvious
dislike of her subject dominates the story.

The "Lady's" speech also introduces the motif of passing judgment, one of
the most important in Tolstoy's novel, and emphatically absent in Chekhov's
story. On a critical evening in Karenina's life, the evening of the ball, Tolstoy has
her say: "No, I will not cast a stone" (I, XXII). The phrase alludes to the scene,
in the Gospel according to John (8: 1-11), of the woman taken in sin: "[Jesus]
said to them, 'He that is without sin among you, let him first cast a stone at
her.'" The lady with the dogs' phrase is modeled on the biblical "judge not, that
ye be not judged" and has similar connotations. Both phrases, about casting
a stone and about judging, have acquired in the language of the twentieth-
century a quasi-proverbial function. They nevertheless retain their biblical
associations even as elements of non-religious discourse. Petrushevskaia's
Lady's words, with their religious overtones, thus introduce the motif of
who is entitled to judge a fellow human being. In *Anna Karenina*, this phrase
is one of the details foreshadowing the time when Anna becomes the target
of many a stone. Tolstoy draws a clear distinction between God's judgment

and that of society; but he, nevertheless, subjects Anna to both. Chekhov's characters, in contrast, replace abstract moral judgment with concrete private fears. Gurov keeps looking around while kissing Anna on the street; and while Anna is not afraid of God's judgment, she is incessantly afraid of incurring Gurov's disrespect. In Petrushevskaia's story, the narration itself is the voice of universal condemnation. Potential relief comes from the fact that while the narrator condemns the Lady with the Dogs the reader is free to condemn the narrator for her refusal or inability to empathize. Her meanness and cruelty makes her suspect. This reaction on the part of the reader would therefore be produced by the *absence* of the conventional way of affecting the reader through the unmasking of the narrator. She unmasks herself by being given unlimited freedom to judge, but then there are also those who might agree with her. The author's virtual absence allows for this alternative as well.

Because narrative remains a weapon aimed at the lady, the story emerges as devoid of human compassion. The people surrounding the protagonist do not have any pity for her; she, in turn, feels compassion only for stray dogs. And after her death, the narrator concludes, "not a single dog, as the saying goes, took pity on her (*kak govoritsia, ni odna sobaka ee ne pozhalela*). That is of course idiomatic speech, but the "dogs" spoken of here clearly allude not only to humans but also include "real dogs," specifically the stray ones that the "Lady" had taken care of. This detail finally strips the lady not only of human, but even of her dogs' compassion. The atmosphere of the story is that of a world in which nothing is valued and no one is pitied; thus, even a suicide attempt is interpreted as a farce and a scandalous trick and the notion of faithful dogs mourning their good masters is plainly ridiculed. While in Chekhov's stories human interaction based on love and compassion is rare and precious, in Petrushevskaia's it does not exists. This significant absence accounts for the terrifying vision of the world that emerges in her stories: while Chekhov often makes the lack of human communication, contact and connection into a leading motif of his stories, intimating that this is an important source of human unhappiness and implying that it can be overcome, at least by some people, for Petrushevskaia's narrators it is an issue that does not exist. They do not trouble themselves with the problem of miscommunication because they have no epistemological uncertainties.

In the last paragraph of the story, the void created by the absence of compassion is especially apparent as the narrator arrives at the Lady's death in her account of her life story. She calmly states the facts, or lack of facts: "Still, nobody knows how she actually died, which cot she expired on, apparently from cancer and in agony"; and she explains: "All of this had to end somehow, this abominable life, crippled by God only knows what, but too noisy and stormy for our terms and conditions." She then wonders what happened to the dog and whether it was allowed to wail over its owner's grave, before dismissing the thought by referring once again to the times: "nobody would allow such a thing in these times" (201). Thus if there was "one dog" who mourned the Lady's death, the narrator buries this fact in the flow of her habitual skepticism. Since she already stated that "not a single dog took pity on her" the dog's wailing is dismissed like everything else that does not fit her interpretation. What are these times, one may ask, when not even a dog is allowed to howl at the grave of its dead owner and a human being dies alone and in pain in a hospital bed? The answer must be that these are the times neither of Tolstoy's nor of Chekhov's Anna. The questions that preoccupied Tolstoy and Chekhov are now far less urgent than they once were and their ideas on love and death as important events in a human life are suspect. The Anna Karenina of our time, as Petrushevskaia constructs it, would not be able even to commit suicide to end her torment, and would have to go on living, losing the last shreds of dignity; while the lady with a dog would outlive her love – the substance of her life – and be left with nothing. The Lady's dog is, significantly, "the last of its line" (201).

It is clear that the loud, arrogant, and slightly crazy lady with the dogs carries no resemblance to Anna Sergeevna. Still, her story bears the title of Anna Sergeevna's story and opens with words that unequivocally connect it to Chekhov's, even when stating the opposite. Petrushevskaia's title announces that her story of the end relates to the dominant ethical tradition of nineteenth-century literature, even when it is denied (by the narrator). Chekhov, the last classic of the nineteenth century, opposes the traditional literary treatment of fateful passion by entering into a dialogue with Tolstoy and presenting a radically different way of portraying illegitimate love. He brackets off the social and moral side of the situation and concentrates on love as a force capable of changing one for the better.[22]

His story, therefore, concludes and exemplifies, whether in direct or in negated form, some of the nineteenth-century tradition's premises. Petrushevskaia's "absent author," in turn, denies love and beauty any inherent value by having her character outlive them both and turn into a lonely and unappealing creature. In this story, as in Tolstoy's novel, the motif of passing judgment is central. However, in Tolstoy, it is one of the forces contributing to Karenina's transformation into an angry, unreasonable, vengeful, albeit still pitiable figure; while in Petrushevskaia, it is the only "moral" force operating in a world devoid of feeling. Everything else is discarded as fleeting and useless.

Petrushevskaia, in effect, attempts to show the end not only of the love and life story of her protagonist, but of a whole cultural tradition that exalted morality, love, family, compassion, and other axioms of meaningfulness in human existence, even when it revalued and reinterpreted these. In her vision of contemporary reality, these values are deemed to be illusions, therefore they cannot be reinterpreted or revalued. No one among the present-day writers in Russia better fits the description given by Lev Shestov of Chekhov's poetics: "Stubbornly, sadly, monotonously, during all the years of his literary activity, nearly a quarter of a century long, Chekhov was doing one thing only: by one means or another he was killing human hopes."[23] Chekhov's dialogue with Tolstoy in "The Lady with a Dog," however, is one of many examples to the contrary: it is of course not human hopes that Chekhov is contesting but a prescriptive attitude toward the complexity of human life and emotions. Tolstoy's heroine's passion leads her to ruin; the love of Chekhov's characters gives meaning to their existence. Petrushevskaia seems to be skeptical about both possibilities. In "The Lady with the Dogs," her narrator at least – probably without knowing either writer – seems to side with Tolstoy in condemning stormy passions that lead to fateful consequences, only to go a step further and deprive the character she tells us about even of the compassion allowed Anna Karenina.

By withholding anything but the most indirect authorial presence that serves as a counter perspective to the narrator's interpretation of events, namely the intertextual linkages demonstrated above, Petrushevskaia creates a world of voids that force the reader to fill those somehow. One reason why, most probably, a reader would distrust the narrator and her vision of reality is his or her experience of the Russian literary tradition with its emphasis on humanistic values, the experience called forth by the story's intertextual thrusts and so conspicuously lacking in the narrator. The psychological depth of Tolstoy's novel, the compassionate lyricism of Chekhov's story – these are the elements Petrushevskaia evokes to create a counterpoint to her narrator's voice. They serve as a reminder of the lost world of the nineteenth century and contribute to the melancholy inherent in a requiem. Petrushevskaia's cycle *Requiems* mourns a debate discontinued and a quest terminated – in short, a past irrevocably lost except as echoed in remembrance.

ENDNOTES

[1] See Vladimir Makanin, *Anderground ili Geroi Nashego Vremeni* (Moscow, 1999); Evgenii Popov, *Nakanune Nakanune* (Moscow, 2001); and Sergei Soloukh, *Klub Odinokikh Serdets Untera Prishibeeva* (Moscow, 2002).

[2] See Irina Murav'eva, "*Dva imeni*," *Grani* 43 (1989): 121; Mark Lipovetsky, "*Tragediia i malo li chto eshche*," *Novy mir* 10 (1994): 231; and Maria Vasil'eva, "*Tak slozhilos'*," *Druzhba narodov* 4 (1998): 208–17.

[3] For analyses of "Night Time" see Helena Goscilo, "Speaking Bodies: Erotic Zones Rhetoricized," in *Fruits of Her Plume: Essays on Contemporary Russian Women's Culture*, ed. Helena Goscilo (Armonk, NY: M. E Sharpe, 1993), 135– 63; idem, "Mother as Mothra: Totalizing Narrative in Petrushevskaya," in A *Plot of Her Own: The Female Protagonist in Russian Literature*, ed. Sona Stephan Hoisington (Evanston, IL: Northwestern University Press, 1995), 102–13; and Josephine Woll, "The Minotaur in the Maze: Remarks on Lyudmila Petrushevskaia," *World Literature Today: Russian Literature at a Crossroads* 67 (1993): 125–30. For analyses of "Our Crowd" see Patricia Carden, "The Art of War in Petrushevskaya's 'Our Crowd,'" *Studies in Short Fiction* 34:1 (1997): 39–54; and Woll, "The Minotaur in the Maze." For analyses of "Such a Girl" see Aleksandra Karriker, "Claustrophobic Interiors and Splintered Selves: Petrushevskaya's Prose in Context," *West Virginia University Philological Papers* 41 (1995): 124–31.

[4] B. Meilakh, "*Dva resheniia odnoi problemy*," *Neva* 9 (1956): 187–88.

[5] On Chekhov's treatment of the "adultery theme" see Thomas Winner, *Chekhov and His Prose* (New York: Holt, Rinehart and Winston, 1996), 223. For an analysis of this and other stories constituting what she calls "the Anna Plot" in Chekhov see Caryl Emerson, "Chekhov and the Annas," in *Life and Text: Essays in Honour of Geir Kjetsaa on the Occasion of this 60th Birthday*, ed. Eric Egeberg et al. (Oslo, 1997), 121–32.

[6] Anton Chekhov, "Dama s sobachkoi," in his *Polnoe sobranie sochinenii i pisem v tridtsati tomakh* (PSS), ed. N. F. Bel'chikov et al. (Moscow, 1974–83), 10:132. Subsequent in-text parenthetical references to Chekhov's story indicate the volume and page number. (Translation in *Anton Chekhov: Later Short Stories, 1888–1903*, ed. Shelby Foote, trans. Constance Garnett [New York, 1999]). Subsequent in-text references to L. N. Tolstoi, *Anna Karenina: Roman v vos'mi chastiakh* (Moscow, 1984), indicate the book and chapter numbers. (Translation in *Leo Tolstoy, Anna Karenina: A Novel in Eight Parts*, trans. Richard Pevear and Larissa Volokhonsky [New York, 2000]).

[7] Amy Mandelker, Framing *Anna Karenina: Tolstoy, the Woman Question, and the Victorian Novel* (Columbus: Ohio State University Press, 1993), 91.

[8] Ibid., 115.

[9] Mirrors are also used in Anna Karenina as a potential pathway into self-consciousness, one that Tolstoy's characters do not necessarily follow: Levin looks at himself in the mirror before entering Anna's house and refuses to acknowledge that he is drunk. On the other hand, when Anna looks in the mirror on the last day of her life she does gain an insight into herself. She recognizes herself in the strange woman that is looking at her in the mirror (the "other woman" she referred to in her delirium some months before), and her acknowledgment, "Ah, it's me," is one of the last and decisive factors that drive her to suicide (VII, XXVII).

[10] Julie de Sherbinin traces representations of the biblical sinner in Chekhov and throughout the Russian literary canon. The Christian paradigm of two Marys, the virgin and the whore, which de Sherbinin designates the Marian paradigm, is fixed in popular imagination and in literary representation. Within this paradigm, Anna Karenina represents the sinner, "the woman who would transgress the boundaries of commonly shared religious/social beliefs to commit adultery (her body prostrate at Vronsky's feet after their first amorous encounter, announces literally a fallen woman)." See de Sherbinin, *Chekhov and the Russian Religious Culture: The Poetics of the Marian Paradigm* (Evanston, IL.: Northwestern University Press, 1997), 37, 86.

[11] Winner, *Chekhov and His Prose*, 224.

[12] Vladimir Nabokov, *Lectures on Russian Literature*, ed. Fredson Bowers (San Diego: A Harvest Book Harcourt Brace & Company Bruccoli Clark Layman, 1981), 333.

[13] L.N. Tolstoy, diary entry, 16 January 1900, in *Tolstoy's Diaries*, ed. and trans. R. F. Christian (London: Flamingo, 1994).

[14] Virtually every work on Petrushevskaia makes a note of the unremitting bleakness of her world. See, for instance, Helena Goscilo's "Mother as Mothra" for a look at Petrushevskaia's subversive treatment of the traditional roles of mothers, wives, and daughters. For an analysis of Petrushevskaia's characters' moral disintegration as representative of the disintegration of social norms, and her stories as "testament of an arduous even horrible epoch," see Karriker, "Claustrophic Interiors," 127.

[15] Vladimir Kataev, *Proza Chekhova: Problemy interpretatsii* (Moscow: *Izdatel'stvo Moskovskogo Universiteta*, 1979), 257.

[16] Jan van der Eng, "The Semantic Structure of Lady with a Lapdog," in *On the*

Theory of Descriptive Poetics. Anton Chekhov as Story-Teller and Playwright, ed. Jan van der Eng et al. (Amsterdam: Peter de Ridder Press, 1978), 75·

[17] Petrushevskaia, "*Dama s sobakami*," in her *Dom devushek* (Moscow: *Vagrius*, 1999), 199. Page numbers refer to the original Russian text. The first English translation, by Krystyna Anna Steiger, is included in the present collection following this article.

[18] See Tolstoy, *Anna Karenina*, I, XXII; I, XXIII; II, VII; II, XI; and II, XXIV; respectively.

[19] Percy Lubbock, *The Craft of Fiction* (London, 1954), 38.

[20] Petrushevskaia, "*Dama s sobakami*," 200. In 1976, Brigitte Bardot, the famous French actress who became one of the icons of female sexuality in the United States in the 1950s and 1960s, established the Brigitte Bardot Foundation for the Protection of Distressed Animals.

[21] Ibid. In "Niura the Beautiful" ("Niura Prekrasnaia"), another story of the Requiems cycle, a dog is again a substitute for a close family relationship, in this case an unfaithful husband and nonexistent child: "The husband has long lived on the sly with a girlfriend, and there has been a baby already, but Niura did not manage to have a child and walked everywhere with her dog" (*Dom devushek*, 242).

[22] First drafts of the story stated explicitly: "Made them both better." Chekhov cut the word "better" from this sentence during the last stages of working on the story, trusting the reader to make the conclusion. See K. M. Vinogradova, "*Stranitsa iz chernovoi rukopisi rasskaza 'Dama s sobachkoi,'*" in *Literaturnoe nasledstvo: Chekhov*, vol. 68 (Moscow, 1960), 133–40.

[23] Lev Shestov, *Chekhov and Other Essays* (Ann Arbor: University of Michigan Press, 1996), 4.

XV

The Lady with the Dogs

A SHORT STORY

LYUDMILA PETRUSHEVSKAYA

She is dead now, and he is too; their abominable love affair is over.
And what's interesting about it is that it was over long before their death.
They had already separated long before, about ten years; he was living
somewhere or other, while she came and took up residence at the House
of Creative Workers, as if for effect – she and a dog. Inasmuch as an old
memory of her lived on here, of her escapades and scandals, of their
benders for all the world to see, of the fact that she was the wife of an
eminent artist – well, she had been. At the same time they recalled
that she was also the daughter of an eminent figure from the old days,
and, powerless to do anything about it, they allocated an apartment to
her, and she moved in there with her dog and lived quietly, conversing
loudly only with her dog. "You've gone out of your mind," she would say
to it on the balcony (the neighboring balconies heard her uncommonly
loud voice – there are figures like that, with inherently loud voices,
like leaders, military commanders and orators but, as a rule, just plain
troublemakers).

What the neighboring balconies had heard in the past were the
succulent kisses of greeting, the click-clack of heels, the (equally) loud
voices of guests, the scraping of chairs and the clinking of glasses, and
what especially annoyed everybody were the rich, bright, far-resounding,
innately actor-like, trained voices, in which they had terrible brawls.
They say irons used to fly around the room, but everything stayed in

one piece, arms and heads. It took one splendid moment for the news
to spread that they had separated; it was he who'd chucked the whole
damn thing and gone off to be with some broad. And there you have
it, the coming of the lady with the dog – or dogs, rather, for on more
than one occasion she showed up carrying some vile, filthy, clearly out of
place, embarrassed dog, an outsider, hung over this lady's shoulder like
a fox stole that was all tattered and moth-eaten. The lady would rebuke
her poodle, saying it didn't have the right to persecute this unfortunate
wretch, this carrion, if they wanted to fatten it up. Everybody had the
right to live, this Brigitte Bardot would shout (to her it seemed like she
was telling the dog off quietly), nobody should be persecuted! Persecute
not, and you shall not be persecuted!

And thus she carried on, and people literally recoiled from her, so
strikingly did she herself resemble a disheveled, ratty animal that was
persecuted and, in spite of everything, including the meals in the dining
room, hungry. On her shoulder she'd be carrying around a bewildered
rag in the form of a mongrel, with legs that were filthy up to the elbows,
while a well-groomed poodle, also deeply bewildered, would be running
along beside her, and everybody around would avert their eyes; only
the children gawked. Incidentally, she hated children and also had a
scandalous relationship with her fairly adult child, and time and again
people heard her repeat that animals were the only creatures that had
never bawled her out.

Since the divorce her outward appearance had changed dramatically;
her once voluptuous bust had shrunk, her hands had withered like potato
plants, the hair she once wore proudly and erectly she now hid under
headscarves, and the one and only thing she had left was her love for
baubles, which really dangled from her and jingled all over – in her ears,
around her neck, around her bony wrists. The dogs never bawled her out,
the costume jewelry loved her, and that was all she had left.

She only lost her temper once, which had never happened before,
and revealed her new nature of goody-goody and old maid. When
there was a get-together on the balcony one storey up, and the guests
began click-clacking their heels and talking in rich, loud voices, and
the clatter of dishes rang out, and things flowed and percolated, she
waited till midnight, secretly boiling over, and then richly, soberly and
distinctly, on her own balcony she said a single phrase, which nobody
could decipher, and which some conveyed as "you're keeping my dog

awake," and others as "even a dog needs its rest." In short, something incompatible and incongruous with her goody-goody nature, but clear in its intentions: the time had come for the next generation to celebrate, which was irrelevant to her by now, like everything else. Everybody already knew she had no means of subsistence, her husband had left her the apartment and that was it, she couldn't work anymore – no more than she could've gone back to her job at the institute after the nuthouse, where she'd ended up fresh out of the noose. They'd only just barely been tolerating her at the institute anyway, with her bright clothes, costume jewelry, wild makeup, tardiness and unjustified absences, with her voluptuous promises to manage this deal or that with the help of influential acquaintances, and also with the strange story of somebody's money having disappeared from her room. Nobody caught our lady red-handed, but there was talk; they became seriously apprehensive about her, though they didn't show it, afraid as they were of killing this deeply wounded animal altogether. And that's not the worst of it. In the dead of the night she telephoned two or three women, busy ones with families, to say she was going to hang herself right now and the door was unlocked, so let them come and take her out of the noose. One and all, the women started talking her out of it, but when she called the third one, the first two called each other and summoned the emergency psychiatric ambulance service, who came, threw open the door, and out of fright our lady jumped off the chair with the noose at the ready around her neck, and the telephone receiver in her hand – it was precisely the element of surprise that made her jump, when she saw the white smocks. Otherwise she might not have jumped, her colleagues thought. But a paramedic intercepted the suicide in mid-air, caught her with ease; the cervical vertebrae didn't snap in her fragile, swan-like neck, and she didn't poop her pants or bite off her tongue – no such hideousness occurred in her case.

Still, nobody knows how she actually died, which cot she expired on, apparently from cancer and in agony. All of this had to end somehow, this abominable life, crippled by God only knows what, but too noisy and stormy for our terms and conditions. Nevertheless, not a single dog, as the saying goes, took pity on her, they all just sighed gently, hearkening to distant rumors, and where her own old doggie disappeared to, her poodle, the last of its line, and whether the dog howled over her corpse, or sat by her grave – all of these myths from animal stories can be disregarded, nobody would allow such a thing in these times. Only one thing is clear: that the dog was in for a rough time after the death of its Lady, its one and only.

Translated by Krystyna Anna Steiger

XVI

Russian Postmodernist Fiction and Mythologies of History:Viacheslav Pietsukh's "The Central-Ermolaevo War" and Viktor Erofeev's "Parakeet."

MARK LIPOVETSKY

CONTEXT: MYTHOLOGIES OF HISTORY

It should come as no surprise that postmodernism, with its emphasis on the playful subversion of all authoritative discourses, has a unique approach to the question of history. In her book *A Poetics of Postmodernism*, Linda Hutcheon goes so far as to define this entire trend in fiction as "historiographic metafiction," positing that the combination of metafictional self-reflexiveness with a new artistic philosophy of history is what gives rise to postmodernist poetics.[1] This approach could seem a bit narrow, since it cannot possibly encompass the entire radically diverse range of postmodernist literature, but it seems tailor-made for such significant postmodernist novels as Umberto Eco's *Name of the Rose*, E. A. Doctorow's *Book of Daniel* and *Ragtime*, Milorad Pavic's *Dictionary of the Khazars*, John Fowles's *French Lieutenant's Woman* and *A Maggot*, D.M. Thomas's *White Hotel*, Gabriel Garcia Marquez's *One HundredYears of Solitude* and *The Autumn of the Patriarch*, the novels of John Barth, and, of course, numerous short stories by Jorge Luis Borges. What is different about the postmodernist interpretation of history? Using the work of Hutcheon and other scholars as a point of departure, I suggest concentrating on the following major principles:

1. A rejection not only of the search for any kind of historical truth but of the very teleology of the historical process itself. This feature is certainly connected to postmodernism's fundamental orientation toward relativism and multiple truths. As Linda Hutcheon writes: "Postmodernist discourse

– both theoretical and practical – needs the very myths and conventions they contest and reduce...; they do not necessarily come to terms with either order or disorder ... but question both in terms of each other.... The postmodern impulse is not to seek any total vision. It merely questions. If it *finds* such a vision, it questions how, in fact, it *made* it" (48, emphasis in the original). That is, postmodernism not only establishes multiple variations of the ordering of history but also uncovers the artificial status of such orders; they are not objective, not given, but rather are constructed by the mechanisms of culture and human consciousness. On the level of poetics, this quality reveals itself in the way in which "postmodernism establishes, differentiates, and 'then disperses stable narrative voices (and bodies) that use memory to try to make sense of the past" (118). In other words, in postmodernist poetics the concept of *culture as chaos* is projected on the image of history.

2. Hutcheon argues that postmodernism leads to a "metafictional rethinking of the epistemological and ontological relations between history and fiction" (121). The point here is that in both postmodern literature and contemporary historical scholarship (Michel Foucault, the "New Historicism," Hayden White) the historical process is treated as a complex interaction of myths, discourses, cultural languages, and symbols, that is, as an open-ended *metatext* that is constantly being rewritten. The traditional Aristotelian opposition of history and literature as the real and the possible, as fact and fancy, is destroyed: "Historiographic metafiction shows fiction to be historically conditioned and history to be discursively structured" (120).

3. The understanding of history as an open-ended text naturally gives rise to a particular aesthetic strategy: "Postmodern fiction suggests that to rewrite or to re-present the past in fiction and in history is, in both cases, to open it to the present, to prevent it from being conclusive and teleological" (110). On the one hand, this describes the formation of a particular historical view of the present that in no way differs from the past; both past and present are constantly written and rewritten. On the other hand, here we also see the connection between postmodern philosophy and dialogical poetics, which attempts to expand the "zone of direct contact with inconclusive present day reality."[2]

4. Finally, postmodern intertextuality and irony take on particular importance when this conception of history is given form:

> Postmodern intertextuality is a formal manifestation of both
> a desire to close the gap between past and present of the
> reader and a desire to rewrite the past in a new context...
> Among the many things that postmodern intertextuality
> challenges are both closure and single, centralized meaning...
> The typically contradictory intertextuality of postmodern art
> both provides and undermines context. (118, 127)

As a rule, postmodern intertextuality is of a parodic or ironic cast, making problematic the subject's pretense to historical knowledge of both the past and the present. Hutcheon suggests that this is the fulfillment of Foucault's predictions that the "writing subject endlessly disappears,"[3] emphasizing the dependence of the creative subject on impersonal forms of language or discursive play.

To what extent can these principles be applied to Russian literary postmodernism? To what extent do Russian authors transform typically postmodernist artistic and philosophical concepts? This question is crucial, for Russian postmodernist fiction contains numerous examples of such play with various historical myths and mythologies of the ordering of history. Here we need only recall the works of Vladimir Sharov, in particular, his novels *The Rehearsals* (1992), *Before and During* (1993), *How Could I Not Be Sorry* (1995), as well as Valery Zalotukha's *Great Crusade for the Liberation of India* (1995), Dmitrii Lipskerov's *Forty Years of Chanzhoe* (1996), and Iuri Buida's *Yermo* (1996) and *Boris and Gleb* (1997), among other recent works.

Even a cursory glance at these texts reveals their striking difference from the meta-utopian fiction of the "sixties" authors who also addressed the problem of historical discourses (Vladimir Voinovich's *Life and Extraordinary Adventures of the Private Ivan Chonkin,* Vasily Aksenov's *Island of Crimea,* several chapters of Fazil Iskander's *Sandro of Chegem,* and practically all the fiction of Iuz Aleshkovskii). The authors of the sixties satirized the myths of Soviet history and historiography, but in revealing their absurdity, they tended to operate under the premise that Soviet myths distorted "normal," "rightful" history, which had nonetheless been imprinted in the memories of individuals (that is, sources that are unreliable by definition). As for the authors of the "New Wave," they either seek a kinship between Soviet historical myths and any possible attempt to give order to history forever and always, or go beyond the bounds of the "Soviet world" entirely in order to examine the problem of the absurdity of history and historical consciousness *in general,* as well as the question of the possibility (or rather, the impossibility) of "historical truth" as such.

Such a "new historicism" is central to the fiction of Viacheslav Pietsukh, who himself was initially a history teacher by profession.

VIACHESLAV PIETSUKH: *"THE ENIGMA OF THE RUSSIAN SOUL"* REVISITED.

> Viacheslav Pietsukh: Forgive me once again for repeating myself, but there is good literature and nonliterature.
>
> Elisabeth Rich: Only those categories?
>
> Viacheslav Pietsukh: Only those. All these others are philologists 'fancies.' They also need to earn their bread. It's they who think up all kinds of postmodernisms. We simply never had any postmodernists. What kind of postmodernists can you talk about?... The avant-garde in general – this is pure experimentalism; I repeat, a laboratory.... And results in Russia, as a rule, consist of solid Russian Christian realism.[4]

Pietsukh's very style breaks the boundaries of "Soviet-ness," lending the narrative a strong intertextual dimension. Yet the point is not that Pietsukh paraphrases classical plots in his stories. Far more important is the narration's somewhat stylized tone, which breathes new life into the image of the unhurried, respectable, reliable *narrator,* an image that had been consigned to the realm of generic archeology. Pietsukh actually *narrates* his stories (and his novels, which are written in the exact same manner), using a narrator who is somewhat distanced from the author (unlike the narrators of Aksenov, Aleshkovskii, Tolstaia, and Sokolov).

Pietsukh's narrator presents the author's thoroughly everyday plots in the light of the historical and cultural past. The parallels between the flood in a modest Moscow office and the *Decameron* ("The Flood"), an old woman's disappearance from a crowded communal apartment and *Crime and Punishment (The New Moscow Philosophy),* the story of the hostility between two neighborhoods and old Russian chronicles of war ("The Central-Ermolaevo War"), the fate of an unknown graphomaniac and Pushkin's tragic death ("Allusion") – all seem to arise spontaneously from absurd situations rather than from the author's master plan.

"[T]here is absolutely nothing surprising in the fact that, in our country, where life goes, there goes literature," says the narrator of "The Central-Ermolaevo War," explaining one of Pietsukh's key themes, "and, on the other hand, where literature goes, there goes life; not only do we write the way we live, but we live the way we write."[5] According to this logic, Russian life throughout history, and especially recently, has been naturally literary, with the single stipulation that "literature is a finished version, while life is a rough draft, and not even a very good one" (246). All these declarations draw attention to a purely postmodern blurring of boundaries between the sign and its referent, calling the dependence of "history" on "literature" into question.

The device that lies at the heart of Pietsukh's fiction is paradoxical: it might best be called *intertextual irony*. On the one hand, the natural literariness of Russian life compels the author to *recognize* literary-historical prototypes in the anecdotal conflicts he describes. Moreover, as a rule, this recognition is the prerogative of that very same narrator, a professional man of letters who invariably finds his way into Pietsukh's works. He is the one who locates the author's wild stories in the context of Russian cultural traditions. On the other hand, the direct intertextual connections to the Russian classics only emphasize the discrepancy between "real" events and the familiar stories from nineteenth-century Russian literature and history. Thus "Our Man in a Case," whose title refers to Chekhov's famous short story about the narrow-minded provincial teacher Belikov, presents a contemporary Belikov who is a rather nice, unusually refined, and vulnerable man, whose "fears were not abstractions of the 'what if that happens' variety but were well founded."[6] His death prompts the narrator to comment:

> [O]ne hundred years ago, Belikov the schoolteacher was sent off on his final journey with great pleasure, since he was considered a harmful anomaly, but at the end of this century, everyone felt sorry for Serpeev the schoolteacher. No, say what you will, life does not stand still. (38)

And vice versa: when two of our contemporaries try to resolve conflicts at work through a classic duel (with bows and arrows, no less – no other weapons could be found), when they fire eleven times (since neither of the duelists had ever held a bow in his hands), when an arrow finally hits one of them in the eye, then not only do the ideas of "life's rules" lifted from literature prove absolutely inappropriate, but the fundamental *impossibility* of these ideas become clear. What in the past had been tragedy now becomes tragi-farce. Such transformations are constant motifs in Pietsukh's fiction.

The "class" conflict between the *nouveau riche* and the intellectual ends with the two becoming pals, a friendship that somehow leads to the trashing of the *nouveau riche*'s car and furniture ("The Tragedy of Ownership"). The story of the local poet, which resembles Pushkin's family drama but ends with a concussion and sedatives rather than with the poet's death, in today's terms looks like the script for an absurdist performance piece ("Allusion"). The absurdity is only reinforced by the regular, heart-rending cry of "Comrades, what are you doing! Have you flipped *[ochumeli]* or something? Do you have any idea what you're doing?" (48). In Pietsukh's contemporary *Decameron* ("The Flood"), the plague *(chuma)* is replaced by a burst water pipe, while Boccaccio's orderly system of stories is replaced by completely fantastic tall tales that nonetheless turn out to be gospel truth while remaining unbelievably absurd, like the story about the millions of rubles lost at a card game, which, of course, can never be paid back to the creditor.

Such is the "laughter of life" that results from natural literariness and eventually replaces traditional cultural patterns. The play with literary and historical archetypes compels us to see randomness in place of profound connections, gaps in place of centuries-old traditions, absurd impulses in place of unshakable "rules of life." In *The New Moscow Philosophy*, the lovers of wisdom who investigate the death of an old woman come to the conclusion that

> something's happened to time... The Bible, Christ, the Roman Empire, Spinoza, the encyclopedists, 'liberty, equality, fraternity' – it's all still to come. For a while now, our evil hasn't been what it should be, our good hasn't been what it should be, they've somehow been transformed by seventy-one years of building socialism. (310)

Soviet history, it would seem, has stranded Pietsukh's heroes in pretime, prehistory, and preculture.

Yet Pietsukh goes much further; quite often he projects Soviet discourse onto historically distant situations. "That's just the point, Stepan. It's never gone your way and it never will," says one of the "remnants of the Russian empire" who have miraculously survived the revolution and political oppression in "Three Men under an Apple Tree."

> In our country, even in the time of Nicholas the Bloody [Nicholas I], the social was higher than the personal. Don't even get me started on Ivan the Terrible's struggle with the enemies of the people. And I'll say nothing about the large-scale collectivization under Mikhail Romanov. (113)

Such pronouncements reflect numerous theories on the "origins and meaning" of Soviet history (from those of the turn-of-the-century Russian philosopher Nikolai Berdiaev to Vasily Grossman, author of the 1961 novel *Life and Fate)*. But far more important than this resemblance is the revelation that Russian history was always as inextricably entangled in the absurd as Soviet history, and therefore, the Russian literary classics never "reflected" anything; instead, they continually composed and modeled an *ideal* plan for life. At the same time, according to the author, Russian life itself has invariably been built with literature in mind. "People are required to live with literature in mind, like Christians do with 'Our Father'," (333) according to the protagonists of *The New Moscow Philosophy,* Pietsukh's reinterpretation of Dostoevsky's *Crime and Punishment.* Thus the "natural literariness" of life, as we have seen, merely reinforces the permanent absurdity of existence rather than reversing it.

For Pietsukh, the category of "national character" becomes a form of ironic, provisional compromise with literary tradition, the historical past, and the present. This is what Pietsukh's literature models, uniting the present and the past. And yet when the author talks of Russia and the absurdity of Russian life and Russian history, he creates such a universal context that "Russian national absurdity" looks like an existential and timeless trait. This paradox is central to his story "The Central-Ermolaevo War," which would seem to be an artistic examination of the problem of "national character" and the peculiarities of Russian life.

The story's simple plot, which describes the protracted hostility between young men from two neighboring central Russian villages, is deceptive: from the very first lines of the story, its universal scale is clear. "The Central-Ermolaevo War" is only an arbitrarily selected point in history, one that is no more or less significant than any other. As the narrator contends, the *"compositional"* nature of the Russian soul consists equally of Napoleonic Wars, senseless domestic tasks, arguments with one's wife, and a new religion. Naturally, a place can be found for the Central-Ermolaevo War as well:

> The enigma of the Russian soul is actually very easily explained: the Russian soul encompasses everything. By way of comparison the German soul or, say perhaps, the Serbo-Croat soul ... Not that we have any grounds for supposing their souls to be in any way shallower than ours; indeed, they may well in some respects be more thorough-going, more compositionally sound if you like, as a bowlful of stewed fruit containing fruit is more compositionally sound than a bowlful of fruit consisting of fruit, vegetables, spices and minerals. That said, however, there is no getting round the fact that certain things they do lack. They may, for instance, be brimming with constructiveness but quite hopeless at negating the universe. They may be bursting with entrepreneurial flair, but lack any trace of that eighth note of the octave, that sense of 'let's watch the whole lot go up in flames.' Again, they may be long on national pride, but quite hopeless at building castles in the air. The Russian soul has the lot: constructiveness, negation, flair, pyromania, national pride and castles in the air. Building castles in the air is, in fact, a particular strength. Imagine for a moment that a Russian, from having nothing better to do, has dismantled a shed he actually very much needs, explained to his neighbor why Russia was victorious in the war against Napoleon, and given his wife a good thrashing with the kitchen towel; he then sits back on his veranda smiling peacefully at the loveliness of the day, and is suddenly struck by the thought that it's perhaps time he invented a new religion.[7]

Characteristically, the universalism of national character in this description is defined by a combination of mutually exclusive elements, resulting in either destruction (dismantling "a shed he actually very much needs") or something frankly irrational ("it's perhaps time he invented a new religion"). This theme is elaborated in at least two aspects of the story. First of all, the history of the Central-Ermolaevo War is framed by reflections on the influence of place names, landscape, and climate on the Russian national character (in the spirit of Russian historians such as Vasily Kliuchevskii or Dmitrii Likhachev). But the narrator, as opposed to the authorities, deliberately interprets it either as something destructive or something totally irrational and illogical. The toponymy preserves the memory of "Fedor Ermolaev who dynamited the local church in 1922" (238), or is simply absurd, since

> Golden Beaches boasts a wire factory and the entire town is ankle deep in sunflower seed husks expectorated by the local inhabitants ... the launch visits Third Left Riverbanks rather less than daily, ... the English teacher is the only person in Afrikanida who knows what 'subjective idealism' means. (Ibid.)

The climate "does indeed tend toward divisiveness," (ibid.), while the landscape is called "nothing special" and a "near-desert," although its very lack of anything specific or memorable "leaves you with a sense of obligation. What that obligation might be is anyone's guess" (240). These are the parameters (or perhaps, the absence of parameters) that define the national character from within.

Second, the history of "The Central-Ermolaevo War" is permeated with a network of intertexts that lend it a universal significance. Several cultural languages are combined in this story without doing any damage to consistency. As noted above, one of the most important intertexts of this story is the tradition of the old Russian war chronicle: it is no accident that this little squabble is repeatedly called "internal strife." The story includes the "Battle of Ermolaevo" and a solar eclipse ("the last total eclipse of the sun in the twentieth century" (252), emphasizes the narrator), which exerts a decisive influence on the conflict's outcome (this motif clearly recalls the medieval Russian chronicles, such as *The Igor Tale* and *Zadonshchina)*. The story's characters themselves recognize the "genre memory" of the medieval Russian heroic military tale to some extent, although for them it is mediated through Soviet discourse and Sergei Eisenstein's film *Alexander Nevsky:*

> ...there was only the eerie sound of bicycle chains whistling in the air, heavy breathing on all sides, wide shouting and cursing. Petr Ermolaev furiously dispatched the mechanics, his blows accompanied by the cry of Alexander Nevsky: "He who comes to us with the sword...!" For some reason he did not go on.
>   Papa Carlo battled in silence. (251)

Certainly, Soviet war movies inspired the men to throw Molotov cocktails into the enemy's clubhouse, as well as to interrogate the "prisoner," Abliazov the vet. During the interrogation, the good-natured Papa Carlo plays the role of the cruel inquisitor, while the hangover Abliazov is forced to take on the role of heroic partisan, especially since

> not only did he not know why Svistunov[8] was snooping around in Ermolaevo, he hadn't even known Svistunov was there at all. His ignorance was, in a sense, a blessing, since he was delivered of the temptation to behave dishonorably. He grimaced in terror, and even smiled, but they seared his arm in two places all the same. (248)

A particularly remarkable signal of the characters' involvement in the world of Soviet rhetoric is the poem that Abliazov, while hangover, writes just before the interrogation: "The more you sing and make a racket/The less you worry how much you get in your wage packet" (247). His enemy, Papa Carlo, immediately responds: "That's a real poem, sinuous, and politically correct" (ibid.). Another example of "folk art" is the play written by Medical Orderly Serebriakov: *Home Remedies Spell Trouble.* The man whose Chekhovian name (Professor Serebriakov from "Uncle Vania") is apparently meant to accentuate his intelligentsia roots stages his very own play by casting village youth in the parts, thus recapitulating a typical cliché of Thaw-era "Socialist Realism with a human face." But the play itself, which is described in such detail, ironically revives another cultural tradition, that of Neo-Classicism.

Serebriakov himself explains his play, constantly skipping from one cultural language to another:

> You have to appreciate, comrades, that what we have here is drama, almost tragedy. Because this, this *free-thinking* results in someone's becoming even more ill instead of recovering. One could weep, comrades, but you are hamming it up mercilessly. Now do let's start this scene again from the beginning." (249, italics in the original)

The heroes of this didactic drama are naturally called Vetrogonov ("empty-headed") and Pravdin ("truth"), and the story culminates when they hear the Voice of Reason.

All these cultural languages hark back to highly hierarchical artistic systems, ones that are based on notions of universal Order and the concomitant Rules of Life; this, perhaps, explains why these codes are so intertwined. But the languages of these literary forms are imposed upon absolutely *absurd* and destructive events. Or, to put it more precisely, the absurd plot of "The Central-Ermolaevo War," which starts for no reason and ends because of a solar eclipse, arises from the *intersection* of these literary traditions.

Moreover, all participants in these events are strict followers of the literary Rules of Life: Petr Ermolaev plays Pravdin and in the heat of battle pronounces the "legendary" words of Alexander Nevsky (actually from Eisenstein's film); during the solar eclipse he looks "so much like a priest preparing to commune with the heavens that it fair made your flesh creep" (253). The nickname "Papa Carlo," which comes from Alexei Tolstoy's version of *Pinocchio,* is also associated with the role of *raisonneur.*

Particularly noteworthy is the description of Field Husbandry Day as a kind of deeply ritualized ceremony: this episode can be interpreted as a form of folkloric cultural Order. Here we have a calendar holiday, one that necessarily combines dances and fistfights. However, the holiday culminates in a "catchy song":

> *All the boys from Vologda*
> *Are hooligans and thieving gits.*
> *They jumped a peasant carting dung*
> *And robbed and left him in the shits.* (243)

Note, too, the use of the word "sentimental," so reminiscent of the literary movement that represented the world of the folk as the peak of natural harmony: "'I heard a hunter came across a herd of wild cows twenty kilometers from your Ermolaevo,' says Papa Carlo. 'Perfectly ordinary cows they were, Sentimenthalers, only wild'" (241). Pyotr Ermolaev dismisses these words as "unrealistic."

The combination of "correct" ideas with absurd actions paradoxically gives rise to a sense of the *fullness of life* – and this is typical of Pietsukh's other stories as well: "On the way home the men of Ermolaevo sang songs, and from time to time their leader shouted into the wind, 'This is living, eh lads? This, I reckon, lads, is life!'" (245).

The sense of the fullness of life that grips the characters of the story compels one to understand the *historical value of the absurd*. And the universalistic context of the story does not suggest any other scale. The absurd, on the one hand, appears as a form of freedom and hence as the fullest realization of vital forces – the freedom from various, always limited, orders dictated by culture and history. But against the backdrop of the absurd and destructive "fullness of life," these cultural orders themselves, from medieval heroics to the Socialist Realist canon, are similarly unrealized Utopias, various linguistic *shells* for *normal* human absurdity. The universality of the description of a 1981 model of internal strife convinces one that all other Russian internal strife, from the time of Prince Igor or Alexander Nevsky, followed the same course as the Central-Ermolaevo War: "[A] fundamental law of our life creates multi-talented characters, men with top-heavy destinies, and all sorts of peculiar goings on in which the spirit of the Mongol Horde is palpable" (254).[9]

Here national character resembles a kind of "black box": at its entrance are the culturally regulated "rules of life," while at its exit are the absurd consequences and total ruins of any attempt to impose order. "The Central-Ermolaevo War" reveals a peculiar symmetry in the way in which purely external factors such as toponymy, landscape, climate, and celestial mechanics, as well as such factors as cultural languages and codes, influence "national character." In each case all influences are accepted and ... lead to logically, absolutely unpredictable and usually absurd results. Why? Pietsukh argues that it is precisely because the "Russian soul" encompasses *absolutely all* possible and impossible influences of both culture and nature – and, we might add, it is therefore *chaotic,* according to Prigogine's definition of chaos as the realization of all of a system's possibilities simultaneously. "National character" is utterly lacking in any selectivity or the slightest immunity to these influences. The initial notion of "national character" as a historical constant becomes the complete "chaotization" and dehierarchization of any mythology of history, since all of them, regardless of the cause-and-effect relations that the particular mythology emphasizes, are deconstructed by the chaotic field of "national character," which transforms history into a consistently absurd notion, the only one capable of encompassing the fullness of being. It is "national character" that Pietsukh presents as the paradoxical chaotic mechanism for giving rise to an inevitably absurd metatext of history, one that is equally absurd in both the past and the present.

Moreover, the absurd effect arises at the expense of the *simultaneous* existence of the high cultural canon dictated by literature and the fantastic, grotesque repetitions of literary plots and conflicts. But where does this great literature come from? From the "rough draft" of normal absurdity – as its *mythology*. Thus history constantly plays itself out as the open-ended, paradoxical transition from order to the absurd, which is mythologized by literature as order and which gives rise to new absurdity. Moreover, it is specifically literature that becomes the teleological justification of historical absurdity. Polemicizing with the teleology of historical progress, Pietsukh proposes his own inverse teleology, which presents literature, or rather, literariness, as the "meaning of history." In Pietsukh's consistently absurd work, historical development takes place in changes not in the present or future but in the *past;* mythologized by history, the past is transformed from a "rough draft" into a "fair copy." If the absurdity of history abolishes the category of time (everything always take place in a disorderly "here and now"), then "natural literariness" directs time from the present to the past: The Central-Ermolaevo War exerts an influence on the epic tradition, but not the other way around. "National character" provides reliable isolation from any kind of "lessons of the past." It is no accident that for Pietsukh the voice of the narrator becomes an idiosyncratic pillar of stability; this voice is always registered in the present and always preserves a "common-sense" tone and cozy, old-fashioned style, no matter what he is writing about, whether it be the legendary past or the anecdotal present. This very "literariness" becomes the narrator's defense against chaos; an ironic defense, but a defense nonetheless. Pietsukh's narrator is not a character but rather a traditional literary function belonging to the space of literature; and he belongs to the "fair copy" rather than the "rough draft." It is the narrator's voice that delineates the boundary between the absurdity of life's "natural literariness" and the conventional order of mythologizing play with life.

Absurdity establishes a rupture with the unified logic of history. Causality loses its force. But the permanence of chaotic "national character" suggests a paradoxical logic (or *paralogy?*) based on absurdity. According to Pietsukh, history irrevocably unites order and entropy, which consequently are expressed in repetitions and unpredictability, in dynamism and inertia, in time and timelessness. Thus history takes on the characteristics of the rhizome, whose multiplicity is homogenous and whose fragmentary nature does not exclude wholeness or the capacity for regeneration from any point.

THE "HISTORICAL" STORIES OF VIKTOR EROFEEV: AN APOTHEOSIS OF PARTICLES.

> *Having written my first essays on de Sade and Lev Shestov as long ago as the beginning of the seventies and having paid my dues to the literature of evil, I am nevertheless probably closer to what may be called a "flickering aesthetics," type of "negative capability" which I view as an attempt to escape the postmodern canon, and which combines suggestive, seditious invention with an alluring laying bare of the devices of any discourse.* [10]

Viktor Erofeev's short stories, like the fiction of Pietsukh, follow a "rhizomatic" model of history. His favorite narrative device is his idiosyncratic *skaz*, which binds together the locutions of different eras, weaving together paraphrases of classical texts with parodies of current *belles lettres,* superimposing naturalistic details on refined intertextual discourse. Moreover, in Erofeev's work the clash of various languages of culture and history invariably leads not to synthesis, not to a universal metalanguage, but to a dissonance that saturates the entire text and displays a deliberate clumsiness and contempt for logic.

Extremely vivid example of such multitemporal *skaz* can be found in "The Parakeet" where multitemporality is not only a characteristic of the consciousness of the narrator but also a property of the chronotope. The speaker in the story is a Russian torturer who belongs simultaneously to the era of the rack and to the era of pinching the scrotum "as a preventive measure," [11] and who is fluent in the language of some kind of "medieval age" and highly contemporary "special" terminology. These playful fusions, which can at times be found within the boundaries of a single phrase, work toward an image of history *without movement,* in which one time creeps into another but all times are subject to the same incontrovertible laws: the laws of the absurd.

But the essential difference between Viktor Erofeev's stories and those of Pietsukh lies in the fact that, in Erofeev, absurdity is expressed first and foremost *through the narrator's voice* (hence Erofeev's devotion to *skaz*), while in Pietsukh's work the narrator is removed from the absurdity of history.

The protagonist of "The Parakeet" is narrational Frankenstein's monster, assembled from the bodies of his cultural ancestors. The story's voice masks a certain archetypal discourse of the torturer, refracted through the prism of Russian history and culture in a new way each time. The mentality represented by the narrator of "The Parakeet" (the torturer, who embodies the discourse of absolute power) is saturated with oxymorons that are the consequence of his total isolation. Erofeev's torturer is entirely certain of his dignity and high professionalism: "We tormented and tortured your son, Yermolai Spiridonovich, we couldn't have done otherwise, we've not been taught any other way."[12] He is convinced of his own profound knowledge of people and the unconditional social usefulness of his trade; hence the patronizing and condescending tone of his letter to the father of the tortured boy. The most important thing for him is his firm knowledge of the *norm.* With wise, fatherly experience, the torturer submits his moral judgments:

> I, thank God, know my business, I earn my bread, and therefore I have an idea of how our kind of people scream on the rack and how those who aren't our kind do. One of ours would never call me a barbarian, because he doesn't think that way, but your scoundrel admitted that he did. He behaved, I regret to inform you, rather cowardly. (373)

> But at the same time, I like the humble sufferers, the ones who only fart and quack when they're on the rack, I respect them, and I wouldn't even swap a sufferer like that for a hundred Englishmen, because torture and suffering are a thing pleasing unto God, and what's an Englishman? – shit and nothing more! (375)

> At this point (or was it, perhaps, earlier) we tore off his
> knackers to teach him not to shoot his mouth off like that
> about his father for no good reason, tore them off and tossed
> them right to the dogs: let them have a little treat... (Ibid.)

And all of the torturer's work, whose terrifying details lend a special persuasiveness to these edifying speeches, is dictated by the imperative to protect the norm from "alien" influences. He sees his main social and personal duty as nipping potential violations of the Norm in the bud, finding the symbol hidden behind any nontrivial action, such as forcing a dead parakeet to take "unnatural flight":

> Well, what if all of a sudden, contrary to our expectations, it up
> and actually was resurrected? In what terms would we explain
> this particular circumstance to our countrymen, so trusting in
> our best intentions? I become lost in fatal conjecture...
> WOULDN'T WE BE FINE FOOLS! (368-69)

Of course, such logic presupposes the potential guilt of everyone, without exception; even a "three-year-old sniveler" is under suspicion, the "villain still does not talk, or pretends not to" (370). Only the torturer himself is above suspicion; he bears the heavy burden of responsibility to the Norms of the people's life. It is precisely the torturer's conviction of the existence of an unshakable order of things that also serves as the justification for his atrocities. As Serafima Roll argues, the main crime turns out to be "an attempt to inquire into the natural order of things"[13] – for the attempt to resurrect a dead parakeet the hapless boy Yermolai Spiridonovich endures terrible tortures culminating in his gruesome death, all of which is described in the torturer's letter to the boy's father.

The combination of sadism and the unwavering attachment to maintaining the "norm" is not the only oxymoron. The very transformation of the *category* of the norm itself is paradoxical. What matters here is not even the executioner's musings on "mankind's great passion for torture"[14] or how "a man will sell out anyone and anything, you just have to approach him slowly, don't scare him – just give him time!" (375). Far more important is the stylistics of *skaz*. Thus the narrator's "terminology" of torture and Soviet bureaucratic clichés are easily transformed into the lexicon and style of folk poetics:

And I struck him, your brown-eyed boy, right in the teeth with all my soul, because I'd grown weary, I took preventive measures, but my fist... well, you, Yermolaich, know. And so his teeth spattering in various directions, *just like pearls from a broken string — they spattered and tumbled."* (372, emphasis added)

When Yermolai Spiridonovich and I came to share that common opinion, we embraced in our joy: *a job well done, I say, is its own reward, bring us, my stalwarts, wine and viands, we shall make merry! And my stalwarts bring us white salmon, suckling pigs and lambs, sundry soufflés and a wine that has the playful name, Madonna's Milk. We ate and then shot the breeze."* (375-76, emphasis added)

There is nothing forced about the conflation of the rack and the poetics of folklore; the transitions are entirely organic — and this is the most terrifying thing of all. If for Pietsukh the language of cultural symbols is a refined version of the absurdity of history, then Erofeev reveals that what appears to be the norm, inculcated both in culture and in history, is open to any pathology, any atrocity. Not only that, but the dogged assertion of the norm (cultural or otherwise; the torturer constantly invokes the authority of "world culture") becomes the triumph of pathology and torture.

The constant paradoxes and dissonance of "The Parakeet" determine not only the narrative structure but something broader: the representation of the (meta)historical discourses of the Russian mentality, which remain constant in time. *Skaz,* which is common to so many of Erofeev's stories (such as "Life with an Idiot," "Berdiaev," "Death and the Maiden," "How We Cut the Frenchman's Throat"), forms the core of his poetics. Here one might use Foucault's term, the "decentralization of the subject": the voice of the narrator, when expressed through multicultural and multihistorical *skaz,* does not actually belong to the narrator as a character anymore; it is only the projection of multiple and multidimensional historical and cultural discourses. But the clash of these discourses and the fragments of cultural codes gives way to a *figure of emptiness* that swallows up the subject, the discourses, cultural codes, and history itself as the aggregate of all those factors. Moreover, it does not matter which of the discourses is accepted as a system of reading: the discourse of power or powerlessness, freedom or violation, liberalism or the ideology of the torturer. The result remains the same. For Erofeev, the synonym of this figure of emptiness is the theme of death and/or insanity. It is death that turns out to be the moment of *unity* of torturer and victim in "The Parakeet":

> "Well, Godspeed!" I said, and I led him by the arm to the ledge of the belfry. "Fly, Yermolushka! Fly, my pigeon!" Spreading his arms out to form a cross, he stepped into the emptiness. For just a minute I was almost seized by the torment of doubt: what if he were to ascend like a turquoise parakeet, to the demons' delight? With a certain disquiet I leaned over the railing and glanced below. Thank God! Smashed!"[15]

In "Death and the Maiden," we have the monologue of a man who has recognized death as the magnificent mystery of *unity* and who therefore commits a senseless murder for the sake of existential self-actualization. Murder is presented by the narrator-protagonist as "proof of the boundless possibilities of our reason, which has become the master of the most implacable and destructive force,"[16] "transforming blind chance into the triumph of will and handicrafts" (ibid.). It is worth noting that the hero's passion for death is inseparable from his strong desire for a woman – the murdered girlfriend. Comprehension of death once again runs out to be essential for living life to the fullest.[17]

Yet there, as in his other stories, Erofeev contextualizes the discourse of his narrator. The narrator's reflections on death as a unique performance ("a strong feeling of genre" [ibid.]) is offset by apparently "alien," "healthy" opinions: "the most fashionable murder of the season" (129), "the Komsomol burial service ... after the service a young priest bursting with health spoke of the ties between science and religion" (133). The narrator's speech is based on oxymoronic combinations of refinement and naturalistic vulgarity, but his victim speaks exactly the same language. This victim belongs to the same circle, in which "both foul language and 'Nabokov' are described as 'okay' " (ibid.). But the "unattainable example of Stalin's sense of humor" (131) – the phrase "love conquers death," which runs through the entire story as a leitmotif – ultimately imparts a *discursive significance* to the protagonist's monologue.

Thus his imagined speech at the graveside of the girl he killed is begun with the famous words "Brothers and sisters!" (136) – these are the very same words with which Stalin began his speech to the Soviet people after the Nazis invaded the USSR. Behind the protagonist's pathology we see the norm of Russian history, which invariably proves that love (for the tyrant, for power, for the idea) really does conquer death. The loss of a sense of *existential limits* as the norm of historical being, the identification of death with effective spectacle, and, in the final analysis, the transformation of death into a game: here we find those conditions thanks to which the narrator attains unity with his beloved, with society, with history. This is an epic situation, but one that has been turned inside out: here the blurring of ontological boundaries and concomitant values becomes the precondition for epic unity: "We're racing along the outlying road. The noise of the forest. And everything is good. Stalin is right. Gorky is right. We are all right. 'Man' has a proud ring about it. Love conquers death" (137).

By analogy, the murder of the wife in "Life with an Idiot" ultimately identifies the intellectual narrator with the idiot (who is also a rapist, a murderer, a lover, and Lenin). The story begins with the narrator's punishment: he must choose a madman from a mental institution and live with him for a fixed period of time. One of the mental patients looks remarkably like the narrator himself, but he is rejected in favor of Volodia, the "idiot" of the story's title. By the end of "Life with an Idiot," the narrator has himself been committed to that very asylum and realizes that the man he rejected in the beginning was actually he. Erofeev consciously provokes the reader's disgust and confusion. But the paradox of his fiction is that he completes the collapse of the "grand narratives" of Soviet culture, at times in literally nauseating detail, demonstrating the process in which words that once held power are literally transformed into excrement and carrion.[18]

In such a model of the world, the position of the martyr turns out to be the only reliable one. But typically for Erofeev, this role, as a rule, is given to the child, who traditionally embodies the infinite renewal of life. Like Yermolai Spiridonych from "The Parakeet," and the boy from the story "Galoshes," these characters are at great pains to adapt to the conditions of the lethal game, and they seek understanding ("He kept trying to help me to understand, he aided himself, you see, with his little hand"[19]). They gullibly accept historical norms and imitate them: "Each holiday, the boy imitated the street and weighed out the decorations: stars, slogans, portraits of the leaders; and he led a parade of tin soldiers and carved chess figures on the bed"[20]. But even the everyday road from home to school demonstrates alienation from life; it becomes a procession around the circles of hell. "Galoshes" begins with the scene of the boy's death:

> The boy feverishly grabbed hold of the fire escape. He was afraid of climbing higher, and as for going down, he was afraid of the stones. The third-grader stood below and threw rocks at him. One rock hit his back, the other hit his shoulder, the third, finally, ended up in the back of his head. He shouted weakly and flew down, back first. 172)

Then come exile ("Grandma shoved the boy out the door" [173]), spitting ("the third-grader magnanimously spat in his face" [174]), and ridicule. Moreover, as he depicts the class as it laughs at the boy, squealing and barking, the author suddenly changes angles, which radically expands the temporal and spatial boundaries of this particular scene:

> They laughed: Gorianova, who went away on a two-year business trip with her husband; the fidgety Artsybashev would subsequently become a rather famous man of letters and join the writers' union... Sokina, with her skinny legs, laughed, but the red-headed fool Trunina was lucky; her husband was a member of the Central Committee (true, of the Komsomol)... Iudina would outlive them all: on her ninetieth birthday, she would walk into the communal kitchen in a colorful bathing suit. The shocked neighbors would burst into applause... Shchapov the warrant officer, who received a concussion in the colonial campaign, Chemodanov the karate expert, and Wagner, breastless Wagner, crowed with all their might. Baklazhanova, Mukhanov, and Klyshko laughed their way into the passageway, like some sort of fruit.[21] (176)

This infinitely expanding image of the cruelly laughing class is life itself, in its motley diversity. And the child in this scene — because of his sufferings — looks like a saint (the teacher notices a halo around his head). The target of universal malice, he gains a unique perspective from which he can see the future lives of his laughing classmates.

Here life's continuity is based on the mythological paradigm of sacrifice, which lies beneath the oxymorons of plot and style in Erofeev's stories. But sacrifice does not serve as a renewal of being and does not presuppose resurrection. The cyclical order of myth is replaced by a structure that once again resembles the "dissipative orders," which, as specialists in self-organizing chaos assert,

> can survive only by remaining open to a flowing matter and energy exchange with the environment. In fact, matter and energy literally flow through it and form it, like the river water through the vortex...The structure is stabilized by its flowing. It is stable but only relatively – relative to the constant flow required to maintain its shape.[22]

One can apply this idea to Erofeev's representation of history, with the sole stipulation that *here fluidity is paradoxically expressed in the endless self-destruction and self-negation of all the constituent elements of the system, but only by performing this function does the system continue to exist.*

In the fiction of Pietsukh and Erofeev, history certainly lacks the aura of "objectivity." It is relative and pathological, born of cultural myths and the anecdotes that make a mockery of them. It is senseless and infinite, self-destructive and eternal. Nevertheless, in the works of these authors, the world of history is "already made"; the hero only participates in it while submitting to the logic of the game of history, the logic of a demythologizing reproduction of the mythology of history and culture.

On the other hand, the very nature of postmodernist playfulness thoroughly undermines such a fundamental category of history as *time*. In both Pietsukh and Erofeev, history becomes timelessness, which is explained by the fact that the interactions of heterogeneous cultural languages and symbols in their works are expressed through the motifs of destruction, loss of meaning, and death. The perception of history *as emptiness filled with heterogeneous ideas of history* quite logically becomes the next step in the development of the historical consciousness of Russian postmodernism. These ideas are also of a mythological cast, but they are myths that are aware of their status as creations, of their literary (rather than divine) origins. We have the opportunity to see how these myths are composed before our very eyes, *in order that they become real as soon as possible*. Moreover, if humor predominates in the works of Pietsukh and Erofeev, in the form of parodic periphrases of various quotations, they are surprisingly earnest in their approach to history as a literary artifact. The difference, apparently, is a consequence of an altered relationship between the author and the historical character. Each occupies an opposing position in relation to history: the character looks at history from within; the author looks from without, thereby creating the distance necessary for the ironic deconstruction of "historical consciousness." In this sense, Pietsukh's author-narrator, who directly comments on his characters' actions, and Erofeev's extra-textual author, who hides behind the *skaz* narrator, have much in common: The deliberately literary style of Pietsukh's narrator creates the essential ironic distance no less effectively than the conspicuous absence of an authorial voice in Erofeev's stories. When the authorial voice is not only not hidden but also pointedly identical to that of historical characters, then we have a new situation in which the author locates himself within the historical context and takes part in its creation, just like the characters. In this case the play with mythologies of history cannot be separated from metafictional devices: metafiction becomes meta-history.

ENDNOTES

[1] Linda Hutcheon, *A Poetics of Postmodernism. History,Theory, Fiction* (NewYork/London: Routledge, 1988).

[2] M. Bakhtin, *The Dialogic Imagination: Four Essays*, ed. Michael Holquist, trans. Caryl Emerson and Michael Holquist (Austin: University ofTexas Press, 1981), 39.

[3] Michel Foucault, *Language, Counter-Memory, Practice* (Ithaca: Cornell University Press, 1977), 116.

[4] Elizabeth Rich, *Russian Literature After Perestroika*. Special Issue of South Central Review 12: 3-4 (1995): 136-37.

[5] V. Pietsukh, "The Central-Ermolaevo War," trans. ArchTait, in *The Penguin Book of New Russian Writing: Russia's Fleurs du Mal*, ed.Viktor Erofeev and Andrew Reynolds (London: Penguin Books, 1995), 219-220.

[6] V. Pietsukh, *Ia i prochee* (Moscow: *Khudozhestvennaia literatura*, 1990), 35.

[7] V. Pietsukh, "The Central-Ermolaevo War," 237.

[8] The militiaman whose presence seems suspicious to the men from Central [Author].

[9] Subsequently, in his novel *ROMMAT* (Romantic Materialism), Pietsukh places this hypothesis at the foundation of an artistic idea; the Decembrist Uprising of 1825 is described as a prank played by young Russians hungry for life, in the spirit of "The Central-Ermolaevo War."

[10] Viktor Erofeev, "Russia's *Fleurs du Mal*," in *New Russian Writing: Russia's Fluers du Mal*, ed. Viktor Erofeev and Andrew Reynolds (London: Farrar, Straus & Giroux, 1991), xxviii.

[11] Viktor Erofeev, "The Parakeet," trans. Leonard J. Stanton, in *Glasnost: An Anthology of Russian Literature Under Gorbachev*, ed. Helena Goscilo and Byron Lindsey (Ann Arbor: Ardis, 1990), 372.

[12] Ibid.,

[13] Serafima Roll, "Re-surfacing:The Shades ofViolence inViktor Erofeev's Short Stories," unpublished manuscript, 12.

[14] Erofeev, "The Parakeet," 374.

[15] Ibid., 376.

[16] Viktor Erofeev, *Izbrannoe ili Karmannyi apokalipsis* (Moscow, Paris, New York;TheThirdWave, 1993), 131.

[17] A number of motifs common to Viktor Erofeev's works are without a doubt rooted in the culture of high modernism.Thus the treatment of murder in "Death and the Maiden" clearly echoes Andre Gide's novel *Les Caves duVatican* (I

am grateful to Anita Mozhaeva for this observation).

[18] Curiously, Brodsky described this very same strategy in 1975: "'Carrion!' he exhaled, grabbing his belly/but he will prove farther away/than the earth from the birds,/because carrion is freedom/ from cells, from/the whole: an apotheosis of particles" (Josef Brodsky, *Sochinenia Iosifa Brodskogo* (Sankt-Petersburg: *Pushkinskii Fond* 3 (1994): 12). Quoted from the translation by Marian Schwartz in *Russian Studies in Literature* 30: 1 (Winter 1993-94): 51.

[19] Erofeev "The Parakeet," 369.

[20] Erofeev *Izbrannoe,* 173.

[21] Note that the classmates' names are clear anagrams of the names of members of the Moscow Union of Writers who played an active role in the attack on the independent almanac *Metropol'* (1979), whose editors included Aksenov and Viktor Erofeev. Balkazhanov is an obvious distortion of Grigory Baklanov, Mukhanov is Ivan Ukhanov, Klyshko is Nikolai Klychko, and Trunina is Iuliia Drunina. Some of the names are left unchanged: the black marketeer Verchenko is named after Iurii Verchenko, who was then the organizational secretary of the Union of Soviet Writers (i.e., the KGB representative).

[22] John Briggs and F. David Peat, *Looking Glass Universe: The Emerging Science of Wholeness* (New York: Simon and Schuster, 1984), 169.

XVII

Psychosis and Photography: Andrei Bitov's "Pushkin's Photograph."

SVEN SPIEKER

THE POSTUTOPIAN SUBJECT: MODERNISM – SOCIALIST REALISM – POSTMODERNISM

The following discussion is devoted to Bitov's concept of the human being and the implications that concept has for the process of remembering. For evidence we shall draw principally on "Pushkin's Photograph *(1799-2099)"[1]* (*Fotografiia Pushkina (1799-2099)* which forms a part of *Teacher of Symmetry (Prepodavatel' simmetrii).[2]* These texts belong to the group of Bitov's texts which were written and published after *Pushkin House (Pushkinsky dom)[3]* and complicate the notion of Bitov's involvement in postmodernism by masquerading as modernist texts in many of the stylistic and formal aspects. "Pushkin's Photograph" confirms the suspicion that Bitov's postmodern attitude manifests itself least of all in the more formal aspects of his writing.

We will begin our analysis with a brief discussion of the changing conceptualization of the subject from modernism to postmodernism:

a) The modernist subject is marked by its preponderance over historical time. Modernism sees the individual (especially the artist) at the forefront *(avant-garde)* of innovation. The innovating subject/artist occupies an eccentric position vis-à-vis the historical past. As modernism regards the past (as well as the transcendent future) in general as non-historical, the modernist subject is free to invent, rewrite, and alter its own past and biography at will.[4]

b) In its approach to the subject, socialist realism occupies a middle position between modernism and postmodernism. It does not share the modernist indifference towards the past. Socialist realist art is replete with eclectic historicizing elements. At the same time, however, socialist realism shapes history according to its own ideological needs. The attitude of the socialist realist artist is post-historical rather than ahistorical. That attitude assumes that the Utopian future has already become reality within the *hic et nunc* of the socialist state. History has found its *telos* in the socialist state where everything is new and innovative, including the past. Here, formal innovation is redundant as such innovation is already inherent in the new reality created by the socialist state. In this way, the socialist realist subject loses its innovative edge and its eccentric position vis-à-vis time and society. Its formal innovations are no longer needed and its Utopian visions are relegated to the realm of historical oblivion. Like the modernist subject, its socialist realist counterpart has no relevant (personal) history. Unlike the latter, however, it conceives of itself as the very token of the arrival of a Utopian outside from which the modernist had felt forever separated.

c) A number of traits link the postmodern subject with its socialist realist counterpart.[5] The former, too, does not share the modernist insistence upon the irrelevance of the past. However, where both modernism and socialist realism perceive the past as essentially ahistorical, postmodernism nevertheless restores to the past its historicity.[6] The modernist rewritings and mystifications of the past acquire in themselves the status of historical facts as the non-existent past has already happened. While postmodernism does restore to the subject its historical context, the exact parameters of that context are forever elusive and unidentifiable. In this way, the past becomes opaque and invisible. The postmodern subject searches for (its own) history without being able to find it. The self accepts as real any historical fiction offered to it. In this way, the self becomes "the other." The ontological equivalence between I and other is axiomatic in postmodernism. This equivalence contrasts sharply with the eccentric position of the subject in high modernism. In postmodernism, the ego loses the modernist hegemony over the realm of history and becomes a "weak" subject.[7]

The weak subject of postmodernism manifests itself in the figure "I = Someone Else." Typologically, that figure unfolds into two different types of postmodern subject, psychotic and narcissistic.[8] For the psychotic individual as much as for its narcissistic counterpart, inside and outside, self and other are equivalent. Both are prone to confuse fiction and fact, present and past, in and out, etc. For Freud, both narcissism (neurosis) and psychosis are symptomatic of the constraints placed upon the ego both by outside reality and by the demands of the id.[9] The neurotic contents himself with the repression of the impermissible urge and with the concomitant denial of its reality. He renounces the real object and shifts his libidinal desire, firstly, to an imaginary substitute, and then, secondly, back to a repressed object. The neurotic becomes a master at avoiding that part of reality which is unbearable to him.

By contrast, the psychotic individual replaces outside reality altogether and constructs for himself an alternative reality according to the demands of the id.[10] In this way, the psychotic fundamentally alters the relations between the inside (the ego), on the one hand, and outside reality, on the other.[11] While the neurotic merely seeks to muffle the influence of the id (remaining otherwise faithful to the super-ego and outside reality), the psychotic loses any contact with the real world and lives inside his own psyche as if it were the outside. Neurosis as well as psychosis are symptomatic of the patient's attempt to bring about a *restitutio ad integrum*, an effort to restore the former equilibrium between id and ego, inside world and outside reality, by returning to an archaic *Urzustand*. In this sense, the symptoms of neurosis and psychosis are indicative of an attempt at self-healing through regression.

2. PSYCHOSIS AND POSTMODERNISM IN "PUSHKIN'S PHOTOGRAPH"

2.1. The Difficult Outside

It is especially the psychotic substitution of inside for outside which plays a role in Andrei Bitov's texts. The author's protagonists in *Pushkin House*, "Pushkin's Photograph" and other texts live in reality as if in another world.[12] In "Pushkin's Photograph," psychotic confusion has a particularly high profile. In the introductory frame, Bitov tells the story of a writer (Bitov's *alter ego*) who has left the capital in order to join his family in his country cottage and to resume writing. The main narrative focuses upon one of the fictitious writer's many unfinished texts. It involves a young philologist being sent from the year 2099 into the Pushkinian era. His mission in traveling to the distant past is to produce a photographic image of the live Pushkin. However, that mission fails. The representatives of past high culture, and most notably Pushkin himself, withdraw into obscurity whenever the hero activates his recording equipment, leaving the protagonist in a state of constant emotional confusion.

In the introductory frame, the equivalence between inside and outside models both relations in space and the psychology of the fictitious writer. The opposition between inside and outside is no longer productive for him. Bitov's writer evidently leaves the city in order to reestablish a proper distinction between inside and outside, or image and real thing *(veshch'; delo)*. In the following segment, the deictic there *(tam)* and here *(zdes')* indicate his desire for a strong delineation of city and countryside. The countryside represents that realm where inside and outside may once more be experienced as separate. The city, by contrast, is characterized by a semiotic practice in which signs substitute for absent referents, obliterating separation and distance amidst the proliferation of technologies of communication:

> I am trying to make something here, anything, as long as it's something, because where I come from [*tam, otkuda ia*] you can't make anything because of *connections to the world*, not work, but to the whole world, to the tele-world: -phone, -vision. (55-56)

In its emphasis upon communication and the way in which urban space renders irrelevant the crossing of spatial boundaries, Bitov's analysis appears strikingly "postmodern." Bitov's fictitious writer, however, believes that he can escape the effects of this development. He endorses the traditional semanticization of city (official space) and countryside (nonofficial metaspace) in Soviet fiction. Here, the city appears as a place of constraint and captivity, whereas rural life offers a niche which restores to the individual a sense of freedom.

Watching the outside world through the window of his attic, Bitov's writer establishes a relationship with the outside which restores to it the quality of a horizon of transcendence. Sitting on his veranda, he muses upon the waning day:

> it was as if everything that life has drawn for us during the day out of clouds, shadows, grass, and fences had now been completely erased. It hadn't turned out right and life had smeared it with her eraser. (15)

In this description, a transcendent, immaterial essence manifests itself in the transient phenomena of the material world (*zhizn'*). Epistemological and perceptional obscurity characterize the outside for Bitov's writer throughout: "may be I'll fail to describe the view from the window for the hundredth time" (17). What we see at work here is a negative dialectic whose comfort consists in the total opposition of inside and outside. Even where the outside may not be positively known or depicted, it still exists as a negative counter position to the immanent here and now.

Increasingly, however, Bitov exposes his alter ego to instances which undermine the latter's confidence in the comforting negativity of his position. These instances suggest that the writer's assumption of a strict separation of inside and outside or city and countryside may have been an illusion. The name which the writer gives to the possibility of a confusion between name and object or outside and inside is that of a generalized text (*"tekst"*). The immobile text threatens the dynamism of beginning anew and, consequently, the negative knowledge of the fictitious author's fragmentary writings: "As I'll begin now, but starting where? With this or with that? [...] the paper turns yellow, the text fades, and nothing moves" (18).[13] The dissolution of oppositions such as in and out within the general metaphor of the "text" is axiomatic in postmodern thinking.

Bitov's writer reacts to the confusion between inside and outside with bouts of schizoid delusion. He appears to see himself from a distance: "as if I were looking at myself from upstairs, from the attic" (15). In another instance, he is incapable of telling present from past, or fact from fiction:

> [. . .] these clocks are still chiming in the past tense, a sonic past perfect, and somehow remind me – and I am already confused about which direction I'am looking in from the middle-temporal point of my Adler (that is tapping away now in my typewriter). (19)

Later on, his confusion leads the writer to abandon any attempt to control his own writing: "and I can't synchronize events any more than this" (27). The inability to experience time in a historical sequence is, as we shall see, one of the most characteristic traits of psychosis.

2.2. The Invisible Past: Igor Goes Psychotic

The central narrative repeats the major motifs from the frame story: the "weak" *sujet* (Igor's journey from the present to the past cannot be marked as an event in time and space) and the hero's inability to participate mimetically in the outside (all of Igor's attempts to take a photographic picture of Pushkin fail). Both the macroworld of official culture which launches Igor Odoevtsev on his trip and the microcosm of the hero's individual psyche are modeled in accordance with the psychotic attempt to restore psychological balance by replacing the reality principle (consciousness, the outer world) with the subconscious (the inner world).

The conflict at the bottom of the psychotic imbalance in 'Pushkin's Photograph" is the death of the father. The lost father, in 'Pushkin's Photograph," is none other than the father of Russian post-Petrine culture, Alexander Pushkin. The question as to how to mourn the death of Pushkin represents one of the most painful issues in Russian intellectual history of the 19th and 20th centuries. The modernist view of the past as unhistorical also crystallizes in the figure of Pushkin. The past survives, in such texts, merely in the form of forbidden sanctuaries which are off-limits for the inhabitants of the future.[14] In Futurist manifestoes, the national poet figures as a metonymy connoting the redundancy of history as a whole. In his manifesto "!Budetliansky" (1914), Velimir Khlebnikov writes:

> We discovered that the man of the twentieth century carries
> a thousand-years-old corpse (the past) and bends under the
> burden. We were finally able to give his height back to the
> man by throwing off that pile of the past (Tolstoys, Homers,
> Pushkins." (194)[15]

The reverse side of the modernist myth of the non-historical past is the view that the true Pushkin has, in fact, not yet been born. In his essay "Word and Culture" (1921), Osip Mandelshtam rejects the Futurist projection of the past as irrelevant. At the same time, however, Mandelshtam, too, participates in the modernist myth of the past as non-historical and nonexistent. He reverses the assumption that the past is dead and charges that, on the contrary, it has not yet arrived: "I want the new Ovid, Pushkin, Catullus, and I am not satisfied by the historical Ovid, Pushkin, Catullus."[16]

The death of the historical Pushkin at the hands of the Russian avant-garde is reversed by the poet's resurrection during the mid-1930s. In a massive campaign culminating in the Pushkin anniversary of 1937,[17] Stalinist culture canonizes the "dead" Pushkin as the true ancestor of socialist realism. The historical Pushkin returns to the canon of Russian culture – as the principal character in numerous fictional anecdotes about his life.[18] The celebrations of the year 1937 serve as the historical precedent of the poet's "300-th anniversary" in "Pushkin's Photograph." Both the official culture which sends Igor on his trip and Igor himself compensate the loss of Pushkin with the construction of an alternative reality in which the poet is still alive.

For Bitov's protagonist, Pushkin's death represents an unbearable reality. The following segment illustrates the traumatic loss of identity in which it results: "he could not manage without him. Without Pushkin he himself was gone" (44). The regular process of mourning a lost object or person involves the gradual withdrawal of libido from everything that was once connected with that object.[19] In some cases, however, the understandable resistance against such forgetting is so intense that the bereaved person loses any sense of reality and denies the death of the loved one. In these cases, the process of mourning is interrupted and replaced by psychotic hallucination.[20] Such is precisely the case with Igor Odoevtsev who creates for himself a substitute reality in which the unbearable loss never occurred in the first place. In Igor's fantasy world, Pushkin is not dead and the possibility of forestalling his death is real. Several times, the hero seeks to reverse the poet's tragic demise: "he had the incomparable opportunity of correcting previous mistakes" (45). In the year 1837, Igor seeks to intercept Pushkin on his way to the fatal duel with d'Anthes with a box of penicillin.

The "Pushkin theme" in Bitov's writings is always connected to the poet's death and the difficulty of accepting it. In the essay "A Memory of Pushkin" (*Vospominanie o Pushkine*) (1985), Bitov reflects upon the death of Pushkin, his canonization within the archive of culture and the question of the representation of the past in general. The author bemoans the determining influence, in public memory, of Pushkin's tragic and untimely death upon our perception of the poet's life and his works. According to Bitov, everything in Pushkin's biography is perceived from the vantage point of its end. In the same essay, Bitov discusses a paradox in the reception of the poet which is characteristic of "Pushkin's Photograph" too. The author writes that the impression of knowing Pushkin's biography down to the most minute detail stems from the confusion of fiction and fact, or canonized history, on the one hand, and the actual past, on the other. The inability of telling Pushkin's biography from his writings produces a psychotic ambivalence which cannot distinguish between truth and fiction: "in this sense we know about Pushkin more than we do about any other person in Russia, and yet we know him less than we know anyone else."[21]

As was the case with the fictitious writer, Igor Odoevtsev, too, cannot recognize history for what it is. To him, the past is reduced to an indifferent grey blur where real and false, image and object cannot be distinguished. Igor's behavior during his journey into the Pushkinian past exemplifies the psychotic urge to treat the sign as if it were the real thing. Like any psychotic, he lives in a world in which he finds a code, but no message. Bitov's protagonist suffers from an inability to relate to things as meaningful signs pointing to a referent beyond themselves. While the neurotic lives in a fully semioticized world where everything refers to everything else (the neurotic suspiciously anticipates the opinions of other individuals), the psychotic, by contrast, refers to signs as if they were real objects, a confusion which precludes any possibility for real communication. The psychotic experiences the overturning of the usual link between the word, on the one hand, and the object which it denotes, on the other: "If we ask ourselves what it is that gives the character of strangeness to the [. . .] symptom in schizophrenia, we eventually come to realize that it is the predominance of what has to do with words over what has to do with things."[22] In psychosis, the words themselves are treated as if they were things, not signs: "[T]he thing – the object in all its reality – has been lost, leaving only the word to be clung to."[23]

As a result, all of Igor's efforts to intercept history appear futile and hallucinatory. The demise of the object is irreversible as fiction and fact, present and past, inside and outside appear hopelessly entangled. Igor's inability to accept the sign for what it is leads to his perennial confusion of words and things. His attempt at *restitutio ad integrum* is consequently doomed to failure. This failure corresponds with Freud's theory of the confusion of signifier and referent in psychosis: "These endeavors [. . .] set off on a path that leads to the object *via* the verbal part of it, but then find themselves obliged to be content with words instead of things" (X,

302). Instead of meeting the real Pushkin, Igor becomes acquainted with the latter's negative doubles, "Apushkin" and "Nonpushkin" (*Nepushkin*). Bitov's protagonist cannot make any distinction between history and its representations. He finds himself forced to refer to historical events as if they were present ones, and to fictions as if they were reality. Even before he is launched on his trip, Igor is beset by a schizoid delusion and a general loss of reality. This is the case especially when the protagonist is listening to the session of the "jubilee council" entrusted with the preparations for Pushkin's 300th birthday:

> [...] he felt as if he had lightly taken his head from his shoulders the way you would a nozzle, and now (it immediately shrank to the size of an apple, very neat) he turned it in his hands with surprise [...] as if it were not his own ...(22)

Moments later, a similar incident of character split occurs. Igor sees his own head roll away from him: "Igor's little head slipped of his palm – that shiny sphere from the ball bearing rolled along the isle ..." (23) A deluded, illogical view of reality is typical of Bitov's protagonist throughout the session. Thus he loses any sense of identity with his own body: "having grown unused to himself, to his body, which he had not felt for a long time, he was not afraid of being noticed" (44).

The psychotic confusion of signs for things is in evidence throughout Igor's journey into the Pushkinian past. Any reality beyond these sign-things remains fully inaccessible to the hero: "he saw only quotations from what he knew; the rest (everything!) merged in a continuous and dangerous delirium of a completely inaccessible reality" (37). Like any psychotic individual, Bitov's hero also turns into a projection screen for the reality which surrounds him. Bitov plays particular attention to the schizoid elements in his protagonist's behavior. Thus, he has no identity other than that of the fictional characters of *Petersburg-text*: "He felt he was at the summit of time. And he joyfully strode down from it, feeling himself Onegin, Bashmachkin, and Makar Devushkin simultaneously" (33). At the end of his mission, he falls into a state of psychotic delusion. Igor experiences the flood of 1824 as Pushkin's fictional character Eugene from the poem *Bronze Horseman* which was written ten years after the historical event. The hero's insanity at the sight of his flooded home is, in fact, that of Pushkin's character. In this way, not even the psychosis of

Bitov's protagonist may be referred to as belonging to "him" and defining his proper identity: "Igor burst out laughing and started to run, gone mad like Eugene, muttering lines of Pushkin's future poem ..." (57-58).

2. 3. Experiencing History

In "Pushkin's Photograph" history has existence only to the extent that it excludes the spectator. The present's intervention in the past cannot in any way alter it and Igor is unable to shoot a photographic picture of the live Pushkin. The hero's inability to produce a *Lichtbild of* the poet exemplifies the psychotic inability to exercise memory, to produce an imprint and image *(Bild)* of the past. At the same time, Bitov emphasizes that the impossibility of producing Pushkin's photograph is not due to the excessive distance and elusiveness of history which characterizes modernist thinking. Invisibility, in Bitov's psychotic world, is no longer the hallmark of the transcendent other world. On the contrary, Igor's inability to participate mimetically in history is the result of the absence of any secret, of a kind of overexposure due to the lack of any distance between the gaze of the spectator (the present) and the past. In Bitov's recent fiction, the modernist non-historicity of the past and its consequent openness to manipulation have been replaced by the conviction that any attempt to give representation to the past has the status of a fiction. At the same time, however, Bitov's psychotic protagonists have lost any ability to distinguish between such fiction and the reality which they replace. Postmodernism does not deny the existence of history. Rather, it denies that it can be told, written, or indeed photographed.

Bitov's psychotic characters may be defined only in terms of that which they are not. In that sense, "Pushkin's Photograph" also illustrates the postmodern abolishment of the subject, its usurpation by the other. Emotions of loneliness and emptiness correspond with these impressions, "feeling of absolute loneliness and abandonment" (38). Analogously, blindness and the inability to comprehend are the leitmotifs of Igor's stay in the Pushkinian era. He does not so much experience the other in terms of the self but, conversely, his own self in terms of the other.

2. 4. False Luminary Scripts: Nabokov – Odoevsky

The invisibility of the past in "Pushkin's Photograph" represents something of a topos in postmodern Russian prose of the last three decades.[24] Diachronically, this motif refutes the modernist assumption that the past is not historical. In other words, history becomes once again inaccessible and remote. With regard to Andrei Bitov, the motif of the invisible or inaccessible past must be traced to an author who represents something of a missing link in the sequence from Russian modernism to Soviet postmodernism, Vladimir Nabokov. For Nabokov, any attempt to represent history through semiosis has the status of a falsification. The emblem of the falsification of the past, according to Nabokov, is the photograph. The latter partakes in a theatre of images with no original. In the novel *Invitation to a Beheading (Priglashenie na kazn')* (1938), Nabokov directly thematizes the photograph as an image which has no referent in reality. His protagonist is continuously deceived by photographic pictures which substitute for non-existent events. Every photographic picture merely refers to another one: "

> No, it was only the semblance of a window; actually it was a glazed recess, a showcase, and it displayed in its false depth – yes, of course, how could one help but recognize it! – a view of the Tamara Gardens."[25]

Later Nabokov's protagonist Cincinnat dreams about the possibility of a distinct boundary line between copy and original in the face of a surrounding reality in which the copy seems to have risen to the place of its original: "It exists, my dream world, it must exist, since surely there must be an original to the clumsy copy" (93).

For Nabokov, the death of the historical past, too, is intimately connected to photographic activity. His essay "Pushkin, or Truth and Verisimilitude" (*Pushkin, ili pravda i pravdopodobie*) (1937)[26] is one of the most pertinent pretexts for Bitov's "Pushkin's Photograph." Here, the representatives of the early photographic age seem to be mourning their own death at the hands of the new technique: "all celebrities of the second half of the nineteenth century now looked like distant relatives who were dressed in black as if mourning for the lost colorful Life."[27] In his essay, Nabokov discusses at length the question of Pushkin's photograph and its relevance for our perception of the poet's life and works. He interprets the fact that no photograph was taken of Pushkin during the poet's lifetime as a guarantee of the continued historicity of the past. Pushkin continues to live in the "other world" of a pre-semiotic darkness. The past is alive but, at the same time, it may not be intercepted. The darkness *(t'ma)* of history prefigures the motif of the invisible past as we encounter it in "Pushkin's Photograph":

> Just think about it: had Pushkin lived for another 2 or 3
> years, we would have had a photograph of him. One more
> step and he would have stepped out of the darkness so rich
> with nuances and filled with colorful hints [...]. (531)

Where modernism manipulates the past at will, Nabokov declares all such manipulations misrepresentations. In this way, history itself becomes dark, invisible and unknowable.

The pretexts for Bitov's treatment of the impossibility of catching a glimpse of the historical past are by no means confined to Nabokov or Russian modernism. The motif of the unidentified past in "Pushkin's Photograph" has another crucial subtext in Vladimir F. Odoevsky's Utopian fragment *The Year 4338. Letters from Petersburg* (1835, 1840).[28] "Pushkin's Photograph" makes a direct reference to Odoevsky 's Utopia: "we are as naïve imagining the technological future in our times as Prince Odoevsky was in Pushkin s, imagining the distant future all hung about with air balloons" (28). Odoevsky's text represents a sequence of fictitious letters containing the notes of a mesmerizer who assumes the personality of a Chinese person and travels through Russia in the 44th century. At that time, Russia has evolved into a technical and scientific Utopia which dominates half of the globe (the other half being dominated by China). Moscow and Petersburg have become one large urban conglomerate. The harsh Russian climate has artificially been transformed into a temperate one. This motif is taken up in "Pushkin's Photograph" where Igor Odoevtsev is struck by the strange dryness of the Petersburg weather. In Odoevsky's Utopia, a considerable part of the former Saint Petersburg is contained under the roof of the vast Museum *(Kabinet redkostei)*, a collection of historical artifacts reminiscent of the museums centers in Bitov's story. Odoevsky's text is based upon the premise that utopia is a place outside of historical time. As the future becomes the present, the past is progressively forgotten: "Future generations will be so preoccupied with present that, much more than we, they will become alienated from the past."[29] Since most of the (written) documents from the past have perished or turned unintelligible, the text of history is dark and impenetrable for the historians of the future. Even "two thousand dissertations" cannot reconstruct the etymology and meaning of a defunct word, such as "Germans" *(nemtsy)* (44).

Odoevsky's future lives in anticipation of a return of Halley's comet in the year 4339, a year from the present of the narrative. In that year, the comet has been predicted to collide with (and presumably destroy) the earth. The mesmerizer travels to Russia specifically to study how its inhabitants live with the certainty of apocalypse (417). In psychoanalytical terms, their reaction displays all the hallmarks of neurotic repression. Unable to cope with their own fears of the comet, the Russians avoid any contact with the subject. Only in a state of hypnosis can they be moved to confess to their anxiety.

Bitov's dialogue with Odoevsky focuses upon the question of history and the (im)possibility of its mnemonic reconstruction. In The Year *4338,* the dilapidated remnants of the past (such as the Moscow Kremlin) are conceived as symbols of the inscrutability of time and history. By contrast, Bitov rewrites in a psychotic key the neurotic avoidance which is a characteristic of Odoevsky's protagonists. It is not the repression of history but, on the contrary, its replacement by a new past that characterizes Bitov's future. Here, a (predictable) past replaces the (unpredictable) future which threatens Odoevsky's Utopia. Bitov's postutopia lovingly recreates history down to the most minute detail. The past is resurrected within the *hic et nunc* of the present in the guise of monuments and decorations in "the epoch of successful preservation of nature and monuments" (20). Instead of being exposed as falsifications or manipulations (as is the case with Nabokov), the fictions of history in Bitov's text all have the status of history themselves.

In "Pushkin's Photograph," the past has become totally transparent and (literally) accessible. Within the post-historical museums of the future, fiction and fact, name and real thing, present and past mingle. The transcendent past is resurrected *in toto* within the immanence of the here and now: "We will restore the whole of former culture down to the tiniest detail…" (23). Within the archive of official culture, the past continues to exist in the form of quotations and photographs: "Our great scientific achievement enabled us to produce photographs of Gogol, Chaadaev…" (20). The "jubilee council" and the cultural establishment which it represents are depicted as a psychotic archive which usurps the past and subsumes it under its own representational regime: "the epoch of successful preservation of nature and monuments." Bitov, of course, targets the rhetoric of Soviet propaganda during the 1950s and 60s, the pathos with which it propagated the conquering of the universe. At the same time, "Pushkin's Photograph" connotes the eagerness with which the Stalinist archive of official culture has appropriated and reshaped the cultural heritage. In Bitov's text, official culture is eager fully to conquer time and space: "…the whole Universe is delighted by our achievements in the field of the subjugation of time" (22). The historical sites, preserved or resurrected, represent the festive decoration for the session of the "jubilee council," devoted to the preparations for the festivities surrounding the 300th anniversary of Pushkin's birth:

> The idea of moving the meeting of the jubilee council from
> the Sputnik of United Nations (SUN) to ancient Earth,
> where Pushkin lived, could not but have a positive effect on
> the atmosphere, comrades, of the meeting. (19)

In "Pushkin's Photograph," the archive of official culture appears as a culture of the simulacrum.[30] Simulation abolishes any sequentiality between the signifier and the denoted object (referent). The distinction between original and copy, or anteriority and posteriority vanishes: "[…] under the dome of the Tower a historic lawn was restored" (20), the product of painstaking effort in which "original" fragment and subsequent recreation mingle. Bitov's museum centers suspend the operation of the museum. If *Pushkin House* opens with the image of the museum fractioned into its many constituent parts, "Pushkin's Photograph" presents the inverse vision of complete preservation and inclusiveness. The museum as a metaspace devoted to the preservation of the past has become identical with that which it exhibits. The preservative cupolas produce a virtual reality which redefines that very reality: "Igor's throat tickles from the dryness of the Petersburg air, and this descendant of the Neva floods is thirsty. Yes, how everything has changed – it really is dry" (22). In this way, the museum becomes the world. The exhibits no longer appear as metonymical displacements of a larger whole. Postmodern memory does not pursue the representation of an absent past through the agency of signs. Instead, the signs themselves usurp the past. No difference can be told between present and past, representation and real thing, remembering subject and remembered object.

The *sujet* of Bitov's text further illustrates the equivalence between in and out, present and past, before and after. Traditionally, (time) travel represents the classic case of a narrative based upon the irreducible ontological difference between inside and outside. Traveling through time presupposes an act of transcending (the flight or journey through time) which involves the successful experience of otherness (the future or the past). In the classic narrative of time travel, the protagonist experiences the outside with the hindsight of his own time. It is this *Verfremdungs-perspektive* which acts as the prerequisite for the genre's didactic potential (Montesquieu). In "Pushkin's Photograph," on the other hand, the secure vantage point on the outside from the stability of the inside (the hero's own present) vanishes. Thus, Igor's journey into the Pushkinian past is depicted not as a departure which could be marked as movement in time or space: "he realized that he was absent in this century just as he had been absent from it before his arrival" (38). The psychotic subject is incapable of structuring its experience as a temporal sequence. The fact that the hero's journey has no palpable effect also represents a departure from the *sujet* of traveling in Bitov's earlier prose, where generally the move from the city to he country has a therapeutic effect on the traveler.

Still, Bitov's protagonist does not return to the future empty-handed. However, the photographs and voice recordings which Igor brings back with him from the past do not yield any insight into the past. His holographic negatives and slide recordings resist development and translation into the logical language of the real:

> They developed Igor's slides, listened to the tapes... They confirmed the diagnosis. No, there was nothing to reproach Igor for; he had not exposed or erased anything. But only a shadow, like the wing of a bird flying up before the lens, came out. One was struck, however, by the unusual, senseless beauty of individual shots [...] the storm that preceded the cloud that had inspired the port to write "The last cloud dispersed by the storm..."; [...] the waves carrying coffins... and all the rest of the shots were of water and waves. (59)

The psychotic cannot escape his own fantasy world. The loss of reality as a result of its substitution by a secondary reality constructed in accordance with the demands of the id cannot be avoided. Igor's images are themselves psychotic to the extent that they oppose any distinction between in and out, fiction and fact, before and after. Their *sujets* are strictly peripheral and irrelevant when compared to the canonized events which they allegedly precede ("the storm that preceded the cloud..."). Instead of a utopian outside, Igor's images visualize "nothing," emptiness, and absence. To look at history one must be excluded from it. Bitov's psychotic heroes, alas, have lost the (neurotic) ability of looking away. They look right on and see – nothing.

ENDNOTES

[1] Cited here as "Pushkin's Photograph."

[2] Although previously published separately, *"Fotografiia Pushkina"* entered the collection *Chelovek v peizazhe* as one of six constituent narratives of the longer *Prepodavatel' simmetrii*. *Prepodavatel' simmetrii* was published for the first time in 1987 in the journal *Iunost'*. The English translation of "Fotografiia Pushkina," by Priscilla Meyer, is in *The New Soviet Fiction. Sixteen Short Stories*, comp. Sergei Zalygin (New York: Abbeville Press, 1989): 15-59. All in-text reference are to this edition.

[3] The distinction between those of Bitov's texts written and published after the publication of *Pushkinsky dom* in the Soviet Union (1987), on the one hand, and those re-published after this publication, on the other, is important for any formulation of Bitov's post-*Pushkinsky dom* prose poetics. The most important text belonging to the former category, apart from *Prepodavatel' simmetrii*, is *Chelovek v peizazhe* (1982).

[4] I. P. Smirnov, *"Ot avangarda k postmodernizmu. (Temporal'naia motivika),"* in *Semantic Analysis of Literary Texts. To Honor Jan van der Eng on the occasion of his 65th Birthday*, ed. E. de Haard (Amsterdam, 1990), 525.

[5] On the constitution of the subject in postmodernism, See A. Easthorpe, "Eliot Pound and the Subject of Postmodernism," in *After the Future. Postmodern Times and Places*, ed. G. Shapiro (Albany, 1990), 158-177; B. Johnson, "Poetry and its Double: Two 'Invitations au voyage'," in *The Critical Difference. Essays in the Contemporary Rhetoric of Reading*, ed. Barbara Johnson (Baltimore: Johns Hopkins University Press, 1981), 23-51.

[6] See L. Hutcheon, *A Poetics of Postmodernism. History, Theory, Fiction* (New York/London, 1988), 87-101; Smirnov, *"Ot avangarda k postmodernizmu,"* 526-527.

[7] "For the postmodern subject is [.. .] no longer an absolute sovereign, a ruler or a master [...]" (W. Welsch, *Unsere Postmoderne Moderne*, (Weinheim, 1991), 316).

[8] I. Smirnov, *Bytie i tvorchestvo* (Marburg/Lahn, 1990); Smirnov gives a typology of narcissistic/schizoid postmodernism, defining it as a viewpoint which can conceive of the immanent self only in terms of the other. "According to this model, there is nothing immanent, only the other." Narcissistic postmodernism, on the other hand, defines that which is immanent as the transcendent. Here, the subject becomes absolute and posits itself as its own object (208). I. Smirnov, "Geschichte der Nachgeschichte: Aur russisch-sorachigen Prosa

der Postmoderne," in *Modelle des literarischen Strukturwandels*, ed. M. Titzmann (Tubingen, 1991), 205-219.

⁹ Z. Freud, *Gessamelte Werke*. I-XVIII (London, 1940), XIII, 388. Literary critics have frequently interpreted (and celebrated) the psychotic's withdrawal into another world as an act of (joyous) liberation from the (political, economic, cultural, linguistic) constraints of reality. This appropriation of psychosis for the study of literature has tended to weaken the concept's Freudian roots. For Freud, psychosis is always accompanied by an acute experience of suffering due to the loss of reality. For an interpretation of psychosis as liberation, see especially G. Deleuze/F. Guattari, *Anti-Oedipus. Capitalism and Schizophrenia* (Minneapolis, 1983).

¹⁰ "The ego [...] creates for itself a new outside and inside world. There can be no doubt about the fact that [...] this new world is constructed in accordance with the desires of the id [...]" (Freud,1940/XIII, 389).

¹¹ Freud reports the case of a young woman who is in love with her brother-in-law. At her sister's deathbed, the woman cannot but think of her brother-in-law who would now be free to marry her. This unforgivable thought, however, is immediately forgotten, a process which initiates the psychological pain. The neurotic reaction, in this context, is to «devalue» (entwerten) reality by suppressing the inadmissible urge (the love for the brother-in-law). Its psychotic counterpart would consist in the downright denial of the sister's death. See Freud 1940/XIII, 364.

¹² Discussions of psychosis in the postmodern context have frequently suffered from the metaphorical elasticity of the term psychosis itself. It is worth noting that in "Pushkin's Photograph," such motifs/symptoms as the equivalence between inside and outside, the disappearance of difference, posthistoire, the world as a text, and, in particular, psychosis itself are directly quoted on the level of the narrated world. Bitov's text as a whole has an abstract, expository quality which almost gives it the quality of a metatext on Soviet postmodernism.

¹³ The postmodern metaphor of a generalized text which dissolves the vertical relations between sign and referent appears throughout "Pushkin's Photograph": "to harness myself to the reins of my attic, to drag it through the impassable text." (15)

¹⁴ See, for example, the "House of Antiquity" in Zamjatin's dystopian novel *My* (Engl. 1924).

¹⁵ V. Khlebnikov, *Sobranie sochinenii* (1933).

¹⁶ O. Mandelshtam, *Sobranie sochinenii v triekh tomakh*, II (Washington, 1971), 224. In the same essay, Mandelshtam writes: «yesterday has not been born yet, it

has not really happened" (334).

[17] The 100th anniversary of Pushkin's death. Also the year when Bitov was born.

[18] In 1936, Daniil Kharms satirizes the proliferation of Pushkin anecdotes which were circulating at the time by publishing his own fictitious mini-narratives about the historical Pushkin. D. Kharms, *"Anekdoty iz zhizni Pushkina,"* in *Polet v nebesa. Stikhi. Proza. Dramy. Pis'ma* (Leningrad, 1991).

[19] Freud 1940/X, 430

[20] Ibid., 430

[21] A. Bitov, *"Vospominanie o Pushkine,"* *Znamia* 12 (1985): 195. Bitov's argument has larger implications. For the author, in effect, charges that any act of archivization and commemoration (not just Pushkin's) fosters and indeed presupposes the perception that the commemorated object is dead once and for all. Instead of contributing to the "resurrection" of the past, its representation in and through the archive of culture closes it. In *"Vospominanie o Pushkine,"* Bitov uses the consecration of the famous Pushkin monument in Moscow (1880) to illustrate this point. According to the author, the monument reminds the spectator not so much of the living presence of its object but, on the contrary, of his death. When the poet's body is relegated from the epistemological darkness of the "other" world (the realm of the dead) to the public square, any hope is finally dispelled that he or his spirit might return at some unknown point in the future: "Before the monument Pushkin had been a mystery, but after its unveiling he became the mystery, entombed in bronze: the monument is open, the mystery is closed" (197). At this point, then, begins the (psychotic) invention of an alternative reality, a reality in which Pushkin's monument and the poet's death have no existence. Thus, Bitov wants to introduce an alternative view on Pushkin which reverses the effects of archive, monument, and school curriculum. Bitov seeks to forget anything which reminds him of Pushkin's death. Instead, the author proposes a psychotic reading of Pushkin's texts. He suggests that the poet's work be read in reverse chronological order, so as to avoid having to deal with the tragic event of the year 1837.

[22] Freud 1940/X, 299.

[23] S. Frosh, *Identity Crisis. Modernity, Psychoanalysis and the Self* (New York, 1991), 157.

[24] See Smirnov, *"Ot avangarda k postmodernizmu,"* 527.

[25] V. Nabokov, *Invitation to a Beheading*, trans. Dmitri Nabokov (New York: Capricorn Books, 1959), 76.

[26] Like Bitov, Nabokov cannot "catch up" with the poet: "I try to follow him with my eyes but he runs away from me only to appear again"(530). V. Nabokov,

"Pushkin, or Truth and Verisimilitude (*Pushkin, ili pravda i pravdopodobie*), " in *Priglashenie na kazn'. Romany. Rasskazy. Kriticheskie esse. Vospominaniia* (Kishinev, 1989), 149-272. This motif is directly cited in "Pushkin's Photograph." Bitov's protagonist "was drawn into the chase" (45).

[27] Ibid., 529.

[28] Reference to Odoevsky is included in the name of Bitov's hero (Odoevtsev).

[29] V. F. Odoevsky, "The year 4338 (1835). Letters from Petersburg," in Leland Fetzer, ed. and trans., *Pre-Revolutionary Russian Science Fiction: an Anthology* (*Seven Utopias and a Dream*) (Ann Arbor: Ardis, 1982), 39.

[30] The simulacrum has become one of the most prominent postmodern metaconcepts suggesting the blurring of the in/out distinction. For definitions of the simulacrum and its postmodern interpretation, see J. Baudrillard, "Simulacra and Simulation," in *Selected Writings* (Cambridge: Polity, 1988), 166-184.

XVIII

The "Traditional Postmodernism" of Viktor Pelevin's Short Story "Nika"

O. V. BOGDANOVA

The work of Viktor Pelevin, one of the brightest and most talented contemporary Russian writers, draws attention to itself for the breadth of the postmodern tools used by the writer to create an image of a postmodern "text-world," the surprising philosophical fullness of his artistic texts, and his ability, rare for contemporary Russian literature, to combine the playful postmodern literary traditions of the present with the serious, thought-full traditions of classical Russian literature. As a prominent representative of postmodern literature, which seemed to have broken with the literary traditions of Pushkin's nineteenth century, Pelevin surprisingly subtly and organically inherits the literary features of the classical past. On this intertextual unity Pelevin builds and expresses his authorial originality and distinctiveness.

Pelevin's short story "Nika" opens with an almost exact quotation from Ivan Bunin's well-known short story "Gentle Breath," which tells of the youthful, "frivolous" and "carefree" schoolgirl Olia Meshcherskaia, of her gentle breath, her love, and her tragic death. Bunin's story closes with: "And now this gentle breath is dissipated again in the world, in this cloud-covered sky, in this cold spring wind" (165).[1] Pelevin's narrative opens with:

> Now that her gentle breathing has dissolved back into the world
> — into this cloudy sky and this cold spring wind — and the volume
> of Bunin lies here on my knees like a heavy brick, I lift my eyes
> occasionally from the page to look over at her photograph,
> which has survived by chance, hanging on the wall.[2]

Pelevin's repetition of Bunin's words orients us from the first syllable toward the Russian classic and the eternal theme of Russian literature: love. Olia Meshcherskaia is established as the original prototype for Pelevin's heroine; the underlying features of Bunin's Olia are reflected in Pelevin's Nika.

For those who haven't read Pelevin's story, it is obvious that the appeal to Bunin is intentional. On the one hand, it is summoned by a desire to draw attention to the recurrence of similar life circumstances; on the other, it is used as a pointer to literary tradition. For those who have read Pelevin's story it is even more obvious that his reference to Bunin's story is intentional and dictated by a desire to both mystify and enlighten the reader. The invocation of "Gentle Breath" by a contemporary writer "compels" the reader to accept the events that happen to the cat as conflicts of human life (the writer does not mention [disclose] the "zoomorphism" of his heroine until the very last sentence). The allusion also lends an ironic, playful beginning to the narrative, both mystifying and deciphering the text: comparing Bunin's volume to a heavy brick (90) adds a light, playful and ironic coloration to the narrative, while continually reinforced markers of Bunin's text[3] repudiate the phantasmagoria ("unrealness") of depicted events. This obscuring/exposing calls attention to the story's involvement with Bunin's text, creates intertextual linkages, and brings the postmodernist thesis – "world as text and text as world" – into effect.

In this way, the ending of Bunin's narrative becomes the beginning of Pelevin's: "Gentle Breath" is picked up in "Nika," forming a distinct circle (or spiral) that signifies continuity on the level of theme (love), in the "key" of the narrative (lyrical subjective confession), and in the system of characters (Pelevin's heroine is first and foremost Buninesque).

In "Gentle Breath," Olia Meshcherskaia is distinguished by her "grace, elegance, [and] a lively and intelligent look in her eyes," her "joyful, uncommonly lively eyes," her ability to look at everything "with bright and lively eyes," her ability to be "the most elegant, carefree, and happy," and her gift for performing any movement "with [...] ease and grace" (Bunin, 94-95); "at fifteen everyone said she was a beauty" (161). Nika is also "young and full of energy," (Pelevin, 96) endowed with "natural elegance" and a "lithe body" with "delicate curves". Her "greenish eyes" radiate "mystery" and her being is suffused with the "reflected glimmer of a supreme harmony" (93) – "she appeared like some perfect work of art" (101). Bunin says of Olia that "no one danced as well as Olia Meshcherskaia. No one skated as gracefully as she" (162). Of Nika, Pelevin writes:

> She never used the lift, but always ran down the steps with swift silent steps. I don't think it was out of any kind of physical vanity – she really was so young [...] that it was easier for her to dash down the stairs in two minutes, scarcely touching them as she went, than to spend the same amount of time waiting for the arrival of a humming, coffin-like cabin [...] (96).

The heroines' external resemblance reinforces their inherent kinship: for example, the way that Olia's ability to listen "with a demure expression on her face," (Bunin, 162) appears again in Nika: "God only knows what she was thinking about, but my words were certainly not penetrating her lovely little head. I might just as well have been talking to the sofa she was sitting on" (Pelevin, 92). Olia was "totally unconcerned with the admonitions given her by her teachers" (Bunin, 160). Nika "didn't give a damn about anything I said either" (Pelevin, 95); moreover, "Nika herself, sitting only a foot away, was as inaccessible as the spire of the Kremlin's Spasskaya Tower" (ibid.).

Just as Olia is easy and changeable in her treatment of admirers (Bunin, 162), so too Nika is inconsistent with her affections:

> When she buried her head in my chest, I slowly ran my fingers down her neck and imagined another palm on that delicate curve – a hand with pale, slim fingers and a ring with a small skull, or a coarse, hairy hand bearing blue anchors and dates – sliding along her throat just as slowly, and I felt that the change would leave her heart entirely untouched. (Pelevin, 90)

The hero observes of Nika's lover: "I had long suspected that Nika liked his kind, animals in the fullest sense of the word, and she would always be attracted to them, no matter whom she herself might resemble" (ibid., 101).

Furthermore, the resemblance shared by the heroines extends to their chosen ones. Olia Meshcherskaia is shot on the platform of the train station by a certain "Cossack officer, ugly and coarse in appearance and having nothing in common with the class of people to which Olia Meshcherskaia belonged" (Bunin, 163). Nika's lover is also characterized unpleasantly: "he had expressionless eyes, vulgar colorless moustaches and a strong air of self-importance" (Pelevin, 101), "[once] I saw him rummaging in the dustbins, still maintaining that same air" (ibid.) – clearly, he is not of Nika's circle.

It is interesting that Nika has a naturally "feline-like lithe body" following on Bunin's portrayal (notice) of a feline essence (aspect) in Olia. This is particularly evident in the conversation between the principal, who "was sitting [...] quietly knitting behind her desk," (Bunin, 162) and Olia: "'You'll listen quite carelessly, as bitter experience has taught me,' the principal said, [sic] *pulled the thread, making a swirl on the polished floor, which Olia watched with curiosity*; she raised her head [...]"[4] (ibid.). The italicized words picturesquely convey Olia's "feline" interest in the ball of thread and her kitten-like desire to play with it.

In Pelevin's story, the narrator's remarks about Nika's diary ("I used to dream of discovering what she thought of me, but it was pointless trying to get any answers out of her, and she kept no diary that I could have read in secret" [Pelevin, 93]) or the fact that he never once saw her with a book (ibid.) seem inexplicable and unmotivated, yet are easily explained once one recalls that Olia Meshcherskaia, herself, carried a diary and read books ("my father's books" [Bunin, 165])[5]. In other words, even dissimilarity reveals the connections and comparisons between the heroines as envisaged by Pelevin (i.e., carried/didn't carry a diary, read/didn't read books). Over the course of Pelevin's narrative, the fascination with Olia Meshcherskaia sets off and adds to the fascination (and tragic quality[6]) of Nika's image, *a priori* predisposing us to a stronger sympathy with the latter.

Pelevin's intention to underline the "recognizability" of his heroine, her "closeness" to Olia, reveals itself in seemingly insignificant details that are, in fact, echoes of Bunin's words. The graveside "porcelain wreath" (Bunin, 161) and "porcelain medallion" which holds a photograph of the young schoolgirl reverberate in Pelevin's "old Kuznetsov porcelain sugar-bowl" (Pelevin, 92). In this instance, both porcelain and the name Kuznetsov[7] take on playing roles. "Porcelain" will even be heard again in the mention of "small herds of porcelain mammoths that had wandered out of the depths of millennia into the future and on to millions of Russian sideboards" (ibid., 94). Treading on the heels of Bunin, who changes the "porcelain" wreath into a "dead" wreath (165) over the course of his narrative, Pelevin makes the "old Kuznetsov porcelain sugar-bowl" a repository of the "dead," "old junk" (92) of the past – "a storehouse for all the proofs of the reality of existence which I had gathered through life" (ibid.).

Other linkages refer to the properties of various other materials. For example, in "Gentle Breath" Olia writes in her diary about "a silk handkerchief" with which she covers her face (Bunin, 164); in Pelevin's story, one of the guests offers to behave more strictly with Nika so that she becomes "smooth as silk" (91) (i.e., compliant). Bunin's "rose-tinged evening" (162) imparts particular traits to one of Pelevin's heroines, turning the "pink-haired old janitor" (Pelevin, 102) into an old woman who looked "like a dried rose" (ibid., 100).

The "natural calendar" of "Gentle Breath" is also maintained in "Nika." Both stories describe the time of year as Spring – in Bunin: "It's April, but the days are gray" (161); in Pelevin: "It was a day in March, but the winter was still hard" (98) – and have the same weather conditions: "the weather had become fine again [...] it had become chilly" (Bunin, 164); compared to "soon it will be spring [...]. But it was still cold" (Pelevin, 100). The parallelism is obvious even in the sentence structure.

Olia Meshcherskaia's natural/organic qualities also embellish the story about Nika. Bunin describes Olia thus:

> Her schoolmates took pains to comb their hair frequently and meticulously, to move gracefully – but not Olia; she was worried about nothing! Not of ink stains on her fingers, nor of a flushed face, disheveled hair, or of scraping her knee in a fall. Everything that distinguished her from all the others during her last two years at school [...] came to her without any effort on her part, unnoticed [...]. (162)

Pelevin endows Nika not only with natural and instinctive, but also intentionally physiological features: "[...] if I might borrow a term from physiology, for her I was the irritant which produced certain reflex reactions" (90) – "in the final analysis she was shallow and vain, and her needs were purely physiological: a full belly, a good sleep, and enough physical affection to maintain a sound digestion" (93). At the end of the story this crudeness becomes pardonable when it is revealed that the subject under discussion has been a cat, not a young woman. To Olia Meshcherskaia's behaviour (and charm), Pelevin adds elements from a "primitive human" behaviour model, like a female Mowgli or Tarzan (e.g., the relationship between Nika and those around her: "my friends [...] made no secret of their disdain when she wasn't around. Not a single one of them, of course, considered her an equal" [91]).

Despite several repellent aspects to Nika and her behavior,[8] the writer portrays her *world* (a term that is also present in Bunin's story[9]) as alluring and attractive to the narrator. Its elemental and organic quality, its simplicity and clarity are imbued with

> an illusory spiritual content. In her animalistic ways [...] there was some reflected glimmer of a supreme harmony, a glimpse of the elusive goal that art seeks hopelessly to attain. I began to think that this simple life was truly beautiful and meaningful [...]. (Pelevin, 93)

The spontaneity and independence of Nika's character, her inherent freedom, which reveals itself in both her nocturnal strolls ("I had noticed long before that she went out for short periods at night"[10] [Pelevin, 99]) and her autonomy from the burden of cultural (that is, "others'") knowledge,[11] separates her from the hero-narrator's circle of acquaintances and charms with its simplicity and artlessness. "Suddenly" the hero realizes that he is "genuinely interested in her world" (93). The desire to know "what [...] her soul consisted of" (95) springs up in him. He wants to understand "her simple walks" (97).

To understand Nika's personality, however – her manner of behaving and thinking – realistically (within the limits of narrative space) involves a switch in focus from her world to the world of the hero, to an awareness of him through his other. The hero's world stands out contrapuntally, founded on "mental constructs" that "cluster like flies on the surface of any object reflected on the retinas of [his] eyes" (Pelevin, 95). It is a world in which "the constant clamor of thoughts [...] had dug a deep rut out of which they could no longer escape" (ibid.); a world the hero "was thoroughly sick of, and from which [he] had no way out" (ibid.). In this world "nothing really new had happened [...] for a long time, and [the hero] hoped that by being close to Nika [he] would be able to discover some new, unfamiliar way of *feeling and living*"[12] (ibid.).

The above italicized verbs may be read as an echo of Pushkin's "To live he hurries and to feel makes haste."[13] In combination with "Russian spleen," "the longing for the new" (Pelevin, 97), and the turn to "eternal questions" (already encountered in, "But what, in that case, did her soul consist of?" [95]), these words are clearly oriented towards the traditional hero of

Russian classical literature – the "superfluous man." A confirmation of this may be found in the words of Pelevin's narrator himself, who says that he "*once again* [...] felt on [his] shoulders the weightless but unbearable burden of solitude"[14] (95). In this context "once again" can be read as something that happened to the hero today (not long ago) and also that happened sometime (long ago) and not to him alone.

Identifying the hero's condition as one of "solitude" is a signal to define the "superfluous" hero of the story more precisely as Lermontovian. The sentence a littler further on, "I had begun to find her company dull" (Pelevin, 96), describes even more distinctly the Pechorin-like features of the hero. In keeping with this, the "swarthy southern charm" (90) of the heroine-"barbarian,"[15] can be read as an allusion to Lermontov's Bela. The adjectives "weightless" and "unbearable"[16] are also contrasted in a Pechorinesque manner. Finally, the characteristic admonition of Pechorin: "You're speaking of a pretty woman as if she were an English horse" (Lermontov, 80), is circuitously related to Pelevin's text (Pelevin's variant is about a Siamese cat).

In the Russian classical literary tradition, the "superfluous" hero is accompanied by a representative of "the charming ideal" – ("A wild creature, sad and pensive, / Shy as a doe and apprehensive"[17]) – a girl who is, as a rule, from the village, provincially modest, pure and trusting, open and passionately loving, and "forever" faithful (Tatiana – Onegin; Bela, Mary, Vera – Pechorin; and later, the loyal Turgenev girls as they stand next to the "new" heroes). In Pelevin's story, however, it is obvious that the "superfluous man" is accompanied by a different type of woman than that of classical literature: one that is unconventional and atypical in relation to the "superfluity" of the first third of the 19th century. In contrast to the heroines of Pushkin or Lermontov, Pelevin has created the image of a heroine still primitive and natural but no longer gentle, pliant, modest, and obedient; instead, she is lively and independent with clearly delineated self-respect, slightly haughty and with accentuated pride, naively empty-headed and unintentional in her feelings, and unburdened by "artificial" intellect.

Indications of a (somewhat) similar type may be found in Russian classical literature in the portrayal of Natasha Rostova.[18] She distinguishes herself through her unfiltered perceptions of the surrounding world, loses herself in the thrill of her feelings, "doesn't deign to be intelligent,"[19] and is described by Leo Tolstoy himself as "a strong, handsome, and fertile woman"[20] in the epilogue of the novel.[21]

In Russian (classical) literature, however, the sphere in which this type of heroine manifests is narrowly localized and has limited reach. The Russian female "charming ideal" is overshadowed and crowded by the male hero — she merely attends to him, accompanying the plot and throwing his internal world into relief. The "female world," despite all its fullness of meaning and wholeness, is, as a rule, found in the shadows: not Tatiana but Onegin; not Vera or Mary, but Pechorin; not Olga but Oblomov; not Sonya but Raskolnikov. In large part this type of heroine is at odds with the traditions of Western literature: Carmen remains the clearest and most frequently interpreted figure in various types of art when the world and even the name of her male counterpart(s) has almost been forgotten.

Pelevin's story breaks as much with the canon of classical Russian literature as with that of the Western tradition. He renders the worlds of both the hero and the heroine as fully-valued and equal. No longer pushed into the background by the world of the hero, the heroine's world rightfully and successfully competes with it.

Even the name of the heroine has been chosen in order to affirm (confirm) her strength and inner power, and to demonstrate the "vibe" of her world. "Veronika" is from the Ancient Greek for "bringing victory"[22] and means "leading to victory," or even "victory" itself. Not by chance does the hero use Nika — a shortened form of the heroine's name — as an echo of the name "of her near namesake, the headless, winged goddess" (Pelevin, 91). In this context the allusion to the "headlessness" and "wingedness" of the goddess is significant: the transfer of "headless" to Nika-the-cat reads as a synonym for "not very clever" (or perhaps "uneducated" — "she had never even heard of [many things]" [Pelevin, 91]), but still "winged," that is, sublime or inspired (by living nature and not numb reason).

Thus, two worlds come together in Pelevin's story: the obviously independent and the obviously oppositional. As is well known, however, the problem of "the double" is a romantic problem. From this stem the romantic motives ("a romantic [...] term" [Pelevin, 94]) and imagery which form the artistic space of the story. Moreover, romanticism's ethic and aesthetic is superposed and superimposed on the adventure romance (almost all the categorological accoutrements of pirate life — "blue anchors," "masts," a "Jolly Roger" ["a ring with a small skull"], and others — flicker throughout the story). This mixture of romanticism and romance does not bother Pelevin; instead, it strengthens his multi-colored, postmodernistically compiled, (dis)organized picture of a universe built out of the chaos of mutually exclusive contradictions and coexisting contrasts.

Romantic "duality" is developed from the very first lines of the story: the "swarthy *southern* charm" of the heroine is opposed "geographically" to the "barren *northern* country" (90). The weather/climate contradictions of the latter are established in the sentence, "It was a day in March, but the winter was still hard" (98), i.e., November-like, opposing "spring" to "autumn." The heroine "was life condensed" and "everything about her contradicted the very meaning of the word [die]" (97). Nika's relationship to her surroundings is internally contradictory and is reflected in the very structure of sentences: "My friends weren't overtly rude to her, *but* they made no secret of their disdain" (91). The protagonists of the story "were together *every day*" but understood that they would "*never* be genuinely close." The heroine had a "simple life," the hero – "nothing but fictions"; the heroine was "entirely free," the hero – dependent on the "inventions of others." Nika's world is open and endless, like the forest in which she wanders that begins "beyond the wide dusty vacant lot"; while the hero's world is closed-in – "[...] she was finding the monotonous seclusion of our life irksome"[23] (96). The contrast is portrayed even at the level of adjectives, for example, in the already mentioned pair: weightless – unburdened, as well as others. In some of the narrator's turns of phrase a meaningful duality is created even in the absence of an express opposite: "She was much younger than me" (90) (she is young therefore he is old); a mention of Nika's "ancient homeland" projects itself onto the not-ancient contemporary world; the adverbial phrases "by chance" and "by the whim of fate" (90) are uttered twice within the space of two paragraphs, thereby signaling an opposition to the usual rules of cause and effect.

Meanwhile, the "double-ness" of Pelevin's world is not in the romantic-past but a postmodernist-present. For the writer, the peculiarity of Nika's opinion on her surroundings becomes the starting point for an irrational worldview: "objects only existed for her as long as she was using them, and then they disappeared" (91). For the hero, however, objects were "storehouses" for "fragments of the past" preserved as "proofs of the reality of existence" (92).

> To throw out an old pair of cracked spectacles is to admit that the entire world seen through them is gone forever, or on the contrary, which is the same thing, it doesn't exist yet

– that world lies somewhere in the kingdom of imminent non-existence. (Ibid.)

Nika's world is subjective, unstable, mobile, irrational and unknowable (not because it is thus in her consciousness but because "[...] it would be too complicated for Nika" otherwise [101]). Juxtaposed to this, the world of the hero must be objective, finite, stable, rationalistic and knowable, i.e., real.

The creation of a logical opposition, however, between Nika's perception – primitive, natural, and unspoiled by civilization – to the realistic (or so it originally seems) means by which the hero comprehends the world is carried out inconsistently. Despite a superficial counter-positioning to Nika, the hero easily (and imperceptibly) moves to the subjective level of world-perception. On this level, subjectivism and irrationality are motivated not by the animal nature of the perceiving subject but by the particularities of thought-consciousness and the character of the perceived object itself, that is, the present-day world. From this emerges a typically postmodernist formulization of a hero for whom "the world around [...] is only a system of mirrors with various curvatures" (102), for whom "everything in the world is interwoven, and the links of cause and effect can never be traced or restored" (98), and who muses,

> who can tell whether or not by giving up a seat in the underground to some spiteful old woman we have condemned the children of Zanzibar to starvation?[24] The extent of our foresight and responsibility is too limited, and in the final analysis all causes lead back into infinity [...].[25] (98)

The image of a "mirror-world" is intensified by the image of a "book-world," the contours of which are created using large and concrete details. The image of a book occurs in the very first paragraph of the story – in the mention of Bunin's tome, heavy like a brick (90). The narrator comments that Nika does not read books (93) and quotes from the book he is reading by G. Gazdanov (98-99). The names of V. Nabokov and N. Chernyshevskii are referred to in the text, and reading between the lines one finds the names of Pushkin, Lermontov, Turgenev, and Blok. The narrator says about himself: "I fell asleep over my book" (99), and "[...] I woke with my book on my knees" (100). With regard to the contents of books, he concludes that "almost every book and every poem was dedicated to Nika" (99). He even catches himself at a certain moment "resembling a young Chernyshevskii."[26]

The text of "Nika" is connected in the same kind of circuitous, associative manner to L. Vygotsky's article "Gentle Breath, by I. Bunin,"[27] with which Pelevin was undoubtedly acquainted when he wrote his story. Vygotsky's conclusion takes the following form:

> The story is, after all, called "Gentle Breath." It produces in us an effect that is almost diametrically opposed to the impression caused by the events themselves. The true theme of this story is the gentle breath, not the muddled life of a provincial schoolgirl. Its fundamental trait is the feeling of liberation, lightness, the crystal transparency of life, none of which can be derived from the literal events. (ibid., 154)

Vygotsky's suggested interpretation of the "lightness" of Bunin's story finds its playful development in Pelevin. The latter's "lightness", however, exists only in so far as the tragic heroine of the story ironically turns out to be a cat rather than a girl. In fact, it is possible to say that, in its broadest sense, the very text of Bunin's story itself becomes the direct metahero of Pelevin's story.

Pushkin's, "Or at a moving tale my eyes will fill"[28] almost writes itself into the story's text (and indeed can be inferred from the text), creating the literariness of the hero, heroine, situation, conflict, and individual clashes, and demonstrating (on the level of the device) the bookishness of the hero's consciousness and its dependence on other texts. The world of Pelevin's hero is a vast text formed many times over, ready to be altered, recorded and read through in different ways. In his image and likeness a new text is created (written just now) that is lively, fluctuating, and prone to transformations, making possible the substitutions of (or substitutions for) Olia Meshcherskaia for Nika, a girl for a cat, Nika herself for whomever ("whatever she might be called and whatever form she might assume" [Pelevin, 99]), Onegin-Pechorin for the hero- narrator, the hero-lover for a tomcat, love intrigue for a training, real life for illusion, etc. In the text-world of Pelevin value takes the form of "a page from a long-destroyed address book with a telephone number which I had never dialed" (92), an unused ticket to the Illusion cinema "with the stub still intact" (ibid.), and several useless "prescriptions that had never been filled" (ibid.); while the catastrophic nature of perceiving tragedy disappears: even Nika's death "failed to make any particular impression" (97).

Furthermore, "every one of us is an accomplice in a mass of murders" (98), and "the longing for the new is one of the most common forms assumed by suicidal impulses in our country" (97).

Originally appearing as the main idea – almost traditional, even classical – the clash of the "relationship between the sexes" (L. Miller)[29] is essentially altered, assuming the character of a problem of worldview and emphasizing the problem of philosophical originality in perceiving the world. The broadest (and simultaneously narrowest) issue in the relationship between men and women transforms into a question about the relationship between different human types (natural and cultural). In its turn, this emerges as a conflict between various worldviews (romantic and realist, subjective and objective). In the final analysis, the problem is one of postmodernistic unity of multidirectional beginnings – of male and female, human and animal, rational and instinctive, realistic and romantic, logical and irrational, ancient and new, southern and northern, spring and fall, living and dead, etc. – wherein the polarity of opposition gets removed and contrasting pairs ("2") have a tendency to transform (by multiplying or splitting) into 3 or more.[30]

Love intrigue (at the level of theme) and its simulation (at the level of ironic play-mystification) become the most superficial and lightweight layer in perceiving this artistic text. Not content to simply play according to the rules of postmodernism, Pelevin creates a philosophical picture of the contemporary universe. On this background he draws a detailed portrait of a contemporary version of the classical hero(es) of Russian literature, modified by time and circumstances, and preserving within itself an inherent dominant idea of a national type.

Thus, within contemporary Russian literature, Viktor Pelevin's story "Nika" becomes an almost classic model of postmodern play by a contemporary artist with previous literary traditions. Pelevin's text demonstrates the successfulness of postmodern deconstruction in the name of classical and traditional reconstruction – the superficial poetic lightness of the story reveals surprising philosophical depths. Taken together, this indicates a continuation by postmodern literature of the traditions of classical Russian literature.

Translated by Nicola Kuchta

ENDNOTES

[1] Ivan Bunin, "Gentle Breath," in Lev S. Vygotsky, *The Psychology of Art* (Cambridge: MIT Press, 1971), 162. Hereafter cited in text.

[2] Viktor Pelevin, "Nika," in *The Blue Lantern*, trans. Andrew Bromfield, (London: Harbord Publishing, 1997), 90. Hereafter cited in text. Some translations may have been modified – Trans.

[3] The quotation at the beginning of Pelevin's story repeats the object details of Bunin's world as well as his words, in particular, the photographs (Bunin's "Gentle Breath" also begins with a photograph (161)) and the mention of the name of the story's creator.

[4] Italics added – Author.

[5] See also: ibid., 163-4, 165.

[6] Long before the tragic denouement Pelevin inserts the phrase "I never imagined that she could die" (97). With no other explanation for the time being, this phrase gets interpreted as an allusion to Bunin's story, to the tragic death of Olia Meshcherskaia.

[7] From the famous owner of the Saint Petersburg porcelain factory at the turn of the twentieth century, i.e., at the precise moment when the events in "Gentle Breath" take place and of the story's composition (1916).

[8] For example, "The people who surrounded her were no more than talking cupboards [...] and when they called on me, she would most often get up and go into the kitchen" (Pelevin, 91).

[9] See: 164, 165.

[10] Just like Kipling's cat that walks alone.

[11] For example: "Nika was entirely free of the degrading necessity to connect the flames hovering over the rubbish-container with the 1737 Fire of Moscow, or the burping croak of the satisfied crow beside the grocery store with the ancient Roman omen recorded by Julian the Apostate" (Pelevin, 95).

[12] Italics added – Author.

[13] Alexander Pushkin, *Eugene Onegin*, trans. James E. Falen (Oxford: Oxford University Press, 1995), 3.

[14] Italics added. – Author.

[15] Mikhail Iu. Lermontov, *A Hero of Our Time*, trans. Marian Schwartz (New York: Random House Inc, 2004), 36.

[16] Pelevin, 95.

[17] Pushkin, *Onegin*, 47.

[18] The comparison was suggested by L. Miller. See: Liudmila V. Miller, "*Konflict rasskaza V. Pelevina "Nika" v kontekste natsional'noi ésteticheskoi traditsii,*" *Мир русского слова* 1: 1 (2001): 65–69.

[19] Leo Tolstoy, *War and Peace*, trans. Richard Pevear and Larissa Volokhonsky (New York: Alfred A. Knopf, 2007), Vol. 2, Part 5: IV, 548.

[20] Ibid., Epilogue, Part I: X, 1154. The word Tolstoy uses to refer to Natasha, "samka," usually refers to female non-human animals. Its recurrence here emphasizes the parallels between Nika the cat and Olia the woman. – Trans.

[21] Throughout "Nika," Pelevin himself mentions various literary parallels to similar female types. In addition to Ivan Bunin's Olia Meshcherskaia, there is Vladimir Nabokov's Lolita (Olia's disregard of "scraping her knee in a fall" (Bunin, 162) flashes in Humbert's consciousness when he "takes the fat social-democratic elbow in the window next door for the knee of his motionless nymphette" (Pelevin, 102)); the "natural reticence" (ibid., 99) of Gaito Gazdanov's heroine, and even, seemingly alien to this series, Aleksandr Blok's heroine (although, in truth, we are speaking of the "Unknown Woman": "And slowly making her way through the drunks, always unaccompanied, always alone…" (ibid.).

[22] A. N. Tikhonov, L. E. Boyarinova, and A. G. Ryzhkova, *Slovar' russkikh lichnykh imen* [Dictionary of Russian Given Names], (Moskva: Shkol'naia Pressa, 1995), 439.

[23] The word in the original, "*tiagotit'sia*", could mean "to find something a burden"– Trans.

[24] "Zanzibar" here may be taken as an element of playful poetics since Kornei Chukovskii's *Aibolit* [Doctor Ouch – Trans.] fixed it in every Russian's consciousness during childhood: "We reside in Zanzibar / In Kalahari and Sahara/ Up on Mount Fernando Po / Where wallows the Hippo-po/ All along wide Limpopo." My Translation – Trans. (Kornei Chukovskii, "*Aibolit,*" in *Chudo-Derevo / Serebrianyi gerb* (Moscow: Detskaia Literatura, 1967), 86.)

[25] Compare Nika: "The people who surrounded her were no more than talking cupboards that appeared for some incomprehensible reason and then disappeared for reasons equally incomprehensible" (Pelevin, 91). Italics added – Author.

[26] Chernyshevskii was an influential young radical in 19th century Russia (Trans.)

[27] L. Vygotsky, *The Psychology of Art* (Cambridge: The M.I.T. Press, 1971), 145-166 .[28] Alexander Pushkin, "Elegy," trans. Babette Deutsch, in *The Works of Alexander Pushkin*, ed. Avrahm Yarmolinksy (New York: Random House, 1936), 72.

[29] See L. Miller: "In Pelevin's story "Nika," one version of the endless and eternal theme of the relationship between the sexes is realized in its – for a Russian artistic picture of the world – traditional representation" (Miller, "*Konflikt*," 66).

[30] An example of which is the splitting of "romanticism" from "romance".

WORKS CITED

Abraham, Karl. "A Short Study of the Development of the Libido, Viewed in the Light of Mental Disorders" [1924]. In *Selected Papers of Karl Abraham*. London, 1965.

Adorno, T. W. *Noten zur Literatur III*. Frankfurt/Main: Suhrkampf, 1965

Afanas'ev, A. N. *Narodnye russkie skazki*. Moscow: Detgiz, 1958.

Aizlewood, Robin. *Starukha*. Bristol: Bristol Classical Press, 1995.

-----. "Guilt without Guilt." *Scottish Slavonic Review* 14 (1990): 199-217.

Akhmatova, A. A. *Sochineniia*. Edited by G. P. Struve and B. A. Filippov. Washington: Inter-Language Literary Associates, 1967-1968.

Alagova, Tamara and Nina Efimov. "Interview with Tatyana Tolstaya." *World Literature Today (Books Abroad)* 67 (1993): 49-53.

Aleksandrov, A., ed. *Polet v nebesa*. Leningrad, 1988.

Anemone, Anthony. "The Anti-World of Daniil Kharms." In *Daniil Kharms and the Poetics of the Absurd: Essays and Materials*. Edited by N. Cornwell, 71-96. London: Macmillan, 1991.

Anninskii, Lev. "*Put' Vasiliia Shukshina*." In Vasilii Shukshin, *Do tret'ikh petukhov*, 638–66. Moscow: *Izvestiia*, 1976.

Apukhtina, V. A. *Proza V. Shukshina*. Moscow: *Vysshaia shkola*, 1981.

Arnheim, Rudolf. *Art and Visual Perception* (new version). Berkeley-Los Angeles-London: University of California Press, 1974.

Babel, Isaak. Konarmiia. *Odesskie rasskazy*. *P'esy*. Letchworth (Hertfordshire): Bradda Books, 1965.

Bakhtin, Mikhail. *The Dialogic Imagination: Four Essays*. Edited by Michael Holquist. Translated by Caryl Emerson and Michael Holquist. Austin: University of Texas Press, 1981.

-----. *Problems of Dostoevsky's Poetics*. Translated by R. W. Rotsel. Ann Arbor: Ardis, 1973.

-----. *Rabelais and His World*. Translated by Helene Iswolsky. Cambridge, MA: MIT Press, 1968.

Barta, Peter I. "The Author, the Cultural Tradition and Glasnost: An Interview With Tatyana Tolstaya." *Russian Language Journal* 44 (1990): 265-83.

Baudrillard, J. "*Simulacra and Simulation*." In *Selected Writing*. Edited by Mark Poster, 166-184. Cambridge: Polity, 1988.

Bavilsky, Dmitri. "*Znaki prepinaniia #34,*" *Topos* (24/12/02)

Beaujour, Elizabeth. *The Invisible Land: A Study of the Artistic Imagination of Iurii Olesha.* New York: Columbia University Press, 1970.

Birnbaum, Henrik, Thomas Eekman, ed. *Fiction and Drama in Eastern and Southeastern Europe: Evolution and Experiment in the Postwar Period.* Columbus, Ohio: Slavica, 1980.

Boas, George. *The Cult of Childhood.* London: Warburgh Institute, University of London, 1966.

Booth, Wayne. *The Company We Keep: An Ethics of Fiction.* Berkeley: University of California Press, 1988.

Briggs, John and F. David Peat. *Looking Glass Universe: The Emerging Science of Wholeness.* New York: Simon and Schuster, 1984.

Brostrom, Kenneth N. "Ornamentalism." In *Handbook of Russian Literature.* Edited by Victor Terras. New Haven/London: Yale University Press, 1985.

Brown, Deming. *Soviet Russian Literature since Stalin.* Cambridge: Cambridge University Press, 1978.

Brown, Edward J. *Russian Literature since the Revolution.* Cambridge, MA: Harvard University Press, 1982.

Buckley, Jerome Hamilton. *Season of Youth. The Bildungsroman from Dickens to Golding.* Cambridge, MA: Harvard University Press, 1974.

Bunin, Ivan. "Gentle Breath." In Vygotsky, Lev. *The Psychology of Art,* 161-165. Cambridge, MA: MIT Press, 1971.

Carden, Patricia. "The Art of War in Petrushevksaya's 'Our Crowd'." *Studies in short Fiction* 34:1 (1997): 39-54.

Carrick, Neil. "A Familiar Story: Insurgent Narratives and Generic Refugees in Daniil Kharms's *The Old Woman*." *Modern Language Review* 3 (1995): 707-21.

Cassedy, Steven. "Daniil Kharms's Parody of Dostoevskii: Anti-Tragedy as Political Comment." *Canadian-American Slavic Studies* 18 (1984): 268-84.

Catteau, J. "De la Métaphorique des utopies dans la littérature Russe et de son Traitement chez Andrej Platonov." *Revue des Etudes Slaves* 56 : 1 (1984): 47-50.

Cavell, Stanley. *Must We Mean What We Say? A Book of Essays.* Cambridge: Cambridge University Press, 1976.

Chances, Ellen. "Daniil Charms' *Old Woman* Climbs her Family Tree." *Russian Literature* 17 (1985): 353-66.

Charters, Ann, ed. *The short story and Its Writer. An Introduction to Short Fiction.*

Boston: Bedfrod/St. Martin Press, 1999.

Chekhov, Anton. *Polnoe sobranie sochinenii i pisem v tridtsati tomakh*. Edited by N. F. Bel'chikov et al. Moscow: *Nauka*, 1974-83.

Chudakova, M. O. *Poetika Mikhaila Zoshchenko*. Moscow: *Nauka*, 1979.

Chukovskii, Kornei. "*Aibolit*." In his *Chudo-Derevo / Serebrianyi gerb*, 83-93. Moscow: *Detskaia Literatura*, 1967.

Conquest, Robert. *The Great Terror: A Reassessment*. Oxford: Oxford University Press, 1990.

Cooper, J. C. *Illustrated Encyclopedia of Traditional Symbols*. London: Thames and Hudson, 1978.

Cornwell, N., ed. and trans. *Incidences*. London: Serpent's Tale, 1993.

Daniil Kharms and the Poetics of the Absurd: Essays and Materials. Edited by N. Cornwell. London: Macmillan, 1991.

Coveney, Peter. *Poor Monkey. The Child in Literature*. London: Rockliff, 1957.

Curtius, Ernst Robert. *European Literature and the Latin Middle Ages*. Translated by Willard R. Trask. London: Routledge and Kegan Paul, 1979.

Dale, Philip S. *Language Development. Structure and Function*. New York: Holt, Rinehart and Winston, 1976.

Dallin, David J. and Boris I. Nikolaevsky. *Forced Labor in Soviet Russia*. New Haven: Yale University Press, 1947.

Dalton, Margaret. *Andrei Siniavskii and Julii Daniel': Two Soviet "Heretical"Writers*. Wurzburg: Jal-Verlag, 1973.

Dalton-Brown, Sally. *Voices from the Void. The Genres of Lyudmila Petrushevskaia*. New York: Berghahn Books, 2000.

Dedkov, Igor'. "*Posledniye shtrikhi (Vasilii Shukshin)*." In *Vozvrashcheniye k sebe. Literaturno-kriticheskie stat'i: Iz opyta sovremennoi prozy 60—70-kh gg.: geroi, konflikty, nravstvennye iskaniia*, 101—32. Moscow: *Sovremennik*, 1978.

Deleuze, G., F. Guattari. *Anti-Oedipus. Capitalism and Schizophrenia*. London: Athlone, 1983.

Des Pres, Terence. *The Survivor: An Anatomy of Life in the Death Camps*. Oxford: Oxford University Press, 1976.

Diamond, Cora. *The Realistic Spirit: Wittgenstein, Philosophy, and the Mind*. Cambridge, MA: The MIT Press, 1991.

Doležel, Lubomir. *Narrative Modes in Czech Literature*. Toronto: University of Toronto Press, 1973.

Druskin, Ia. "On Daniil Kharms." In Cornwell, *Daniil Kharms and the Poetics of the Absurd: Essays and Materials*, 22-31. London: Macmillan, 1991.

Dubrow, Heather. "The Status of Evidence." *PMLA* 111 (1996): 7- 20.

Duff, David, ed. *Modern Genre Theory.* Essex: Longman, 2000.

Durkin, Andrew. "Narrator, Metaphor, and Theme in Sinjavskji's *Fantastic Tales*." *Slavic and East European Journal* 24: 2 (1980): 133-44.

Easthorpe, A. "Eliot Pound and the Subject of Postmodernism." In *After the Future. Postmodern Times and Places.* Edited by G. Shapiro, 158-177. Albany, 1990.

Eikhenbaum, B. M, Yuri Tynianov, ed. *Russian Prose.* Translated and edited by Ray Parrott. Ann Arbor: Ardis, 1985.

Emerson, Carol. "Chekhov and the Annas." *In Life and Text. Essays in Honour of Geir Kjetsaa on the Occasion of His 60s Birthday.* Edited by Eric Egeberg, Audin J. Morch, and Ole Michael Selberg, 121-32. Oslo: Universitetet i Oslo, 1997.

Eng van der, Jan. "The Semantic Structure of *Lady with a Lapdog*." In *On the Theory of Descriptive Poetics: Anton Chekhov as Story-Teller and Playwright.* Edited by Jan van der Eng, Jan M Meijer and Herta Schmid, 59-94. Amsterdam: Peter de Ridder Press, 1978.

Erlich, Victor. "The Writer as Witness: The Achievement of Aleksandr Solzhenitsyn." In *Aleksandr Solzhenitsyn: Critical Essays and Documentary Materials.* Edited by B. Dunlop et al., 16—27. New York: Collier Macmillan, 1973.

Erofeev, Viktor. "The Parakeet." Translated by Leonard J. Stanton. *In Glasnost: An Anthology of Russian Literature Under Gorbachev.* Edited by Helena Goscilo and Byron Lindsey. Ann Arbor: Ardis, 1990.

-----. *Izbrannoe ili Karmannyi apokalipsis.* Moscow, Paris, New York: The Third Wave, 1993.

Fedorov, Nikolai. *Teoriia obshchego dela.* Vernyi, 1906.

Felman, Shoshana and Dori Laub. *Testimony: Crises of Witnessing in Literature, Psychoanalysis, and History.* New York: Routledge, 1992.

Foucault, Michel. "Language to Infinity." In his *Language, Counter-Memory, Practice.* Ithaca: Cornell University Press, 1977.

Fowler, Roger. "Language and the Reader: Shakespeare's Sonnet 73." In *Style and Structure in Literature. Essays in the New Stylistic.* Edited by Roger Fowler, 79-122. Ithaca, NY: Cornell University Press, 1975.

Frank, Joseph. "Spatial Form in Modern Literature." In *The Widening Gyre*, 3-62. New Brunswick (NJ): Rutgers University Press, 1963.

Freeborn, Richard. *The Rise of the Russian Novel*. Cambridge: Cambridge University Press, 1973.

Freud, Z. *Gessamelte Werke*. I-XVIII. London, 1940.

Frosh, S. *Identity Crisis. Modernity, Psychoanalysis and the Self.* New York, 1991.

Galina, M. "*Literatura nochnogo zreniia. Malaia proza kak razrushitel' mifologicheskoi sistemy*," *Voprosy Literatury* 5 (1997): 3-21.

Geller, L. "*Opyt prikladnoi stilistiki. Rasskaz V. Shukshina kak ob'ekt issledovaniia s peremennym fokusnym rasstoianiem*." *Wiener Slawistischer Almanach* 4 (1979): 95-123.

Geller, Michail. *Andrei Platonov v poiskach shchast'ia*. Paris: YMCA-Press, 1982.

Genette, Gérard. *Narrative Discourse: An Essay in Method*. Translated by Jane E. Lewin. Ithaca: Cornell University Press, 1980.

Gerasimova, A. "OBERIU (*Problema smeshnogo*)." *Voprosy literatury* 4 (1988): 48-79.

Giaquinta, R. "Elements of the Fantastic in Daniil Kharms's Starukha." In Cornwell, ed. *Daniil Kharms and the Poetics of the Absurd: Essays and Materials*, 132-48. London: Macmillan, 1991.

Gifford, Henry. "The Real Thing" (Review of Tolstaia's, *On the Golden Porch*). *New York Review of Books* 36: 9 (June 1, 1989): 3-5.

Ginzburg, Aleksandr, ed. *Belaya kniga po delu A. Sinyavskogo i Yu. Danielya*. Frankfurt am Main: Posev, 1967.

Glinka, M. I. *Ruslan i Liudmila. Volshebnaia opera v 5 deistviiakh*. In Glinka, M., *Polnoe sobranie sochinenii*, vol. 15. Edited by G. V. Kirkor. Moscow: *Muzyka*, 1967.

Gogol', N.V. "*Ob arkhitekture nyneshnogo vremeni*." In his *Polnoe sobranie sochinenii*, VIII, 56-75. Moscow: ANSSSR, 1952.

Gombrich, E.H. "Renaissance and Golden Age." In his *Studies in the Art of the Renaissance*. Vol. I (Chicago: University of Chicago Press, 1985),

Gorky, M. "A. P. Chekhov." In his *Sobranie sochinenii*, vol. 18. Moscow, 1963.

Goscilo, Helena. "Monsters Monomaniacal, Marital, and Medical. Tatiana Tolstaya's Regenerative Use of Gender Stereotypes." In *Sexuality and the Body in Russian Culture*. Edited by J.T. Costlow and St. Sandler and J. Vowles, 204-222. Stanford: Stanford University Press, 1993.

-----. "Perspective in Tatyana Tolstaya's Wonderland of Art." *World Literature Today (Books Abroad)* 67 (1993): 80-90.

-----. "Tolstaian Love as Surface Text." *Slavic and East European Journal* 34 (1990): 40-52.

-----. "Mother as Mothra: Totalizing Narrative in Petrushevskaia." In *A Plot of Her Own. The Female Protagonist in Russian Literature*. Edited by Sona Stephan Hoisington. Evanston: Northwestern UP, 1995.

-----. "Speaking Bodies. Erotic Zones Rhetoricized," in *Fruits of Her Plume. Essays on Contemporary Russian Women's Culture*. Edited by Helena Goscilo. Armonk: M. E Sharpe, 1993.

-----. "Tat'iana Tolstaia's 'Dome of Many-Coloured Glass': The World Refracted through Multiple Perspectives." *Slavic Review* 47: 2 (1988): 280-90.

Greber, Erika. *Textile Texte. Poetologische Metaphorik und Literaturtheorie: Studien zur Tradition des Wortflechtens und der Kombinatorik*. Köln/Weimar/Wien: Böhlau, 2002.

Greenleaf, Monika. "The Sense of Not Ending: Romantic Irony in *Eugene Onegin*." In her *Pushkin and Romantic Fashion: Fragment, Elegy, Orient, Irony*, 205-286. Stanford: Stanford University Press, 1994.

Grekova, Irina. "*Rastochitel'nost' talanta*." (Review of T. Tolstaia's, *Na zolotom kryl'tse sideli...*) *Novy mir* 1 (1988): 252-54.

Grubisic, L. "Laughing at the Void: a Structural Analysis of Kharms's *The Old Woman*." *Oregon Studies in Chinese and Russian Literature*, edited by A. Leong (1990): 221-36.

Guro, Elena. *Sochineniia*. Compiled by G.K.Perkins. Oakland, California: Berkeley Slavic Specialties, 1996.

Gusev, V. "*Imenno zhizn', a ne chto drugoe*." *Literaturnoe obozrenie* 1 (1974): 50–55.

Harkins, William E. "The Philosophical Tales of Jurij Oleša" In *Orbis Scriptus. Dmitrij Tschtieoskij zum 70. Geburtstag*. Edited by Dietrich Gerhardt, 349-54. Munich, 1966.

Harman, Gilbert. *The Nature of Morality: An Introduction to Ethics*. New York: Oxford University Press, 1977.

Harrison, Bernard. *Inconvenient Fictions: Literature and the Limits of Theory*. New Haven: Yale University Press, 1991.

Hartman, Geoffrey. *Minor Prophesies: The Literary Essay in the Culture Wars*. Cambridge, MA: Harvard University Press, 1991.

Hébert, Maurice L. *Hesychasm, Word-Weaving, and Slavic Hagiography*, Munich: Sagner, 1992.

Heffernan, James A.W. *Museum of Words. The Poetics of Ekphrasis from Homer to Ashbery*. Chicago: The University of Chicago Press, 1993.

Heller, Michael. "Vasily Shukshin: In Search of Freedom." Translated by George Gutsche. In *Vasily Shukshin. Snowball Berry Red and Other Stories*. Edited by

Donald M. Fiene, 213-33. Ann Arbor: Ardis Publishers, 1979.

Hollander, John. *The Gazer's Spirit. Poems Speaking to Silent Works of Art.* Chicago: The University of Chicago Press, 1995.

-----. *The Figure of Echo: a Mode of Allusion in Milton and After.* Berkeley: University of California Press, 1984.

Holquist, Michael. "Bakhtin." In *Handbook of Russian Literature.* Edited by Victor Terras. New Haven: Yale University Press, 1985.

Hosking, Geoffrey. *Beyond Socialist Realism. Soviet Fiction since Ivan Denisovich.* New York: Holmes & Meier Publishers, 1980.

Howe, Irving. "Predicaments of Soviet Writing." *The New Republic* (May 11 1963).

Hutcheon, L. *A Poetics of Postmodernism. History, Theory, Fiction.* New York/London: Routledge, 1988.

Inozemtseva, E. *"Platonov v Voronezhe." Pod'em* 2 (1971).

Iser, Wolfgang. *The Fictive and the Imaginary: Charting Literary Anthropology.* Baltimore: Johns Hopkins University Press, 1993.

-----. *The Act of Reading: A Theory of Aesthetic Response.* Baltimore: Johns Hopkins University Press, 1974.

Ivanits, L. "Suicide and Folk Belief in *Crime and Punishment." The Golden Age of Russian Literature and Thought.* Edited by D. Offord. New York: St Martins Press, 1992.

Ivanova, Natal'ia. "Bakhtin's Concept of the Grotesque and the Art of Petrushevskaia and Tolstaia." Translated by Helena Goscilo. In *Fruits of Her Plume: Essays on Contemporary Russian Women's Culture.* Edited by Helena Goscilo, 21-32. Armonk, NY: Sharpe, 1993.

Jaccard (Zhakhar), Zh. F. "Vozvyshennoe v tvorchestve Daniilla Kharmsa." In Sbornik materialov. Edited by V. Sashin. *Kharmsizdat/Arsis:* St. Petersburg, 1995.

Johnson, B. "Poetry and its Double: Two 'Invitations au voyage'." In *The Critical Difference. Essays in the Contemporary Rhetoric of Reading.* Edited by Barbara Johnson, 23-51. Baltimore: Johns Hopkins University Press, 1981.

Kantorovich, V. *"Novye tipy, novyi slovar', novye otnosheniia (o rasskazakh Vasiliia Shukshina)." Sibirskie ogni* 7 (1971): 176–80.

Karlinsky, Simon ed. *The Nabokov-Wilson Letters, 1940-71.* New York: Harper & Row, 1979.

Karriker, Aleksandra. "Claustrophobic Interiors and Splintered Selves: Petrushevskaia's Prose in Context." *West Virginia University Philological Papers* 41 (1995): 124-131.

Kataev, Vladimir. *Proza Chekhova. Problemy interpretatsii.* Moscow: *Izdatel'stvo Moskovskogo Universiteta*, 1979.

Kaverin, V. A. *Epilog: Memuary.* Moscow: *Moskovskii rabochii*, 1989.

-----. *Vechernii den'.* Moscow: *Sovetskii pisatel'*, 1980.

Kharms, Daniil. *Sobranie sochinenii.* Edited by M. Meilakh and V. Erl. Bremen: K-Presse, 1978.

Kolb-Seletski, N.M. "Gastronomy, Gogol' and His Fiction." *Slavic Review* 29 (1970): 35-57.

Kolonosky, Walter "Inherent and Ulterior Design in Sinjavskji's "Pxenc." *Slavic and East European Journal* 26:3 (1982): 329-37.

Korchagina, E. P. *"O nekotorykh osobennostiakh skazovoi formy v rasskaze 'Reka Potudan'."* In *Tvorchestvo A. Platonova.* Voronezh, 1970.

Kotzinger, Suzi. *"Vozvyshennoe u Gogolia: Vlast' ritoriki i vozvyshennoe iskusstvo."* In *Traditsii i novatorstvo v russkoi klassicheskoi literature (...Gogol'... Dostoevsky...).* Edited by Sergei A. Goncharov, 3-24. St. Petersburg: Obrazovanie, 1992.

Kristeva, Julia. *Tales of Love.* New York: Columbia University Press, 1987.

Kuryluk, Ewa. *Veronica and Her Cloth: History, Symbolism and Structure of a "True" Image.* Cambridge: Basil Blackwell, 1991.

Kuselev-Bezborodko, Grigory. *Pamiatniki starinnoi russkoi literatury.* St. Petersburg, 1861.

Lachmann, Renate. *Memory and Literature. Intertextuality in Russian Modernism.* Minneapolis: University of Minnesota Press, 1997.

-----. "Bakhtin and Carnival: Culture as Counter-Culture." *Cultural Critique* 11 (1988): 115-52.

Lakshin, V. *Tolstoi i Chekhov.* Moscow, *Sovetskii Pistael'*, 1975.

Lang, Berel. *Act and Idea in the Nazi Genocide.* Chicago: University of Chicago Press, 1990.

Le Fleming, Stephen. "Vasily Shukshin, A Contemporary Scythian." In Richard Freeborn, R. R. Milner-Gulland, and Charles A. Ward, eds. *Russian and Slavic Literature. Selected Papers in the Humanities from the First International Slavic Conference.* Banff, September 1974, 449-66. Cambridge, MA: Slavica Publishers, 1976,

Lebedushkina, Olga. *"Kniga tsarstv i vozmozhnostei."* *Druzhba narodov* 4 (1998):

200-207.

Lermontov, Mikhail. *A Hero of Our Time*. Translated by Marian Schwartz. New York: Random House Inc, 2004.

Levi, Primo. *If This is a Man / The Truce*. Translated by Stuart Woolf. London: Abacus, 1990.

Lipovetskii, Mark. "*Tragediia i malo li chto eshche*." *Novy Mir* 10 (1994): 229-232.

Lohafer, Susan. *Coming to Terms with Short Story*. Baton Rouge: Louisiana State University Press, 1983.

------. *Reading for Storyness: Preclosure Theory, Empirical Poetics, and Culture in the Short Story*. Baltimore/ London: Johns Hopkins University Press, 2003.

Lonnqvist, Barbara. *Xlebnikov and Carnival*. Stockholm Studies in Russian Literature 9. Stockholm: Almqvist & Wiksell International, 1979.

Lotman, Yury. *Analysis of the Poetic Text*. Edited and translated by D. Barton Johnson. Ann Arbor: Ardis, 1976.

Lourie, Richard. *Letters to the Future: An Approach to Siniavsky-Tertz*. Ithaca: Cornell University Press, 1975.

Lubbock, Percy. *The Craft of Fiction*. London: J. Cape, 1954.

Luzhanovskii, A. V. *Rasskaz v russkoi literature 1820-1850kh godov. Stanovlenie zhanra*. Ivanovo: *Ivanovskii gosudarstvennyi universitet*, 1996.

Maguire, Robert A. "Literary Conflicts in the 1920's." *Survey* 18:3 (1972): 98-127.

Mandelker, Amy. *Framing Anna Karenina. Tolstoy, the Woman Question, and the Victorian Novel*. Columbus: Ohio State University Press, 1993.

Maramzin, V. "*Biobibliograficheskii ukazatel'*." Echo 7 (1980).

Markov, Vladimir. *Russian Futurism*. Berkeley and Los Angeles: University of California Press, 1968.

Markovich, V. M. and V. Schmidt, eds. *Russkaia novella. Problemy teorii i istorii*. St. Petersburg: *Izdatel'stvo St. Peterburgskogo universiteta*, 1993.

Matich, Olga and Michael Haim, eds., *The Third Wave: Russian Literature in Emigration*. Ann Arbor: Ardis, 1984.

May, Charles E. *Short Story Theories*. Athens: Ohio University Press, 1976.

------. *The New Short Story Theories*. Athens: Ohio University Press, 1994.

Meilakh, B. "*Dva resheniia odnoi problemy*." Neva, 9 (1956): 184-188.

Mestrovich, Marta. "Tatyana Tolstaya." [Interview] *Publisher's Weekly* 239 (January 1, 1992): 37-38.

Miller, Liudmila V. "*Konflict rasskaza V. Pelevina "Nika" v kontekste natsional'noi esteticheskoi traditsii*." *Mir rysskaya slova* 1: 1, (2001): 65–69.

http://gramota.ru/biblio/magazines/mrs/mrs2001-01/28_212 (accessed June 7, 2009).

Milne, Lesley. "Ghosts and Dolls: Popular Urban Culture and Supernatural in Lyudmila Petrushevskaia's Songs of the Eastern Slaves and Little Sorceress." *The Russian Review*, 59: 2 (2000): 269-84.

Milner-Gulland, Robin. "Grandsons of Kozma Prutkov: Reflections on Zabolotsky, Oleinikov and Their Circle." *Russian and Slavic Literature*. Edited by R. Freeborn et al., 313-327. Columbus, OH: Slavica, 1976.

------. "Zabolotsky's Vremia." Essays in Poetics 1 (1981): 86-95.

-----. "Beyond the Turning-Point." Corwell, ed. Daniil Kharms and the Poetics of the Absurd: Essays and Materials, 243-67. London: Macmillan, 1991.

Mitchell, W. J. T. *Picture Theory. Essays on Verbal and Visual Representation*. Chicago: The University of Chicago Press, 1994.

Moser, Charles A., ed. *The Russian Short Story. A Critical History*. Boston: Twayne Publishers, 1986.

Mukarovský, Jan. *Aesthetic Function, Norm and Value as Social Facts*. Translated by Mark E. Suino. Ann Arbor: University of Michigan Press, 1970.

Murav'eva, Irina. "*Dva imeni*." *Grani* XLIII: 152 (1989): 99-133.

Nabokov, Vladimir. *Lectures on Russian Literature*. Edited by Fredson Bowers. San Diego: A Harvest Book Harcourt Brace & Company Bruccoli Clark Layman, 1981.

Naiman, Erik. "The Thematic Mythology of Andrej Platonov." *Russian Literature* XXI: 2 (1987).

Nakhimovsky, Alice Stone. "Laughter in the Void: An Introduction to the Writings of Daniil Kharms and Alexander Vvedenskii." *Wiener Slawistischer Almanach* 5. Vienna: Anton Riegelnik, 1982.

Nazarenko, Ia. A. *Istoriia russkoy literatury* XIX veka. Moscow: *Gos. izdatel'stvo*, 1926.

Nemec Ignashev, Diane. "Song and Confession in the Short Prose of Vasilij Makarovi Šukšin." Ph.D. diss., University of Chicago, 1984.

Nevzgliadova, Elena. "*Eta prekrasnaia zhizn'. O rasskazakh Tat'iany Tolstoi*." *Avrora* 10 (1986): 111-20.

Newnham, Richard, ed., *Soviet Short Stories*. London, 1963.

Nietzsche, Friedrich. "The Birth of Tragedy." *Basic Writings of Nietzsche*. Translated and edited by Walter Kaufman. New York: The Modern Library, 1968.

Novikov, Vladimir. "*Oshchushchenie zhanra. Rol' rasskaza v razvitii sovremennoi prozy.*" *Novy Mir* 3 (1987).

Nussbaum, Martha. *Love's Knowledge: Essays on Philosophy and Literature.* New York: Oxford University Press, 1990.

-----. *The Fragility of Goodness: Luck and Ethics in Greek Tragedy and Philosophy.* Cambridge: Cambridge University Press, 1986.

O'Toole, L. M. "*Structure and Style in the Short Story: Dostoevskij's A Gentle Spirit.*" *Tijdschrift voor Slavische Taal — en Letterkunde* 1 (1972): 84-65.

-----. *Structure, Style, and Interpretation in the Russian Short Story.* New Haven: Yale University Press, 1982.

Ognev, A. V. *Russkii sovetskii rasskaz.* Moscow: *Prosveshchenie*, 1978.

Opulskaia et al., ed. *V tvorcheskoi laboratorii Chekhova.* Moscow: *Nauka*, 1974.

Orlov, P. A. *Russkaia sentimental'naia povest'.* Moscow: *Izdatel'stvo Moskovskogo Universiteta*, 1979.

Ouspensky, Leonid and Vladimir Lossky. "The Meaning of Icons." In *The Meaning of Icons*, translated by G.E.H. Palmer and E. Kadloubovsky. Crestwood (NY): St. Vladimir's Seminary Press, 1983.

The Oxford Dictionary of the Christian Church. Edited by F. L. Cross. London: Oxford University Press, 1958.

Papernyi, Z. *Zapisnye knizhki Chekhova.* Moscow: *Sovetskii Pisatel'*, 1976.

Parker, Patricia. *Literary Fat Ladies: Rhetoric, Gender, Property.* London/New York: Methuen, 1987.

Peden, William H. *The American Short Story; Front Line in the National Defense of Literature.* Boston: Houghton Mifflin, 1964.

Pelevin, Viktor. "Nika." In his *The Blue Lantern.* Translated by Andrew Bromfield, 90-104. London: Harbord Publishing, 1997.

Pertsov, Viktor. *My zhivyom vpervye. O tvorchestve Yuriya Oleshi.* Moscow: *Soiuz pisatelei*, 1976.

Peterson, Ronald E. "Writer as Alien in Sinjavskji's "Pxenc." *Weiner Slawisticher Almanach* 12 (1983): 47-53.

Petrovsky, A. V. *Slovar' russkikh licnykh imen.* Moscow: *Russkie slovari*, 1980.

Petrovsky, M. "Morphology of Pushkin's 'The Shot'." In *Problémy poetiki.* Edited by V. I. Briusov. Moscow-Leningrad: *Zemlia i fabrika*, 1925.

Petrushevskaia, Lyudmila. *Dom Devushek.* Moscow: Vagrius, 1999.

Piaget, Jean. *The Language and Thought of the Child.* New York: Meridian Books, (1955) 1973.

Pietsukh, Viacheslav. "The Central-Ermolaevo War." Translated by Arch Tait. In *The Penguin Book of New Russian Writing: Russia's Fleurs du Mal.* Edited by

Viktor Erofeev and Andrew Reynolds. London: Penguin Books, 1995.

-----. *Ia i prochee/* Moscow: *Khudozhestvennaia literatura*, 1990.

Platonov, A. "*Iz zapisnykh knizhek*," *Literaturnaia gazeta*, 48 (November 29, 1967.

-----. "*Zhivia glavnoi zhizn'iu*," *Volga* 9 (1975).

-----. *Razmyshleniia chitatelia*. Moscow: *Sovremennik*, 1980.

-----. *Reka Potudan'*. Moscow, 1937.

-----. *Starik i starukha*. Munich, 1984.

Poggioli, Renato. *The Phoenix: and the Spider*. Cambridge, MA: Harvard University Press, 1957.

Popkin, Cathy. *The Pragmatics of Insignificance: Chekhov, Zoshchenko, Gogol*. Stanford: Stanford University Press, 1993.

Pratt, Mary Louise. "The Short Story: the Long and the Short of It." *Poetics: International Review for the Theory of Literature* 10: 2-3 (1981 June): 175-194.

Propp, V. *Morphology of the Folktale*. 2nd ed. Translated by Laurence Scott. Revised and edited with preface by Louis A. Wagner. Austin and London: Publications of the American Folklore Society, Inc., Bibliographical and Special Series, v. 10, Indiana University Research Center in Anthropology, Folklore and Linguistics, 1968. Originally published as Vladimir Propp, *Morfologiia skazki*. Leningrad: Academia, 1928.

Pushkin, A. S. *Eugene Onegin*. Translated by James E. Falen. Oxford: Oxford University Press, 1995.

-----. "*Ruslan i Liudmila. Poema*." In his *Polnoe sobranie sochinenii* v 10 tomakh. 4th ed. Vol. 4: *Poemy. Skazki*, 7-80. Leningrad: Nauka, 1977.

-----. "Elegy." Translated by Babette Deutsch. In The Works of Alexander Pushkin. Edited by Avrahm Yarmolinksy. New York: Random House, 1936.

Rabinowitz, Stanley J. *Sologub's Literary Children: Keys to a Symbolist's Prose*. Columbus, Ohio: Slavica publishers, 1980.

Reid, Ian. *The Short Story*. NY, 1977

Rich, Elizabeth. *Russian Literature After Perestroyka*. Special Issue of *South Central Review* 12: 3-4 (1995).

Robbe-Grillet, Alain. *Snapshots & Towards a New Novel*. Translated by Barbara Wright. London: Calder and Boyars, 1965.

Roberts, Graham. "A Matter of (Dis)course. Metafiction in the Works of Daniil Kharms." *New Directions in Soviet Literature*. Edited by S. D. Graham, 138-63. London: Macmillan, 1992.

Rowe, William Woodin. *Dostoevsky: Child and Man in his Works*. New York/London:

New York University Press, 1968

Rudalev, Andrei. "*Nastoiashchii rasskaz* (Aleksandr Karasev, *Chechenskie rasskazy.* Moscow: *Literaturnaia Rossiia*, 2008), *Zavtra* 9: 143 (24/09/2008).

Schmid, Wolf. "Skaz." *Russian Literature* 54 (2003): 267-278.

Schopenhauer, Arthur. *The World as Will and Representation.* Translated by E. F. J. Payne. New York: Dover, 1969.

Sendler, Egon. *The Icon. Image of the Invisible.* Translated by Steven Bingham. Redondo Beach, CA: Oakwood Publications, 1988.

Shalamov, Varlam. "*O moei proze.*" *Novy mir* 12 (1989): 58-71.

-----. *Kolymskie rasskazy.* Edited by I. P. Sirotinskaya. Moscow: *Sovremennik*, 1991.

-----. *Sobranie sochinenii v chetyrekh tomakh* [Collected Works in Four Volumes]. Edited by I. P. Sirotinskaia. Moscow: *Khudozhestvennaia literatura / Vagrius*, 1998.

-----. *Kolyma Tales.* Translated by John Glad. Harmondsworth: Penguin, 1994.

Shcheglov, Iu. K. "*Entsiklopediia nekul'turnosti. Zoshchenko: rasskazy dvadtsatykh godov i Golubaia kniga.*" In Zholkovskiii, A. K. and Iu. K. Shcheglov, *Mir avtora i struktura teksta. Stat'i o russkoi literature,* 53- 84. Tenafly, N.J.: Hermitage, 1986.

Shcheglova, Evgeniia. "*V svoem krugu. Polemicheskie zametki o 'zhenskoi proze'.*" *Literaturnoe obozrenie* 3 (1990): 19-26.

Shepherd, David, ed. *Bakhtin. Carnival and Other Subjects. Critical Studies* 3: 2 and 4:1/2. Amsterdam-Atlanta, GA: Rodopi 1993.

-----. Beyond Metafiction: Self-Consciousness in Soviet Literature. Oxford: Oxford University Press, 1992.

Sherbinin de, Julie. *Chekhov and the Russian Religious Culture. Poetics of the Marian Paradigm.* Evanston: Northwestern University Press, 1997.

Shestov, Lev. *Chekhov and Other Essays.* Ann Arbor: University of Michigan Press, 1966.

Shklovskii, Viktor. Tristram Shendi *Sterna i teoriia romana.* Petrograd: *Opoyaz*, 1921.

Shubin, E. A. *Sovremennyi russkii rasskaz. Voprosy poetiki zhanra.* Leningrad: *Nauka*, 1974.

Shukman, Ann. "*Ten Russian Short Stories: Theory, Analysis, Interpretation.*" *Essays in Poetics* II: 2 (1977).

Shukshin, Vasilii. *Do tret'ikh petukhov.* Moscow: *Izvestiia*, 1981.

-----. *Kharaktery.* Moscow: *Sovremennik*, 1973.

-----. *Voprosy samomu sebe.* Moscow: *Molodaia gvardiia*, 1981.

Shur, Anna. "*V. T. Shalamov i A. I. Solzhenitsyn: Sravnitel'nyi analiz nekotorykh proizvedenii.*" *Novy zhurnal* (*The New Review*, New York) 155 (1984): 92-101.

Silowowscy, Wiktoria and Rene. *Andrzej Platonow.* Warsaw, 1983.

Simmons, K.A. "*Zhenskaia proza* and the New Generation of Women Writers." *Slovo. A Journal of Contemporary Soviet and East European Affairs* 3 (1990): 66-78.

Simmons, Sherwin W. *Malevich's Black Square and the Genesis of Supermatism*, 1907-1915. New York: Garland, 1981.

Slobin, Dan I. *Psycholinguistics.* Glenview, Illinois-London: Scott, Foresman & Co, (1971) 1974.

Slovar' russkikh lichnykh imen [Dictionary of Russian Given Names]. Edited by A. N. Tikhonov, L. E. Boyarinova, and A. G. Ryzhkova. Moscow: *Shkol'naia Pressa*, 1995.

Smirnov, I. P. "Geschichte der Nachgeschichte: Aur russisch-sorachigen Prosa der Postmoderne." In *Modelle des literarischen Strukturwandels.* Edited by M. Titzmann, 205-219. Tubingen, 1991.

-----. "Ot avangarda k postmodernizmu. (Temporal'naia motivika)." In *Semantic Analysis of Literary Texts. To Honor Jan van der Eng on the occasion of his 65th Birthday.* Edited by E. de Haard. Amsterdam, 1990.

-----. Bytie i tvorchestvo. Marburg/Lahn, 1990.

Smith, Alexandra. "Carnivalising the Canon: The Grotesque and Subversive in Contemporary Russian Women's Prose: Petrushevskaia, Sadur, Tolstaia, Narbikova." In *Russian Literature in Transition.* Edited by I. K. Lilly and H. Mondry, 35-58. Nottingham: Astra, 1999.

Solzhenitsyn, Aleksandr. *The Gulag Archipelago: An Experiment in Literary Investigation.* Translated by Thomas P. Whitney. New York: Harper and Row, 1975.

Strazds, Robert. *Contemporary Russian Soviet Women's Fiction 1939-1989.* PhD thesis, McGill University, Canada, 1991.

Studies in the Art of the Renaissance. Vol. I. Chicago: University of Chicago Press, 1985.

Sutcliffe, Benjamin M. *The Prose of Life. Russian Women Writers from Khrushchev to Putin.* Madison: The University of Wisconsin Press, 2009.

Terts, Abram. *Fantasticheskie povesti.* Paris: *Instytut literacki*, 1961.

-----. *Mysli vrasplokh.* New York: Rausen Publisher, 1966.

-----. *Fantasticheskii mir Abrama Tertza.* New York: Inter-language literary Associates, 1967.

Teskey, Ayleen. *Platonov and Fyodorov: the Influence of Christian Philosophy on a Soviet Writer.* Wiltshire, Eng: Avebury, 1982.

Todorov, Tzvetan. *Facing the Extreme: Moral Life in the Concentration Camps.* Translated by Arthur Denner and Abigail Pollak. New York: Holt, 1996.

Toker, Leona. *Return from the Archipelago: Narratives of Gulag Survivors.* Bloomington: Indiana University Press, 2000.

-----. "Toward a Poetics of Documentary Prose – from the Perspective of Gulag Testimonies." *Poetics Today* 18 (1997): 187-222.

Tolstaia, Tatiana. *Sleepwalker in a Fog,* translated by Jamey Gambrell. New York: Knopf, 1992.

-----. *White Walls. Collected Stories,* translated by Jamey Gambrell and Antonina W. Bouis. New York: NYRB Classics, 2007.

-----. "*Poet i muza.*" *Novy mir* 12 (1986): 113-119.

Tolstaja-Segal, Elena. "*O sviazi nizshikh urovnei teksta s vysshimi: proza Andreia Platonova.*" *Slavica Hierosolymitana* 2 (1978): 197-198.

Tolstoy, L. N. *Anna Karenina. Roman v vos'mi chastiakh.* Moscow: *Khudozhestvennaia literatura*, 1984.

-----. *Tolstoy's Diaries.* Edited and translated by R. F. Christian. London: Flamingo, 1994.

-----. *War and Peace.* Translated by Richard Pevear and Larissa Volokhonsky. New York: Alfred A Knopf, 2007.

-----. *What Is Art? and Essays on Art.* Translated by Aylmer Maud. London, 1938.

Tomashevsky, Iu. V. ed. *Vspominaia Mikhaila Zoshchenko.* Leningrad: *Khudozhestvennaia literatura*, 1990.

Trask, Willard R. trans. *European Literature and the Latin Middle Ages.* London: Routledge and Kegan Paul, 1979.

Trimpi, Wesley. "Horace's 'Ut pictura poesis': The Argument for Stylistic Decorum." *Traditio* 34 (1978): 29-73.

Tynianov, Iu. N. *Poetika. Istoriia literatury. Kino.* Edited by E. A. Toddes, A. P. Chudakov, M. Chudakova. Moscow: *Nauka*, 1977.

Uspensky, B. A. et. al. "Theses on the Semiotic Study of Cultures." In *Structure of Texts and Semiotics of Culture.* Edited by Jan van der Eng and Mojmír Grygar. The Hague-Paris: Mouton 1973.

Vasil'ev, Vladimir. *Andrei Platonov.* Moscow: *Sovremennik*, 1982.

Vasil'eva, Maria. "*Tak slozhilos'.*" *Druzhba narodov* 4 (1998): 208-217.

Verin, V. "*Andrei Platonov – publitsist.*" *Literaturnaia Gazeta* 2 (January 7, 1987).

Vickers, Brian. *In Defense of Rhetoric.* Oxford: Clarendon Press, 1988.

Vinogradova, K.M. "*Stranitsa iz chernovoi rukopisi rasskaza 'Dama s sobachkoi'.*" In *Literaturnoe Nasledstvo.* Chekhov. Vol. 68, 133-40. Moscow: *Izdatel'stvo Akademii Nauk,* 1960.

Volin, V.M. and D.N. Ushakov, eds. *Tolkovyi slovar' russkogo iazyka.* Moscow: *Sovetskaia entsiklopediia,* 1935-1940.

Vol'pe, Ts. *Iskusstvo nepokhozhesti.* Moscow: *Sovetskii pisatel',* 1991.

Vygotsky, Lev Semenovich. *The Psychology of Art.* Cambridge, MA: The M.I.T. Press, 1971.

Wat, Alexander. *My Century: The Odyssey of a Polish Intellectual.* Foreword by Czeslaw Milosz. Translated by Richard Lourie. New York: Norton, 1990.

Welsch, W. *Unsere Postmoderne Moderne.* Weinheim, 1991.

Wetter, Gustav A. *Dialectical Materialism. A Historical and Systematic Survey of Philosophy in the Soviet Union.* Translated by Peter Hath. New York: Praeger, 1958.

Willcock, Malcolm W. *A Companion to the Iliad.* Chicago and London: The University of Chicago Press, 1976.

Williams, Bernard. *Ethics and the Limits of Philosophy.* Cambridge, MA: Harvard University Press, 1985.

Winner, Thomas. *Chekhov and His Prose.* New York: Holt, Rinehart and Winston, 1996.

Woll, Josephine. "The Minotaur in the Maze: Remarks on Lyudmila Petrushevskaia." *World Literature Today. Russian Literature at a Crossroads,* 67 (1993): 125-130.

Wosien, Maria-Gabriele, ed. *The Russian Folk-Tale. Some Structural and Thematic Aspects.* Munich: Sagner, 1969.

Yakubov, V. "*V kruge poslednem: Varlam Shalamov i Aleksandr Solzhenitsyn.*" *Vestnik Russkogo Khristianskogo Dvizheniia* 137 (1987): 156-61.

Zalygin, Sergei, comp. *The New Soviet Fiction. Sixteen Short Stories.* New York: Abbeville Press, 1989.

Zholkovskii (Zholkovsky), A. K. *Bluzhdaiushchie sny i drugie raboty.* Moscow: Nauka / Vostochnaia literatura, 1994.

-----. "*Ruka blizhnego i ee mesto v poetike Zoshchenko.*" *Novoe literaturnoe obozrenie* 15 (1995): 262-86.

-----. "What Is the Author Trying to Say with His Artistic Work? Rereading

Zoshchenko's Oeuvre." *Slavic and East European Journal* 40: 3 (1996): 458-74.

-----. *Mikhail Zoshchenko: poetika nedoveriia*. Moscow: LKI, 2007 [1999].

-----."*Aristokatratka*." In *Litso i maska Mikhaila Zoshchenko*. Edited by Iu. V.Tomashevskii, 331-39. Moscow: *Olimp-PPP*, 1994.

-----. "*Eccola! (K donzhuanskoi teme u Zoshchenko)*." In his *Inventsii*. Moscow: *Gendal'f*, 1995, 57-71.

Zoshchenko, M. M. "*O sebe, o kritikakh i o svoei rabote*." In M. Zoshchenko, *Uvazhaemye grazhdane*. Edited by M. Z. Dolinskii. Moscow: *Knizhnaia palata*, 1991 [1928].

-----. *Before Sunrise. A Novella,* translated and with afterword by G. Kern. Ann Arbor: Ardis, 1974.

-----. *Sobranie sochinenii v 5 tomakh*. Edited by Iu. V. Tomashevskii. Moscow: *Russlit*, 1993.

-----. *Uvazhaemye grazhdane*. Moscow: *Zemlia i fabrika,* 1927.

-----. *Sobranie sochinenii v trekh tomakh*. Edited by Iu. V. Tomashevskii. Leningrad: *Khudozhestvennaia literatura,* 1987.

Zweers, F. *Grown-up Narrator and Childlike Hero*. The Hague-Paris: Mouton, 1971.

CPSIA information can be obtained
at www.ICGtesting.com
Printed in the USA
LVOW10s1830110118
562713LV00003B/151/P

9 781934 843697